PERFECT
WORLD

10 Rie
Aruga

Research Help /
Kazuo Abe (Abe Kensetsu Inc.)

contents

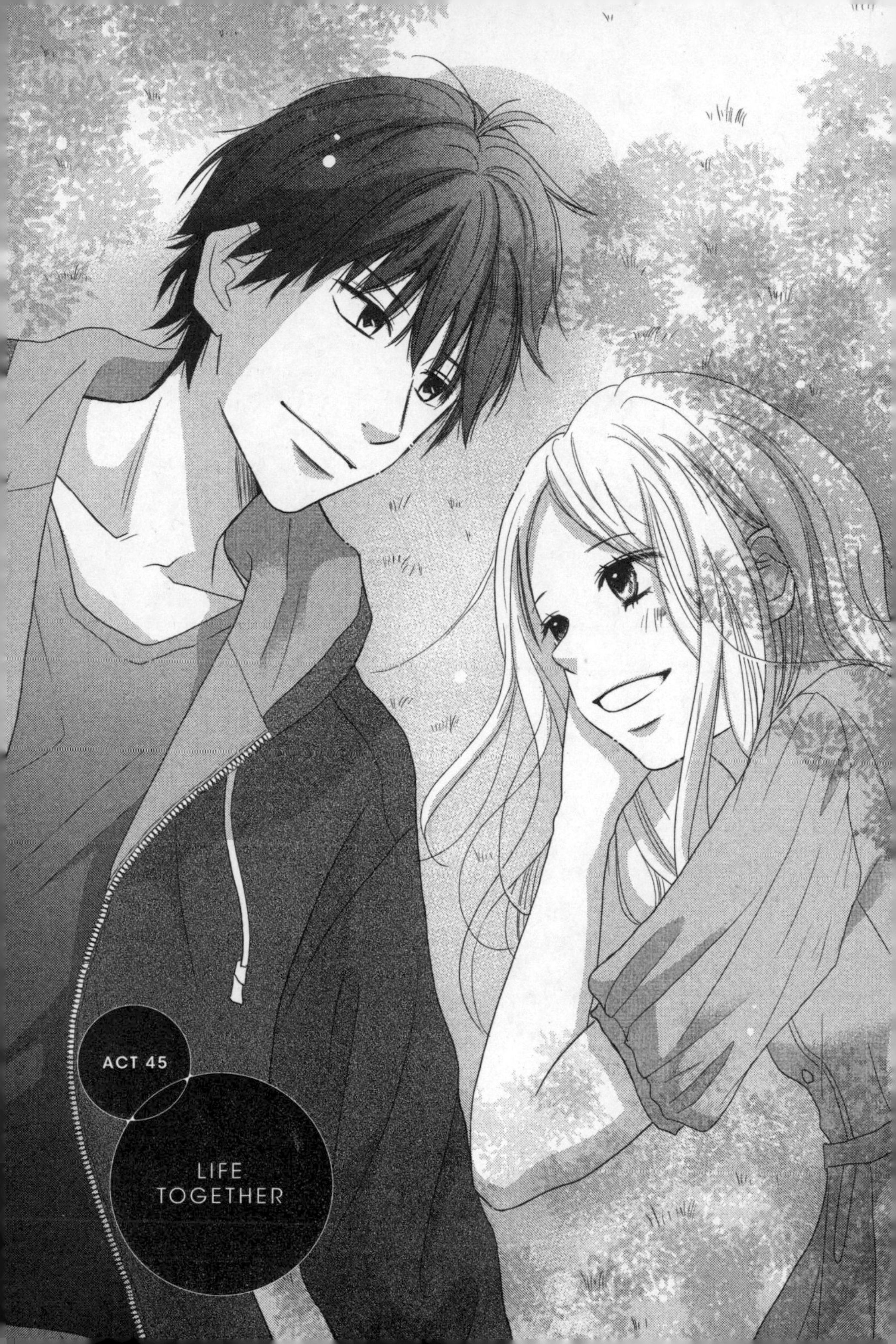
ACT 45
LIFE TOGETHER

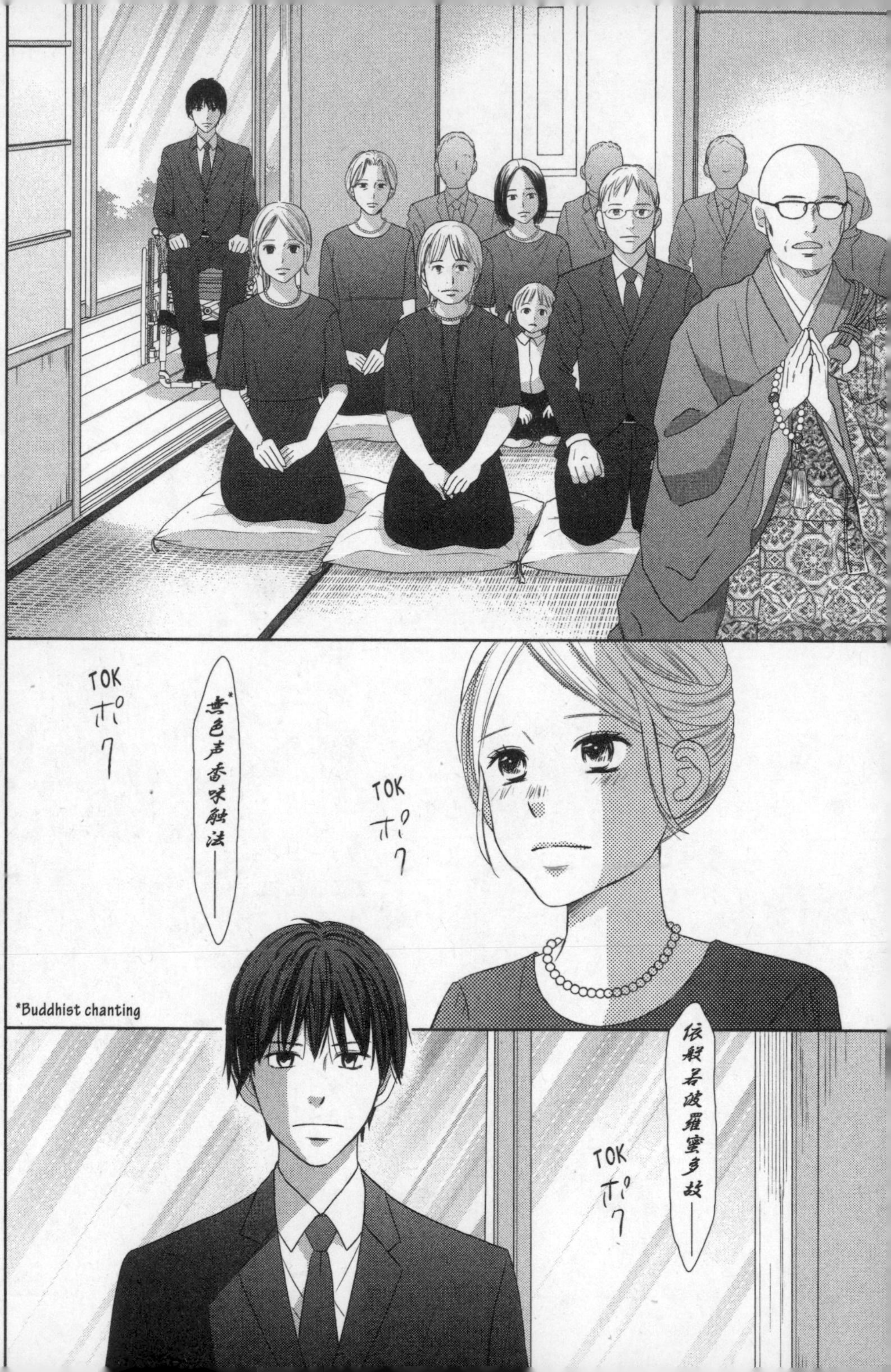
*無色声香味触法——
TOK ポク
TOK ポク
*Buddhist chanting
依般若波羅蜜多故——
TOK ポク

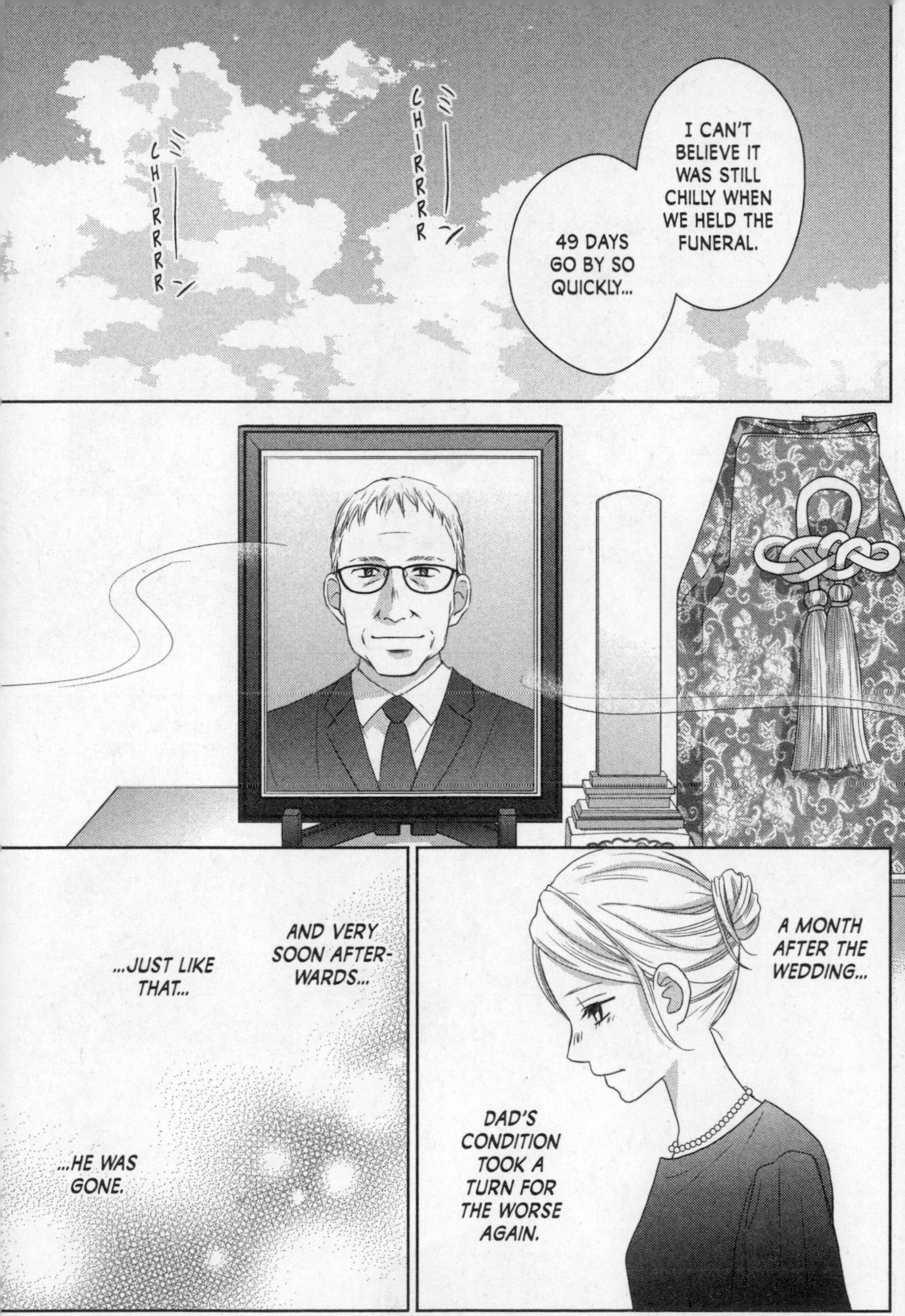
CHIRRRR
CHIRRRR
I CAN'T BELIEVE IT WAS STILL CHILLY WHEN WE HELD THE FUNERAL.
49 DAYS GO BY SO QUICKLY...
A MONTH AFTER THE WEDDING...
DAD'S CONDITION TOOK A TURN FOR THE WORSE AGAIN.
AND VERY SOON AFTER-WARDS...
...JUST LIKE THAT...
...HE WAS GONE.

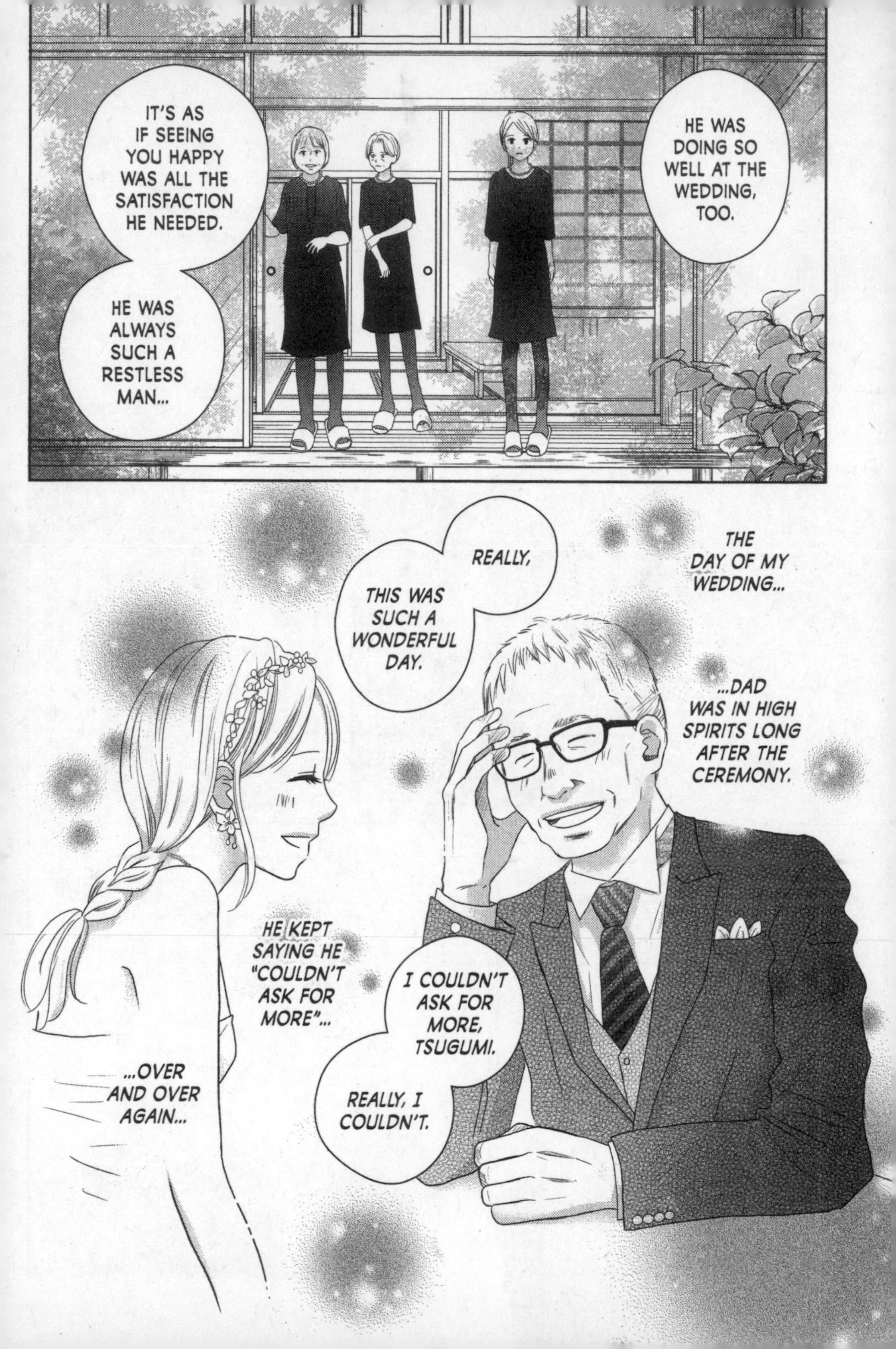
HE WAS DOING SO WELL AT THE WEDDING, TOO.
IT'S AS IF SEEING YOU HAPPY WAS ALL THE SATISFACTION HE NEEDED.
HE WAS ALWAYS SUCH A RESTLESS MAN...
THE DAY OF MY WEDDING...
...DAD WAS IN HIGH SPIRITS LONG AFTER THE CEREMONY.
REALLY,
THIS WAS SUCH A WONDERFUL DAY.
I COULDN'T ASK FOR MORE, TSUGUMI.
REALLY, I COULDN'T.
HE KEPT SAYING HE "COULDN'T ASK FOR MORE"...
...OVER AND OVER AGAIN...

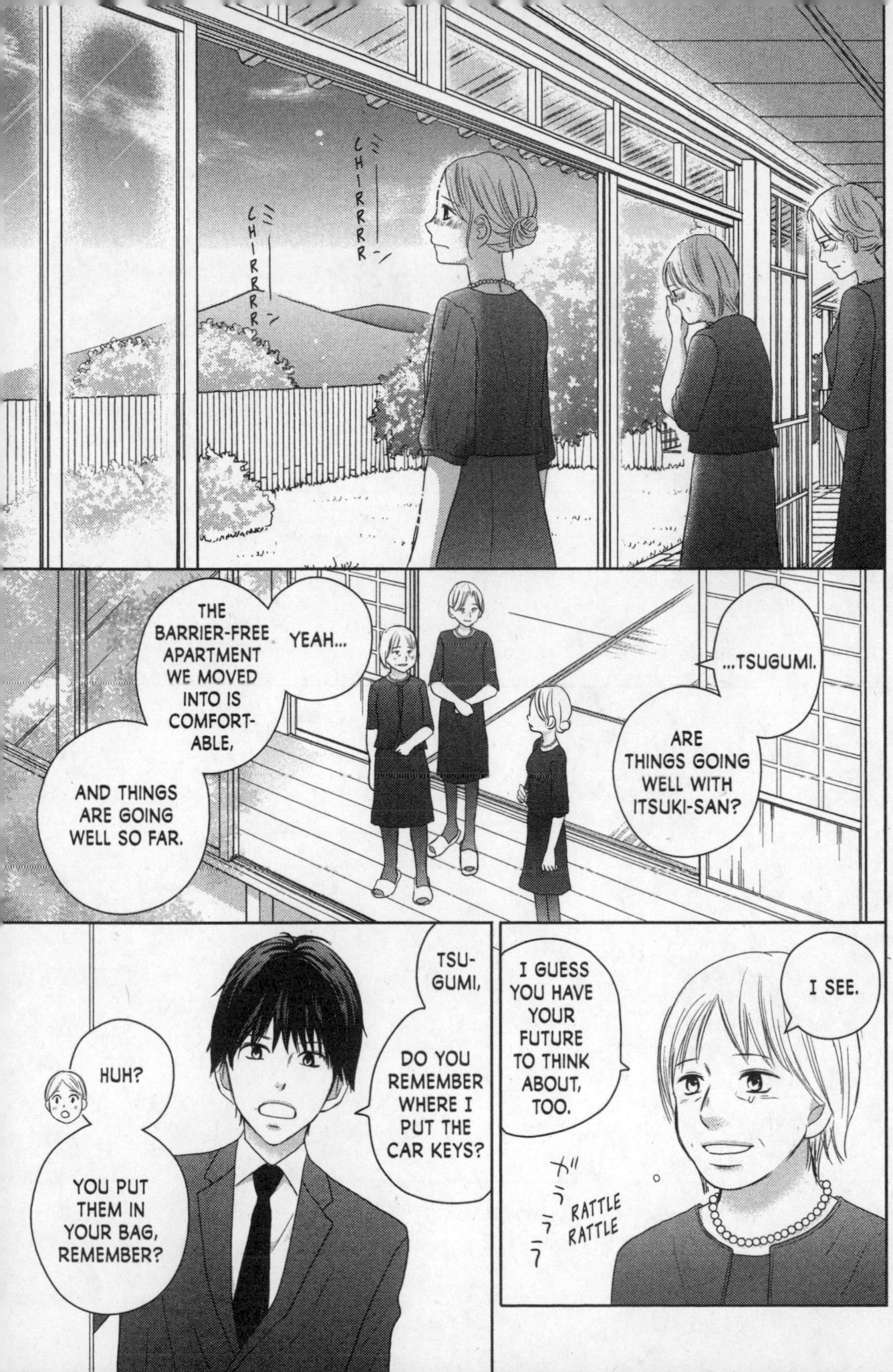
CHIRRRR
CHIRRRR
...TSUGUMI.
ARE THINGS GOING WELL WITH ITSUKI-SAN?
YEAH...
THE BARRIER-FREE APARTMENT WE MOVED INTO IS COMFORT-ABLE,
AND THINGS ARE GOING WELL SO FAR.
I SEE.
I GUESS YOU HAVE YOUR FUTURE TO THINK ABOUT, TOO.
RATTLE RATTLE
TSU-GUMI,
DO YOU REMEMBER WHERE I PUT THE CAR KEYS?
HUH?
YOU PUT THEM IN YOUR BAG, REMEMBER?

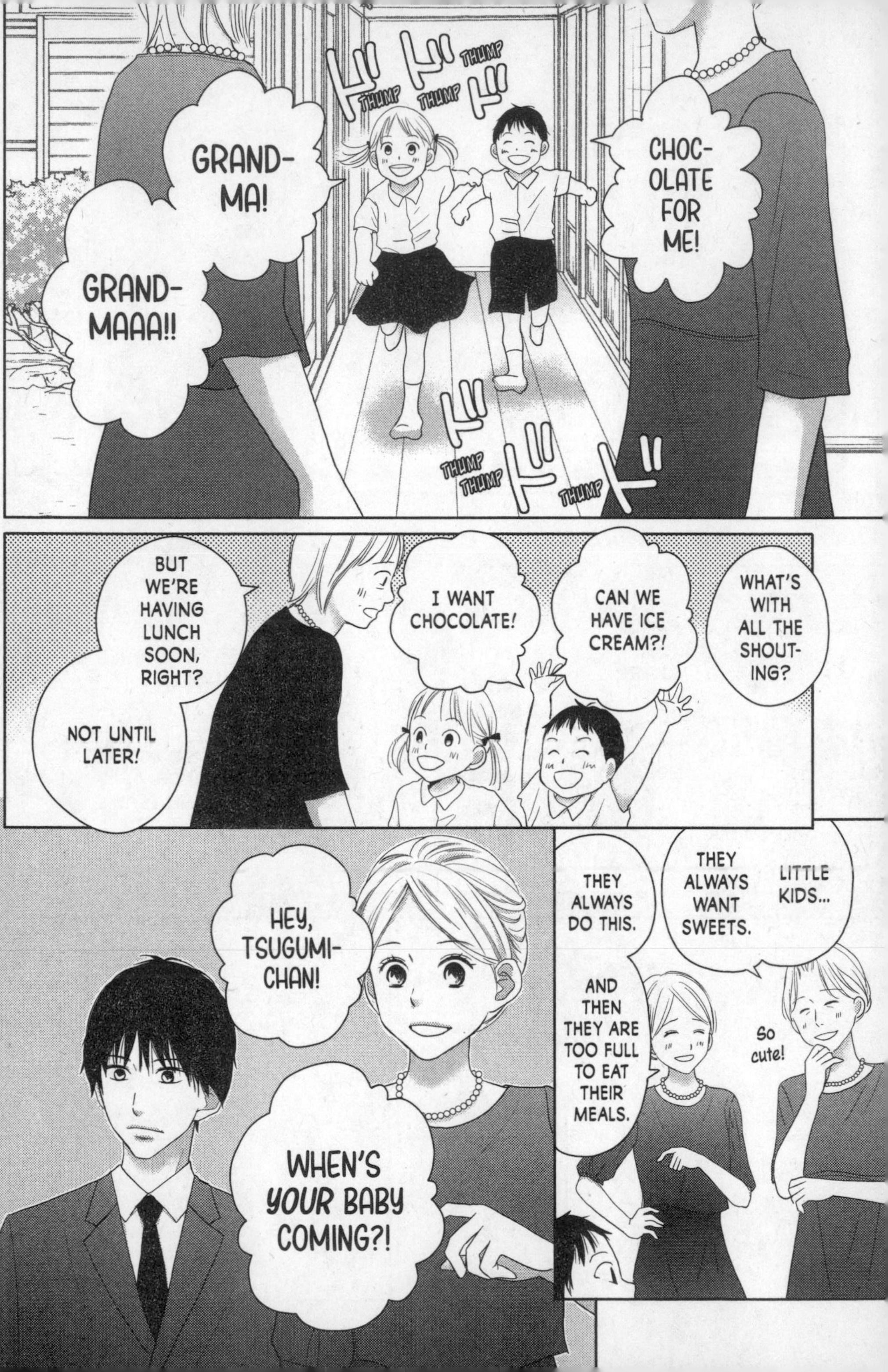
CHOC-OLATE FOR ME!
THUMP THUMP
THUMP
THUMP THUMP
THUMP
GRAND-MA!
GRAND-MAAA!!
WHAT'S WITH ALL THE SHOUT-ING?
CAN WE HAVE ICE CREAM?!
I WANT CHOCOLATE!
BUT WE'RE HAVING LUNCH SOON, RIGHT?
NOT UNTIL LATER!
LITTLE KIDS...
THEY ALWAYS WANT SWEETS.
So cute!
THEY ALWAYS DO THIS.
AND THEN THEY ARE TOO FULL TO EAT THEIR MEALS.
HEY, TSUGUMI-CHAN!
WHEN'S *YOUR* BABY COMING?!

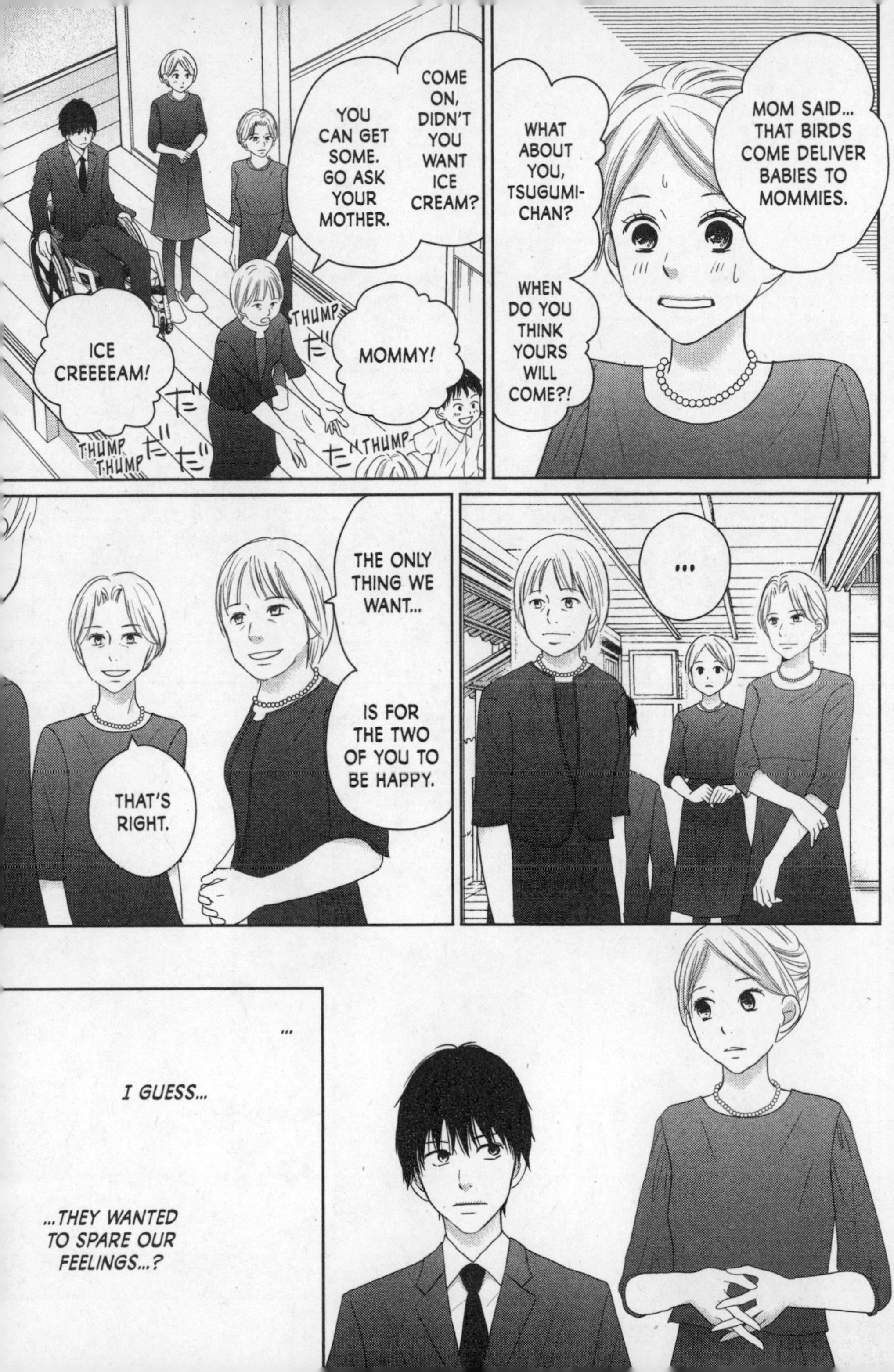
MOM SAID... THAT BIRDS COME DELIVER BABIES TO MOMMIES.
WHAT ABOUT YOU, TSUGUMI-CHAN?
WHEN DO YOU THINK YOURS WILL COME?!
COME ON, DIDN'T YOU WANT ICE CREAM?
YOU CAN GET SOME. GO ASK YOUR MOTHER.
THUMP
MOMMY!
ICE CREEEEAM!
THUMP
THUMP THUMP
...
THE ONLY THING WE WANT...
IS FOR THE TWO OF YOU TO BE HAPPY.
THAT'S RIGHT.
...
I GUESS...
...THEY WANTED TO SPARE OUR FEELINGS...?

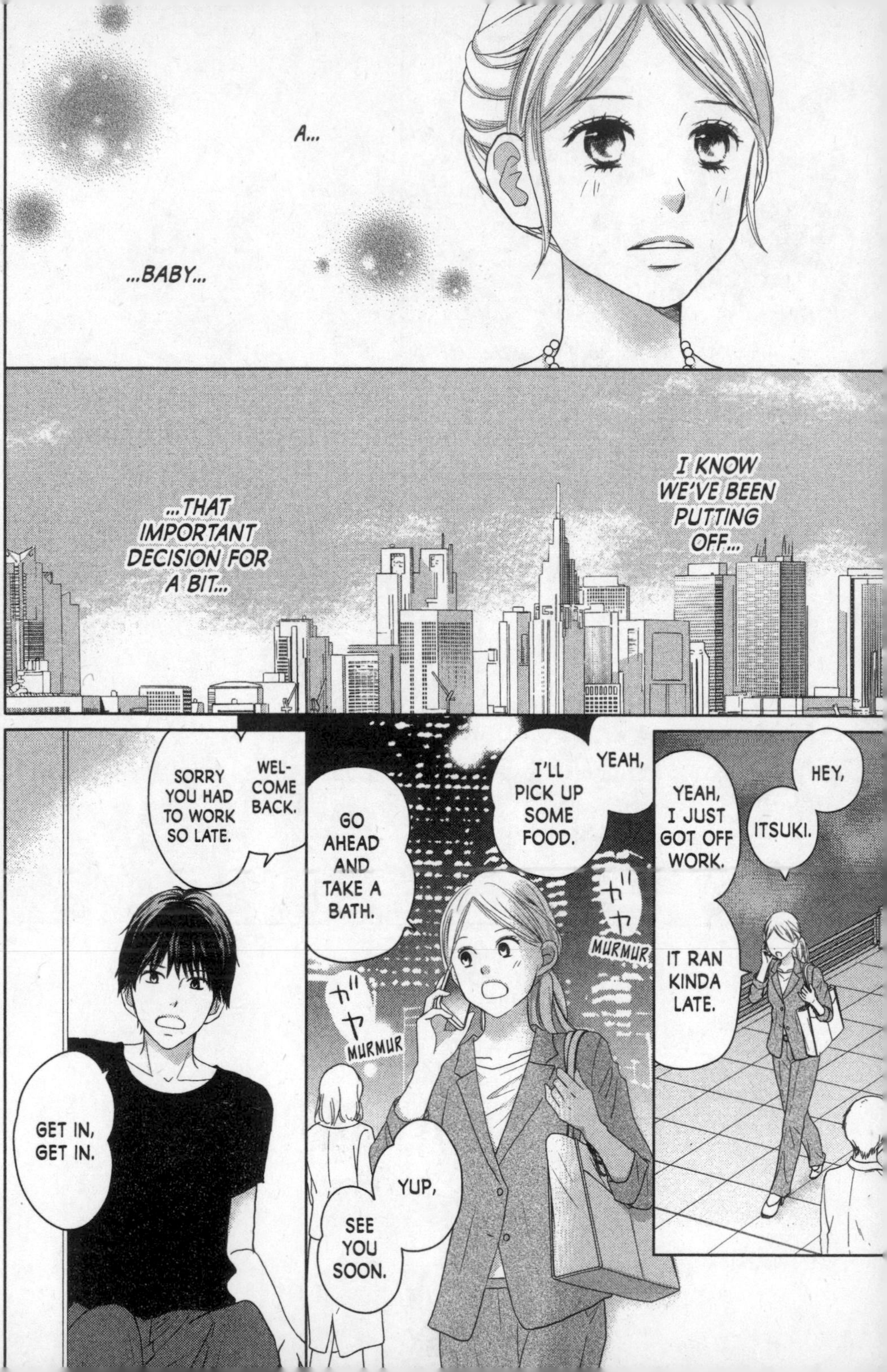
A...
...BABY...
I KNOW WE'VE BEEN PUTTING OFF...
...THAT IMPORTANT DECISION FOR A BIT...
HEY,
ITSUKI.
YEAH, I JUST GOT OFF WORK.
IT RAN KINDA LATE.
YEAH,
I'LL PICK UP SOME FOOD.
GO AHEAD AND TAKE A BATH.
ガヤ
MURMUR
ガヤ
MURMUR
YUP,
SEE YOU SOON.
WEL-COME BACK.
SORRY YOU HAD TO WORK SO LATE.
GET IN, GET IN.

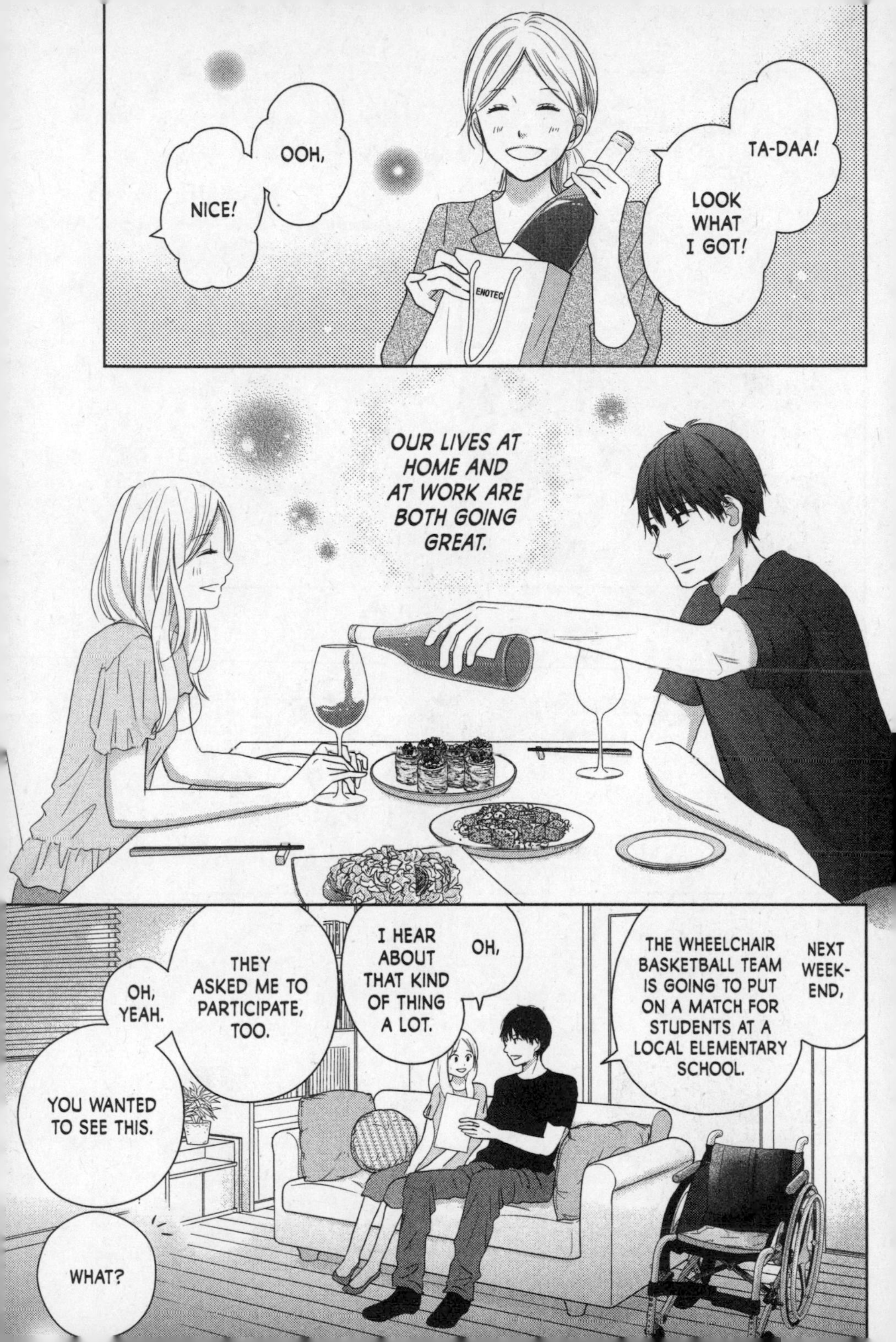
TA-DAA! LOOK WHAT I GOT!
OOH, NICE!
ENOTEC
OUR LIVES AT HOME AND AT WORK ARE BOTH GOING GREAT.
NEXT WEEKEND, THE WHEELCHAIR BASKETBALL TEAM IS GOING TO PUT ON A MATCH FOR STUDENTS AT A LOCAL ELEMENTARY SCHOOL.
OH, I HEAR ABOUT THAT KIND OF THING A LOT.
THEY ASKED ME TO PARTICIPATE, TOO. OH, YEAH. YOU WANTED TO SEE THIS.
WHAT?

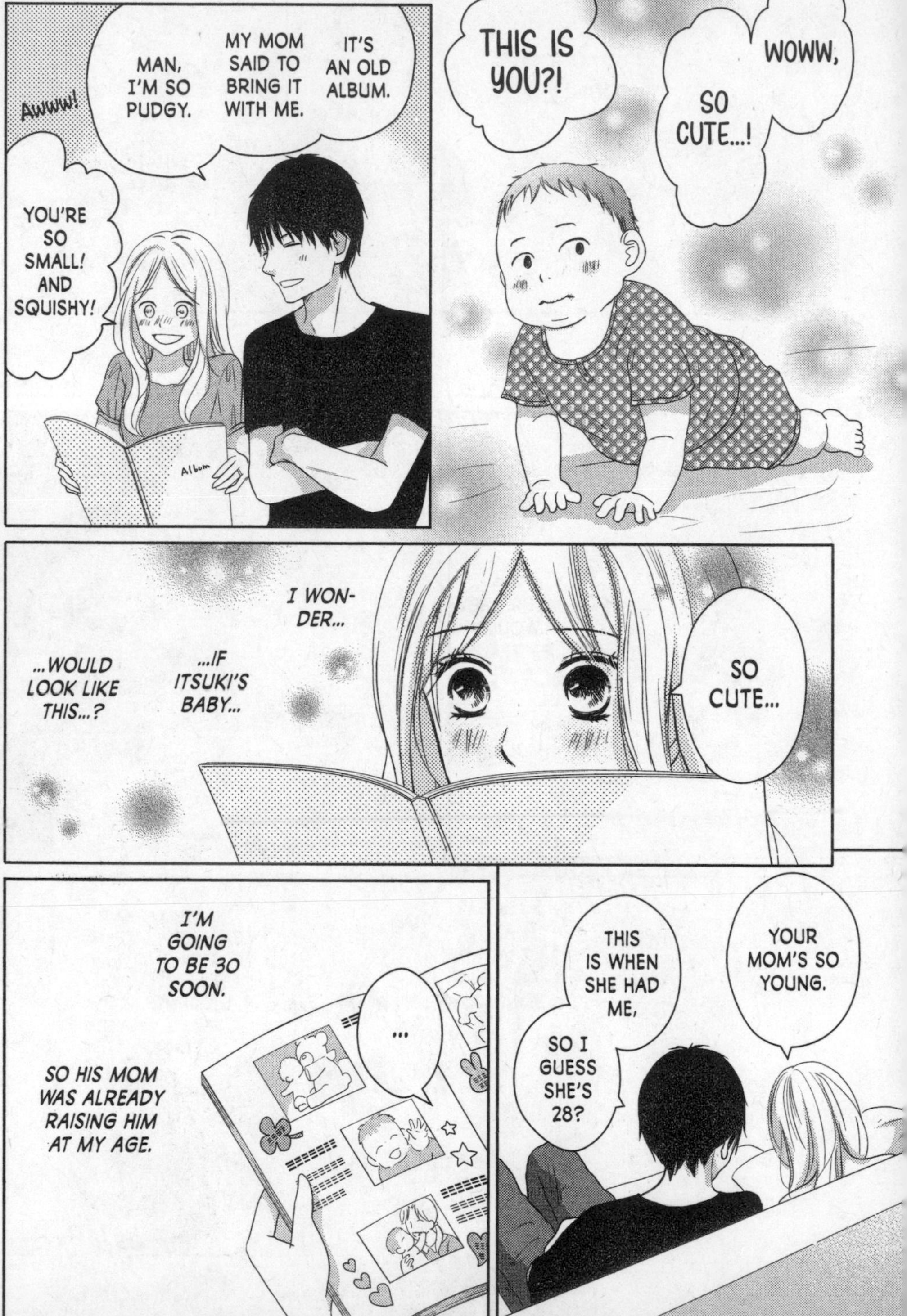
THIS IS YOU?!
WOWW, SO CUTE...!
IT'S AN OLD ALBUM.
MY MOM SAID TO BRING IT WITH ME.
MAN, I'M SO PUDGY.
Awww!
YOU'RE SO SMALL! AND SQUISHY!
Album
SO CUTE...
I WON-DER...
...IF ITSUKI'S BABY...
...WOULD LOOK LIKE THIS...?
YOUR MOM'S SO YOUNG.
THIS IS WHEN SHE HAD ME,
SO I GUESS SHE'S 28?
I'M GOING TO BE 30 SOON.
...
SO HIS MOM WAS ALREADY RAISING HIM AT MY AGE.

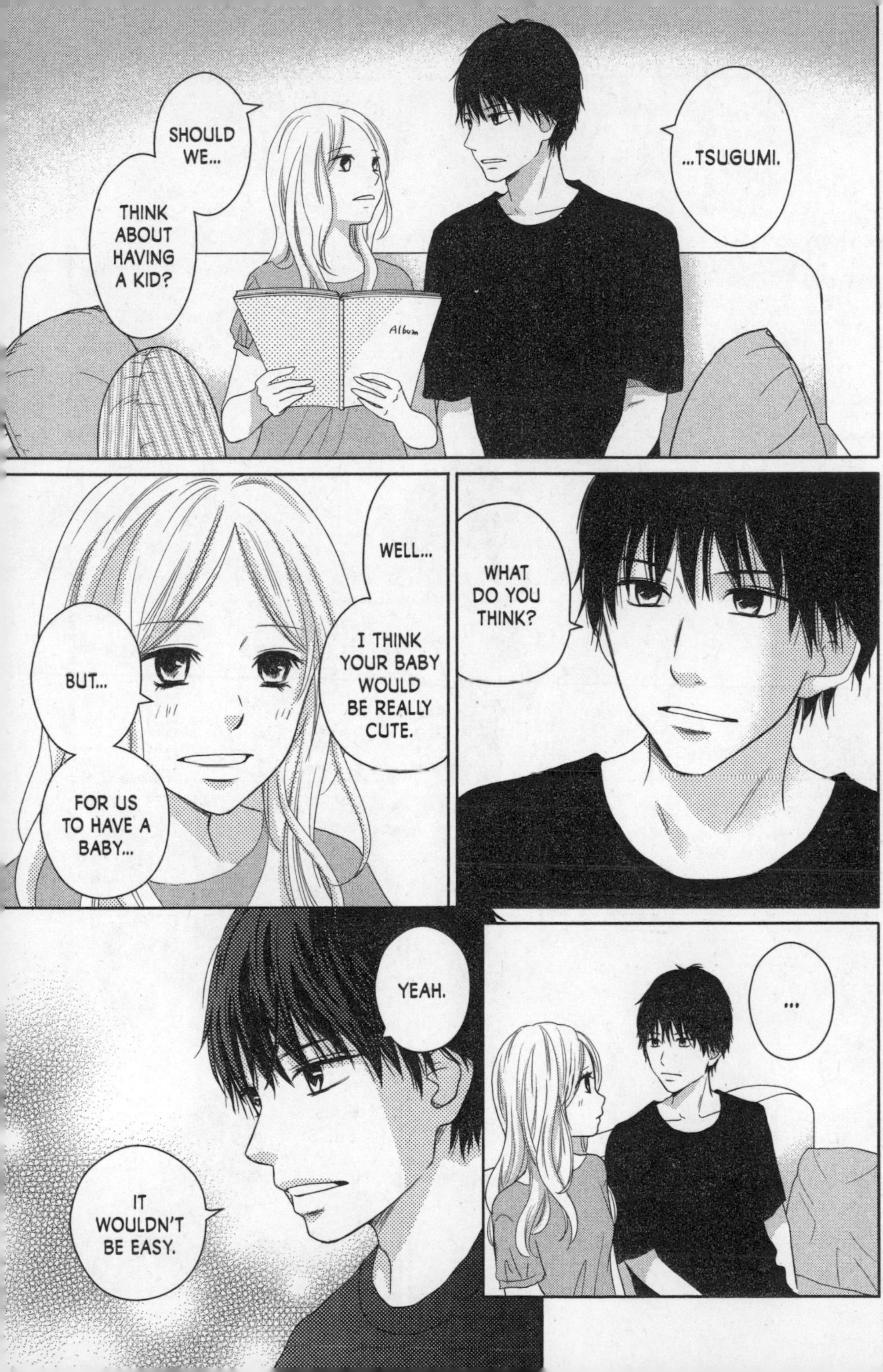
...TSUGUMI.
SHOULD WE...
THINK ABOUT HAVING A KID?
Album
WHAT DO YOU THINK?
WELL...
I THINK YOUR BABY WOULD BE REALLY CUTE.
BUT...
FOR US TO HAVE A BABY...
...
YEAH.
IT WOULDN'T BE EASY.

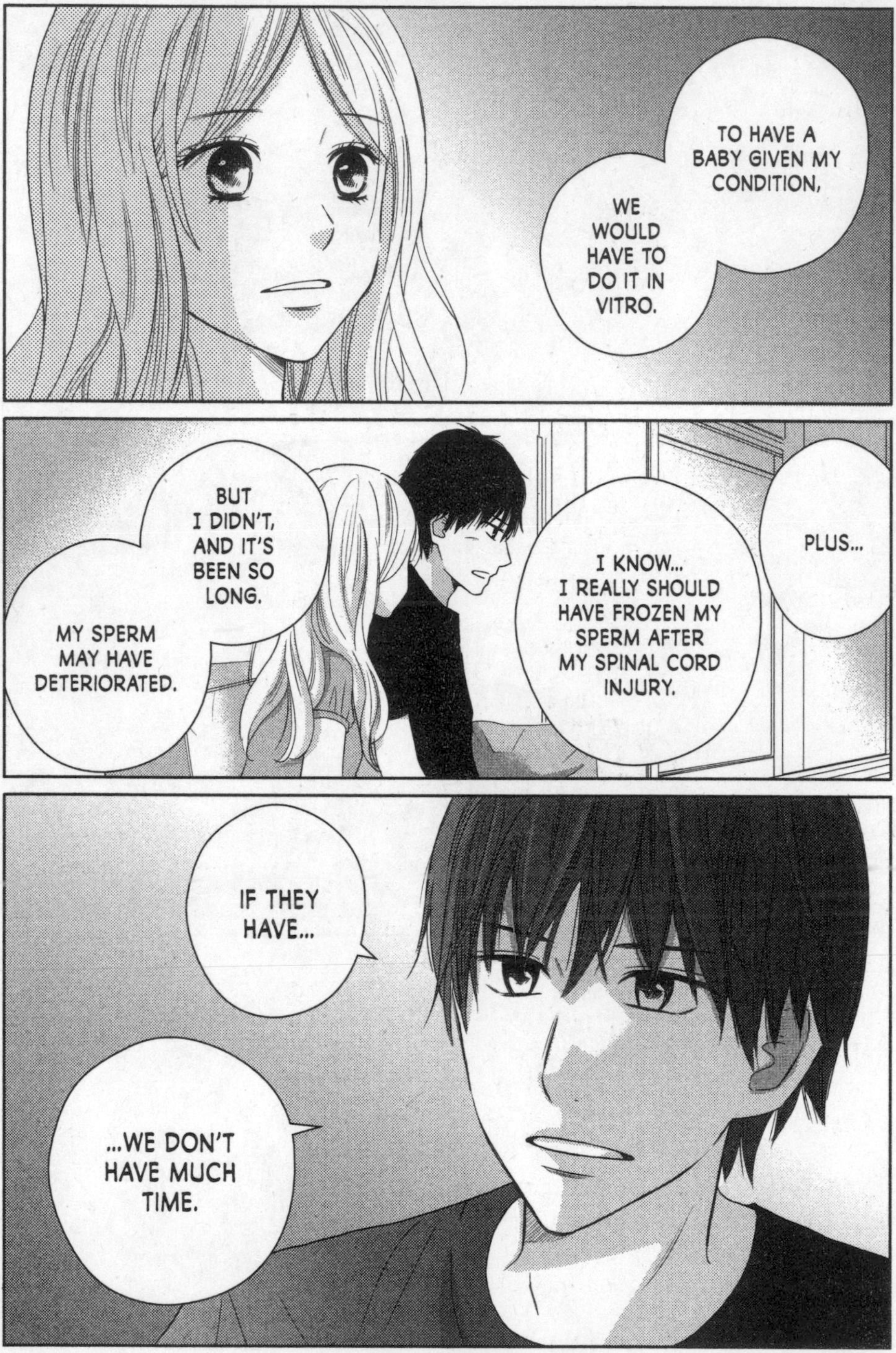
TO HAVE A BABY GIVEN MY CONDITION,
WE WOULD HAVE TO DO IT IN VITRO.
PLUS...
I KNOW... I REALLY SHOULD HAVE FROZEN MY SPERM AFTER MY SPINAL CORD INJURY.
BUT I DIDN'T, AND IT'S BEEN SO LONG.
MY SPERM MAY HAVE DETERIORATED.
IF THEY HAVE...
...WE DON'T HAVE MUCH TIME.

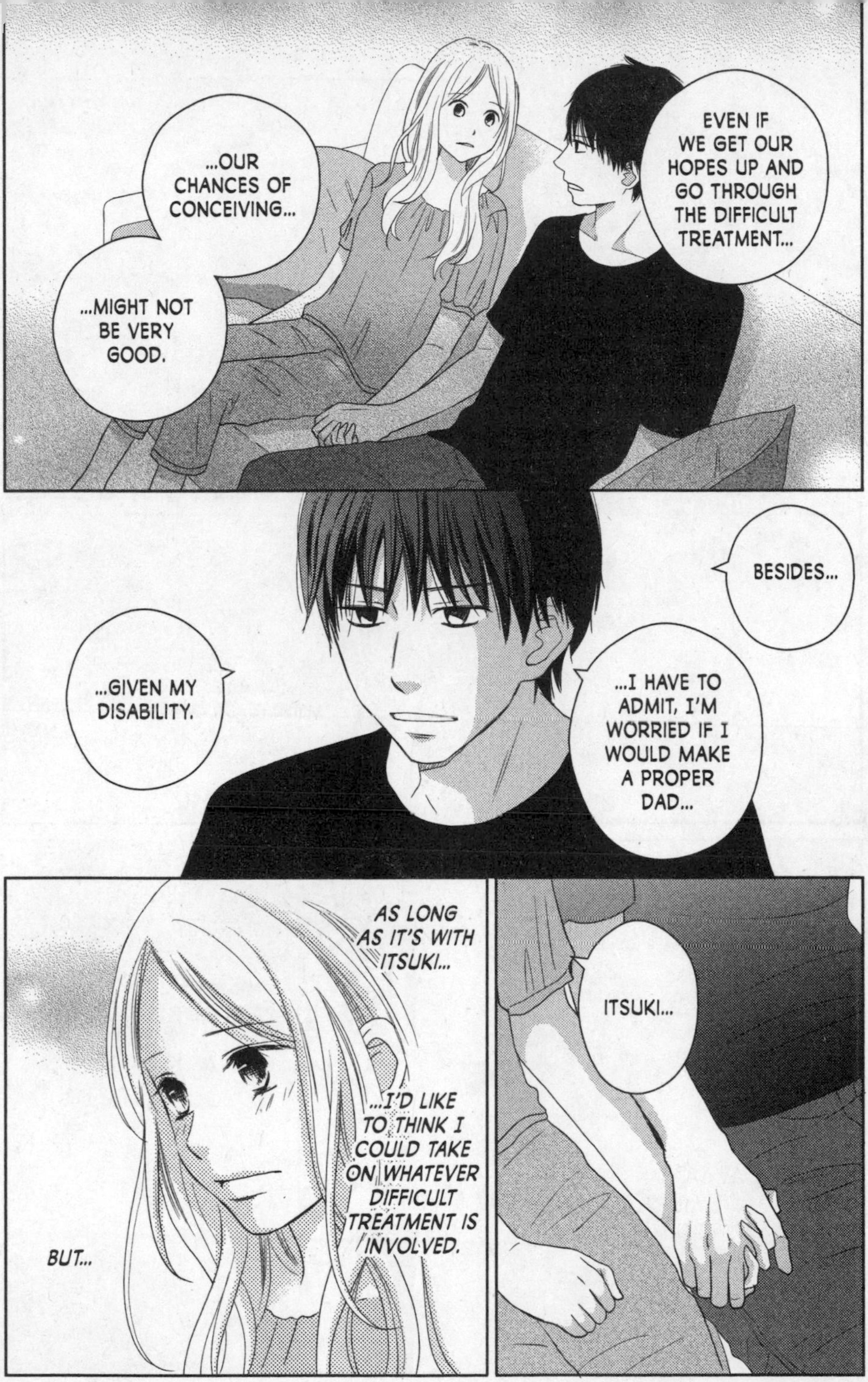
EVEN IF WE GET OUR HOPES UP AND GO THROUGH THE DIFFICULT TREATMENT...
...OUR CHANCES OF CONCEIVING...
...MIGHT NOT BE VERY GOOD.
BESIDES...
...I HAVE TO ADMIT, I'M WORRIED IF I WOULD MAKE A PROPER DAD...
...GIVEN MY DISABILITY.
ITSUKI...
AS LONG AS IT'S WITH ITSUKI...
...I'D LIKE TO THINK I COULD TAKE ON WHATEVER DIFFICULT TREATMENT IS INVOLVED.
BUT...

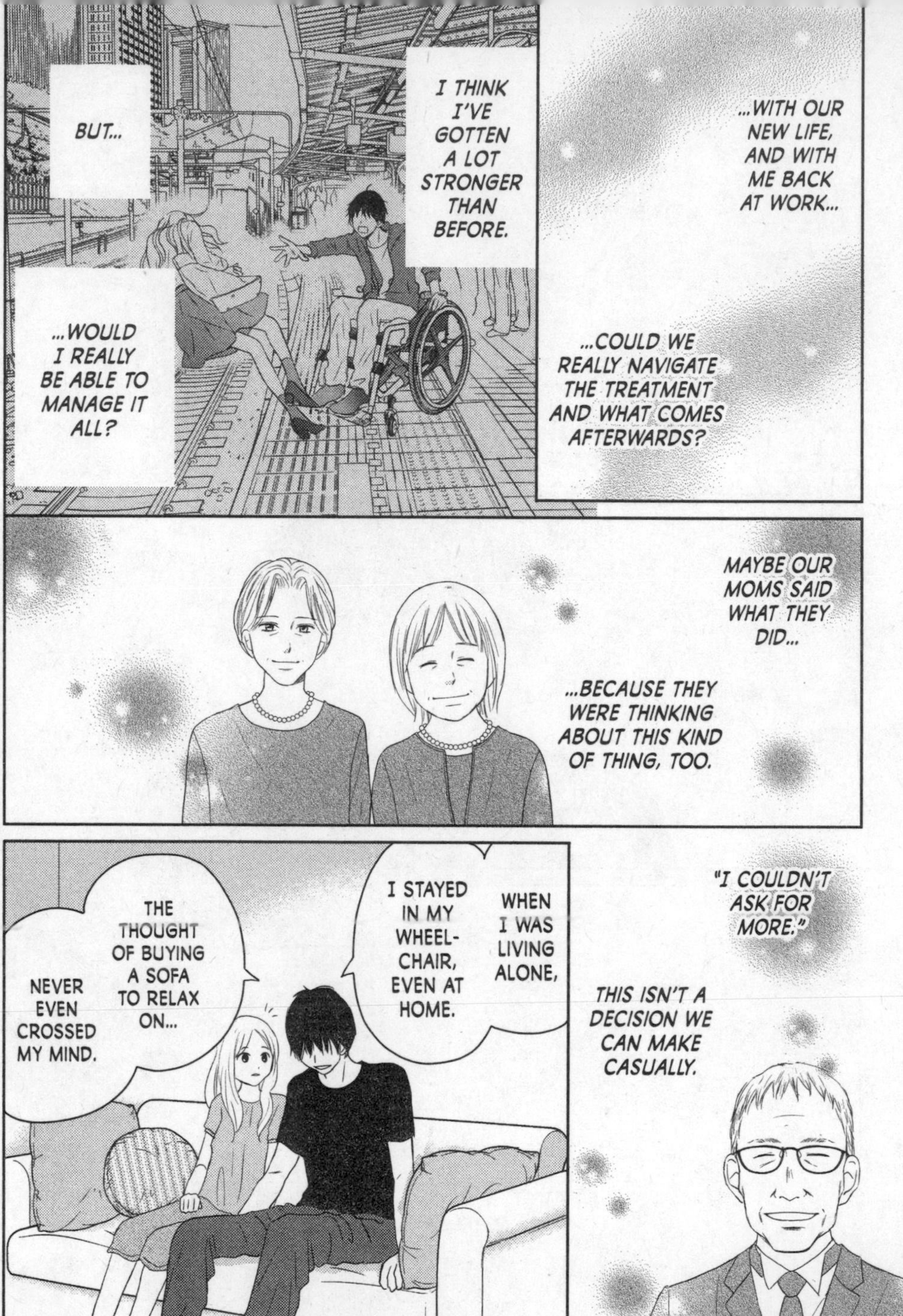
I THINK I'VE GOTTEN A LOT STRONGER THAN BEFORE.
BUT...
...WOULD I REALLY BE ABLE TO MANAGE IT ALL?
...WITH OUR NEW LIFE, AND WITH ME BACK AT WORK...
...COULD WE REALLY NAVIGATE THE TREATMENT AND WHAT COMES AFTERWARDS?
MAYBE OUR MOMS SAID WHAT THEY DID...
...BECAUSE THEY WERE THINKING ABOUT THIS KIND OF THING, TOO.
"I COULDN'T ASK FOR MORE."
THIS ISN'T A DECISION WE CAN MAKE CASUALLY.
WHEN I WAS LIVING ALONE,
I STAYED IN MY WHEEL-CHAIR, EVEN AT HOME.
THE THOUGHT OF BUYING A SOFA TO RELAX ON...
NEVER EVEN CROSSED MY MIND.

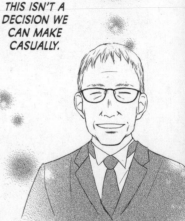

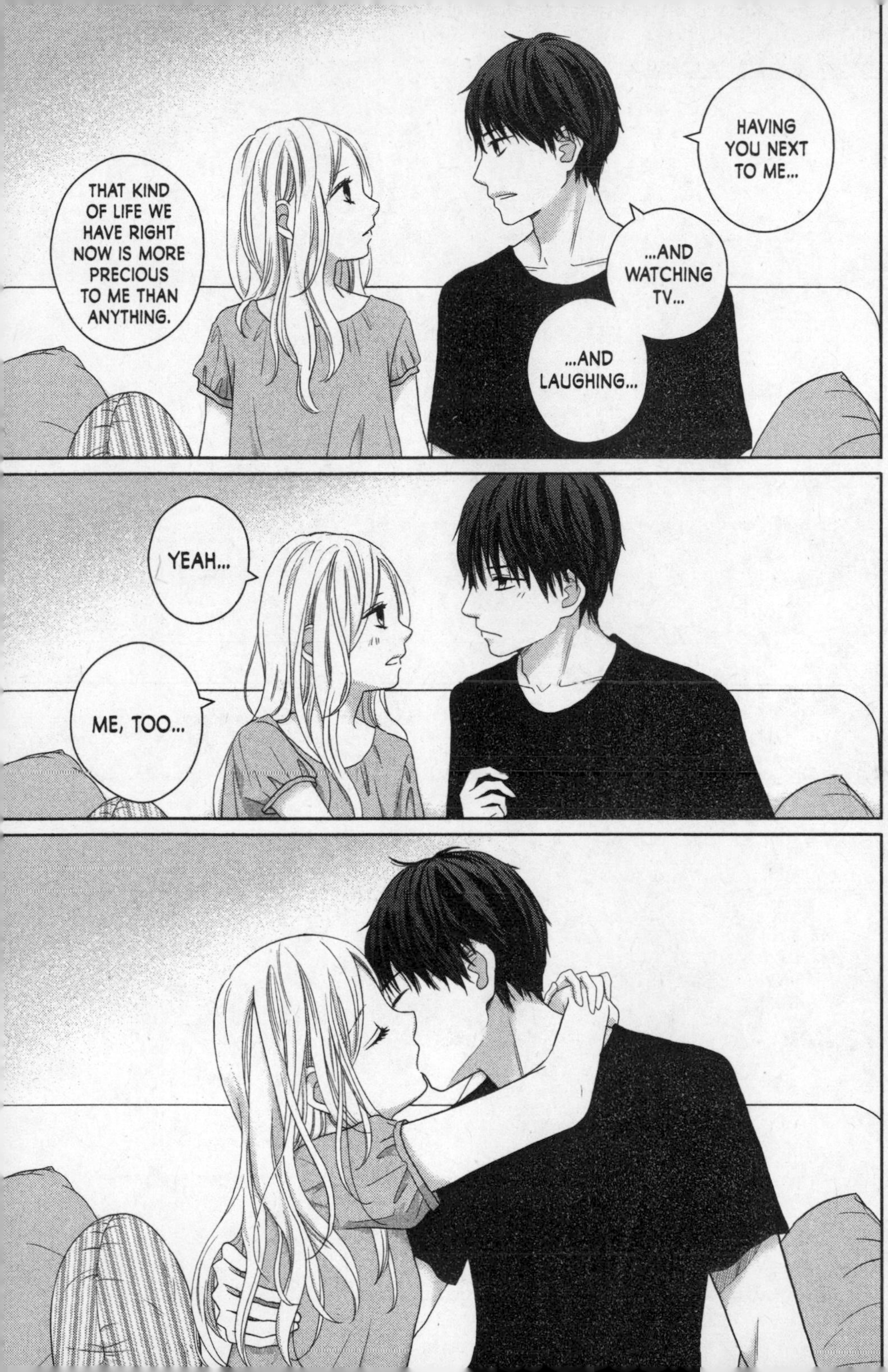
HAVING YOU NEXT TO ME...
...AND WATCHING TV...
...AND LAUGHING...
THAT KIND OF LIFE WE HAVE RIGHT NOW IS MORE PRECIOUS TO ME THAN ANYTHING.
YEAH...
ME, TOO...

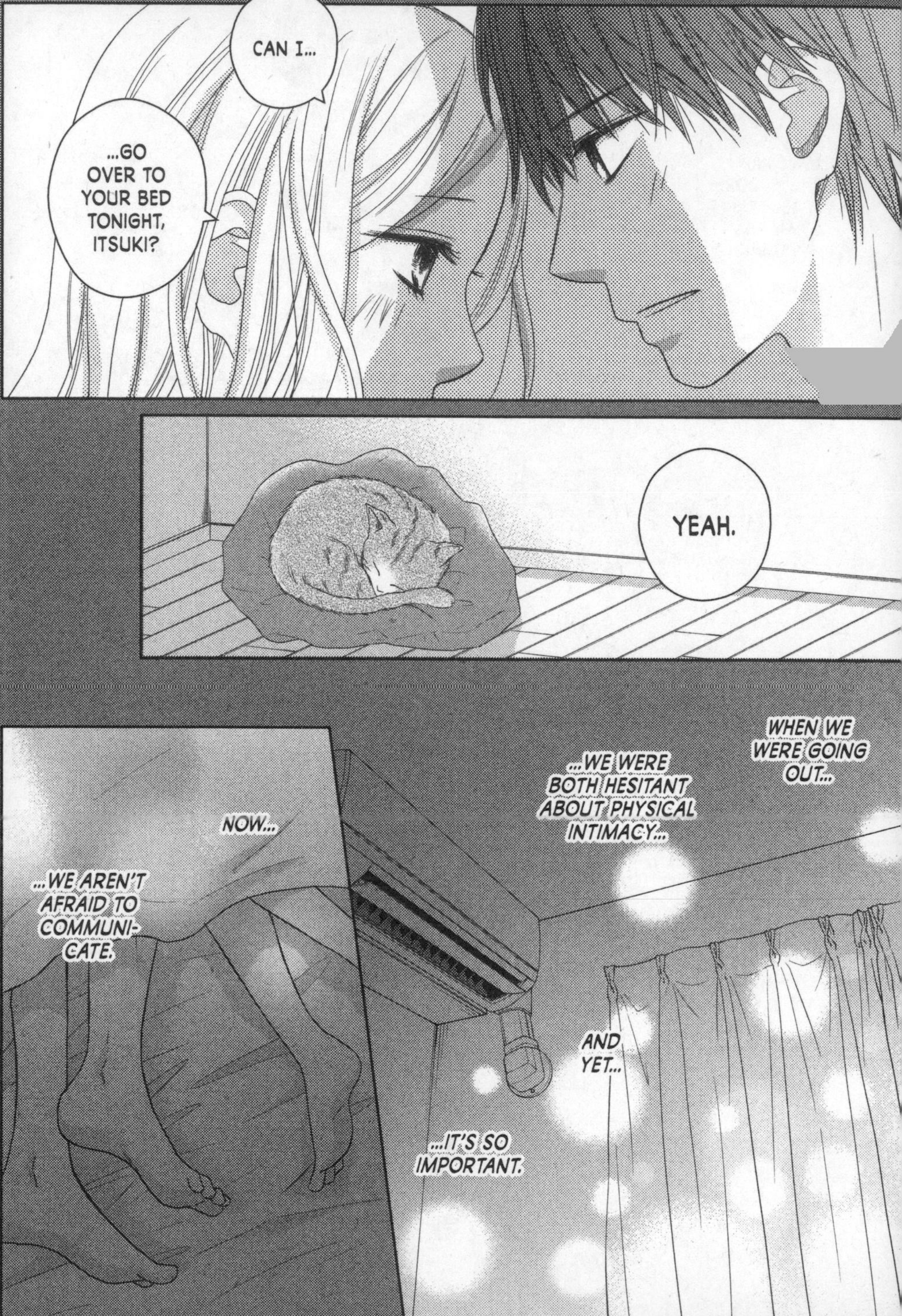
CAN I...
...GO OVER TO YOUR BED TONIGHT, ITSUKI?
YEAH.
WHEN WE WERE GOING OUT...
...WE WERE BOTH HESITANT ABOUT PHYSICAL INTIMACY...
AND YET...
...IT'S SO IMPORTANT.
NOW...
...WE AREN'T AFRAID TO COMMUNI-CATE.

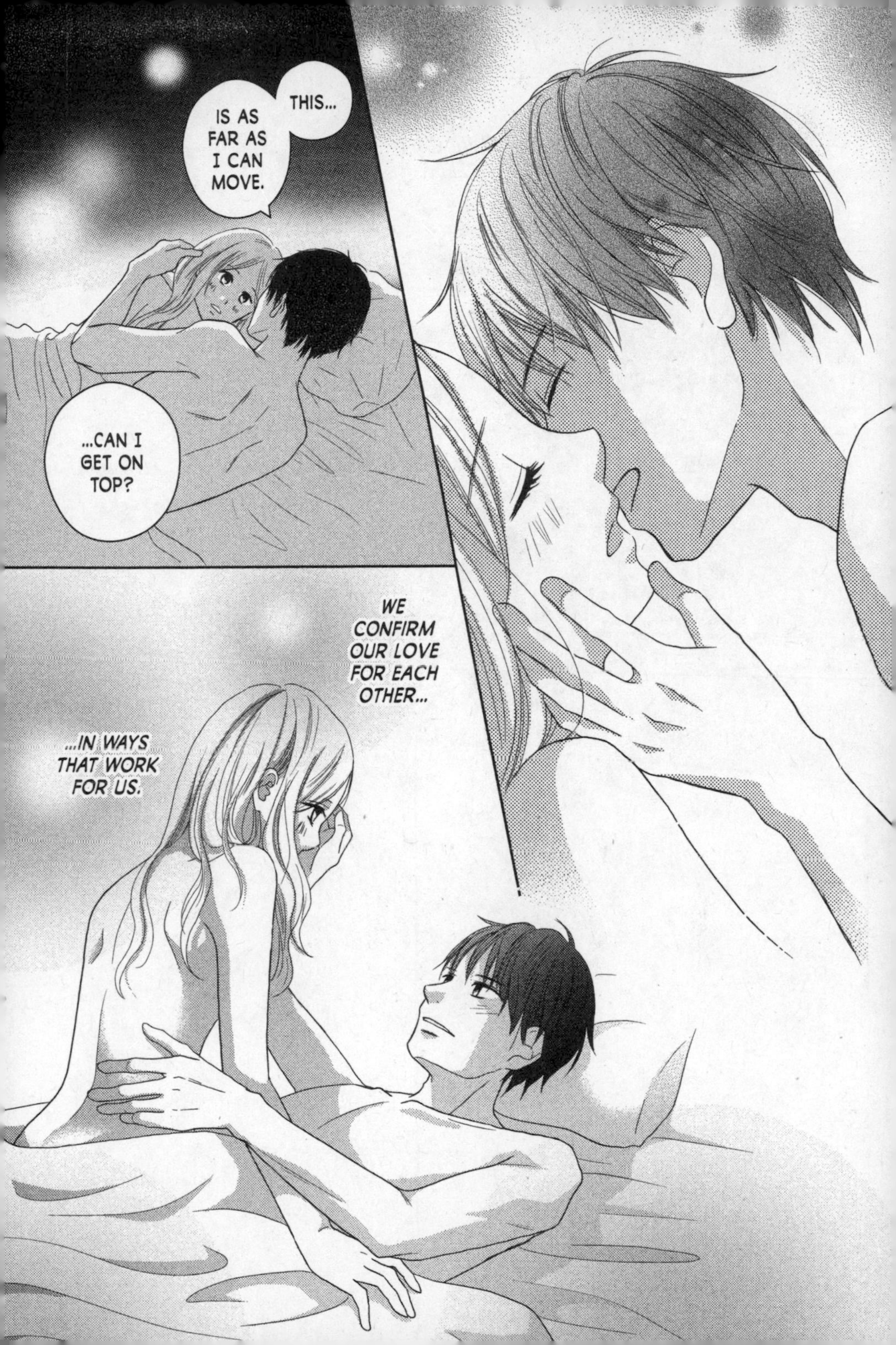
THIS...
IS AS FAR AS I CAN MOVE.
...CAN I GET ON TOP?
WE CONFIRM OUR LOVE FOR EACH OTHER...
...IN WAYS THAT WORK FOR US.

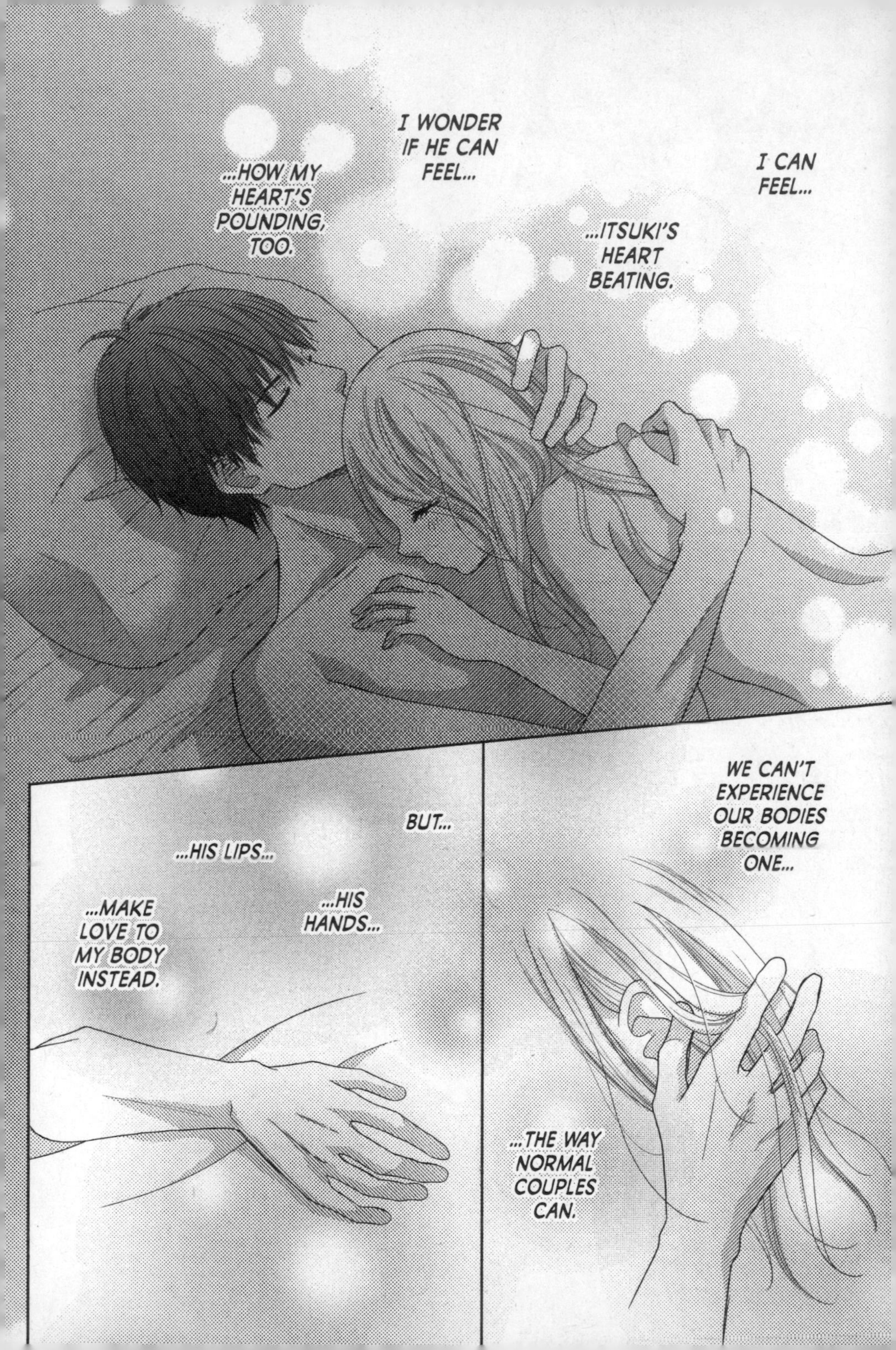
I CAN FEEL...
...ITSUKI'S HEART BEATING.
I WONDER IF HE CAN FEEL...
...HOW MY HEART'S POUNDING, TOO.
WE CAN'T EXPERIENCE OUR BODIES BECOMING ONE...
...THE WAY NORMAL COUPLES CAN.
BUT...
...HIS LIPS...
...HIS HANDS...
...MAKE LOVE TO MY BODY INSTEAD.

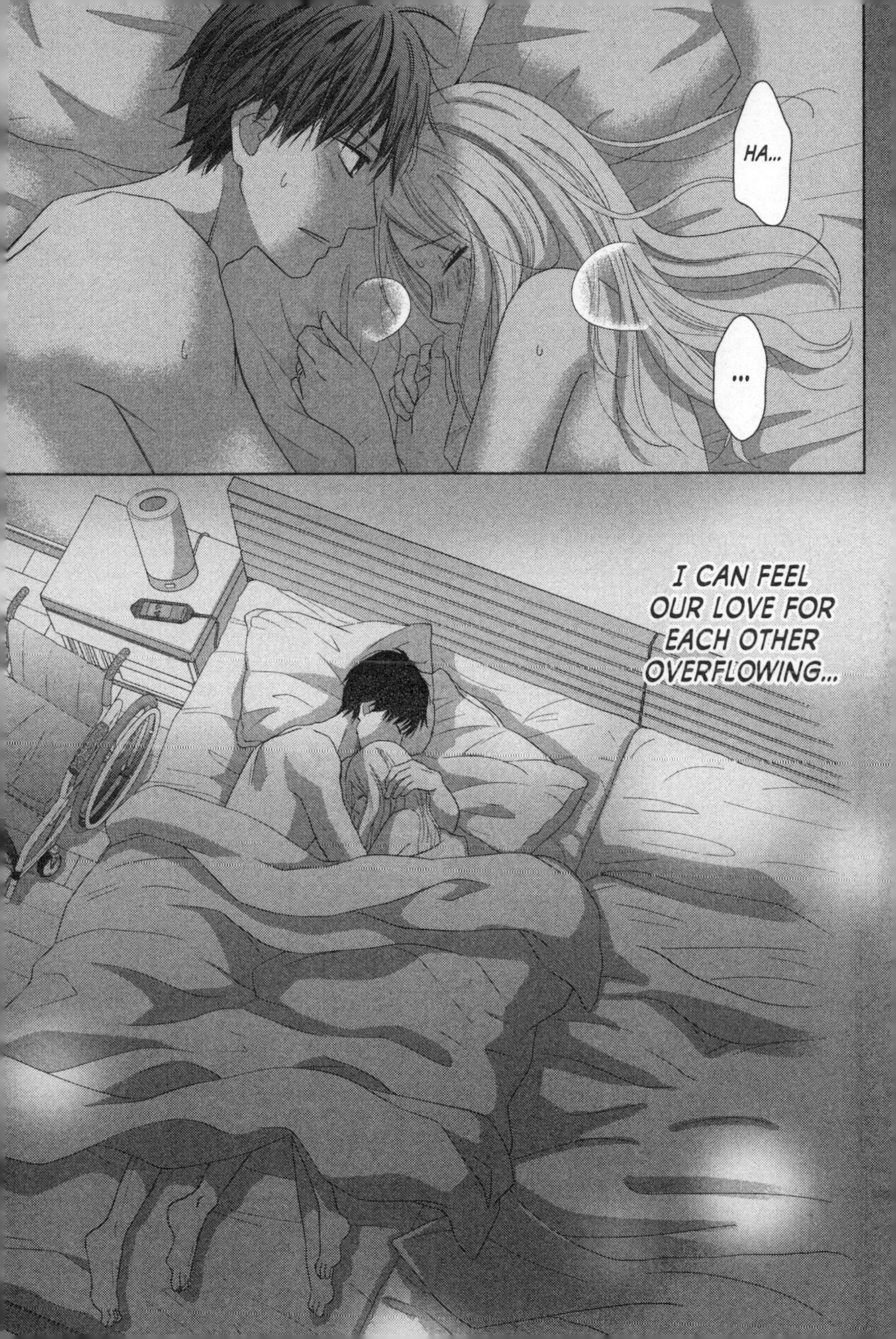
HA...
...
I CAN FEEL OUR LOVE FOR EACH OTHER OVERFLOWING...

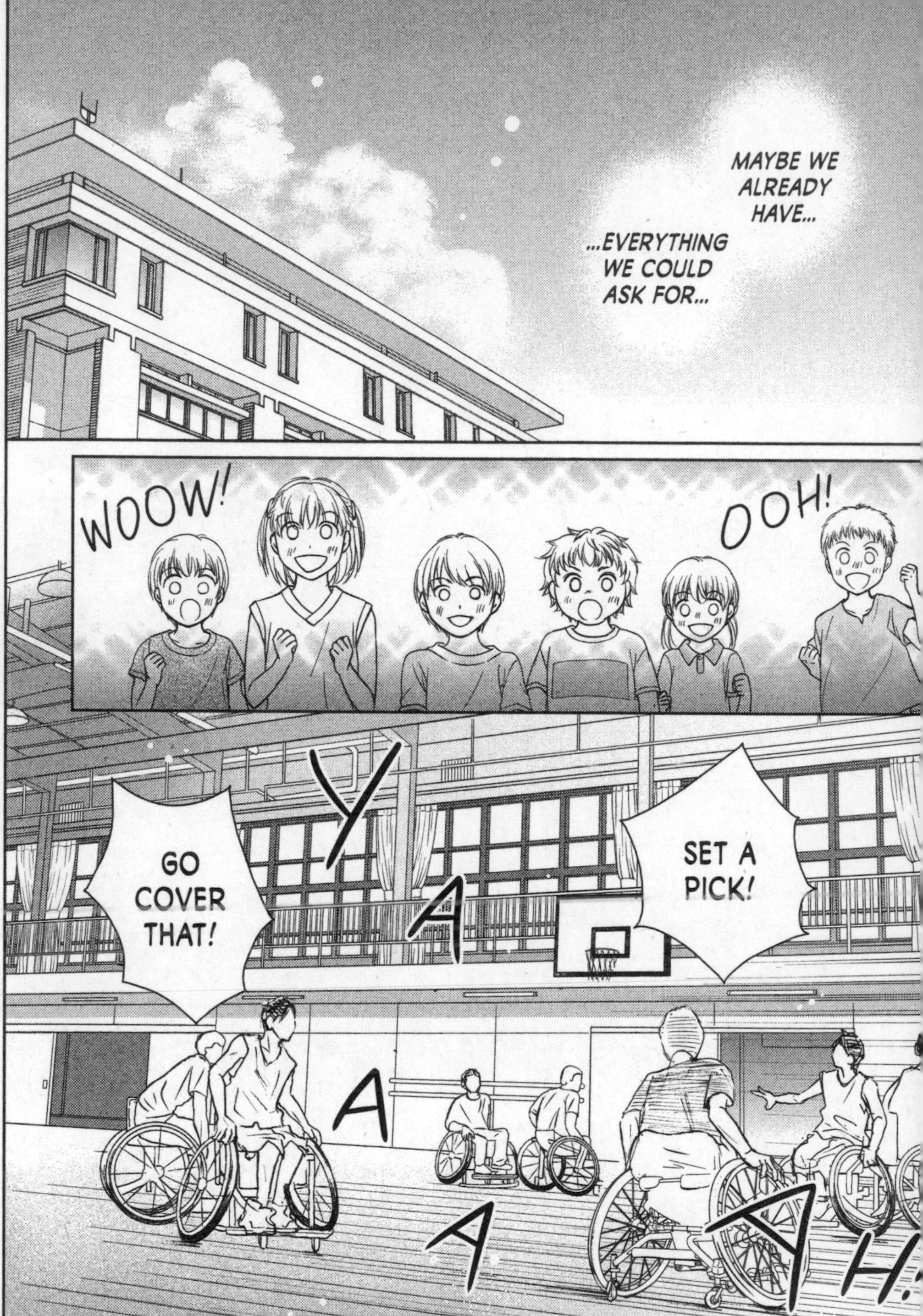
MAYBE WE ALREADY HAVE...
...EVERYTHING WE COULD ASK FOR...
OOH!
WOOW!
SET A PICK!
GO COVER THAT!
YAAAAAH!

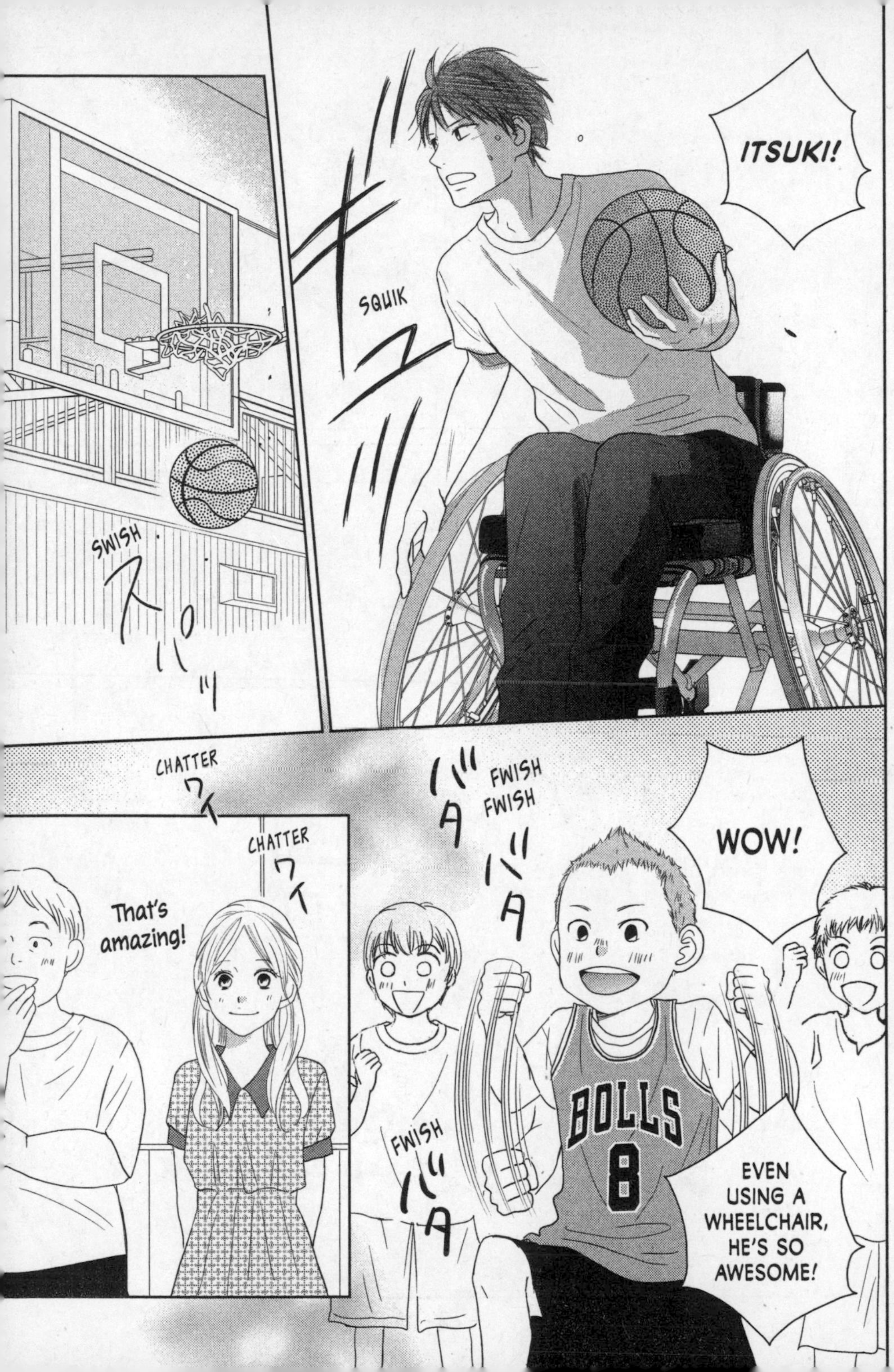
ITSUKI!
SQUIK
SWISH
CHATTER
WOW!
FWISH
FWISH
EVEN USING A WHEELCHAIR, HE'S SO AWESOME!
FWISH
CHATTER
That's amazing!

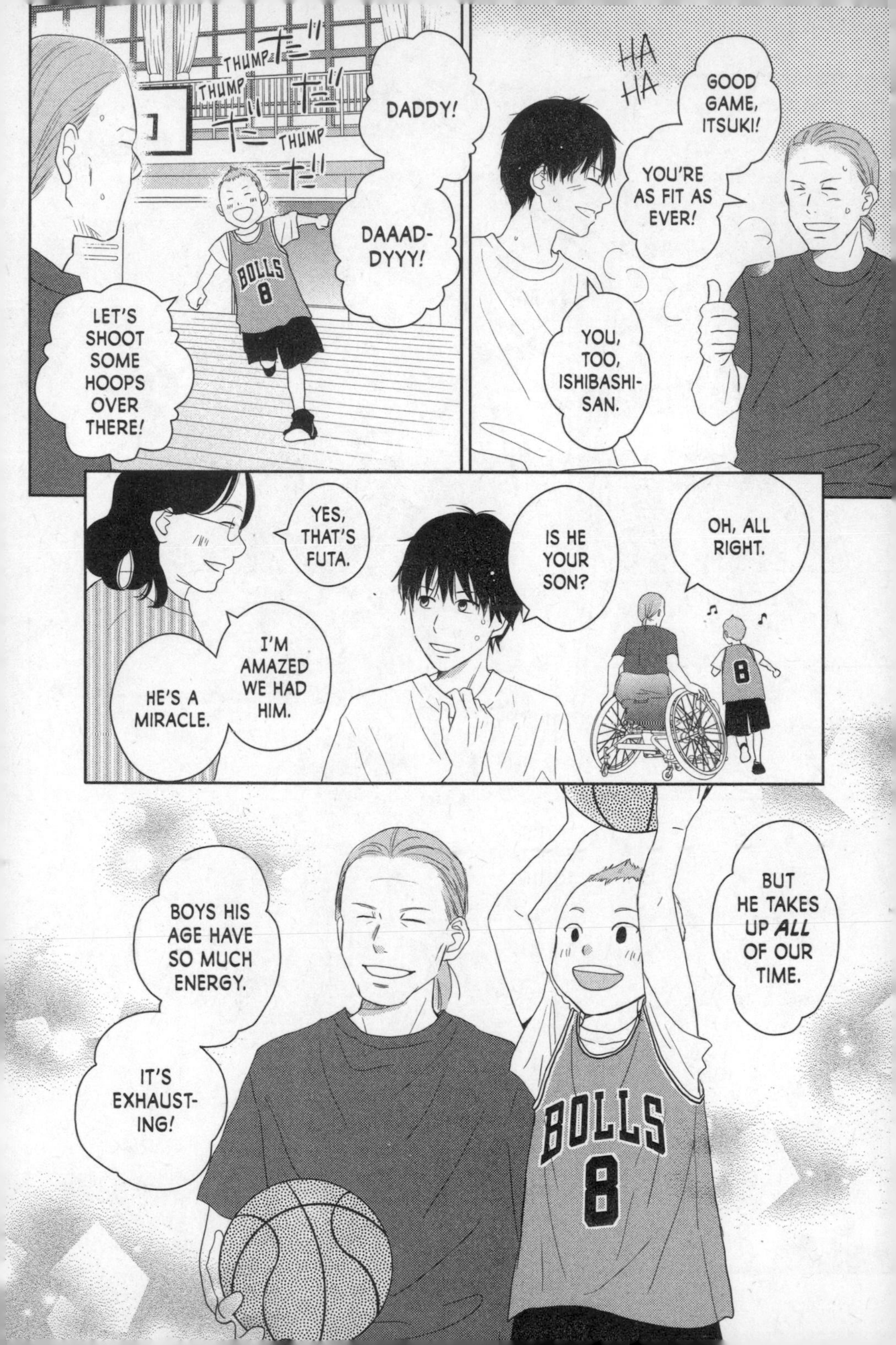
HA HA
GOOD GAME, ITSUKI!
YOU'RE AS FIT AS EVER!
YOU, TOO, ISHIBASHI-SAN.
THUMP
THUMP
THUMP
DADDY!
DAAAD-DYYY!
BOLLS 8
LET'S SHOOT SOME HOOPS OVER THERE!
OH, ALL RIGHT.
IS HE YOUR SON?
YES, THAT'S FUTA.
I'M AMAZED WE HAD HIM.
HE'S A MIRACLE.
BUT HE TAKES UP *ALL* OF OUR TIME.
BOYS HIS AGE HAVE SO MUCH ENERGY.
IT'S EXHAUST-ING!
BOLLS 8

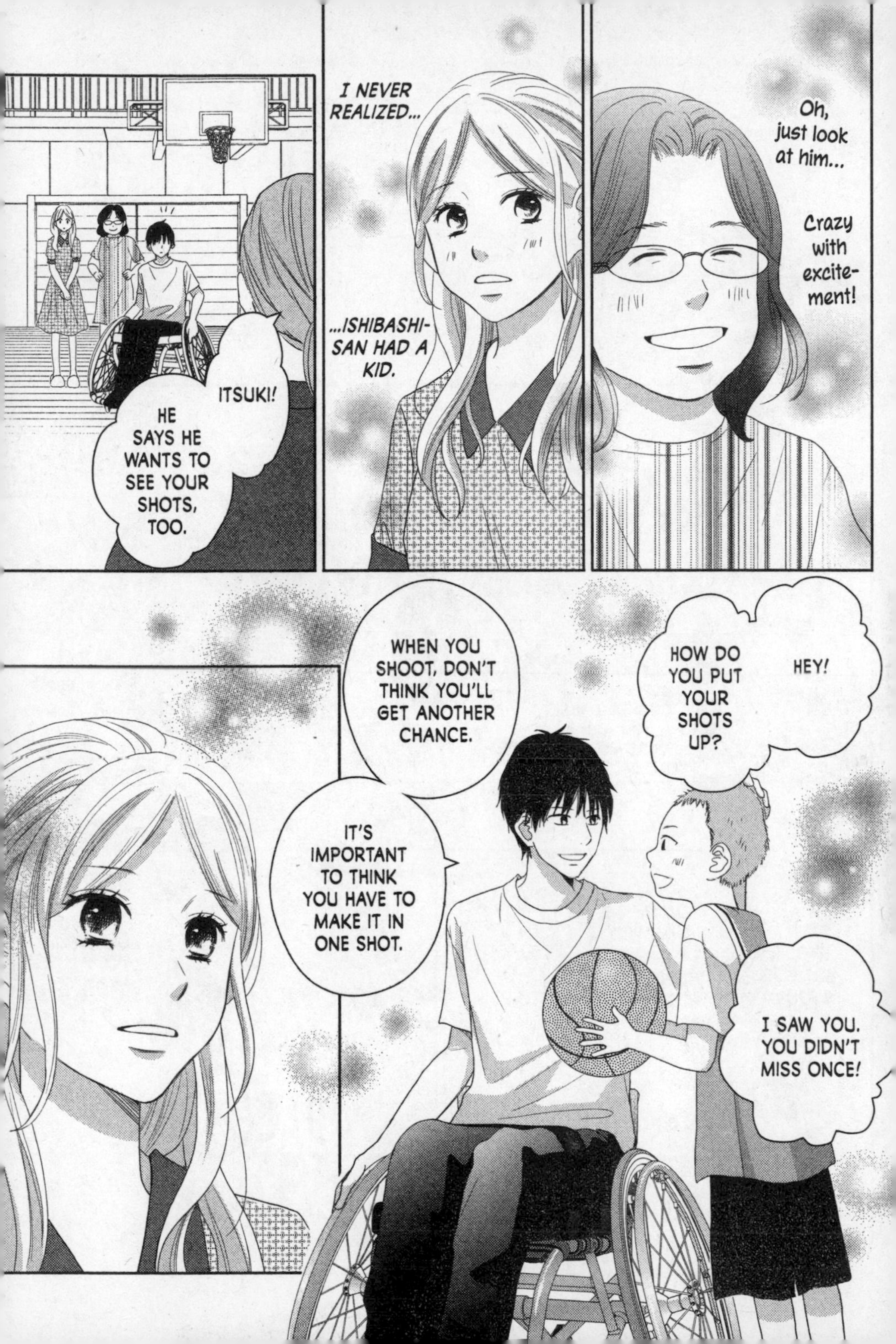
Oh, just look at him...
Crazy with excite-ment!
I NEVER REALIZED...
...ISHIBASHI-SAN HAD A KID.
ITSUKI!
HE SAYS HE WANTS TO SEE YOUR SHOTS, TOO.
HEY!
HOW DO YOU PUT YOUR SHOTS UP?
I SAW YOU. YOU DIDN'T MISS ONCE!
WHEN YOU SHOOT, DON'T THINK YOU'LL GET ANOTHER CHANCE.
IT'S IMPORTANT TO THINK YOU HAVE TO MAKE IT IN ONE SHOT.

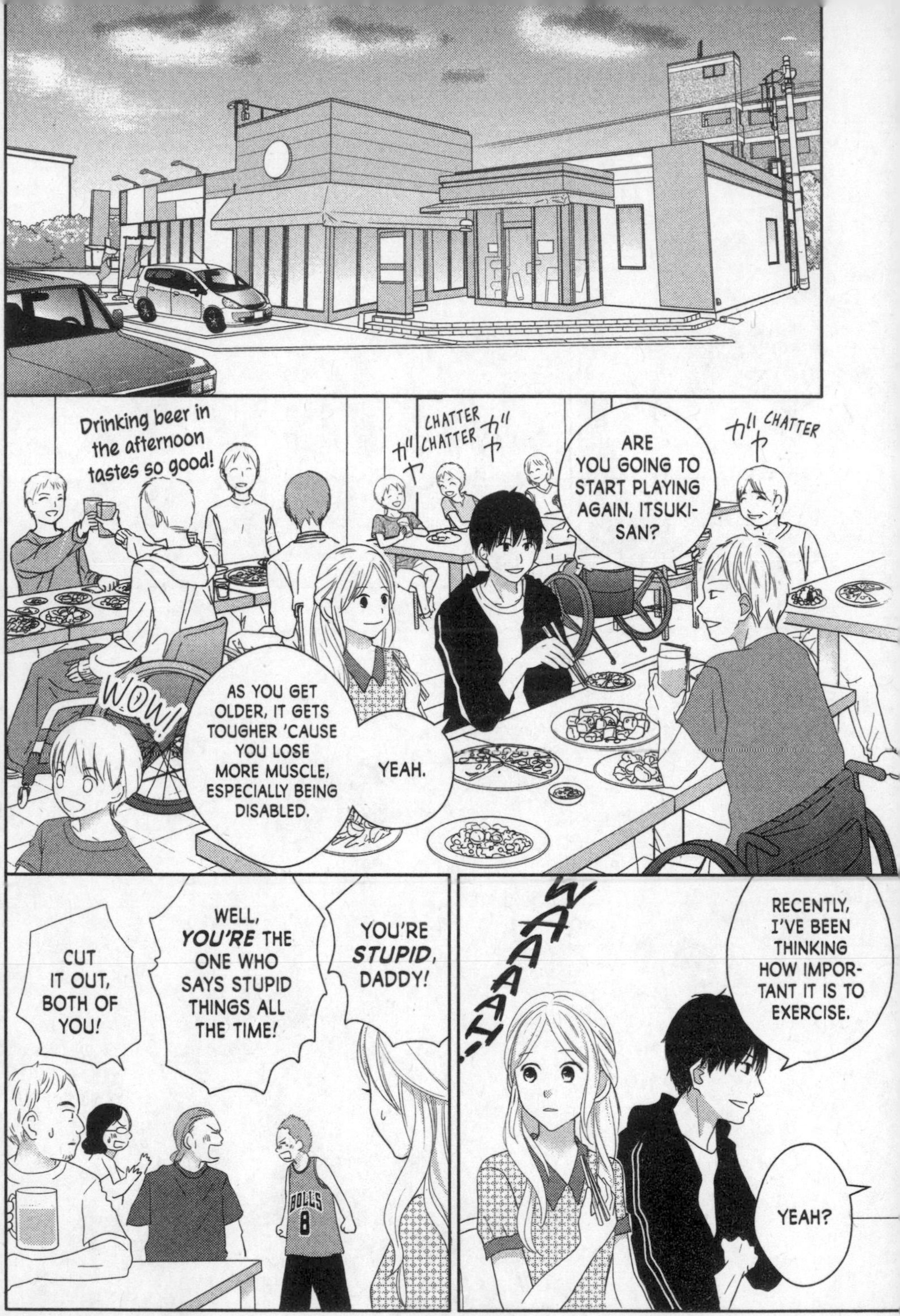
ガヤ CHATTER
ARE YOU GOING TO START PLAYING AGAIN, ITSUKI-SAN?
ガヤガヤ CHATTER CHATTER
Drinking beer in the afternoon tastes so good!
YEAH.
AS YOU GET OLDER, IT GETS TOUGHER 'CAUSE YOU LOSE MORE MUSCLE, ESPECIALLY BEING DISABLED.
WOW!
RECENTLY, I'VE BEEN THINKING HOW IMPORTANT IT IS TO EXERCISE.
WAAAAH!
YEAH?
YOU'RE *STUPID*, DADDY!
WELL, *YOU'RE* THE ONE WHO SAYS STUPID THINGS ALL THE TIME!
CUT IT OUT, BOTH OF YOU!

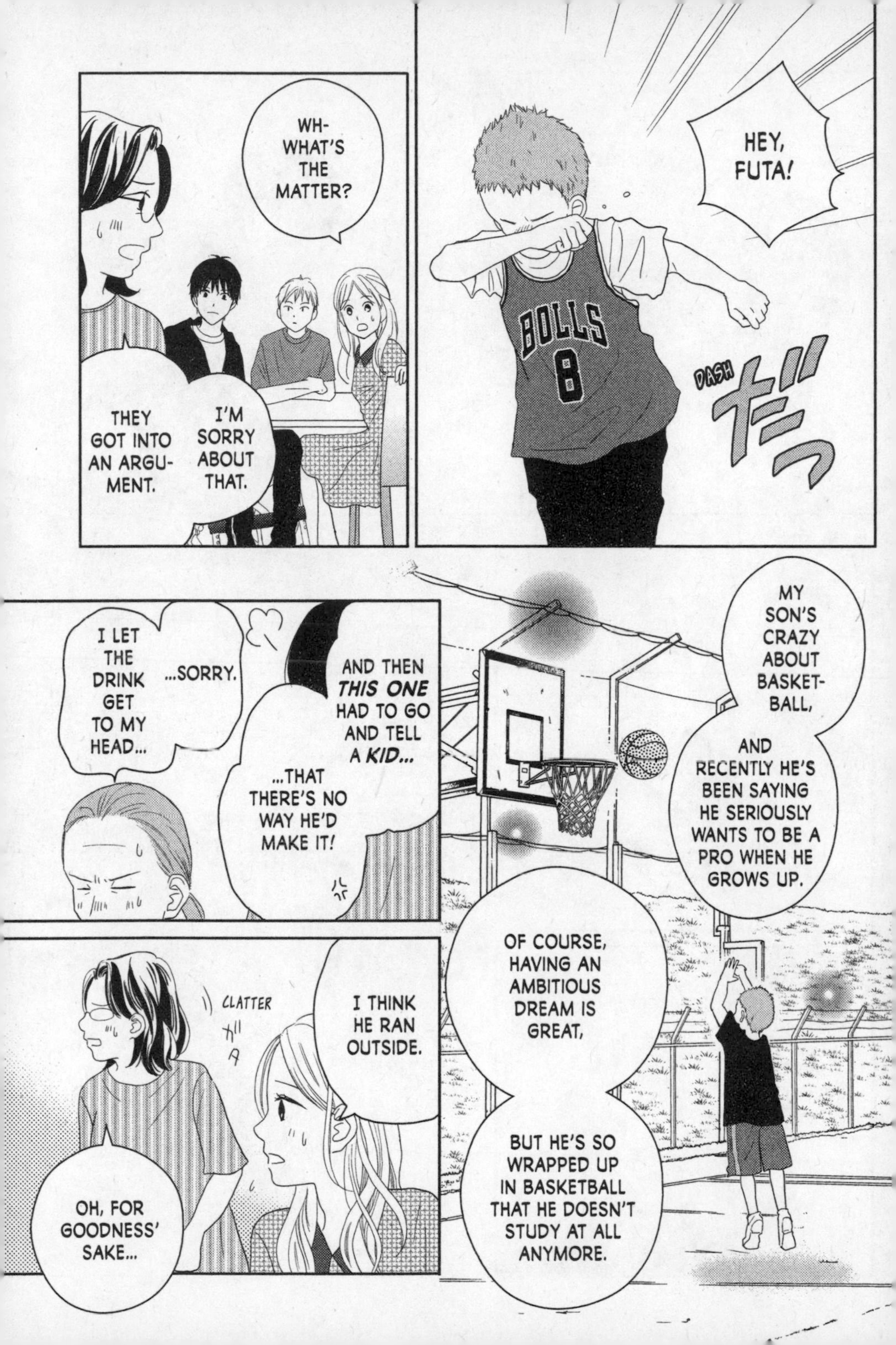
HEY, FUTA!
DASH
WH- WHAT'S THE MATTER?
I'M SORRY ABOUT THAT.
THEY GOT INTO AN ARGU- MENT.
MY SON'S CRAZY ABOUT BASKET- BALL,
AND RECENTLY HE'S BEEN SAYING HE SERIOUSLY WANTS TO BE A PRO WHEN HE GROWS UP.
OF COURSE, HAVING AN AMBITIOUS DREAM IS GREAT,
BUT HE'S SO WRAPPED UP IN BASKETBALL THAT HE DOESN'T STUDY AT ALL ANYMORE.
AND THEN *THIS ONE* HAD TO GO AND TELL A *KID*...
...THAT THERE'S NO WAY HE'D MAKE IT!
I LET THE DRINK GET TO MY HEAD...
...SORRY.
I THINK HE RAN OUTSIDE.
CLATTER
OH, FOR GOODNESS' SAKE...

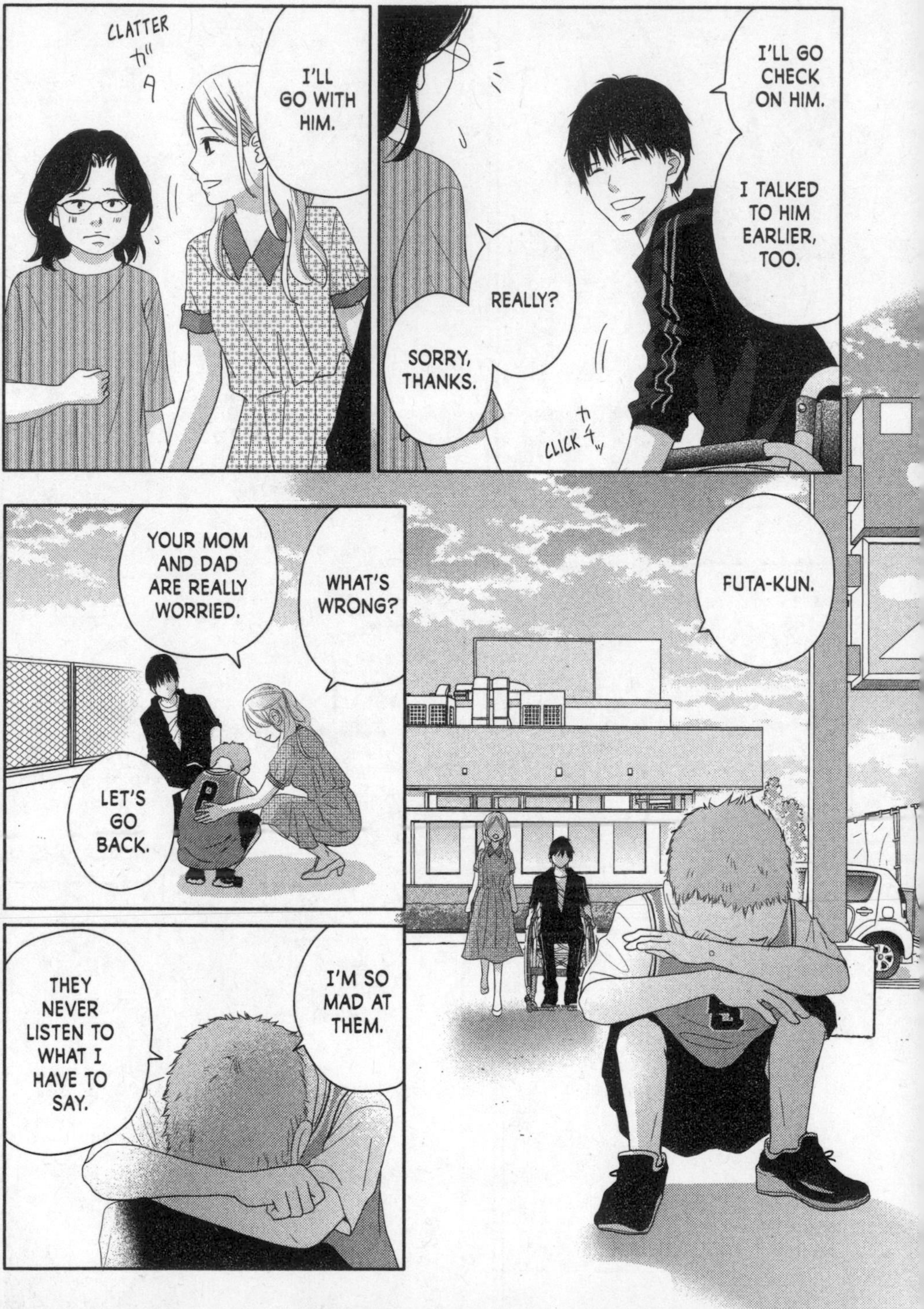
I'LL GO CHECK ON HIM.
I TALKED TO HIM EARLIER, TOO.
REALLY?
SORRY, THANKS.
CLICK
I'LL GO WITH HIM.
CLATTER
FUTA-KUN.
WHAT'S WRONG?
YOUR MOM AND DAD ARE REALLY WORRIED.
LET'S GO BACK.
I'M SO MAD AT THEM.
THEY NEVER LISTEN TO WHAT I HAVE TO SAY.

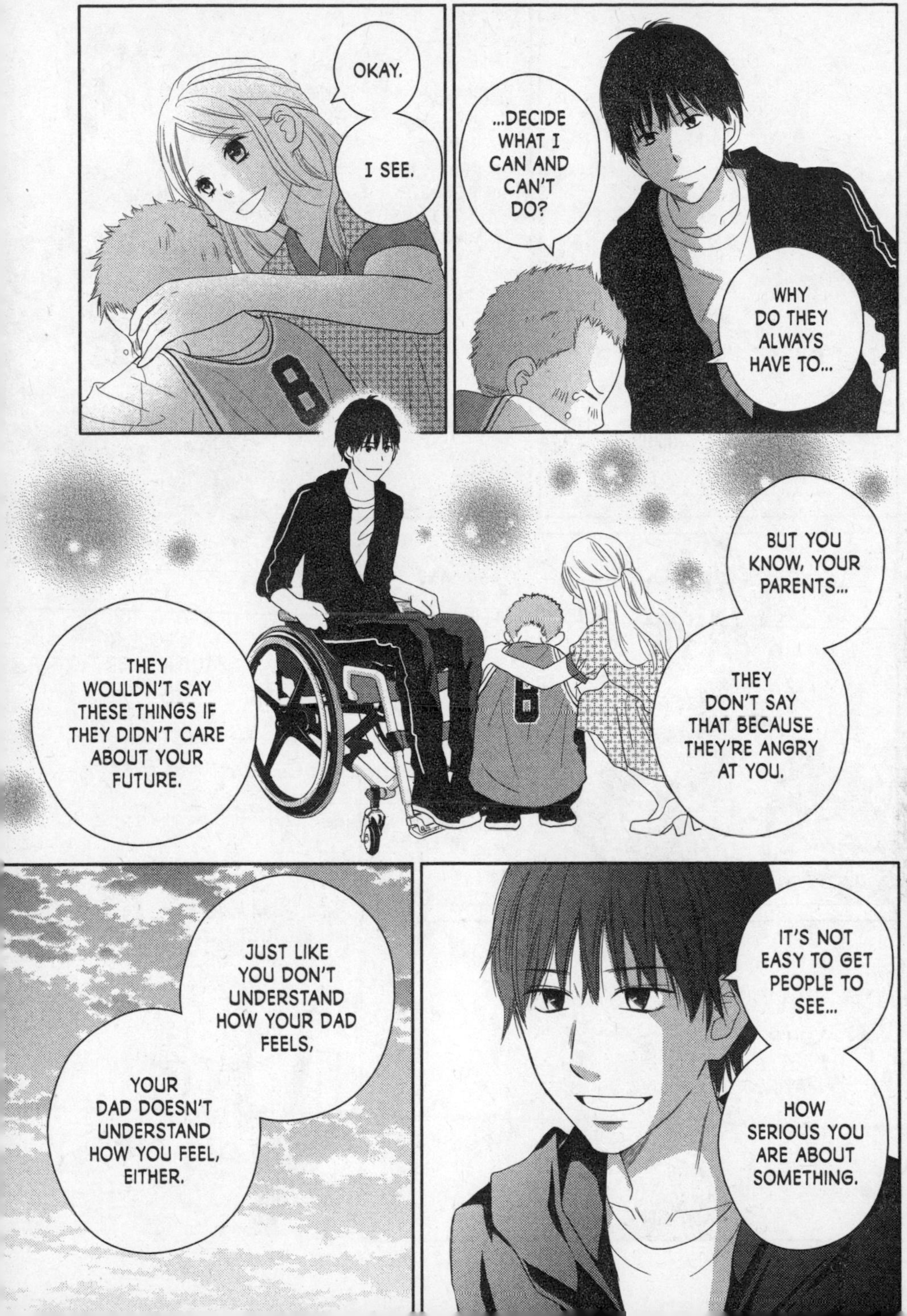
WHY DO THEY ALWAYS HAVE TO...
...DECIDE WHAT I CAN AND CAN'T DO?
OKAY.
I SEE.
BUT YOU KNOW, YOUR PARENTS...
THEY DON'T SAY THAT BECAUSE THEY'RE ANGRY AT YOU.
THEY WOULDN'T SAY THESE THINGS IF THEY DIDN'T CARE ABOUT YOUR FUTURE.
IT'S NOT EASY TO GET PEOPLE TO SEE...
HOW SERIOUS YOU ARE ABOUT SOMETHING.
JUST LIKE YOU DON'T UNDERSTAND HOW YOUR DAD FEELS,
YOUR DAD DOESN'T UNDERSTAND HOW YOU FEEL, EITHER.

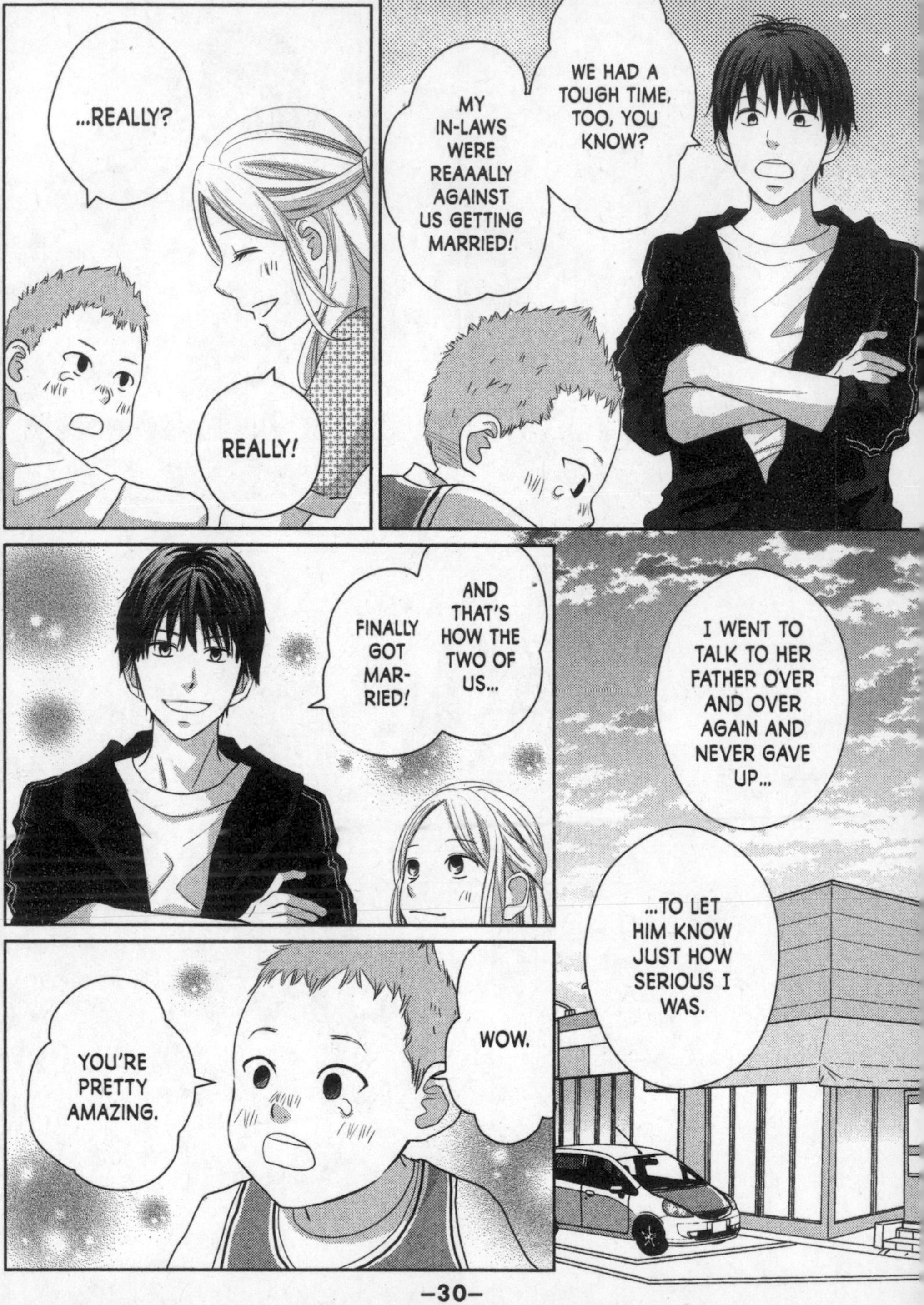
WE HAD A TOUGH TIME, TOO, YOU KNOW?
MY IN-LAWS WERE REAAALLY AGAINST US GETTING MARRIED!
...REALLY?
REALLY!
I WENT TO TALK TO HER FATHER OVER AND OVER AGAIN AND NEVER GAVE UP...
...TO LET HIM KNOW JUST HOW SERIOUS I WAS.
AND THAT'S HOW THE TWO OF US...
FINALLY GOT MAR-RIED!
WOW.
YOU'RE PRETTY AMAZING.

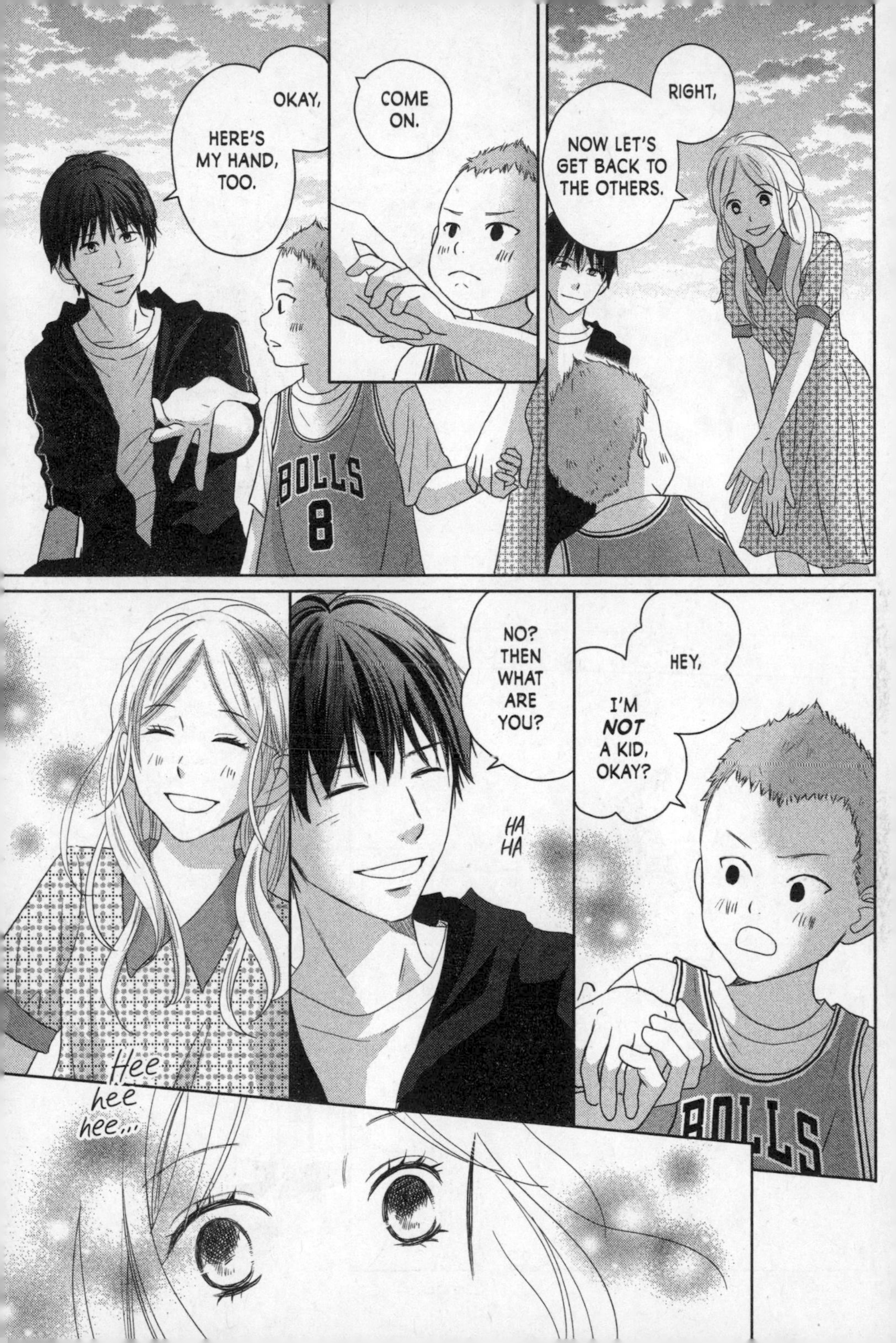
RIGHT, NOW LET'S GET BACK TO THE OTHERS.
COME ON.
OKAY, HERE'S MY HAND, TOO.
HEY, I'M *NOT* A KID, OKAY?
NO? THEN WHAT ARE YOU?
HA HA
Hee hee hee...

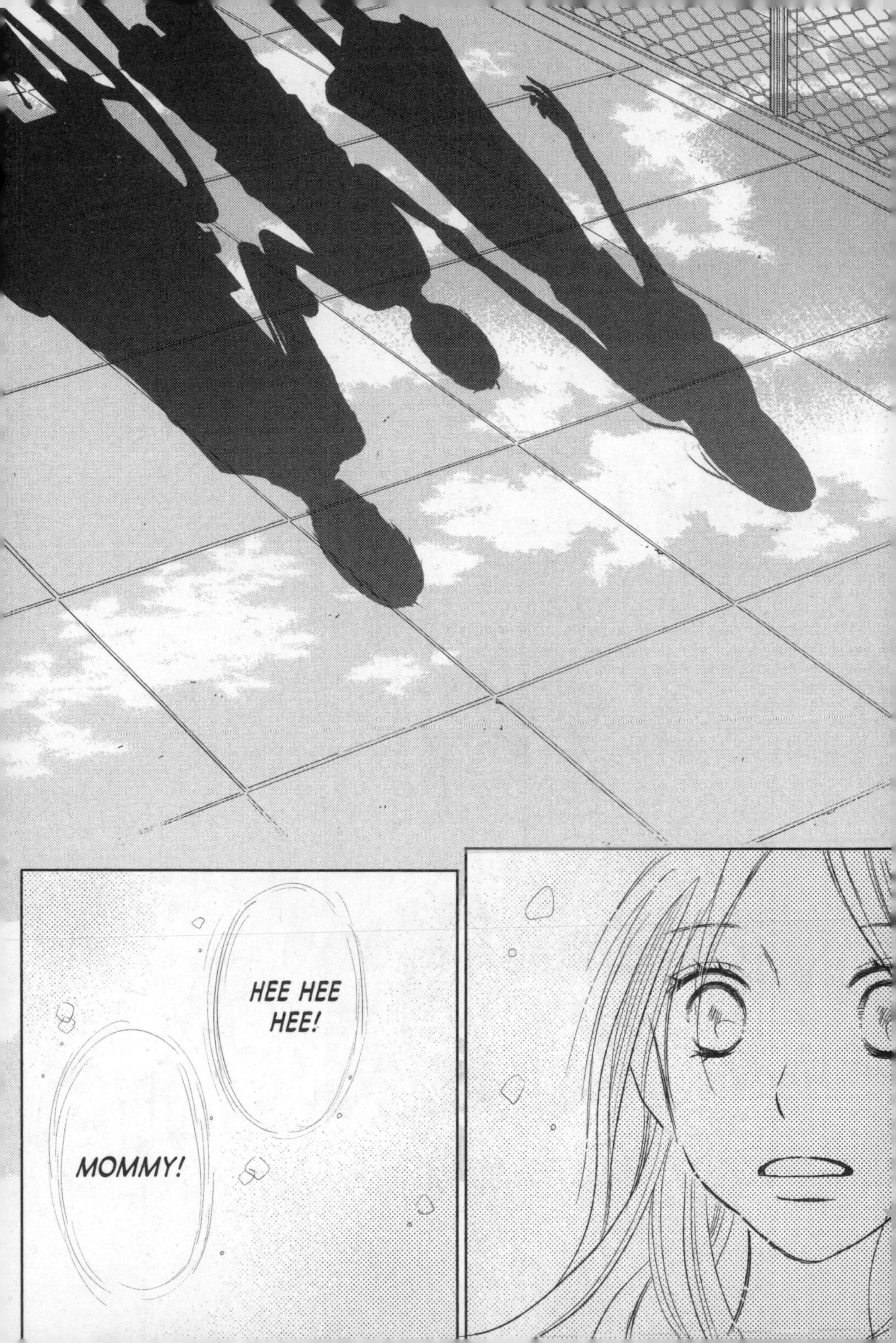
HEE HEE HEE!
MOMMY!

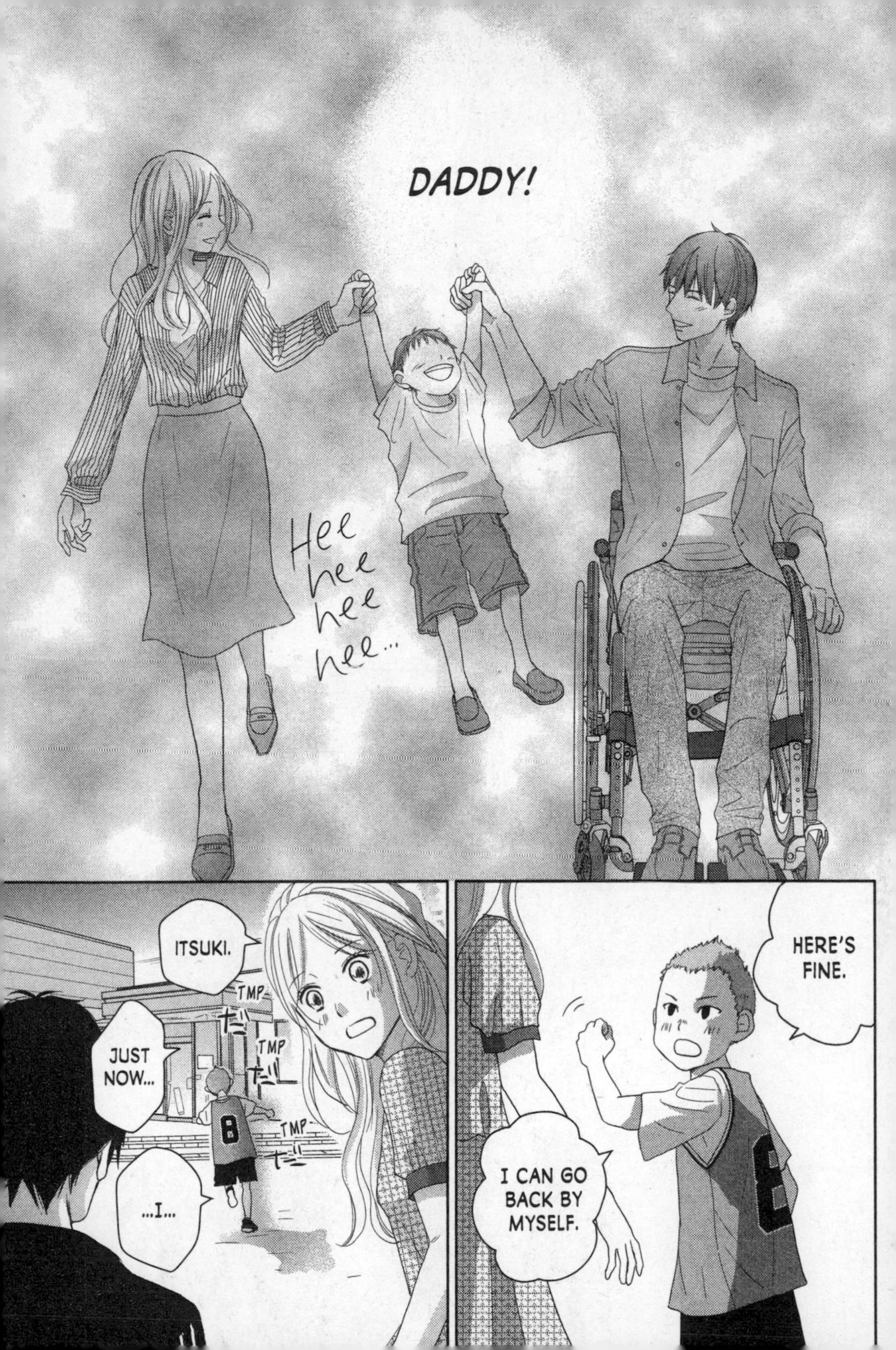
DADDY!
Hee hee hee hee...
HERE'S FINE.
I CAN GO BACK BY MYSELF.
ITSUKI.
TMP
JUST NOW...
TMP
TMP
...I...

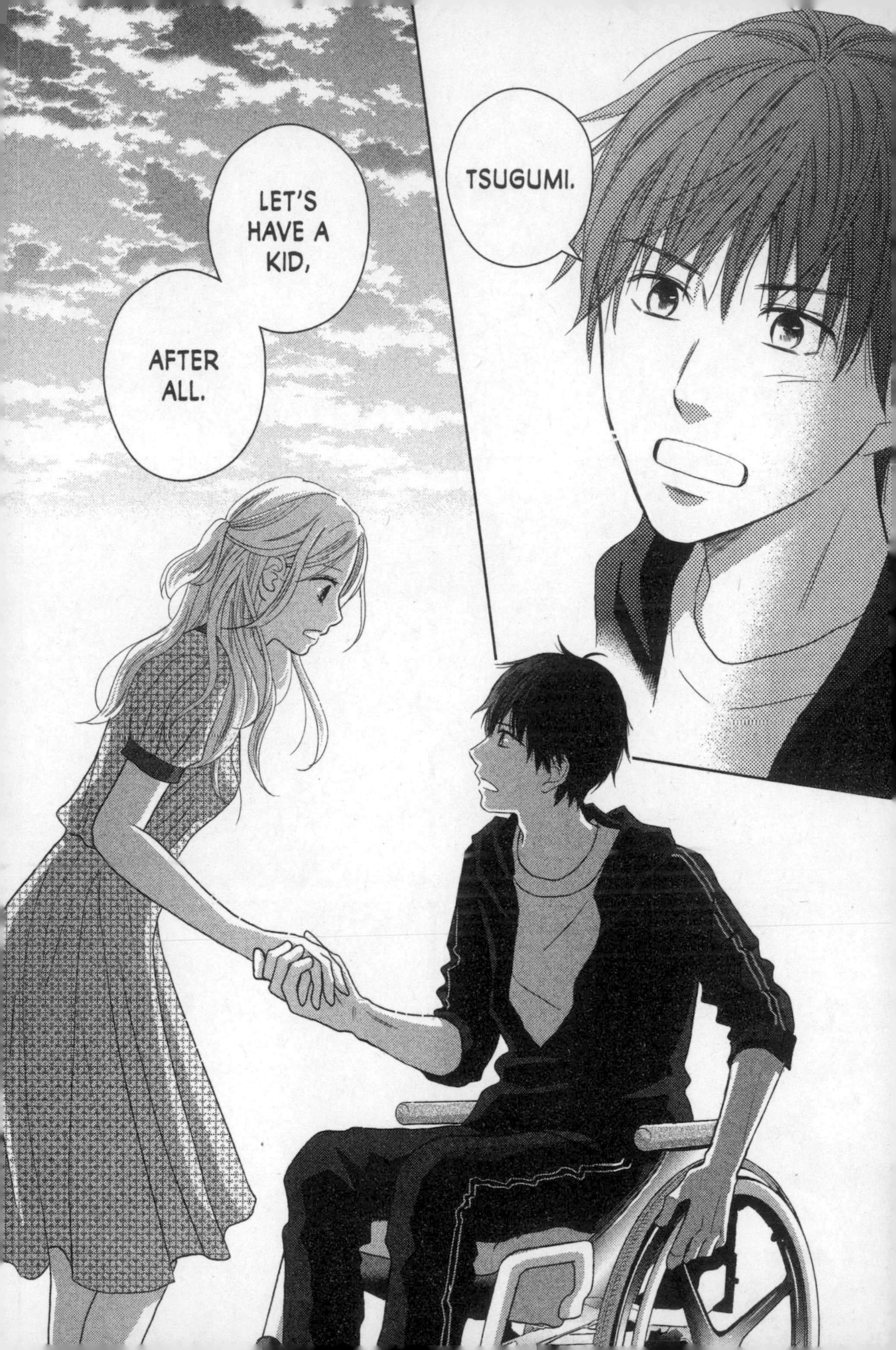
TSUGUMI.
LET'S HAVE A KID,
AFTER ALL.

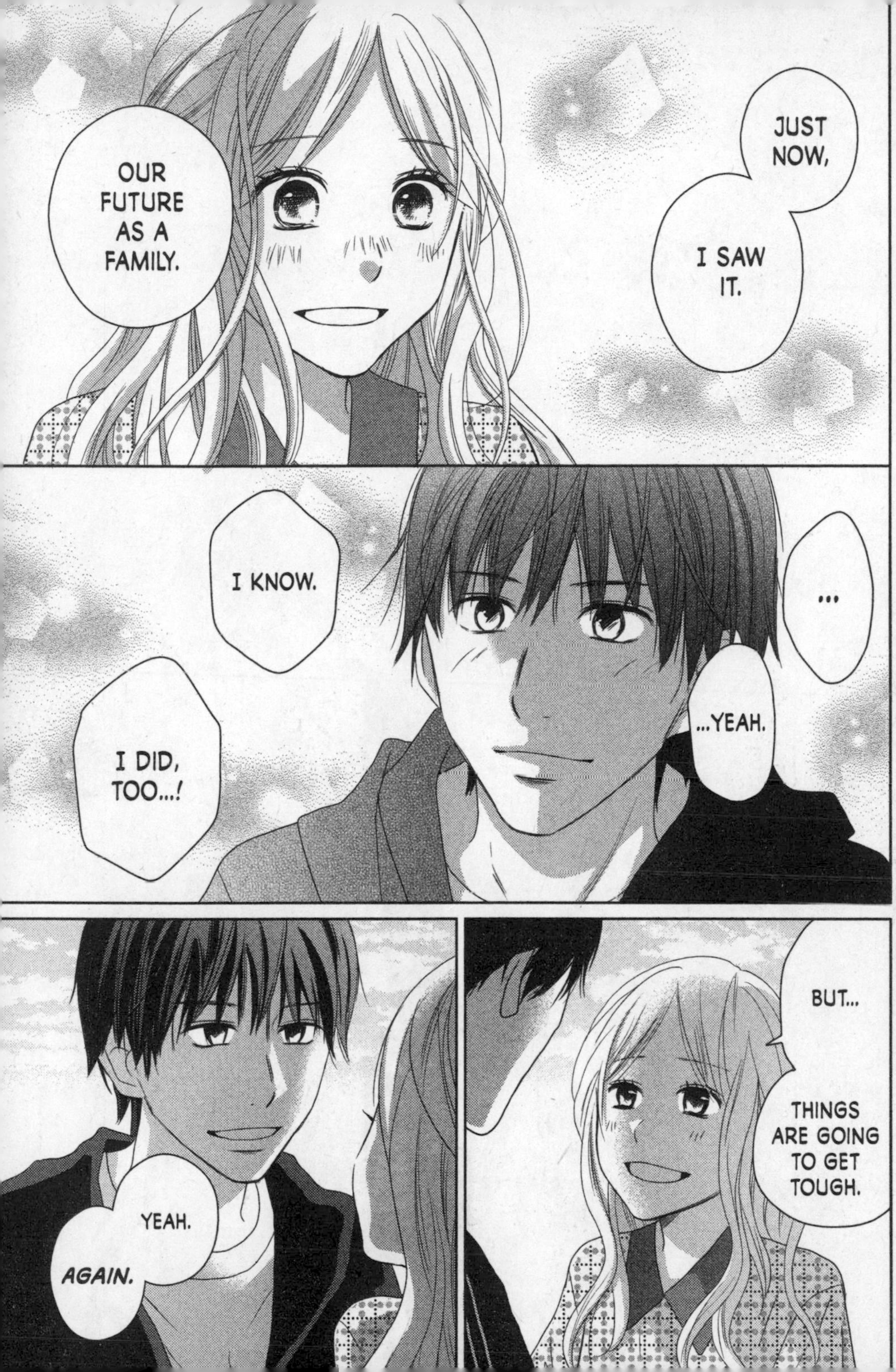
JUST NOW,
I SAW IT.
OUR FUTURE AS A FAMILY.
...
I KNOW.
...YEAH.
I DID, TOO...!
BUT...
THINGS ARE GOING TO GET TOUGH.
YEAH.
AGAIN.

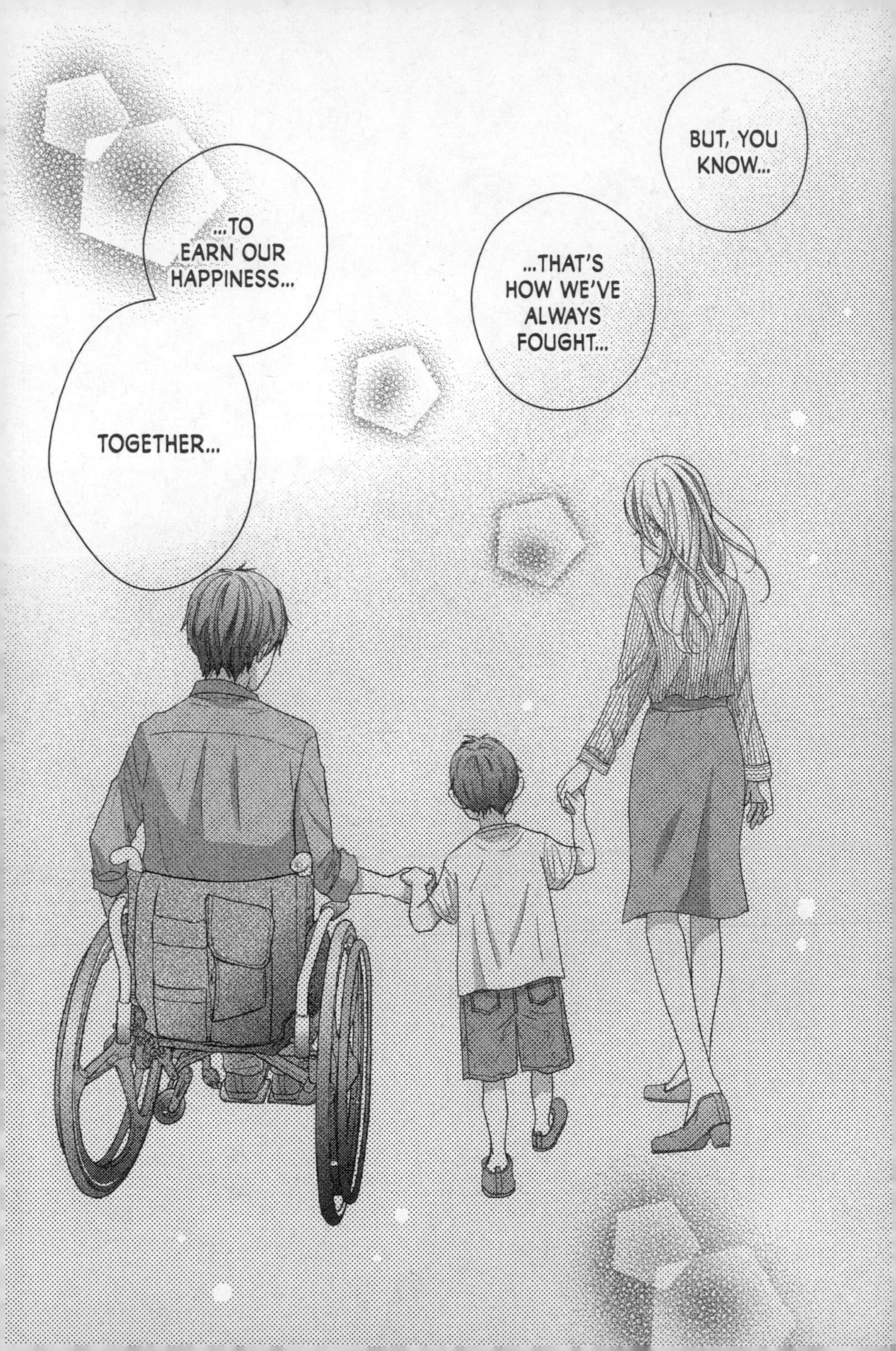
BUT, YOU KNOW...
...THAT'S HOW WE'VE ALWAYS FOUGHT...
...TO EARN OUR HAPPINESS...
TOGETHER...

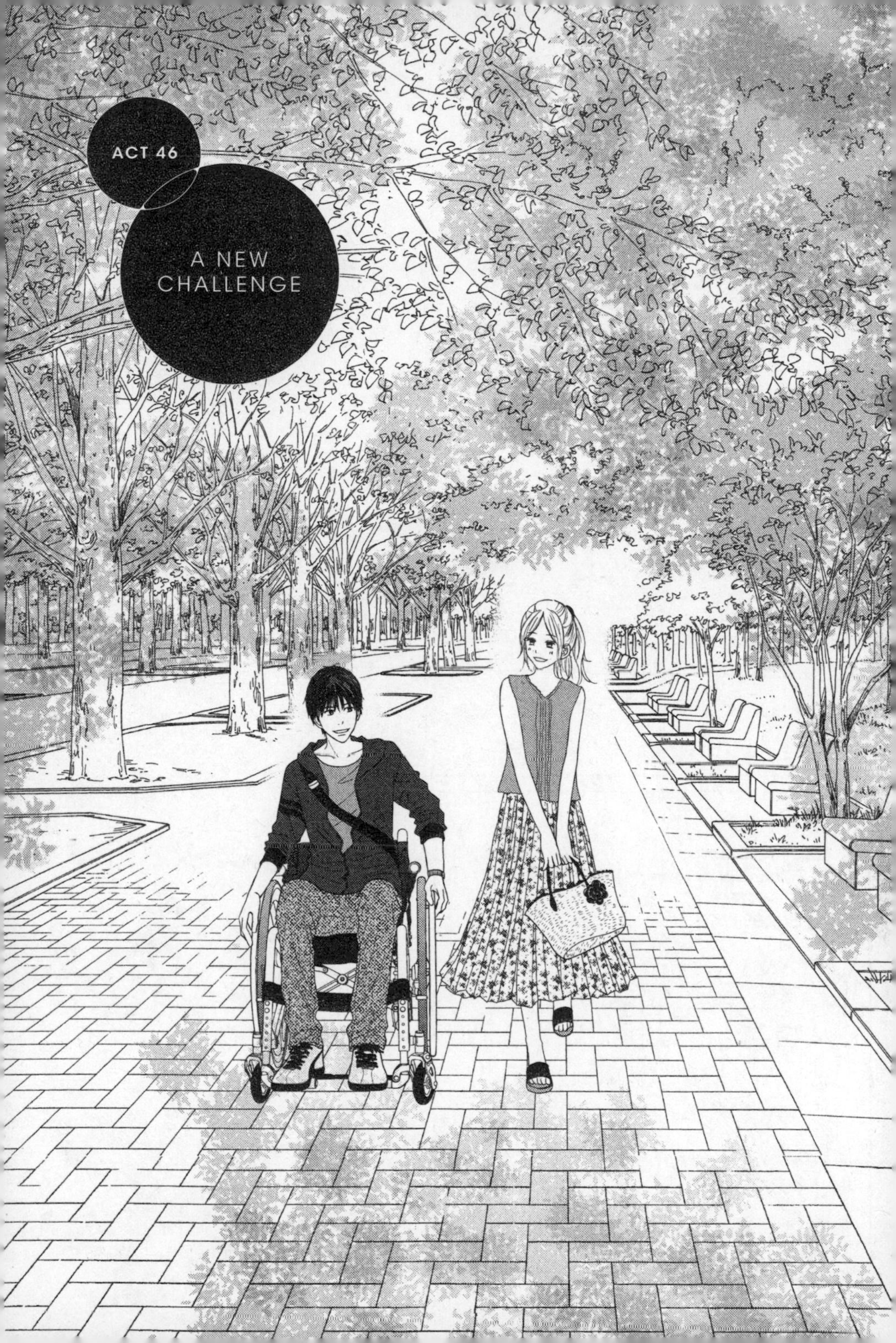
ACT 46
A NEW CHALLENGE

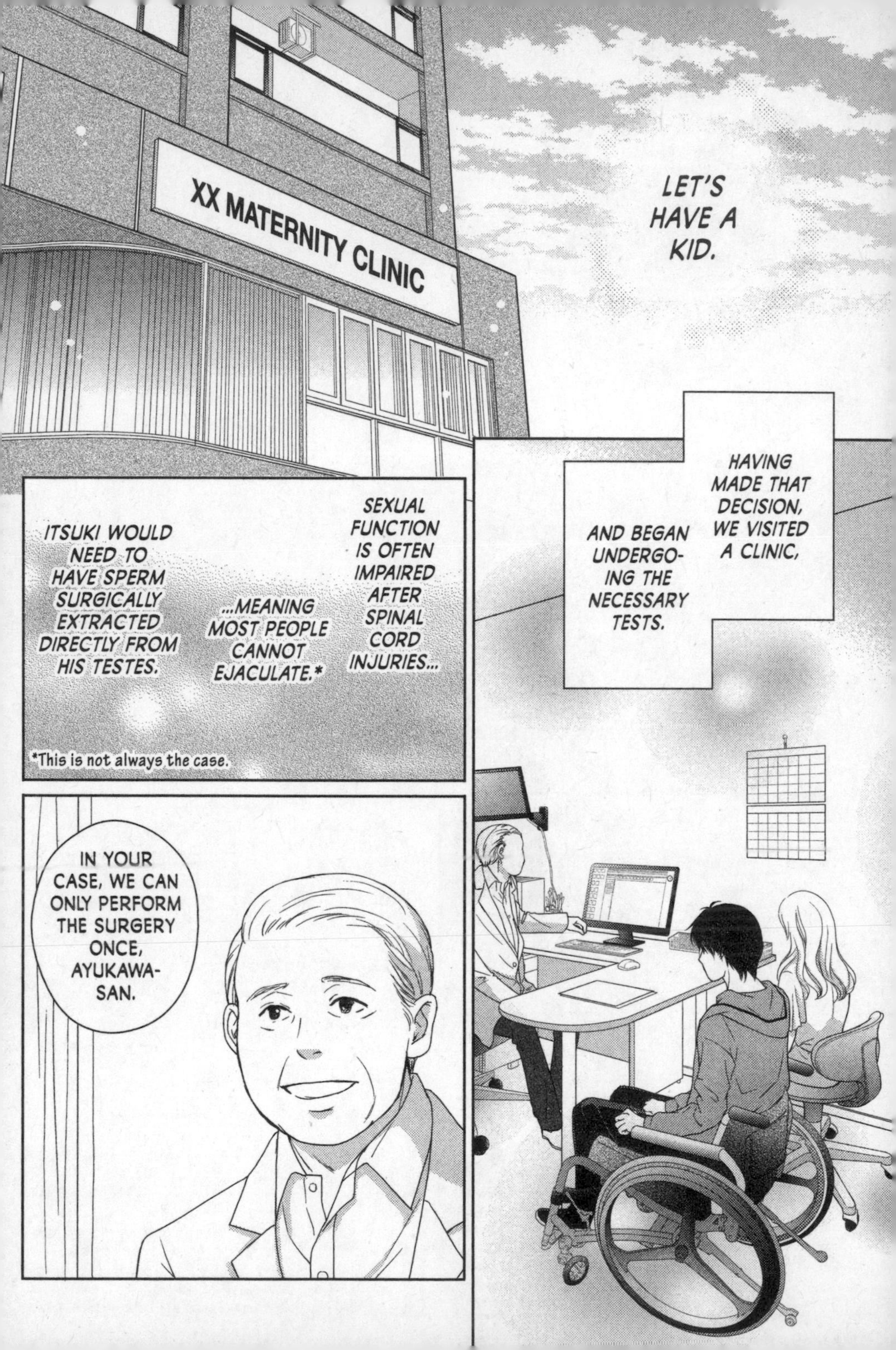
XX MATERNITY CLINIC
LET'S HAVE A KID.
HAVING MADE THAT DECISION, WE VISITED A CLINIC,
AND BEGAN UNDERGO-ING THE NECESSARY TESTS.
SEXUAL FUNCTION IS OFTEN IMPAIRED AFTER SPINAL CORD INJURIES...
...MEANING MOST PEOPLE CANNOT EJACULATE.*
ITSUKI WOULD NEED TO HAVE SPERM SURGICALLY EXTRACTED DIRECTLY FROM HIS TESTES.
*This is not always the case.
IN YOUR CASE, WE CAN ONLY PERFORM THE SURGERY ONCE, AYUKAWA-SAN.

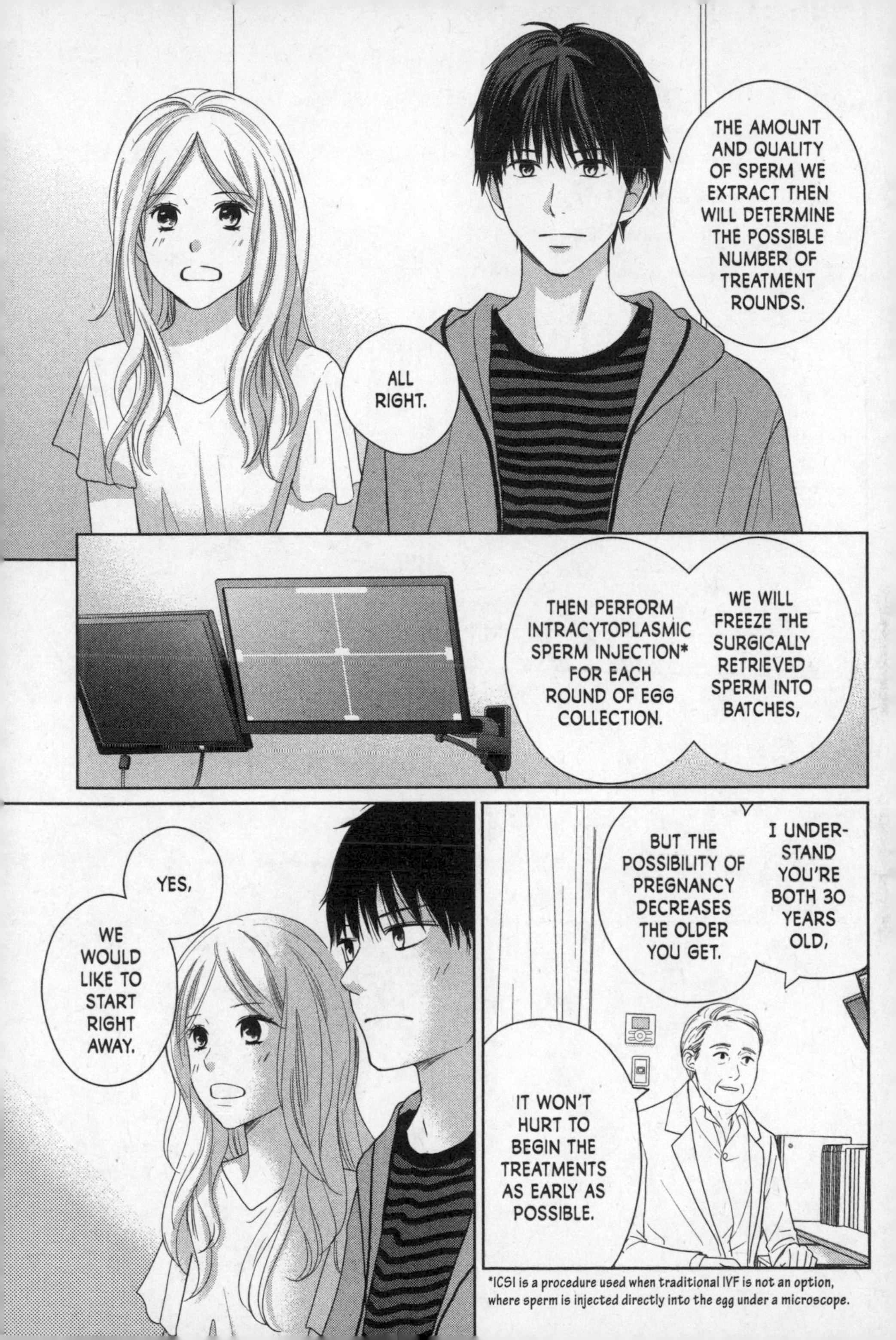
THE AMOUNT AND QUALITY OF SPERM WE EXTRACT THEN WILL DETERMINE THE POSSIBLE NUMBER OF TREATMENT ROUNDS.
ALL RIGHT.
WE WILL FREEZE THE SURGICALLY RETRIEVED SPERM INTO BATCHES,
THEN PERFORM INTRACYTOPLASMIC SPERM INJECTION* FOR EACH ROUND OF EGG COLLECTION.
I UNDER-STAND YOU'RE BOTH 30 YEARS OLD,
BUT THE POSSIBILITY OF PREGNANCY DECREASES THE OLDER YOU GET.
IT WON'T HURT TO BEGIN THE TREATMENTS AS EARLY AS POSSIBLE.
YES,
WE WOULD LIKE TO START RIGHT AWAY.

*ICSI is a procedure used when traditional IVF is not an option, where sperm is injected directly into the egg under a microscope.

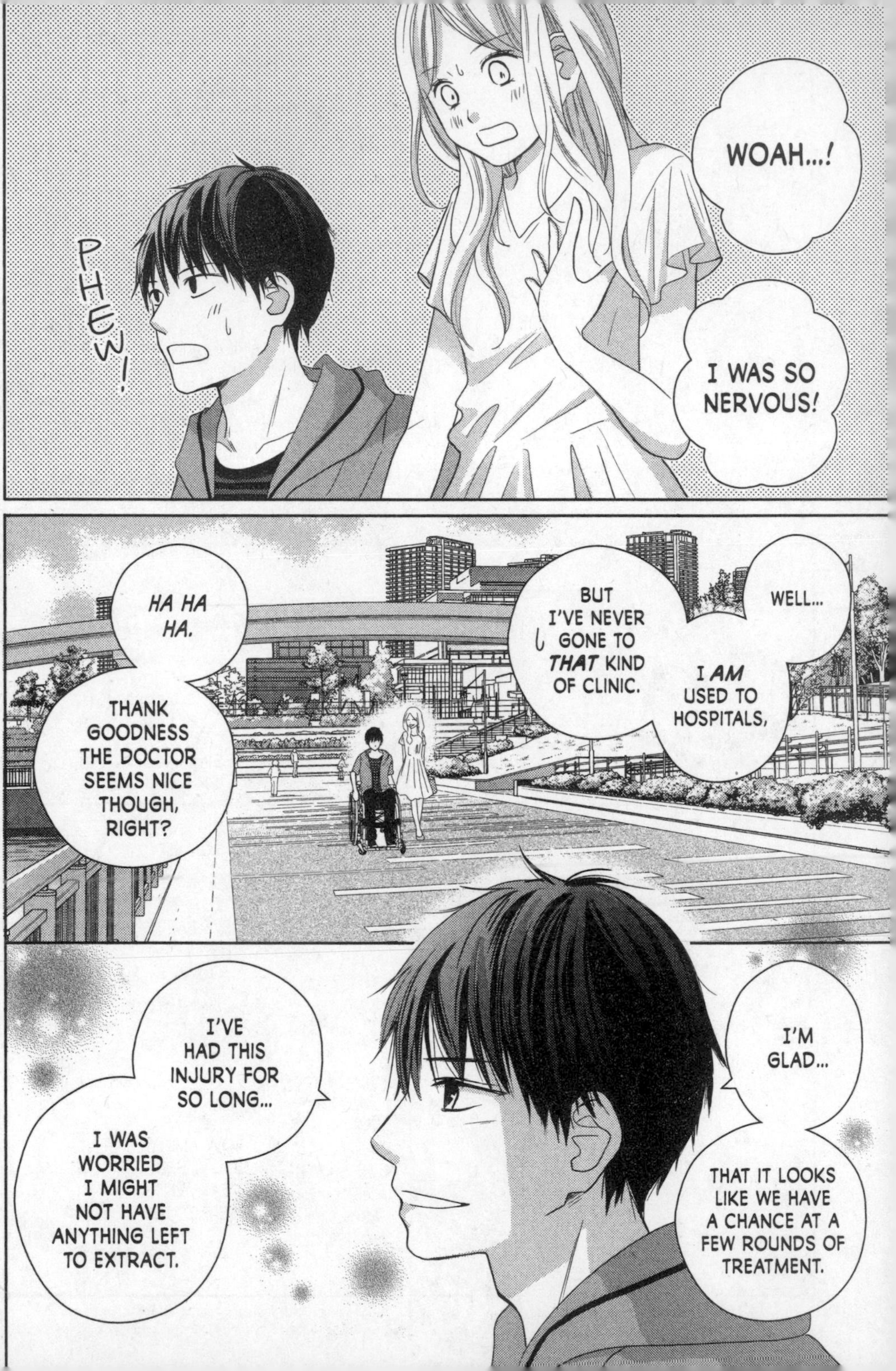
WOAH...!
I WAS SO NERVOUS!
PHEW!
WELL...
I *AM* USED TO HOSPITALS,
BUT I'VE NEVER GONE TO *THAT* KIND OF CLINIC.
HA HA HA.
THANK GOODNESS THE DOCTOR SEEMS NICE THOUGH, RIGHT?
I'M GLAD...
THAT IT LOOKS LIKE WE HAVE A CHANCE AT A FEW ROUNDS OF TREATMENT.
I'VE HAD THIS INJURY FOR SO LONG...
I WAS WORRIED I MIGHT NOT HAVE ANYTHING LEFT TO EXTRACT.

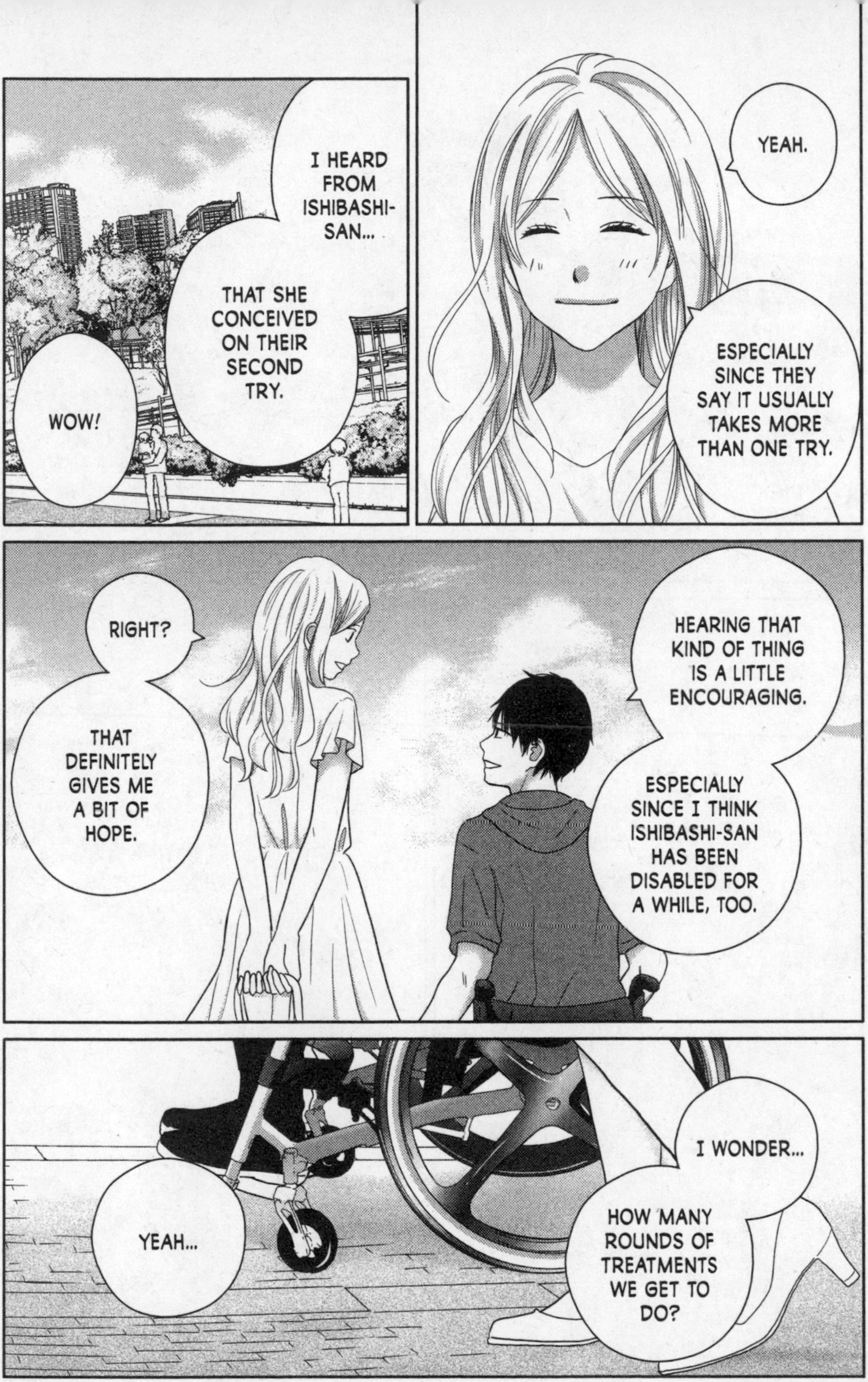
YEAH.
ESPECIALLY SINCE THEY SAY IT USUALLY TAKES MORE THAN ONE TRY.
I HEARD FROM ISHIBASHI-SAN...
THAT SHE CONCEIVED ON THEIR SECOND TRY.
WOW!
HEARING THAT KIND OF THING IS A LITTLE ENCOURAGING.
ESPECIALLY SINCE I THINK ISHIBASHI-SAN HAS BEEN DISABLED FOR A WHILE, TOO.
RIGHT?
THAT DEFINITELY GIVES ME A BIT OF HOPE.
I WONDER...
HOW MANY ROUNDS OF TREATMENTS WE GET TO DO?
YEAH...

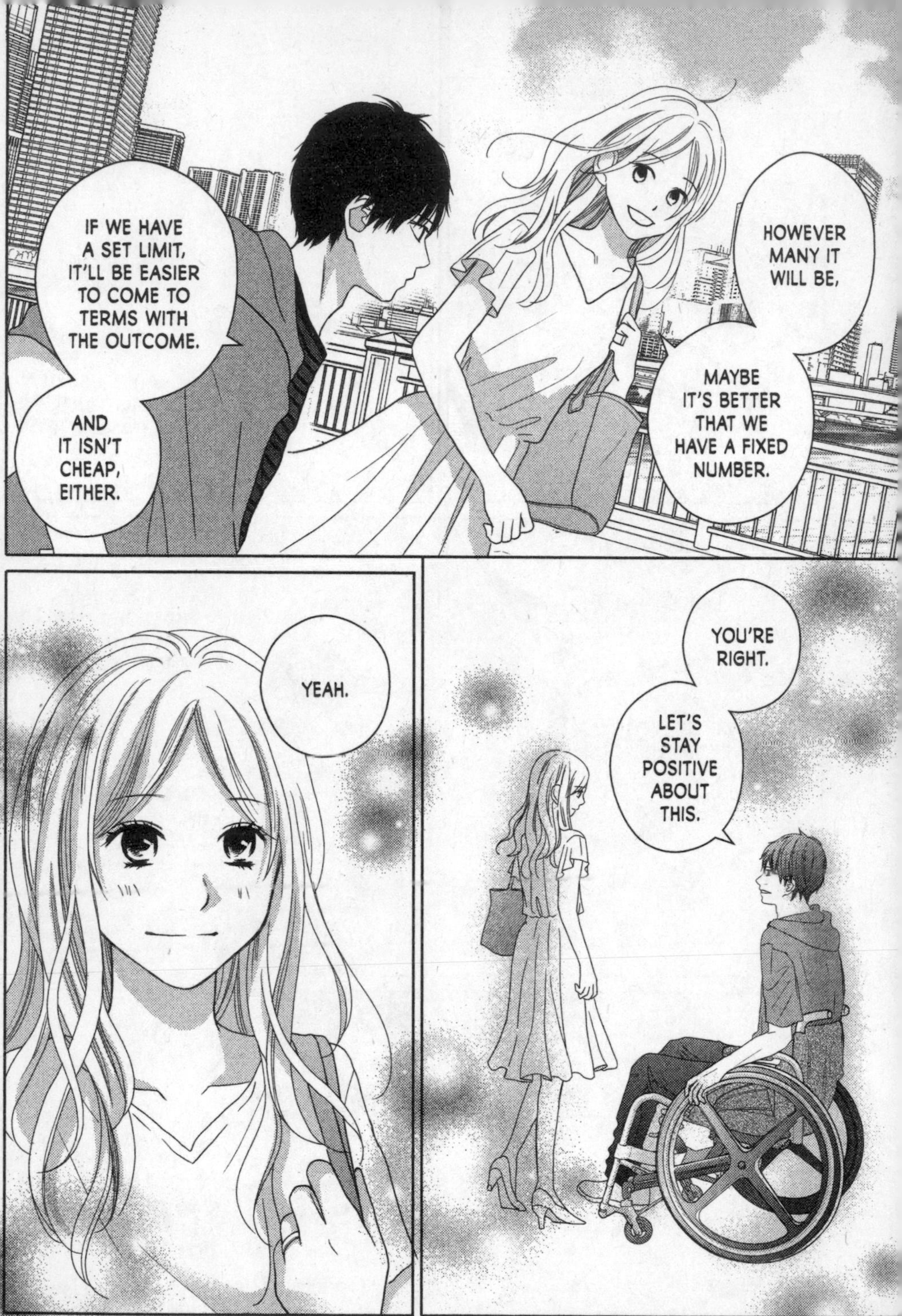
HOWEVER MANY IT WILL BE,
MAYBE IT'S BETTER THAT WE HAVE A FIXED NUMBER.
IF WE HAVE A SET LIMIT, IT'LL BE EASIER TO COME TO TERMS WITH THE OUTCOME.
AND IT ISN'T CHEAP, EITHER.
YOU'RE RIGHT.
LET'S STAY POSITIVE ABOUT THIS.
YEAH.

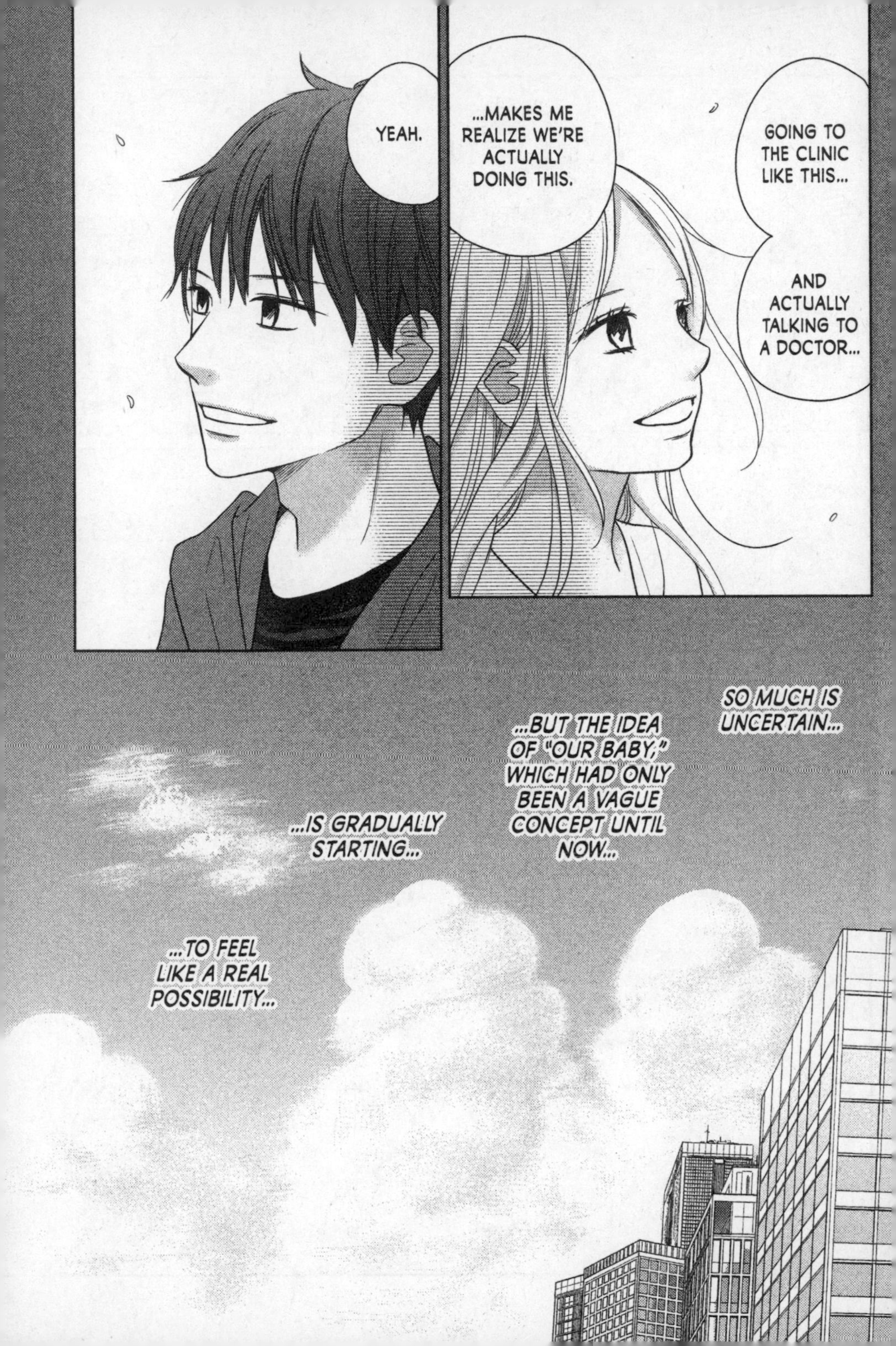
GOING TO THE CLINIC LIKE THIS...
AND ACTUALLY TALKING TO A DOCTOR...
...MAKES ME REALIZE WE'RE ACTUALLY DOING THIS.
YEAH.
SO MUCH IS UNCERTAIN...
...BUT THE IDEA OF "OUR BABY," WHICH HAD ONLY BEEN A VAGUE CONCEPT UNTIL NOW...
...IS GRADUALLY STARTING...
...TO FEEL LIKE A REAL POSSIBILITY...

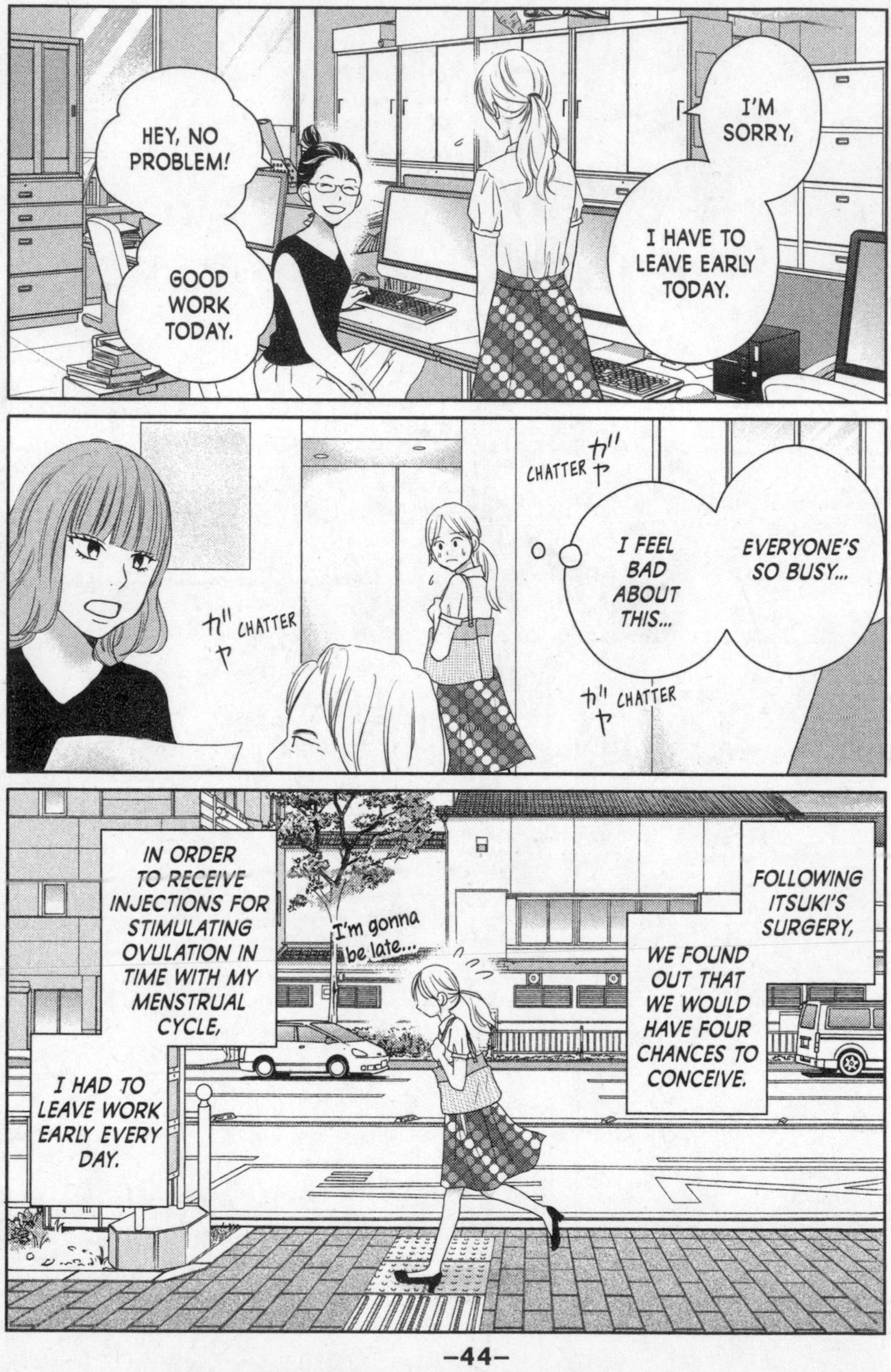
I'M SORRY,
I HAVE TO LEAVE EARLY TODAY.
HEY, NO PROBLEM!
GOOD WORK TODAY.
ガヤ CHATTER
EVERYONE'S SO BUSY...
I FEEL BAD ABOUT THIS...
ガヤ CHATTER
ガヤ CHATTER
FOLLOWING ITSUKI'S SURGERY,
WE FOUND OUT THAT WE WOULD HAVE FOUR CHANCES TO CONCEIVE.
I'm gonna be late...
IN ORDER TO RECEIVE INJECTIONS FOR STIMULATING OVULATION IN TIME WITH MY MENSTRUAL CYCLE,
I HAD TO LEAVE WORK EARLY EVERY DAY.

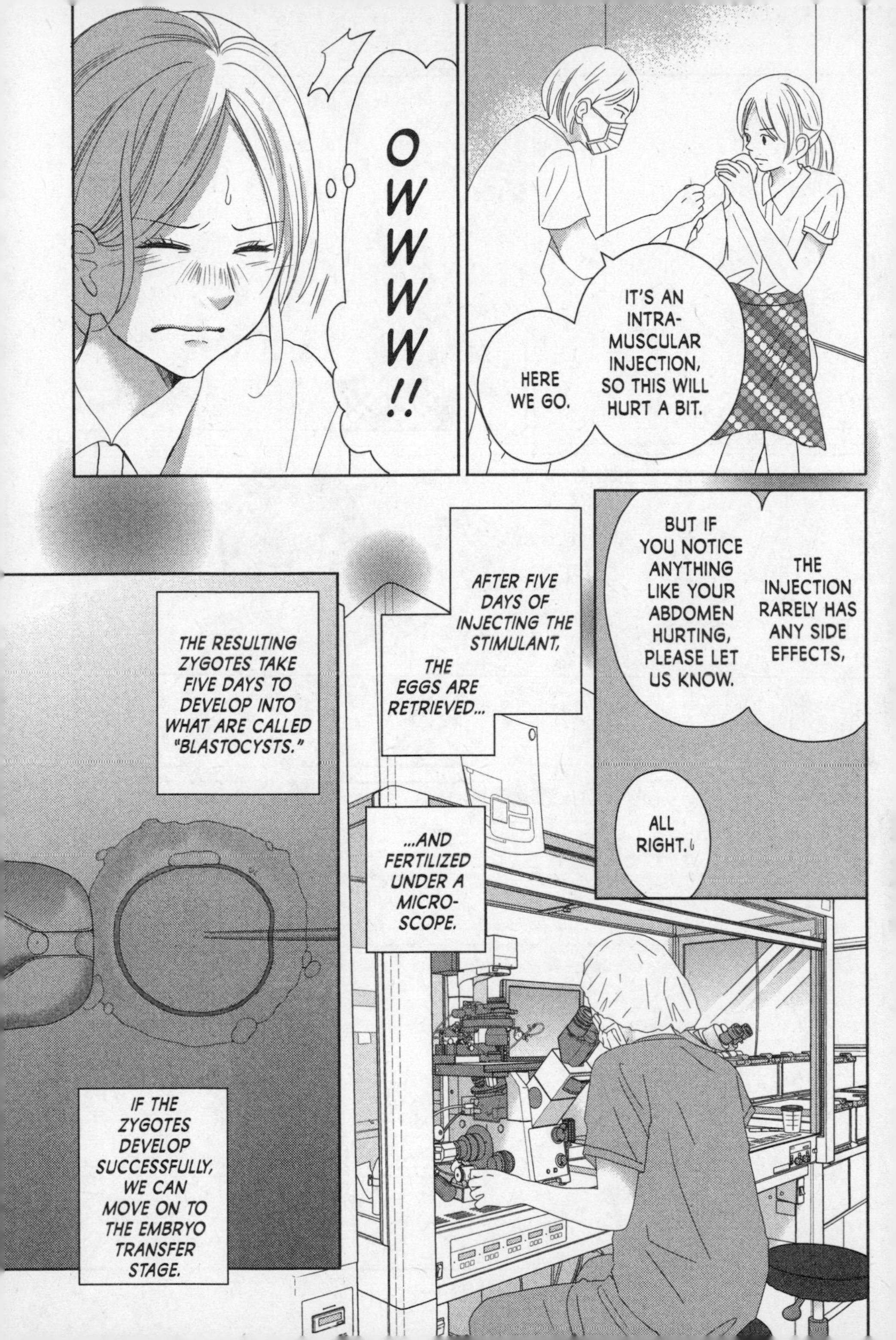
IT'S AN INTRA-MUSCULAR INJECTION, SO THIS WILL HURT A BIT.
HERE WE GO.
OWWWW!!
THE INJECTION RARELY HAS ANY SIDE EFFECTS,
BUT IF YOU NOTICE ANYTHING LIKE YOUR ABDOMEN HURTING, PLEASE LET US KNOW.
ALL RIGHT.
AFTER FIVE DAYS OF INJECTING THE STIMULANT,
THE EGGS ARE RETRIEVED...
...AND FERTILIZED UNDER A MICRO-SCOPE.
THE RESULTING ZYGOTES TAKE FIVE DAYS TO DEVELOP INTO WHAT ARE CALLED "BLASTOCYSTS."
IF THE ZYGOTES DEVELOP SUCCESSFULLY, WE CAN MOVE ON TO THE EMBRYO TRANSFER STAGE.

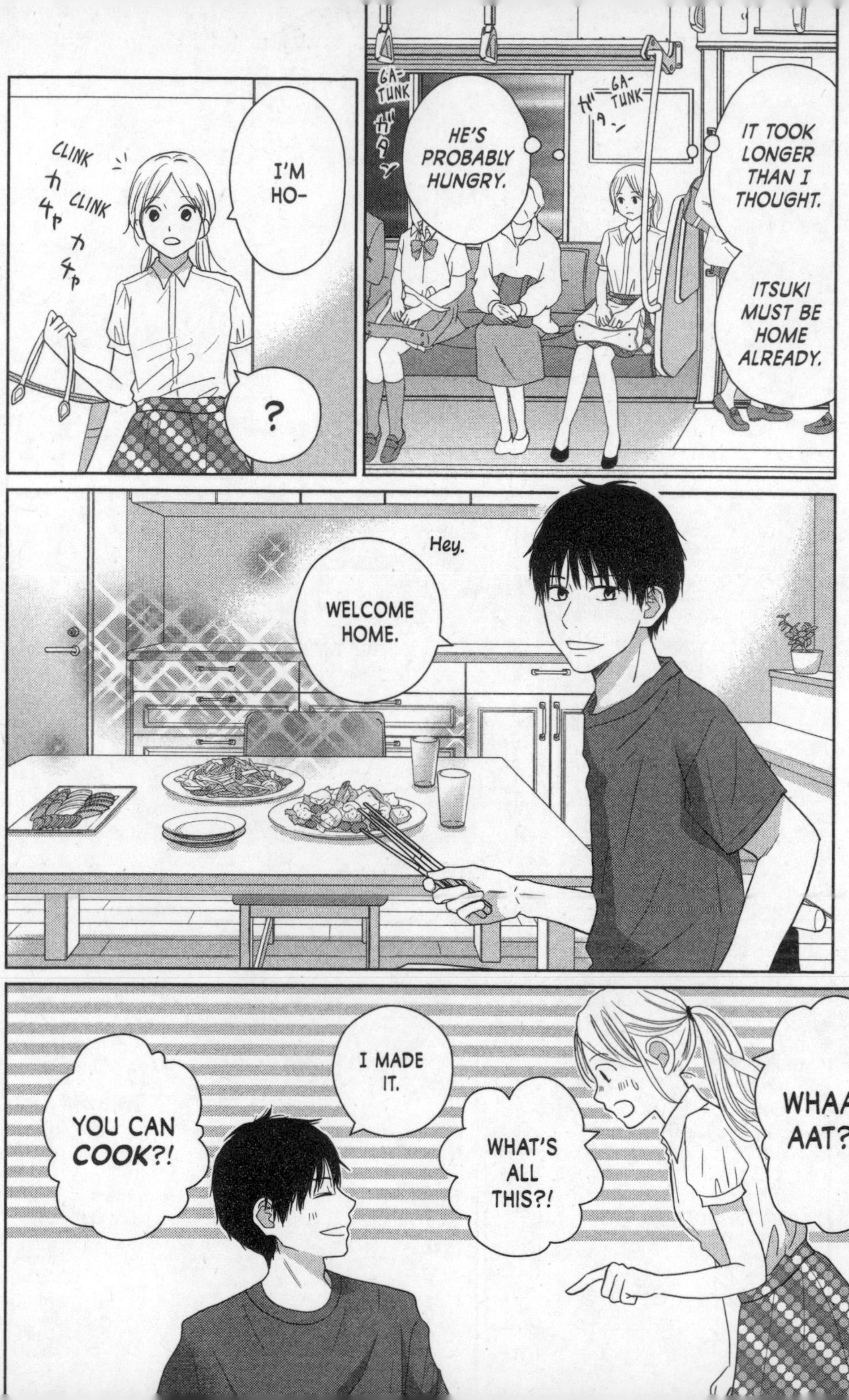
GA-TUNK
GA-TUNK
IT TOOK LONGER THAN I THOUGHT.
ITSUKI MUST BE HOME ALREADY.
HE'S PROBABLY HUNGRY.
I'M HO-
CLINK
CLINK
?
Hey.
WELCOME HOME.
WHAA-AAT?!
WHAT'S ALL THIS?!
I MADE IT.
YOU CAN *COOK*?!

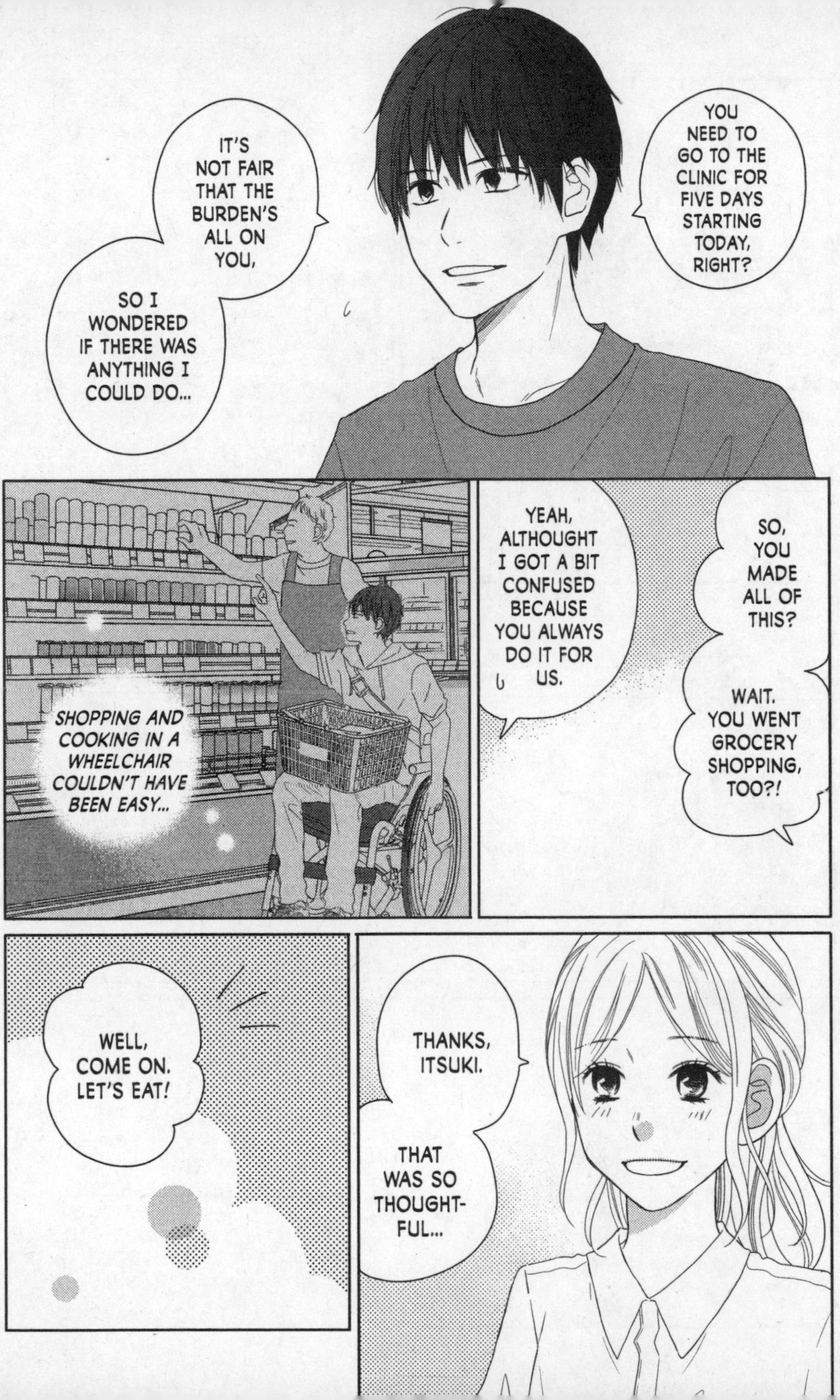
YOU NEED TO GO TO THE CLINIC FOR FIVE DAYS STARTING TODAY, RIGHT?
IT'S NOT FAIR THAT THE BURDEN'S ALL ON YOU,
SO I WONDERED IF THERE WAS ANYTHING I COULD DO...
SO, YOU MADE ALL OF THIS?
WAIT. YOU WENT GROCERY SHOPPING, TOO?!
YEAH, ALTHOUGHT I GOT A BIT CONFUSED BECAUSE YOU ALWAYS DO IT FOR US.
SHOPPING AND COOKING IN A WHEELCHAIR COULDN'T HAVE BEEN EASY...
THANKS, ITSUKI.
THAT WAS SO THOUGHT-FUL...
WELL, COME ON. LET'S EAT!

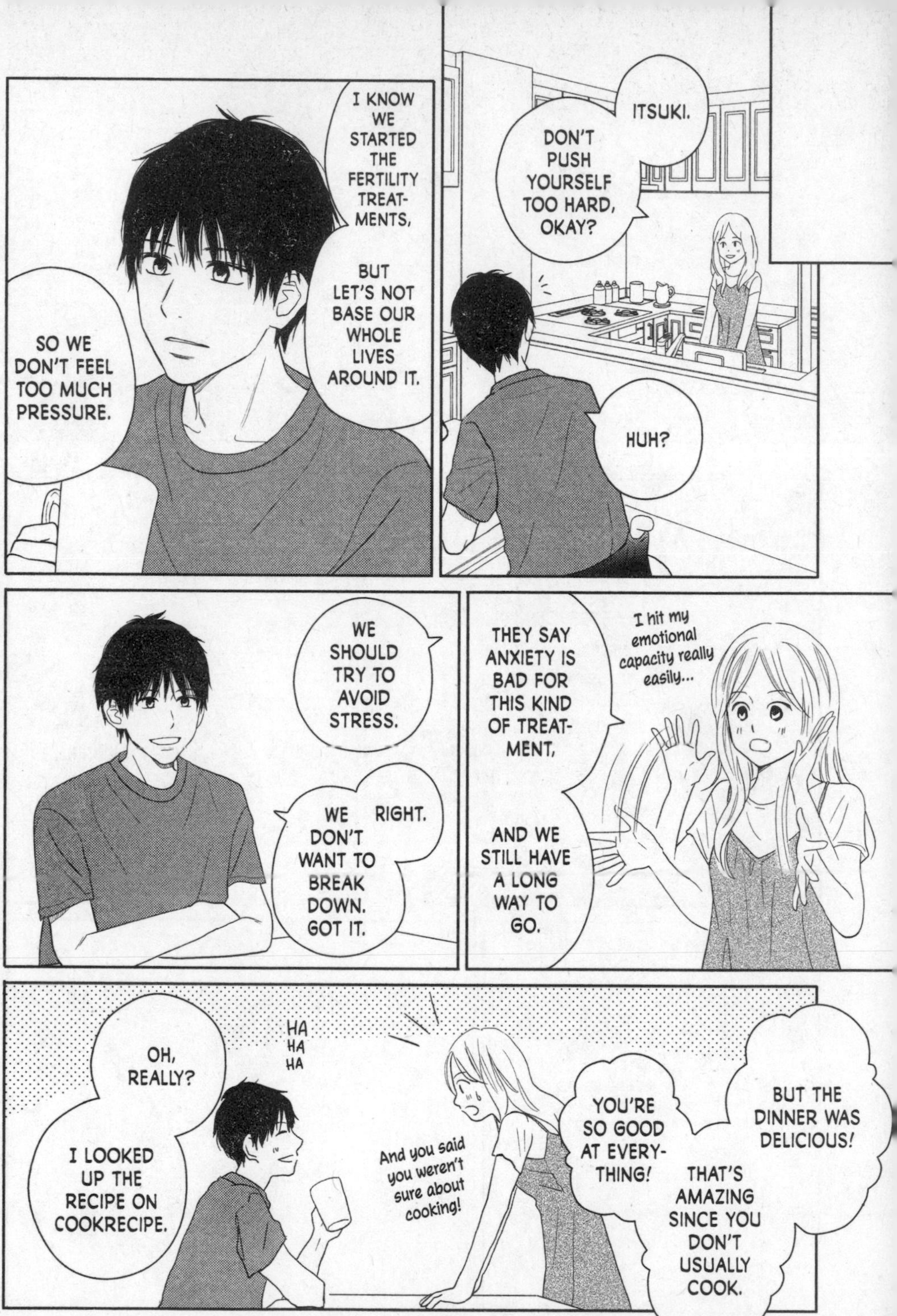

ITSUKI.
DON'T PUSH YOURSELF TOO HARD, OKAY?
HUH?
I KNOW WE STARTED THE FERTILITY TREATMENTS,
BUT LET'S NOT BASE OUR WHOLE LIVES AROUND IT.
SO WE DON'T FEEL TOO MUCH PRESSURE.
I hit my emotional capacity really easily...
THEY SAY ANXIETY IS BAD FOR THIS KIND OF TREATMENT,
AND WE STILL HAVE A LONG WAY TO GO.
WE SHOULD TRY TO AVOID STRESS.
RIGHT. WE DON'T WANT TO BREAK DOWN. GOT IT.
BUT THE DINNER WAS DELICIOUS!
THAT'S AMAZING SINCE YOU DON'T USUALLY COOK.
YOU'RE SO GOOD AT EVERYTHING!
And you said you weren't sure about cooking!
HA HA HA
OH, REALLY?
I LOOKED UP THE RECIPE ON COOKRECIPE.

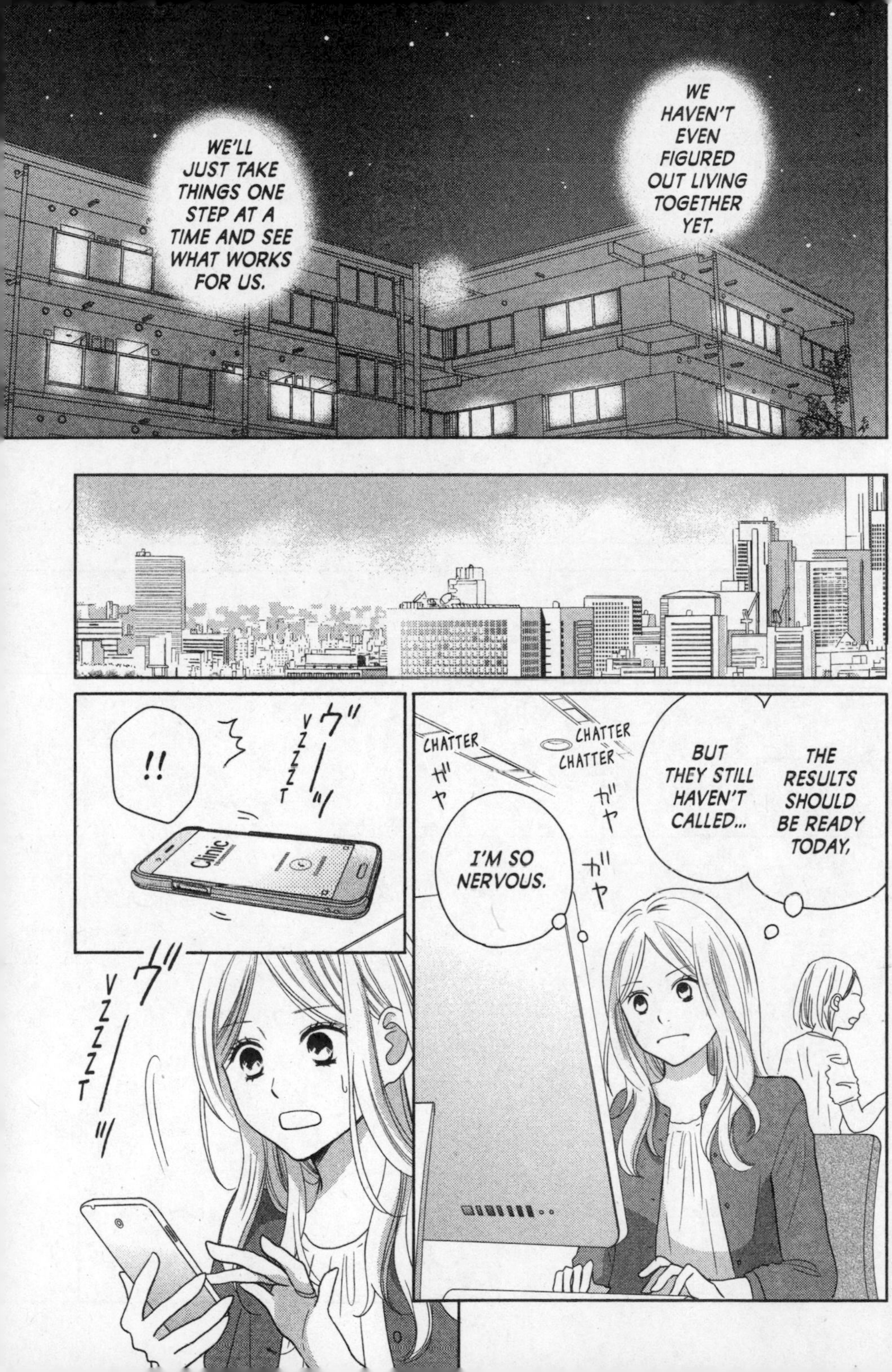
WE HAVEN'T EVEN FIGURED OUT LIVING TOGETHER YET.
WE'LL JUST TAKE THINGS ONE STEP AT A TIME AND SEE WHAT WORKS FOR US.
THE RESULTS SHOULD BE READY TODAY,
BUT THEY STILL HAVEN'T CALLED...
CHATTER
CHATTER
I'M SO NERVOUS.
CHATTER
VZZZZT
!!
Clinic
VZZZZT

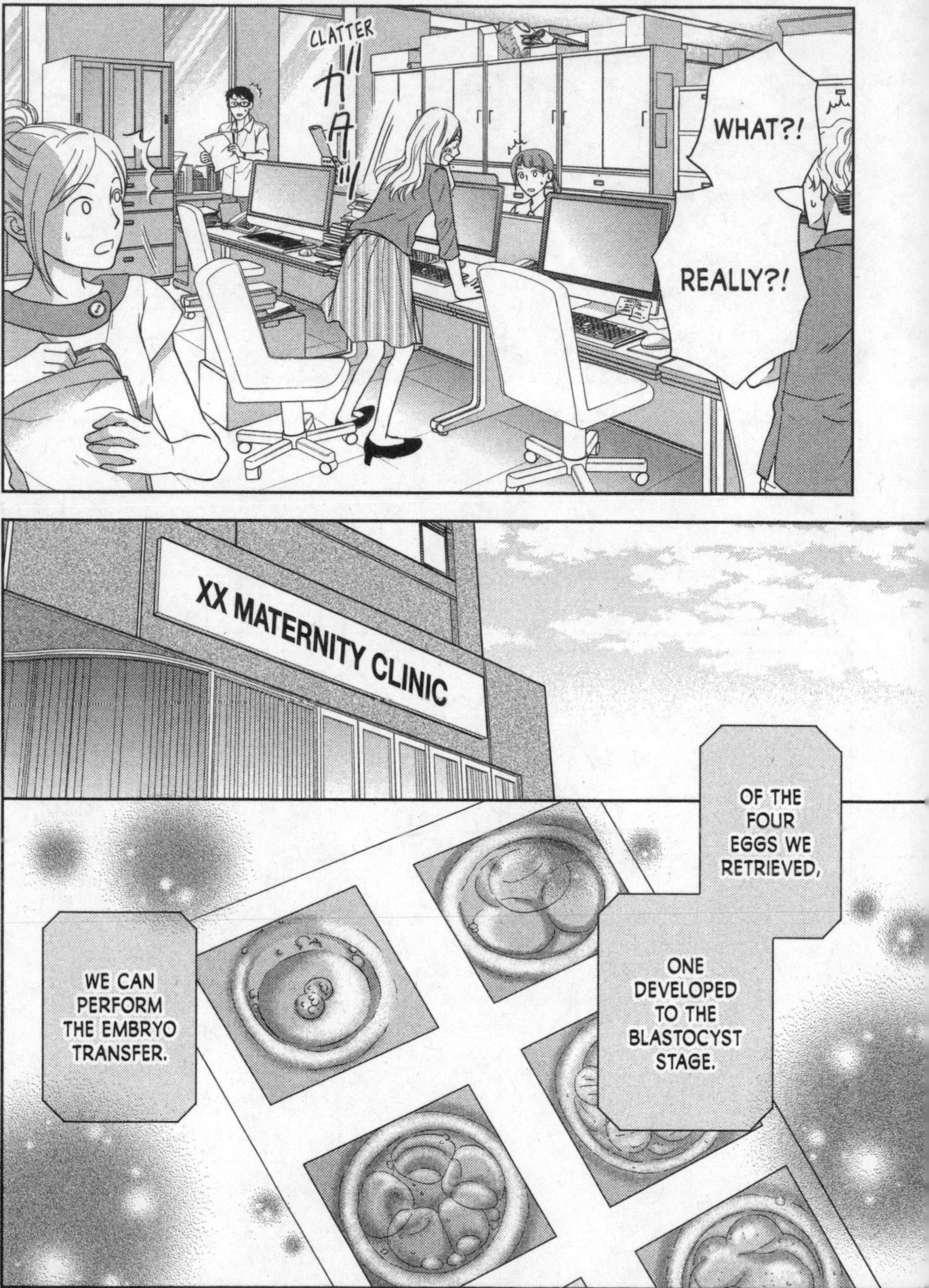
WHAT?!
REALLY?!
CLATTER
ガタ
XX MATERNITY CLINIC
OF THE FOUR EGGS WE RETRIEVED,
ONE DEVELOPED TO THE BLASTOCYST STAGE.
WE CAN PERFORM THE EMBRYO TRANSFER.

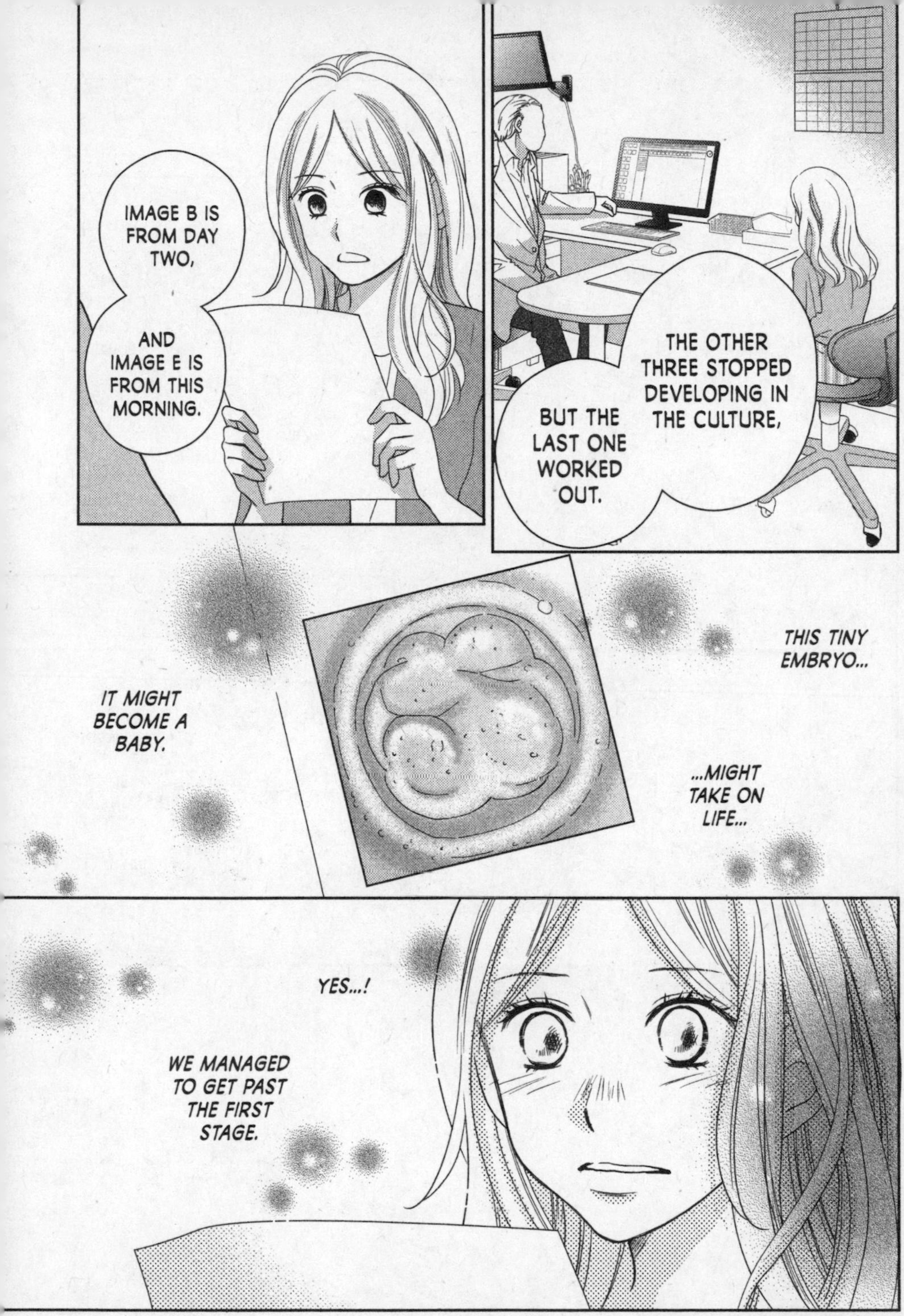
THE OTHER THREE STOPPED DEVELOPING IN THE CULTURE,
BUT THE LAST ONE WORKED OUT.
IMAGE B IS FROM DAY TWO,
AND IMAGE E IS FROM THIS MORNING.
THIS TINY EMBRYO...
...MIGHT TAKE ON LIFE...
IT MIGHT BECOME A BABY.
YES...!
WE MANAGED TO GET PAST THE FIRST STAGE.

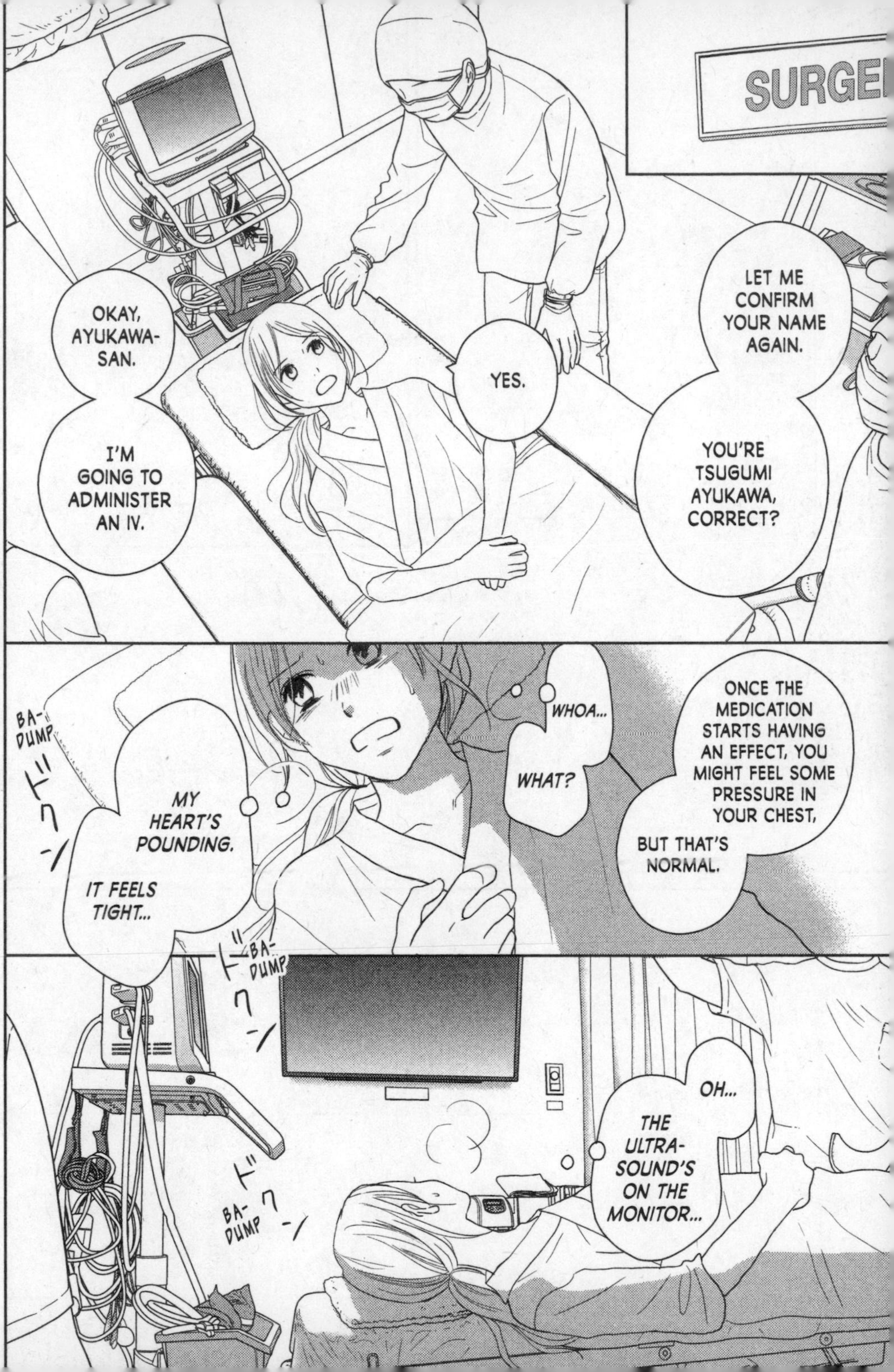
SURGE
LET ME CONFIRM YOUR NAME AGAIN.
YOU'RE TSUGUMI AYUKAWA, CORRECT?
YES.
OKAY, AYUKAWA-SAN.
I'M GOING TO ADMINISTER AN IV.
ONCE THE MEDICATION STARTS HAVING AN EFFECT, YOU MIGHT FEEL SOME PRESSURE IN YOUR CHEST,
BUT THAT'S NORMAL.
WHOA...
WHAT?
BA-DUMP
MY HEART'S POUNDING.
IT FEELS TIGHT...
BA-DUMP
OH...
THE ULTRA-SOUND'S ON THE MONITOR...
BA-DUMP

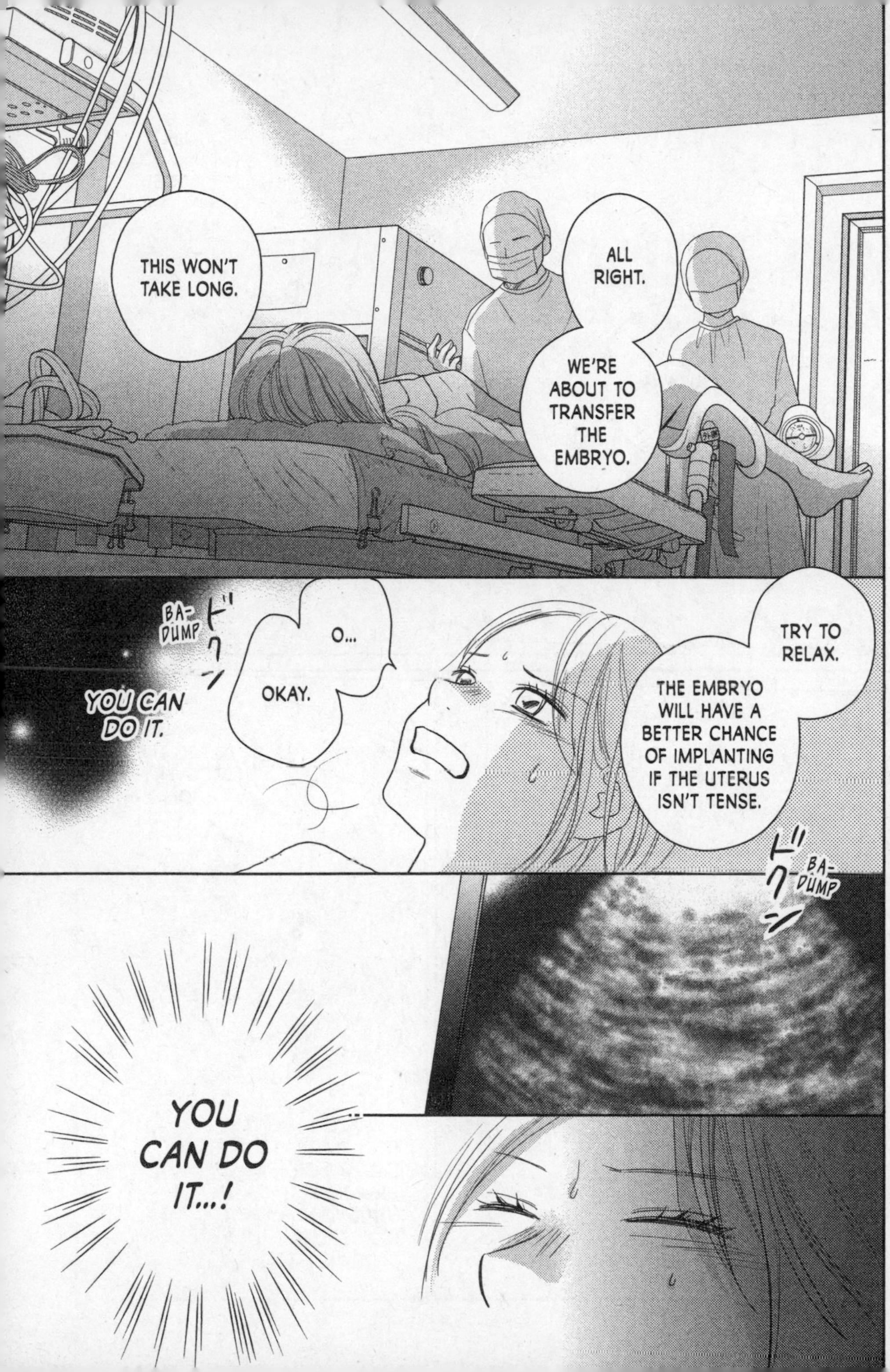
ALL RIGHT.
WE'RE ABOUT TO TRANSFER THE EMBRYO.
THIS WON'T TAKE LONG.
TRY TO RELAX.
THE EMBRYO WILL HAVE A BETTER CHANCE OF IMPLANTING IF THE UTERUS ISN'T TENSE.
O...
OKAY.
BA-DUMP
YOU CAN DO IT.
BA-DUMP
YOU CAN DO IT...!

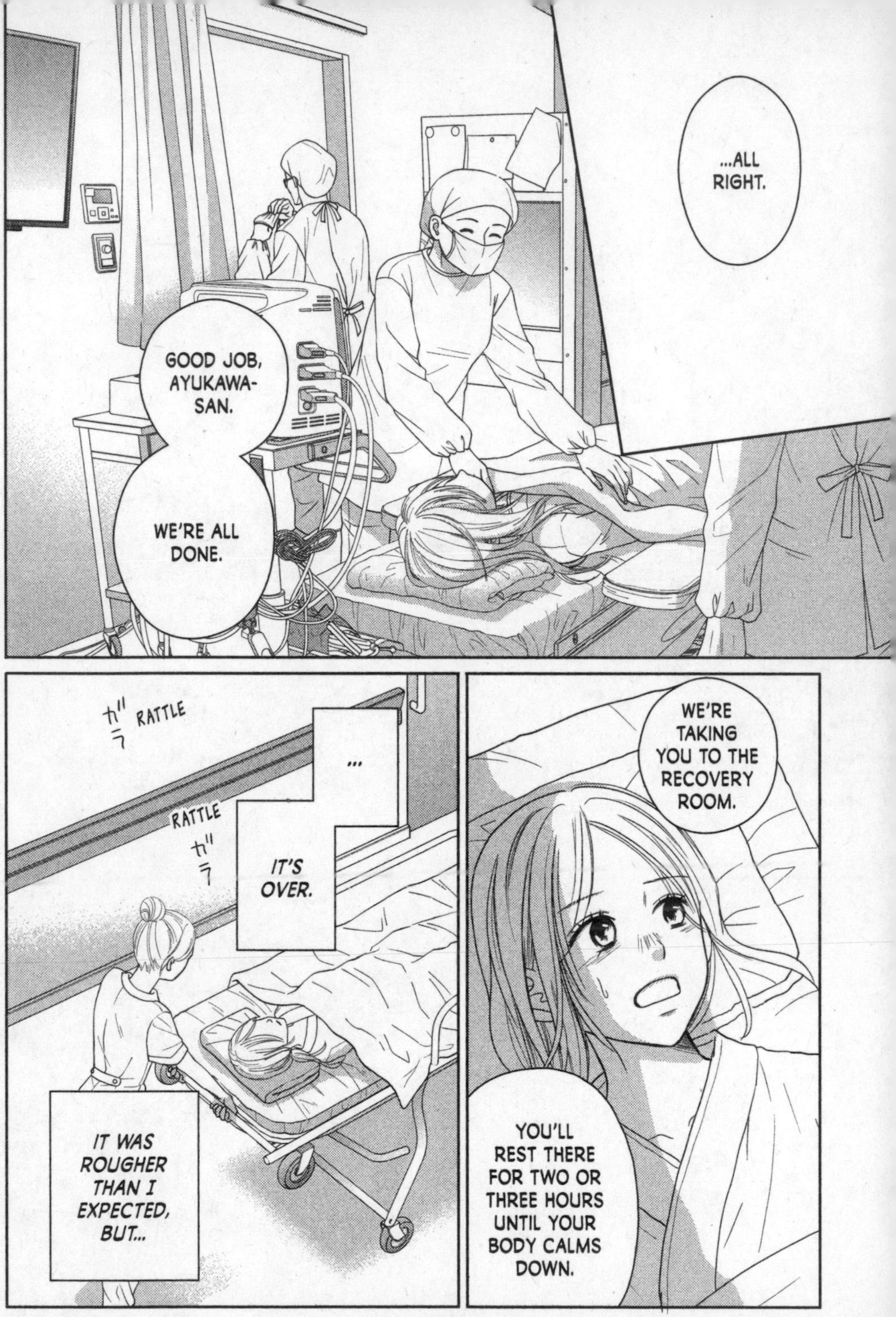
...ALL RIGHT.
GOOD JOB, AYUKAWA-SAN.
WE'RE ALL DONE.
WE'RE TAKING YOU TO THE RECOVERY ROOM.
YOU'LL REST THERE FOR TWO OR THREE HOURS UNTIL YOUR BODY CALMS DOWN.
ガラ RATTLE
RATTLE ガラ
...
IT'S OVER.
IT WAS ROUGHER THAN I EXPECTED, BUT...

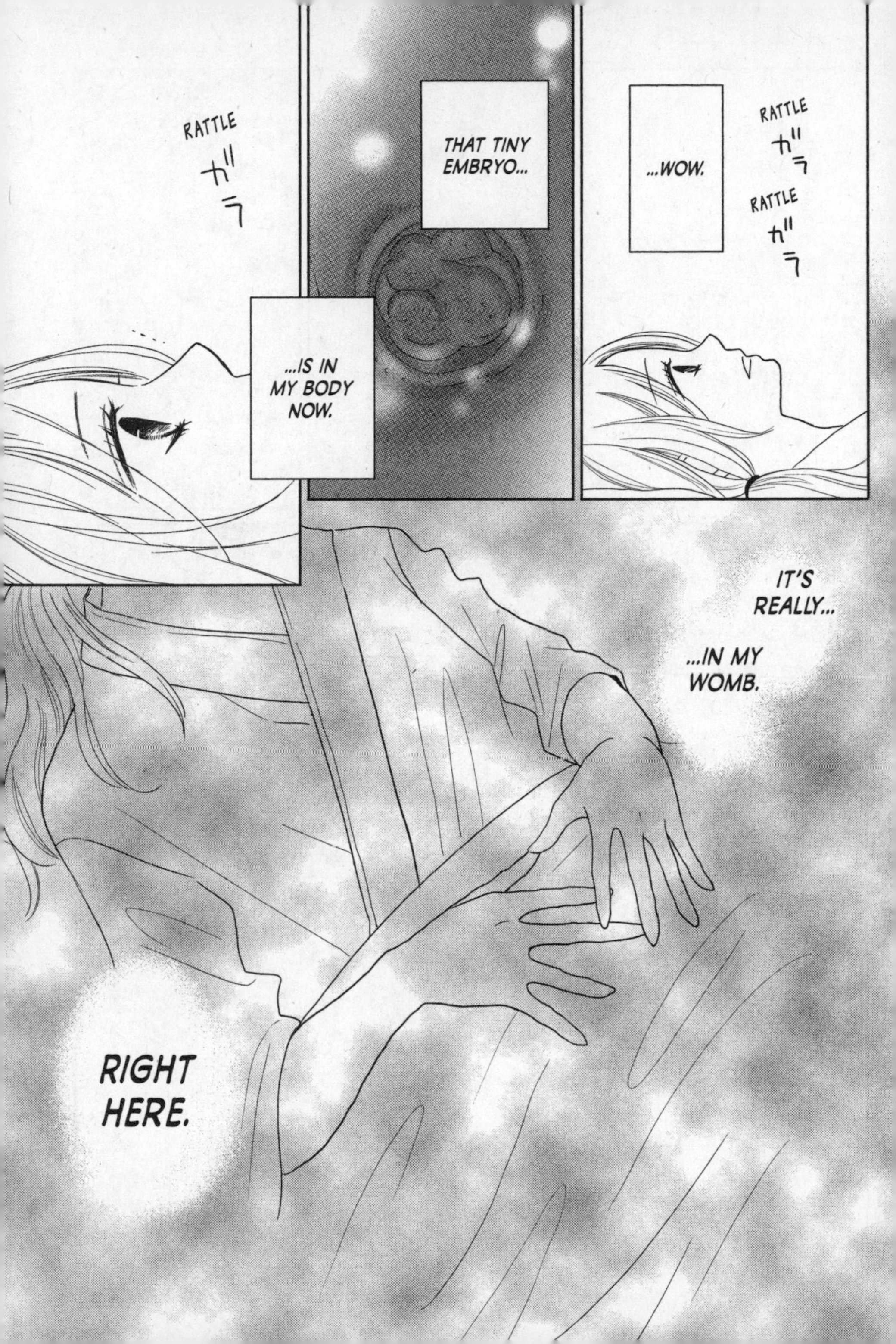
RATTLE
ガラ
RATTLE
ガラ
...WOW.
THAT TINY EMBRYO...
...IS IN MY BODY NOW.
RATTLE
ガラ
IT'S REALLY...
...IN MY WOMB.
RIGHT HERE.

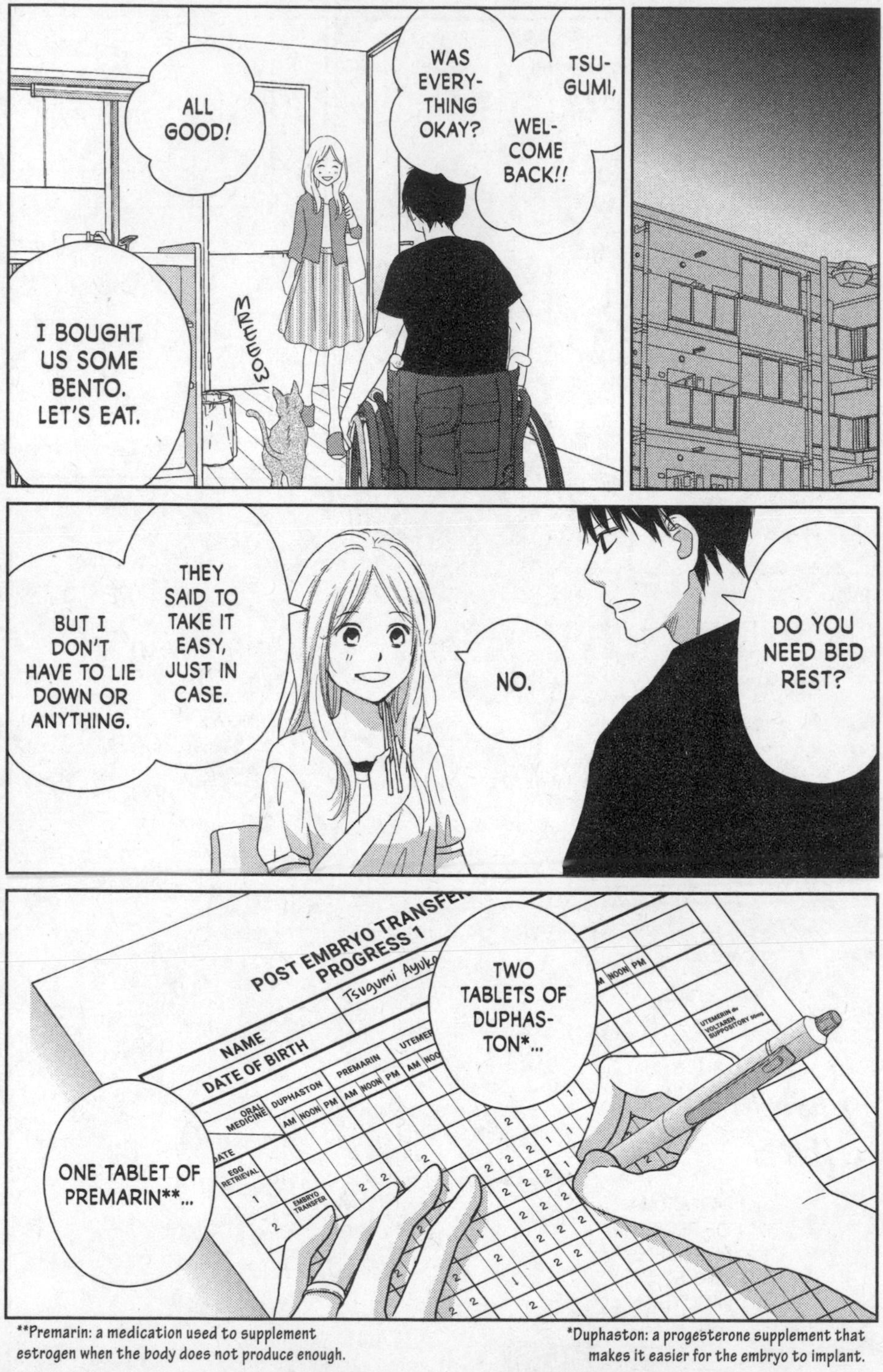
TSU-GUMI, WELCOME BACK!!
WAS EVERYTHING OKAY?
ALL GOOD!
MREEOW
I BOUGHT US SOME BENTO. LET'S EAT.
DO YOU NEED BED REST?
NO.
THEY SAID TO TAKE IT EASY, JUST IN CASE.
BUT I DON'T HAVE TO LIE DOWN OR ANYTHING.
PROGRESS 1
NAME
DATE OF BIRTH
ORAL MEDICINE
DUPHASTON
PREMARIN
AM NOON PM
EGG RETRIEVAL
EMBRYO TRANSFER
TWO TABLETS OF DUPHASTON*...
ONE TABLET OF PREMARIN**...

*Duphaston: a progesterone supplement that makes it easier for the embryo to implant.

**Premarin: a medication used to supplement estrogen when the body does not produce enough.

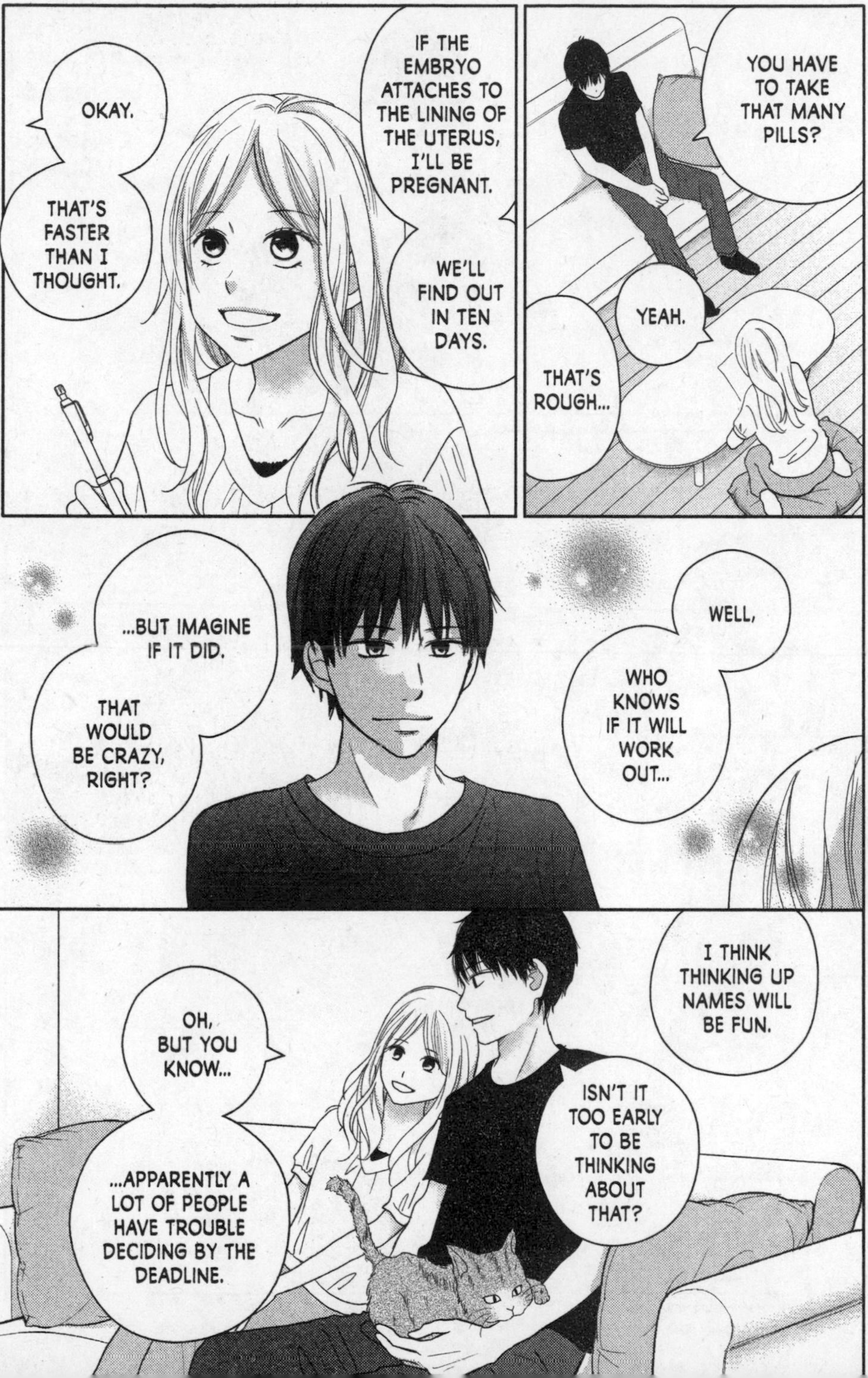
YOU HAVE TO TAKE THAT MANY PILLS?
YEAH.
THAT'S ROUGH...
IF THE EMBRYO ATTACHES TO THE LINING OF THE UTERUS, I'LL BE PREGNANT.
WE'LL FIND OUT IN TEN DAYS.
OKAY.
THAT'S FASTER THAN I THOUGHT.
WELL,
WHO KNOWS IF IT WILL WORK OUT...
...BUT IMAGINE IF IT DID.
THAT WOULD BE CRAZY, RIGHT?
I THINK THINKING UP NAMES WILL BE FUN.
ISN'T IT TOO EARLY TO BE THINKING ABOUT THAT?
OH, BUT YOU KNOW...
...APPARENTLY A LOT OF PEOPLE HAVE TROUBLE DECIDING BY THE DEADLINE.

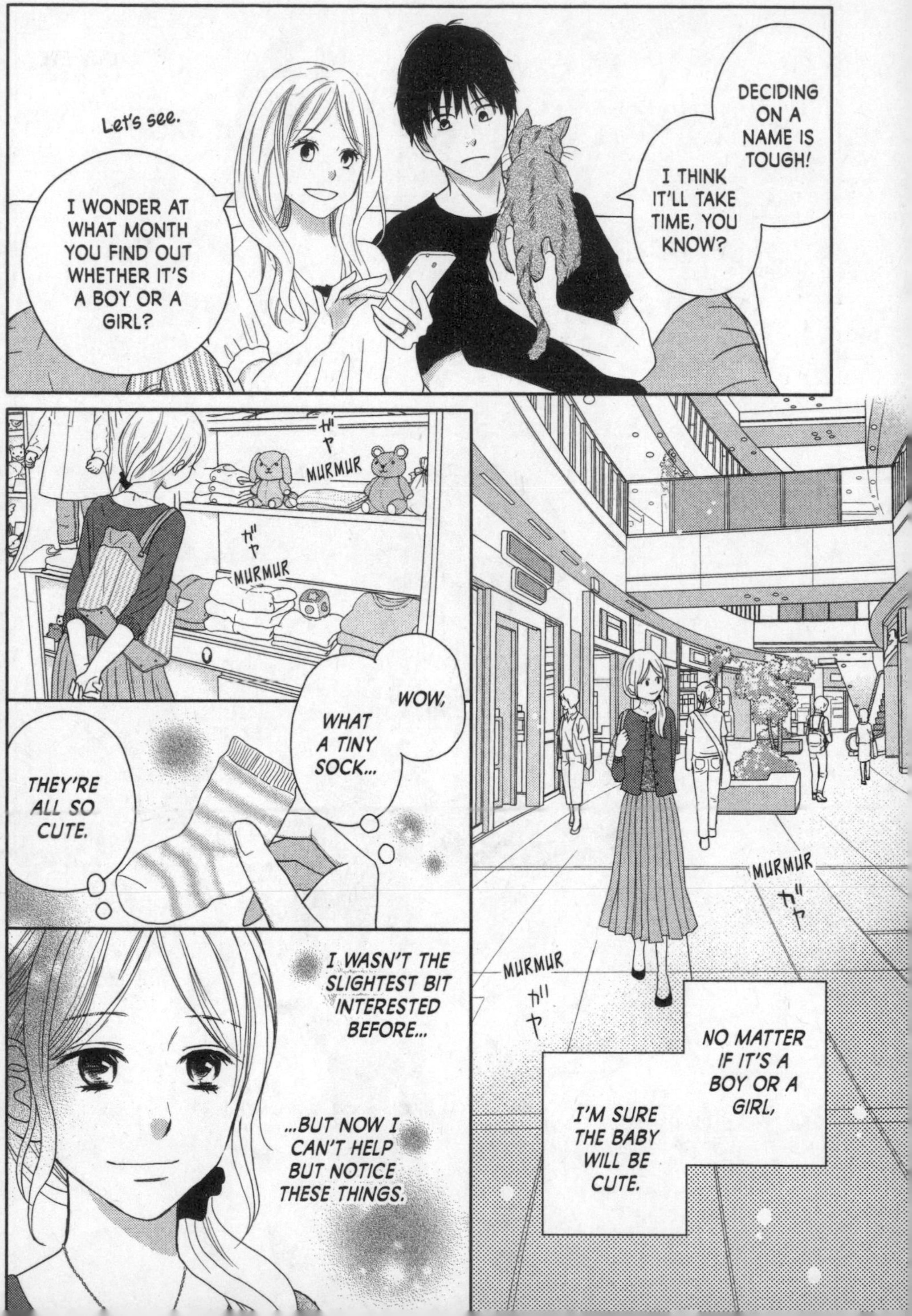
DECIDING ON A NAME IS TOUGH!
I THINK IT'LL TAKE TIME, YOU KNOW?
Let's see.
I WONDER AT WHAT MONTH YOU FIND OUT WHETHER IT'S A BOY OR A GIRL?
MURMUR ガヤ
MURMUR ガヤ
NO MATTER IF IT'S A BOY OR A GIRL,
I'M SURE THE BABY WILL BE CUTE.
ガヤ MURMUR
ガヤ MURMUR
WOW, WHAT A TINY SOCK...
THEY'RE ALL SO CUTE.
I WASN'T THE SLIGHTEST BIT INTERESTED BEFORE...
...BUT NOW I CAN'T HELP BUT NOTICE THESE THINGS.

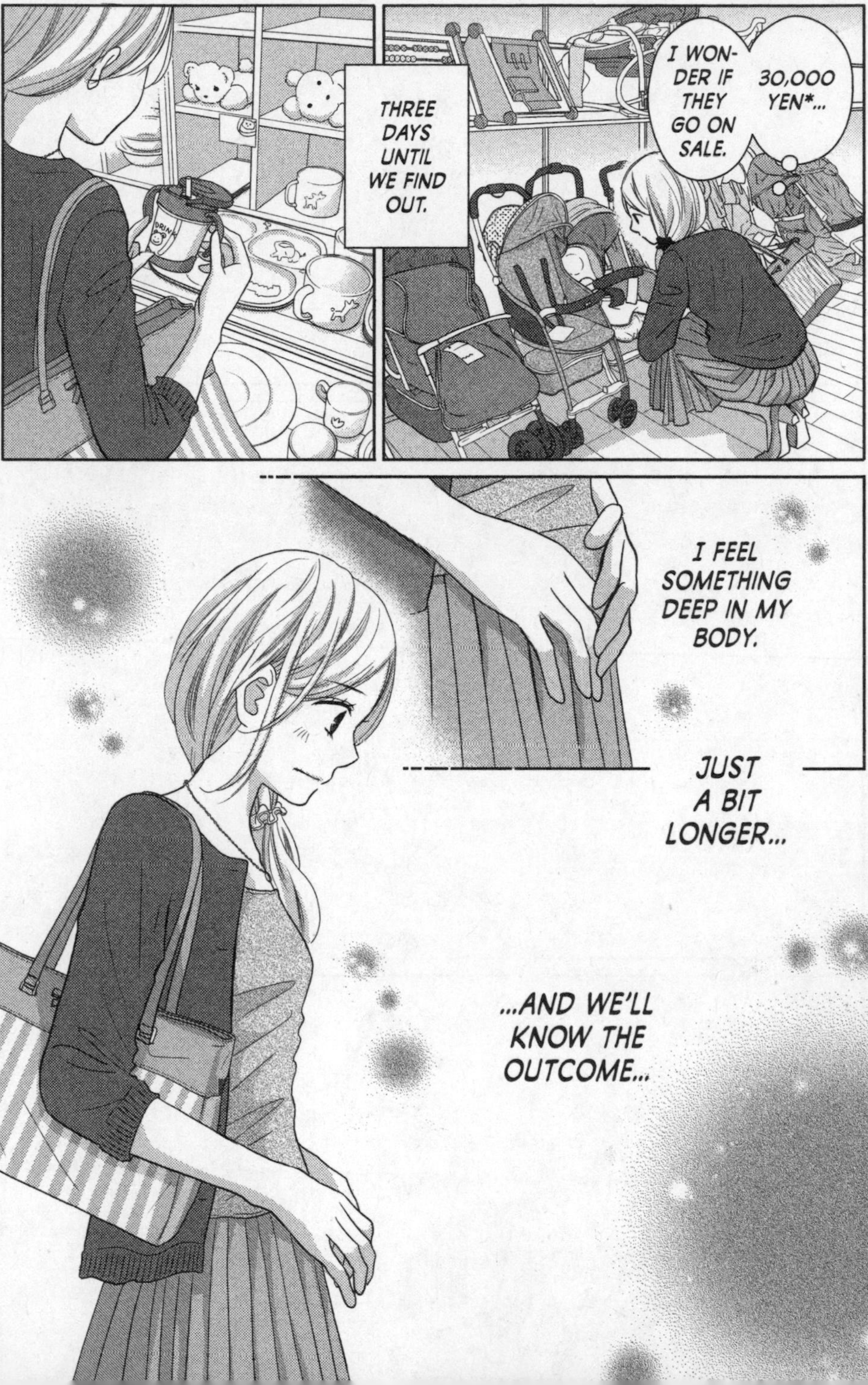
30,000 YEN*...
I WONDER IF THEY GO ON SALE.
THREE DAYS UNTIL WE FIND OUT.
I FEEL SOMETHING DEEP IN MY BODY.
JUST A BIT LONGER...
...AND WE'LL KNOW THE OUTCOME...

*About 300 USD

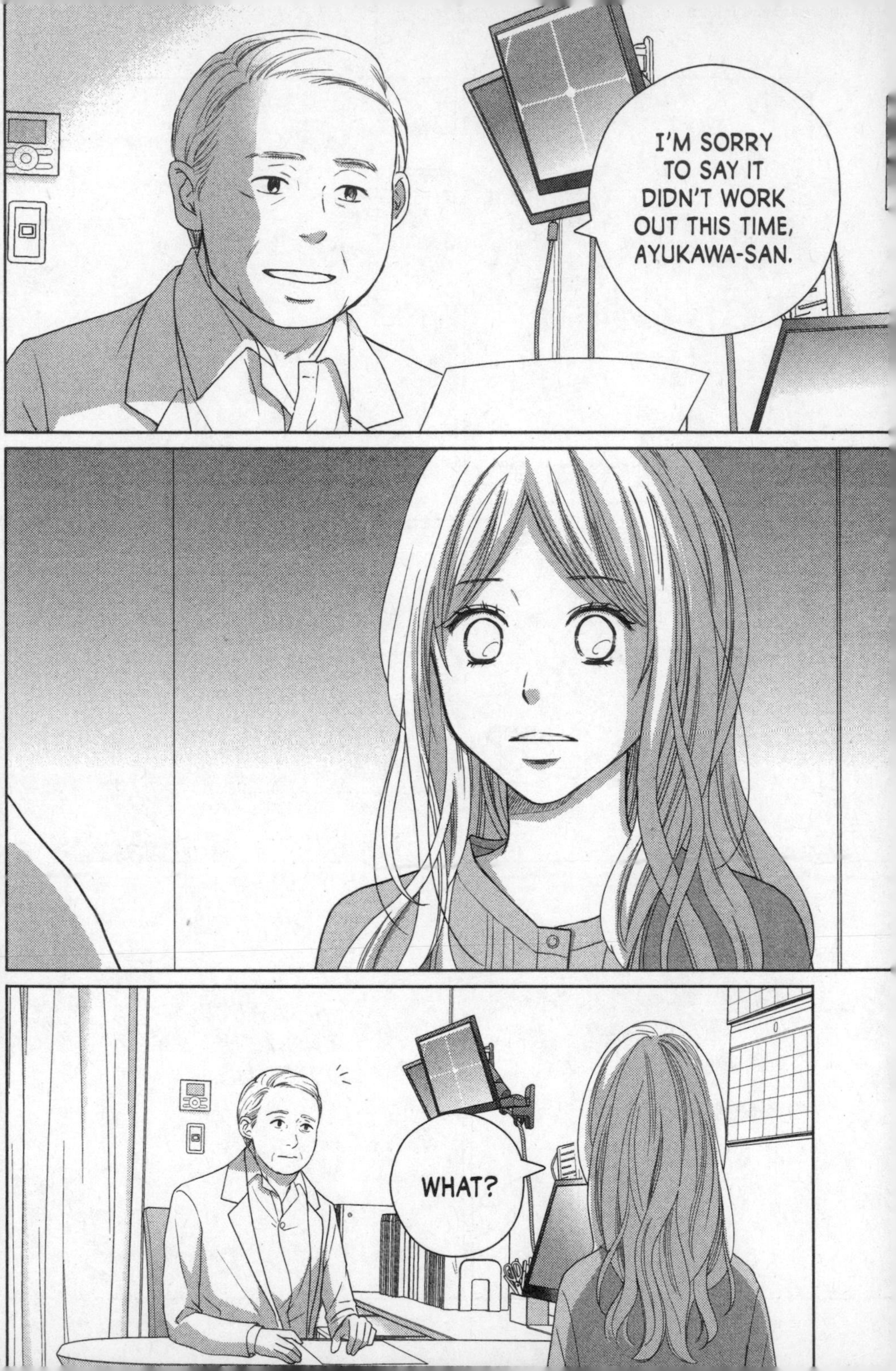
I'M SORRY TO SAY IT DIDN'T WORK OUT THIS TIME, AYUKAWA-SAN.
WHAT?

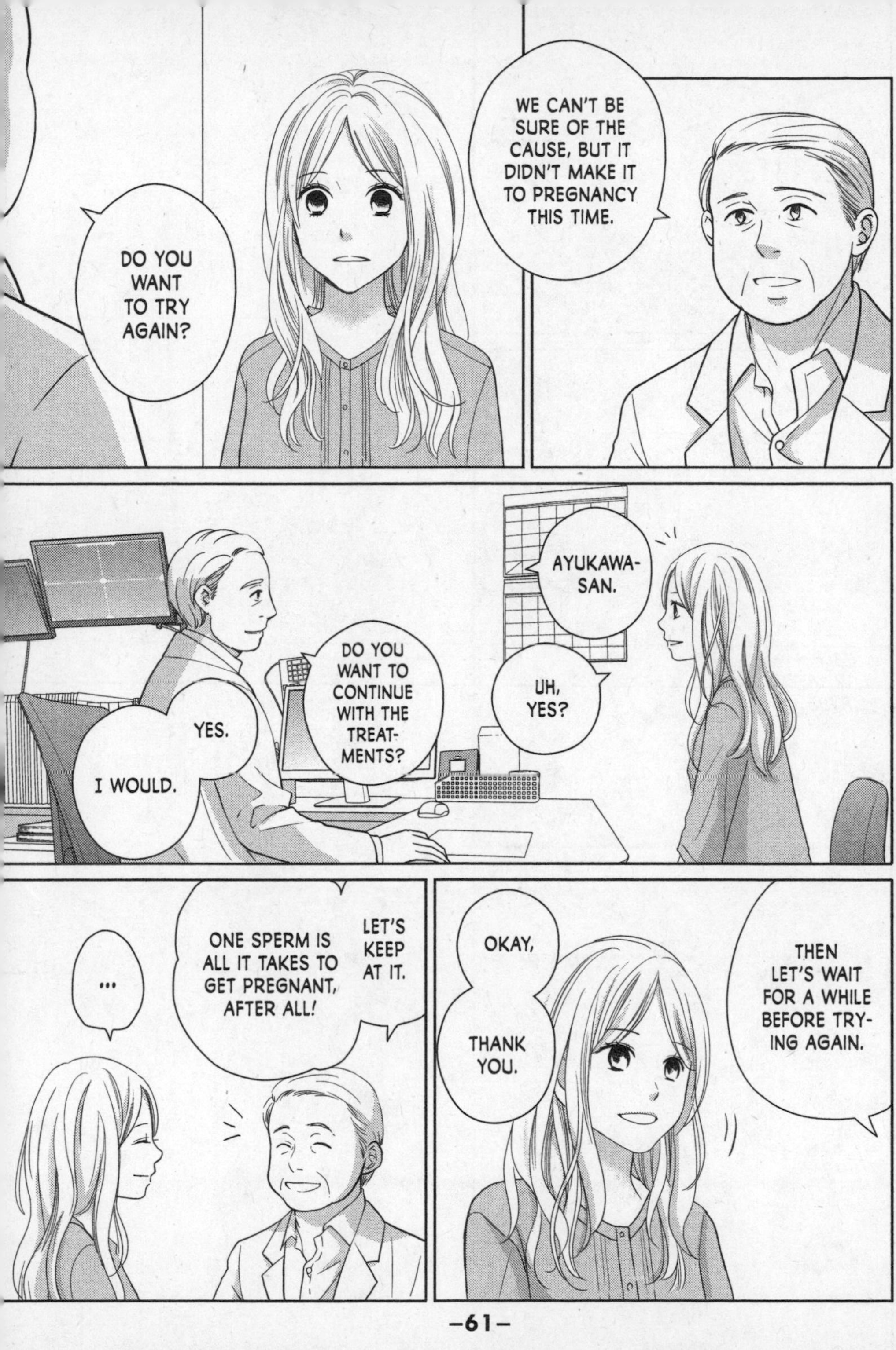
WE CAN'T BE SURE OF THE CAUSE, BUT IT DIDN'T MAKE IT TO PREGNANCY THIS TIME.
DO YOU WANT TO TRY AGAIN?
AYUKAWA-SAN.
UH, YES?
DO YOU WANT TO CONTINUE WITH THE TREAT-MENTS?
YES.
I WOULD.
THEN LET'S WAIT FOR A WHILE BEFORE TRY-ING AGAIN.
OKAY,
THANK YOU.
LET'S KEEP AT IT.
ONE SPERM IS ALL IT TAKES TO GET PREGNANT, AFTER ALL!
...

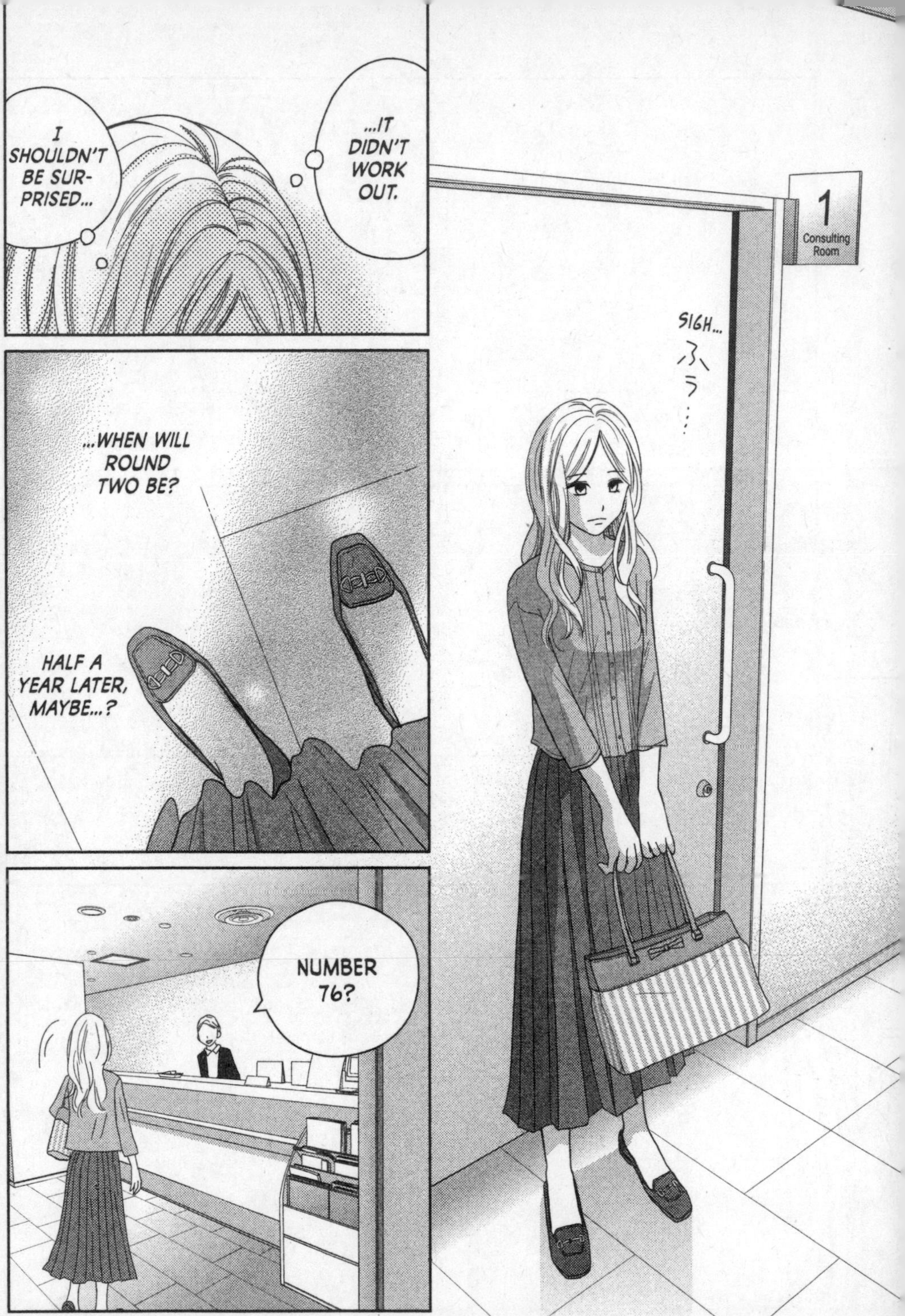
1
Consulting Room
SIGH...
ふら…
...IT DIDN'T WORK OUT.
I SHOULDN'T BE SUR-PRISED...
...WHEN WILL ROUND TWO BE?
HALF A YEAR LATER, MAYBE...?
NUMBER 76?

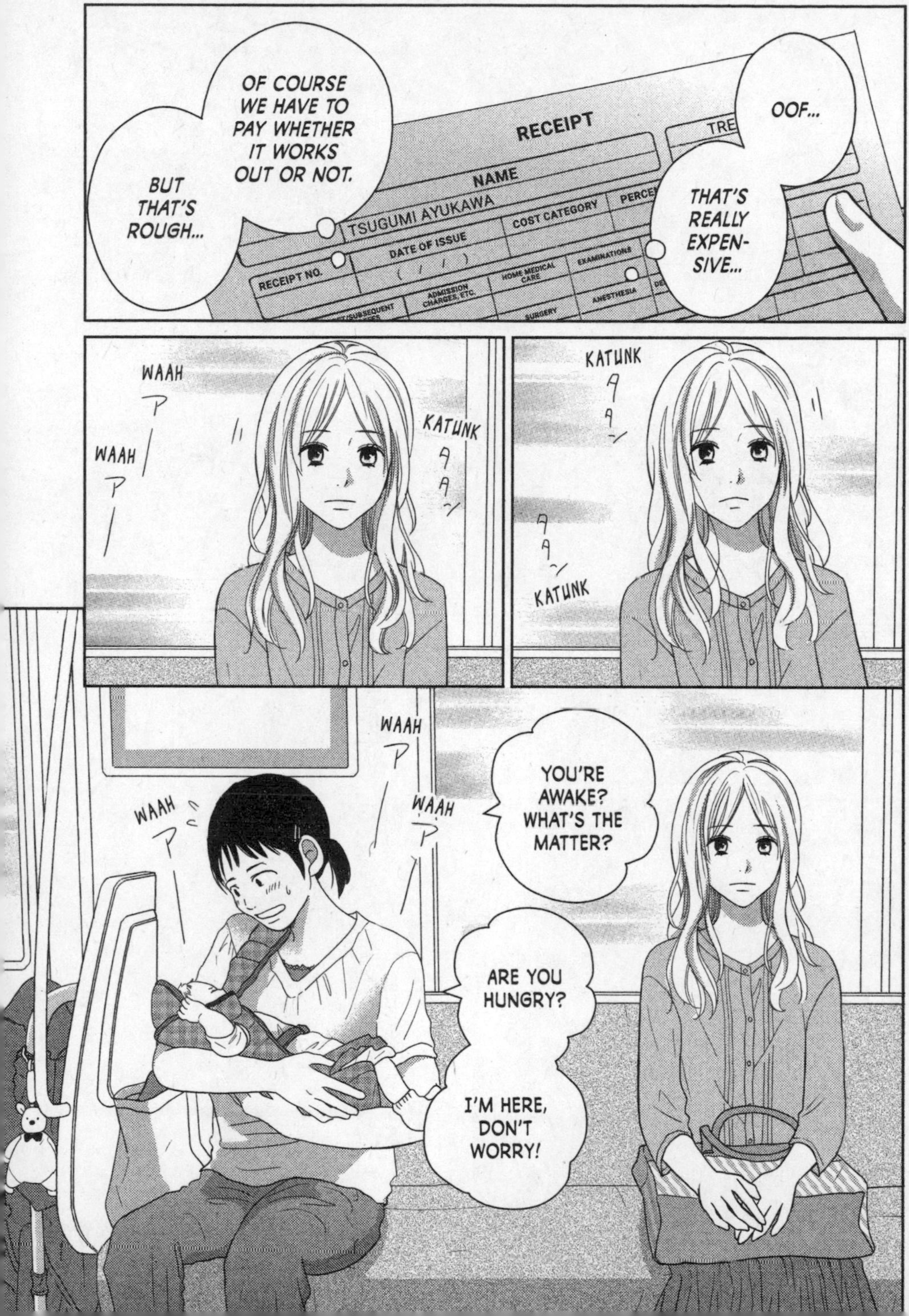
OOF...
THAT'S REALLY EXPENSIVE...
OF COURSE WE HAVE TO PAY WHETHER IT WORKS OUT OR NOT.
BUT THAT'S ROUGH...
RECEIPT
NAME
TSUGUMI AYUKAWA
COST CATEGORY
DATE OF ISSUE
RECEIPT NO.
ADMISSION CHARGES, ETC.
HOME MEDICAL CARE
EXAMINATIONS
ANESTHESIA
SURGERY
KATUNK
KATUNK
KATUNK
WAAH
WAAH
WAAH
WAAH
YOU'RE AWAKE? WHAT'S THE MATTER?
WAAH
ARE YOU HUNGRY?
I'M HERE, DON'T WORRY!

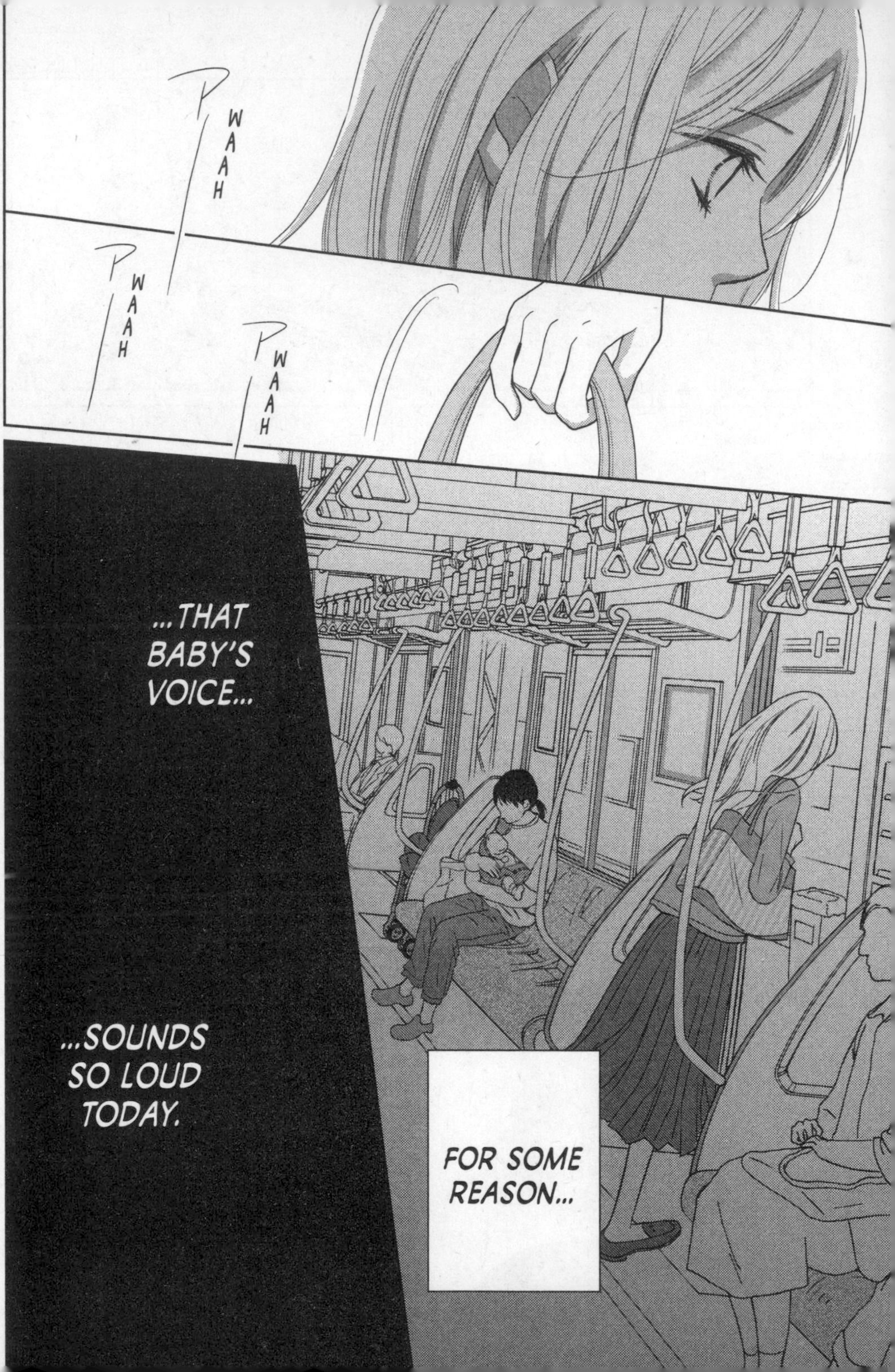
PWAAH
PWAAH
PWAAH
FOR SOME REASON...
...THAT BABY'S VOICE...
...SOUNDS SO LOUD TODAY.

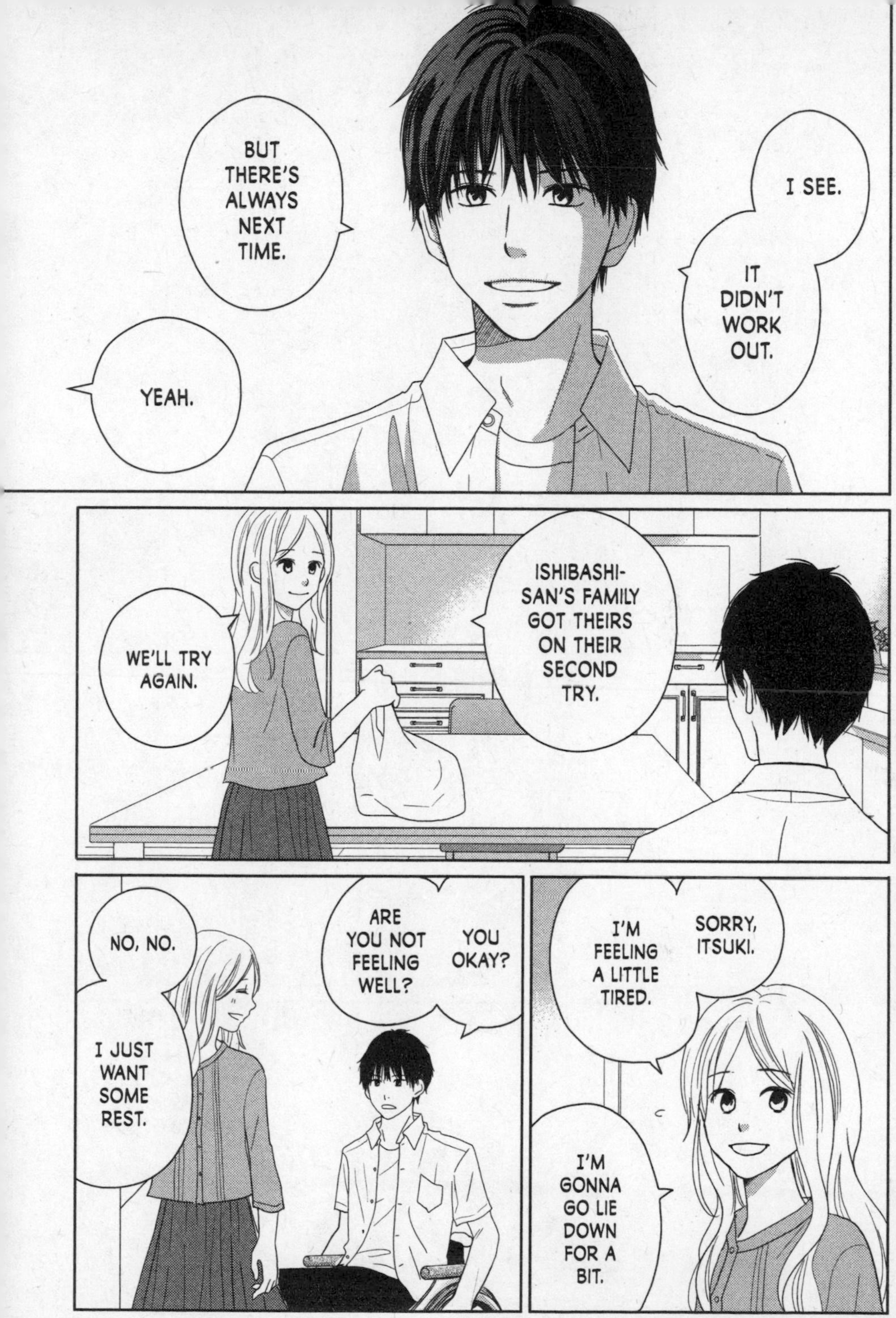
I SEE.
IT DIDN'T WORK OUT.
BUT THERE'S ALWAYS NEXT TIME.
YEAH.
ISHIBASHI-SAN'S FAMILY GOT THEIRS ON THEIR SECOND TRY.
WE'LL TRY AGAIN.
SORRY, ITSUKI.
I'M FEELING A LITTLE TIRED.
I'M GONNA GO LIE DOWN FOR A BIT.
YOU OKAY?
ARE YOU NOT FEELING WELL?
NO, NO.
I JUST WANT SOME REST.

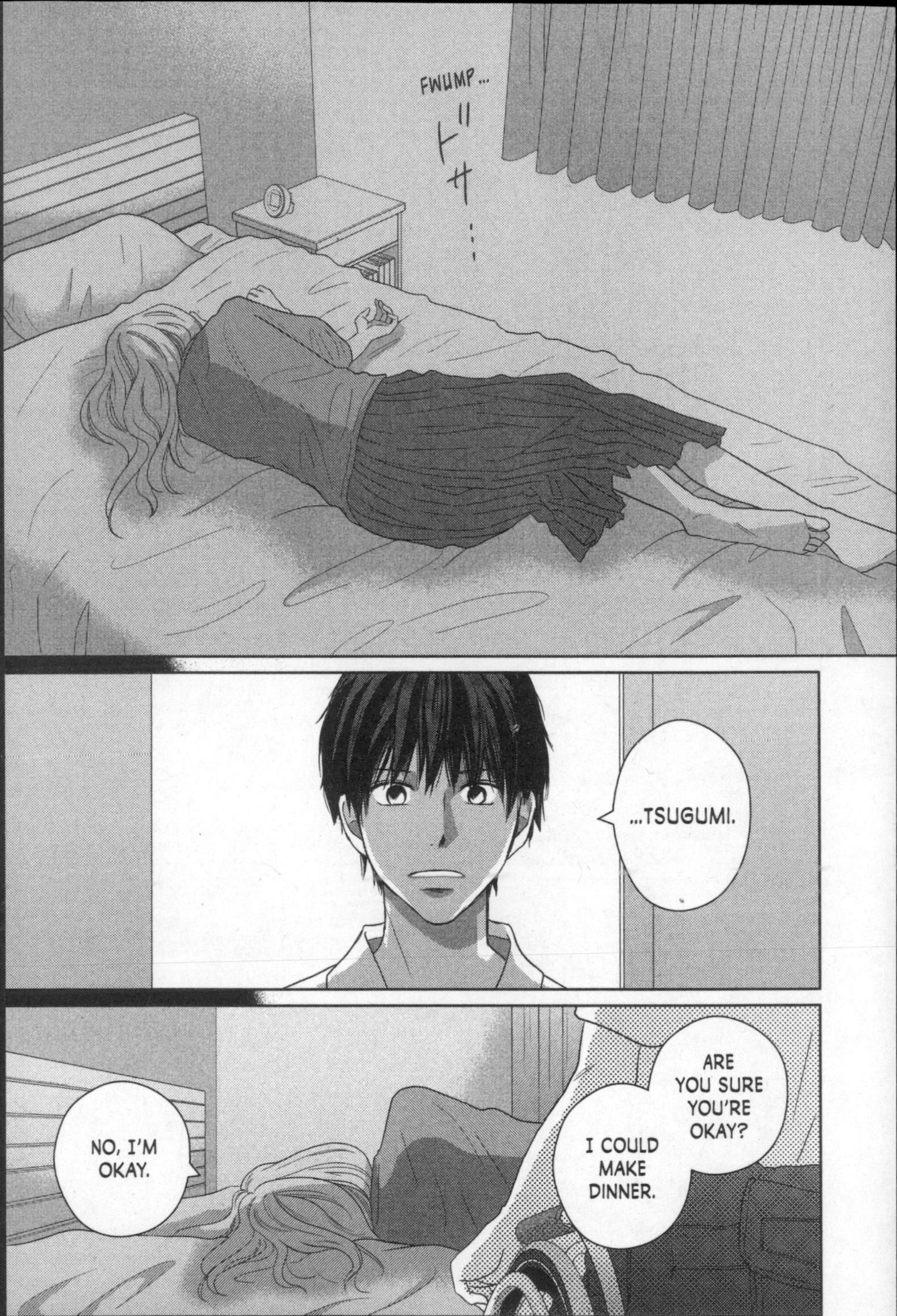
FWUMP...
ドサ…
...TSUGUMI.
ARE YOU SURE YOU'RE OKAY?
I COULD MAKE DINNER.
NO, I'M OKAY.

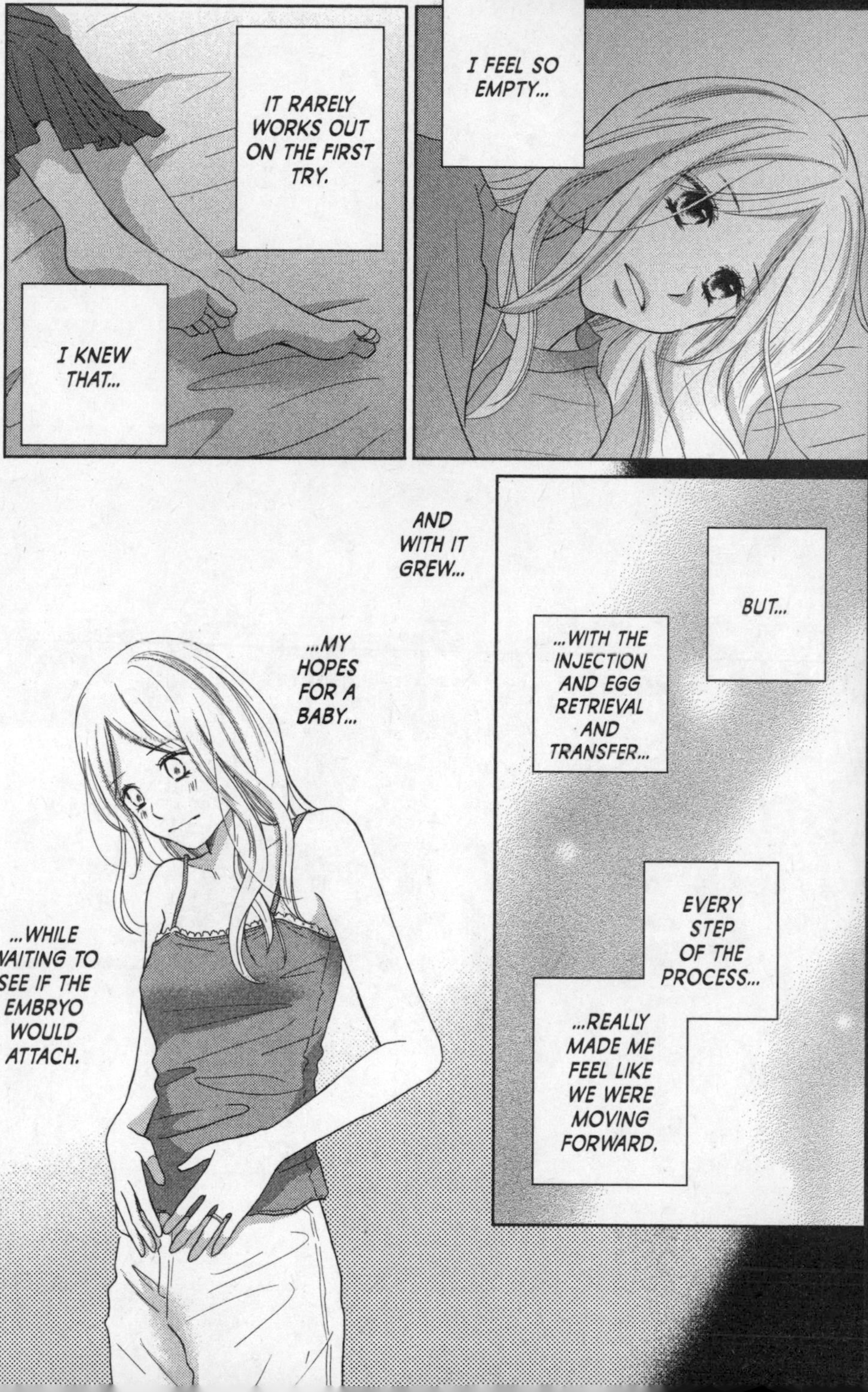
I FEEL SO EMPTY...
IT RARELY WORKS OUT ON THE FIRST TRY.
I KNEW THAT...
BUT...
...WITH THE INJECTION AND EGG RETRIEVAL AND TRANSFER...
EVERY STEP OF THE PROCESS...
...REALLY MADE ME FEEL LIKE WE WERE MOVING FORWARD.
AND WITH IT GREW...
...MY HOPES FOR A BABY...
...WHILE WAITING TO SEE IF THE EMBRYO WOULD ATTACH.

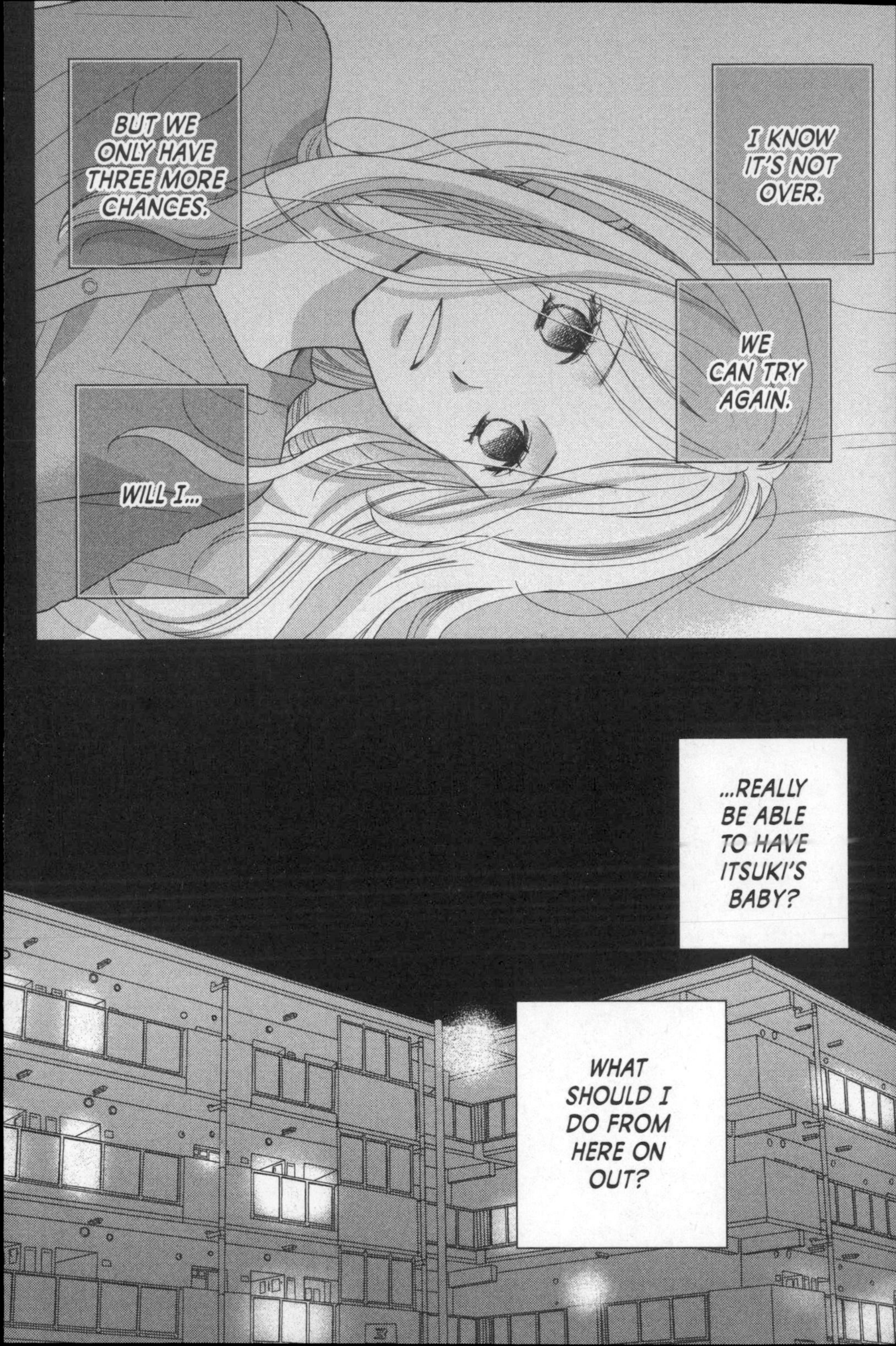
I KNOW IT'S NOT OVER.
WE CAN TRY AGAIN.
BUT WE ONLY HAVE THREE MORE CHANCES.
WILL I...
...REALLY BE ABLE TO HAVE ITSUKI'S BABY?
WHAT SHOULD I DO FROM HERE ON OUT?

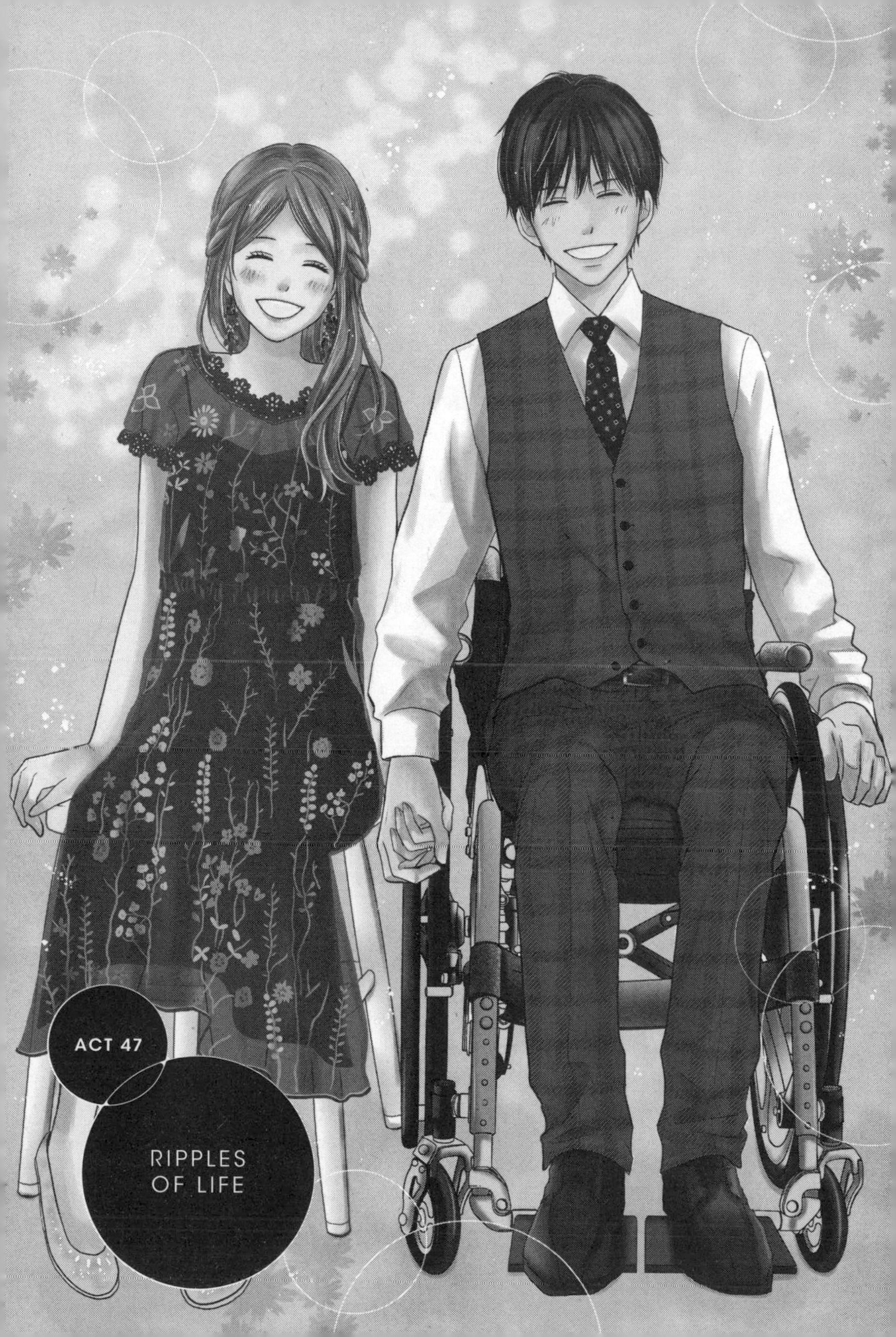
ACT 47
RIPPLES OF LIFE

PERFECT WORLD

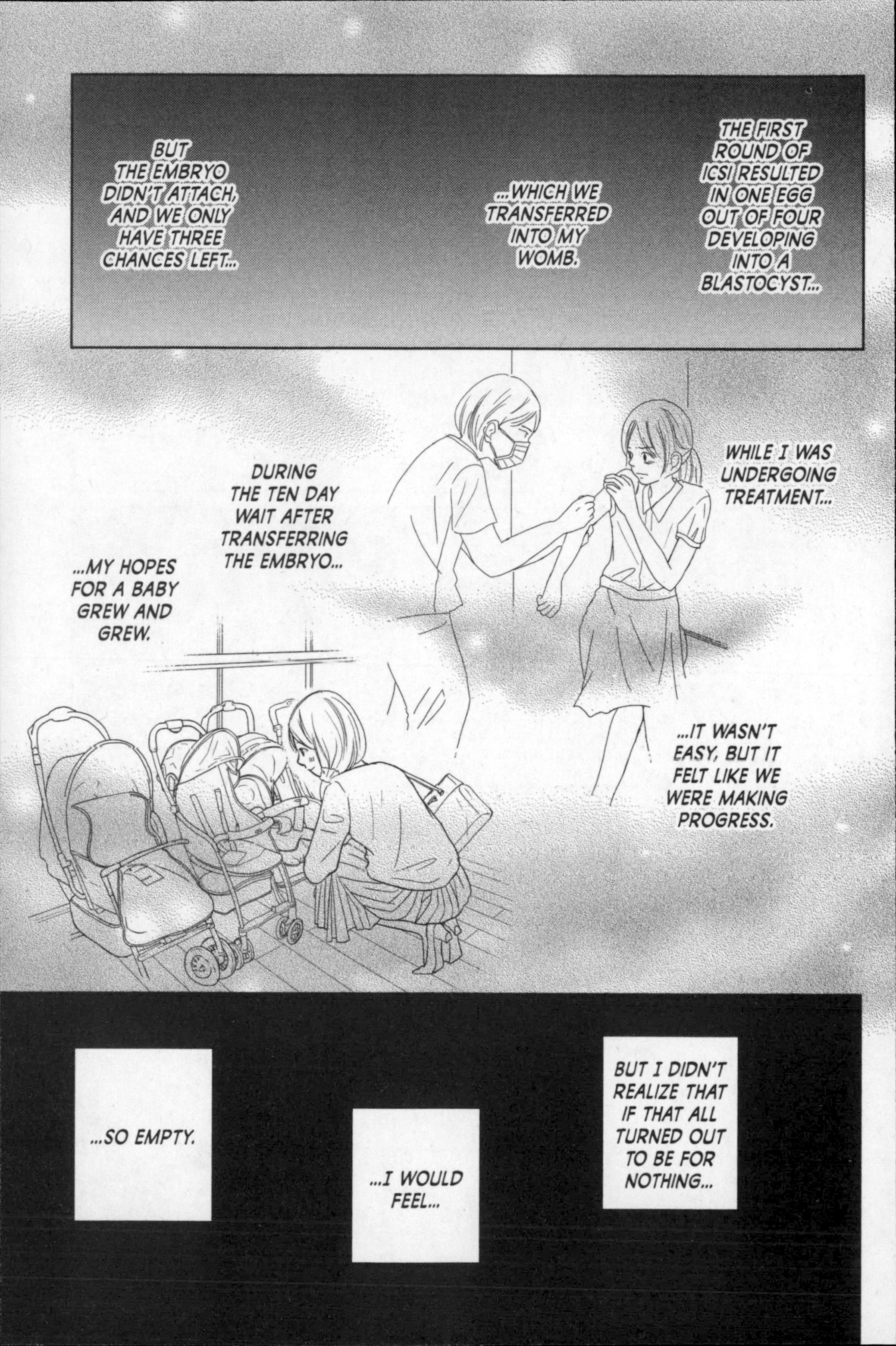
THE FIRST ROUND OF ICSI RESULTED IN ONE EGG OUT OF FOUR DEVELOPING INTO A BLASTOCYST...
...WHICH WE TRANSFERRED INTO MY WOMB.
BUT THE EMBRYO DIDN'T ATTACH, AND WE ONLY HAVE THREE CHANCES LEFT...
WHILE I WAS UNDERGOING TREATMENT...
...IT WASN'T EASY, BUT IT FELT LIKE WE WERE MAKING PROGRESS.
DURING THE TEN DAY WAIT AFTER TRANSFERRING THE EMBRYO...
...MY HOPES FOR A BABY GREW AND GREW.
BUT I DIDN'T REALIZE THAT IF THAT ALL TURNED OUT TO BE FOR NOTHING...
...I WOULD FEEL...
...SO EMPTY.

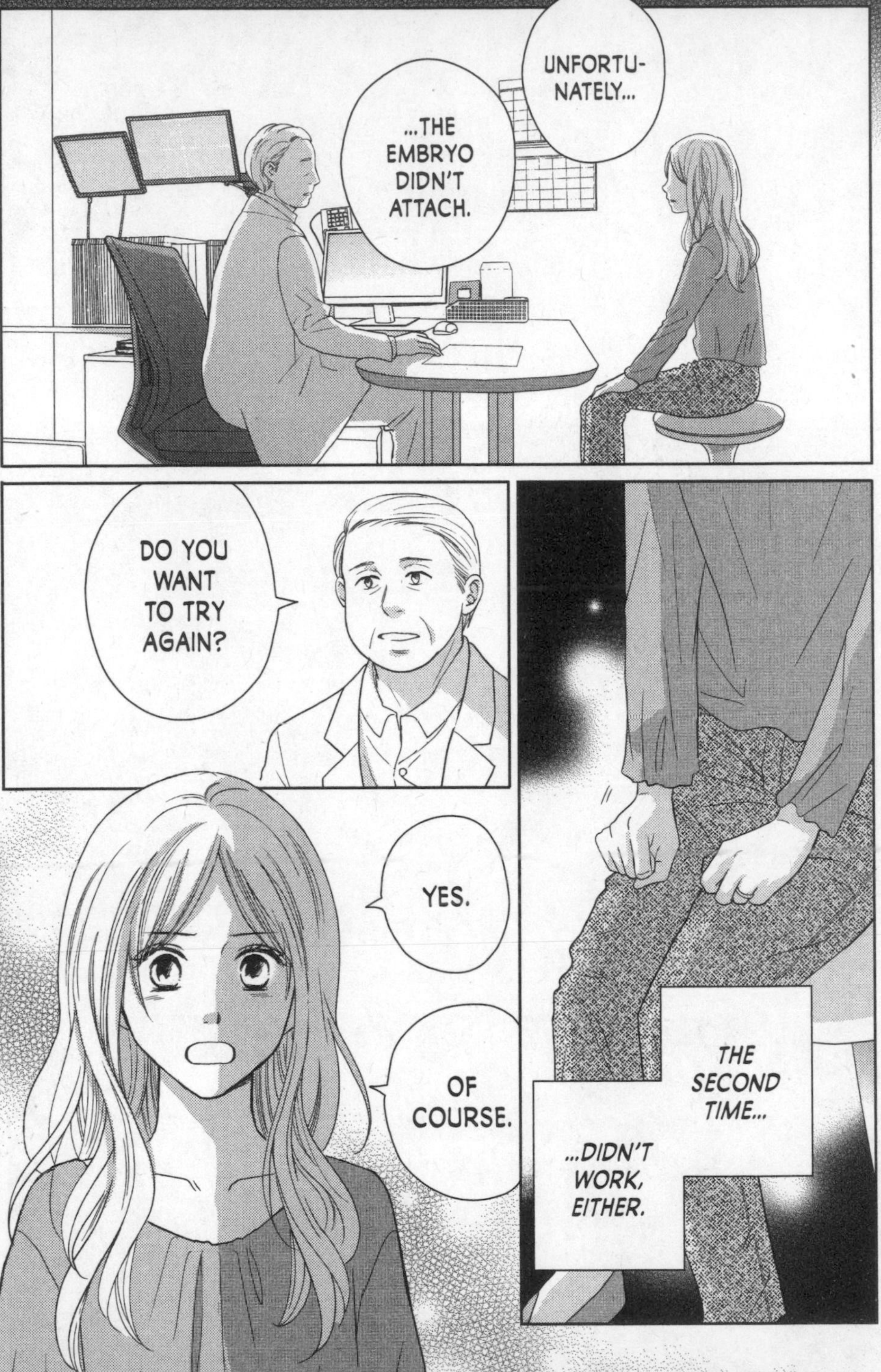
UNFORTU-NATELY...
...THE EMBRYO DIDN'T ATTACH.
THE SECOND TIME...
...DIDN'T WORK, EITHER.
DO YOU WANT TO TRY AGAIN?
YES.
OF COURSE.

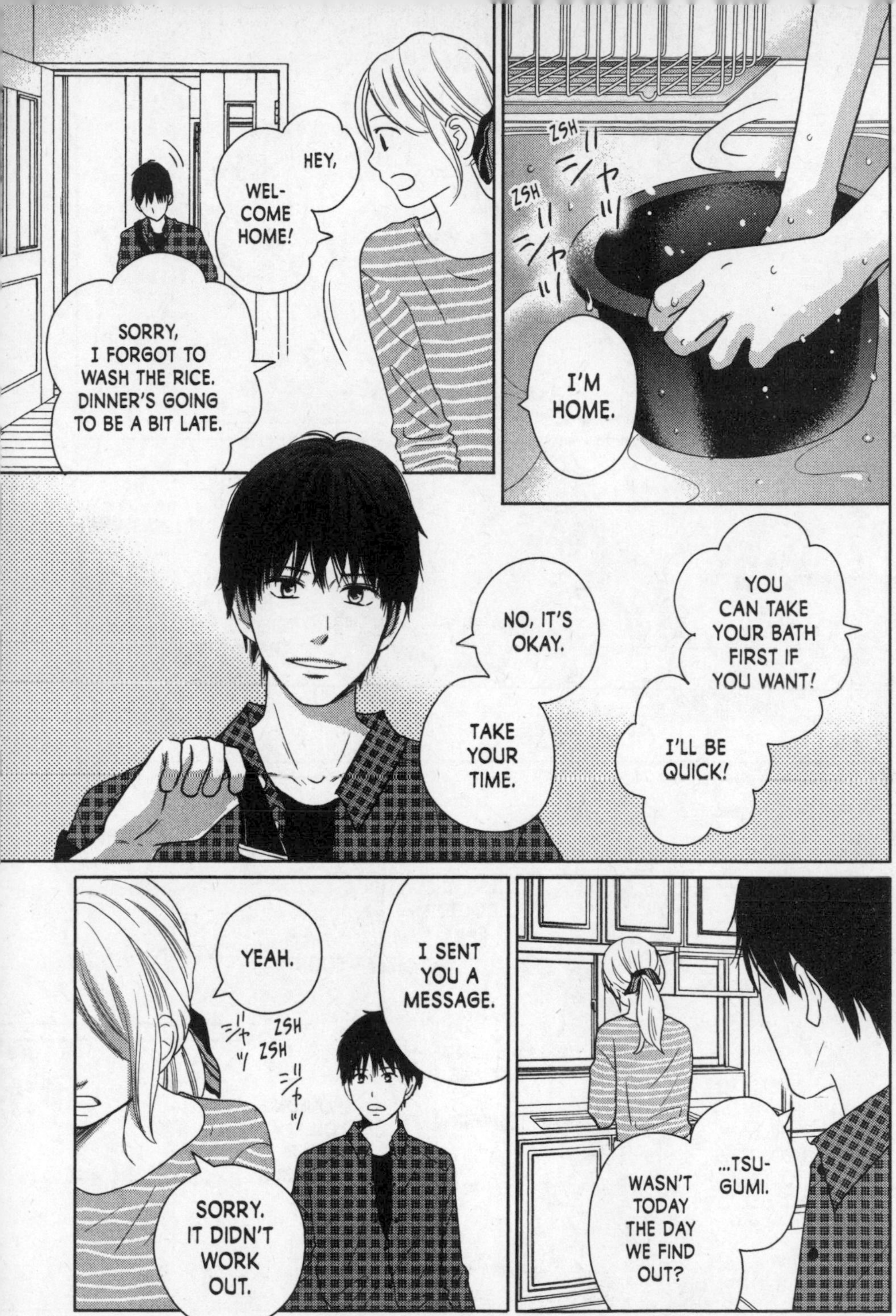
ZSH
シャッ
ZSH
シャッ
I'M HOME.
HEY, WEL-COME HOME!
SORRY, I FORGOT TO WASH THE RICE. DINNER'S GOING TO BE A BIT LATE.
YOU CAN TAKE YOUR BATH FIRST IF YOU WANT!
I'LL BE QUICK!
NO, IT'S OKAY.
TAKE YOUR TIME.
...TSU-GUMI.
WASN'T TODAY THE DAY WE FIND OUT?
I SENT YOU A MESSAGE.
YEAH.
シャッ ZSH
ZSH シャッ
SORRY. IT DIDN'T WORK OUT.

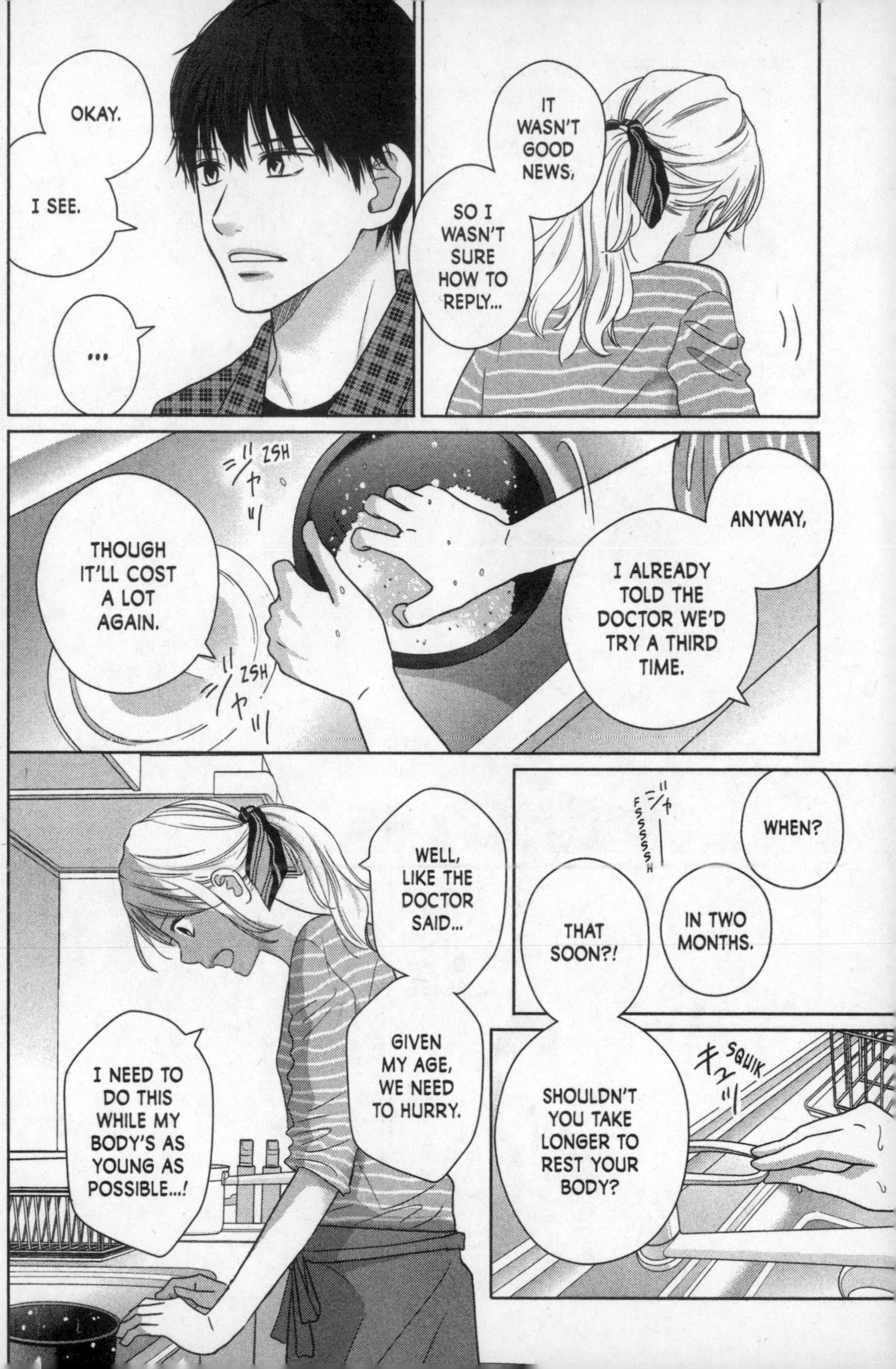
IT WASN'T GOOD NEWS,
SO I WASN'T SURE HOW TO REPLY...
OKAY.
I SEE.
...
ZSH
ANYWAY,
I ALREADY TOLD THE DOCTOR WE'D TRY A THIRD TIME.
THOUGH IT'LL COST A LOT AGAIN.
ZSH
WHEN?
IN TWO MONTHS.
FSSSSSH
THAT SOON?!
SHOULDN'T YOU TAKE LONGER TO REST YOUR BODY?
SQUIK
WELL, LIKE THE DOCTOR SAID...
GIVEN MY AGE, WE NEED TO HURRY.
I NEED TO DO THIS WHILE MY BODY'S AS YOUNG AS POSSIBLE...!

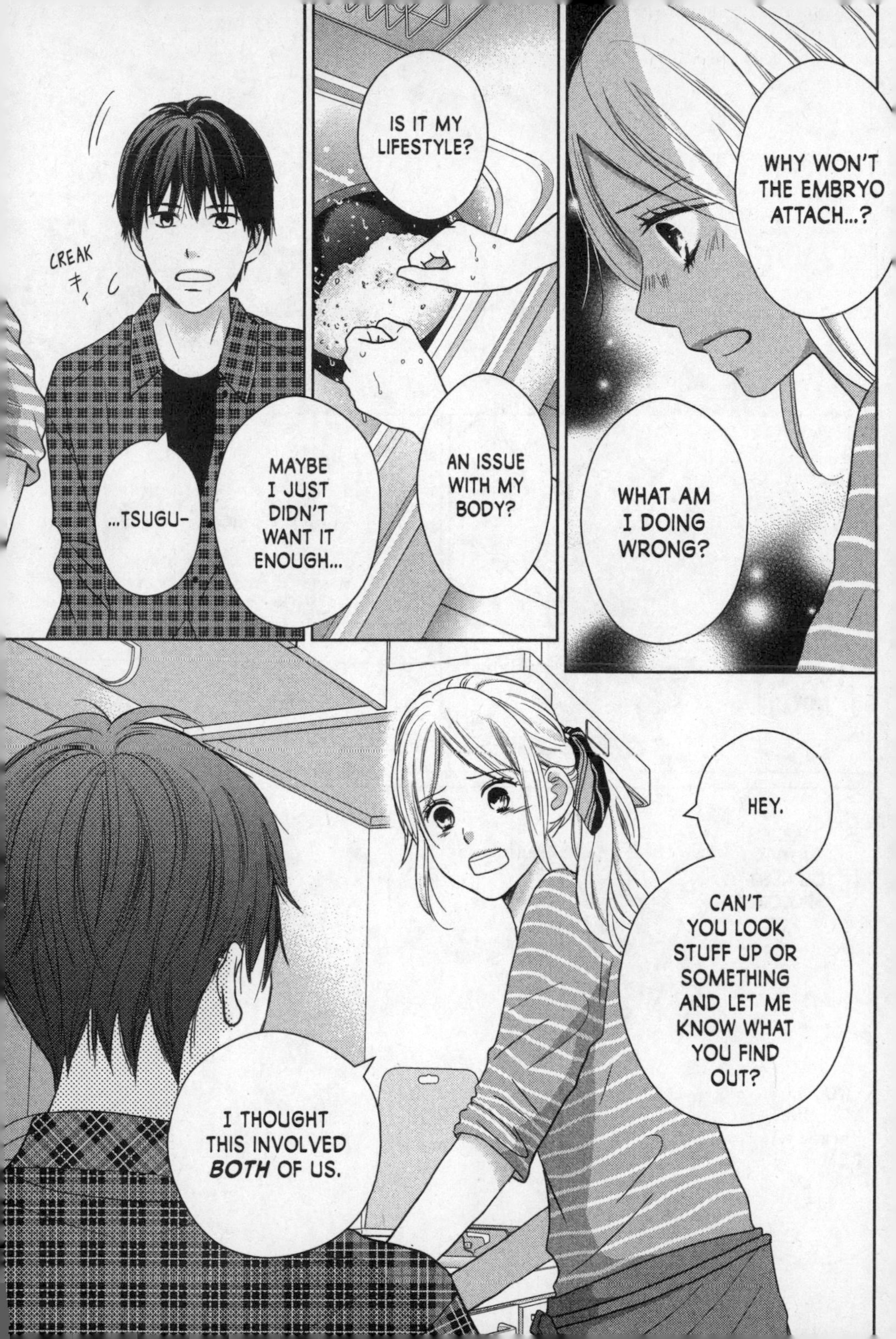
WHY WON'T THE EMBRYO ATTACH...?
WHAT AM I DOING WRONG?
IS IT MY LIFESTYLE?
AN ISSUE WITH MY BODY?
MAYBE I JUST DIDN'T WANT IT ENOUGH...
CREAK
キィ
...TSUGU-
HEY.
CAN'T YOU LOOK STUFF UP OR SOMETHING AND LET ME KNOW WHAT YOU FIND OUT?
I THOUGHT THIS INVOLVED *BOTH* OF US.

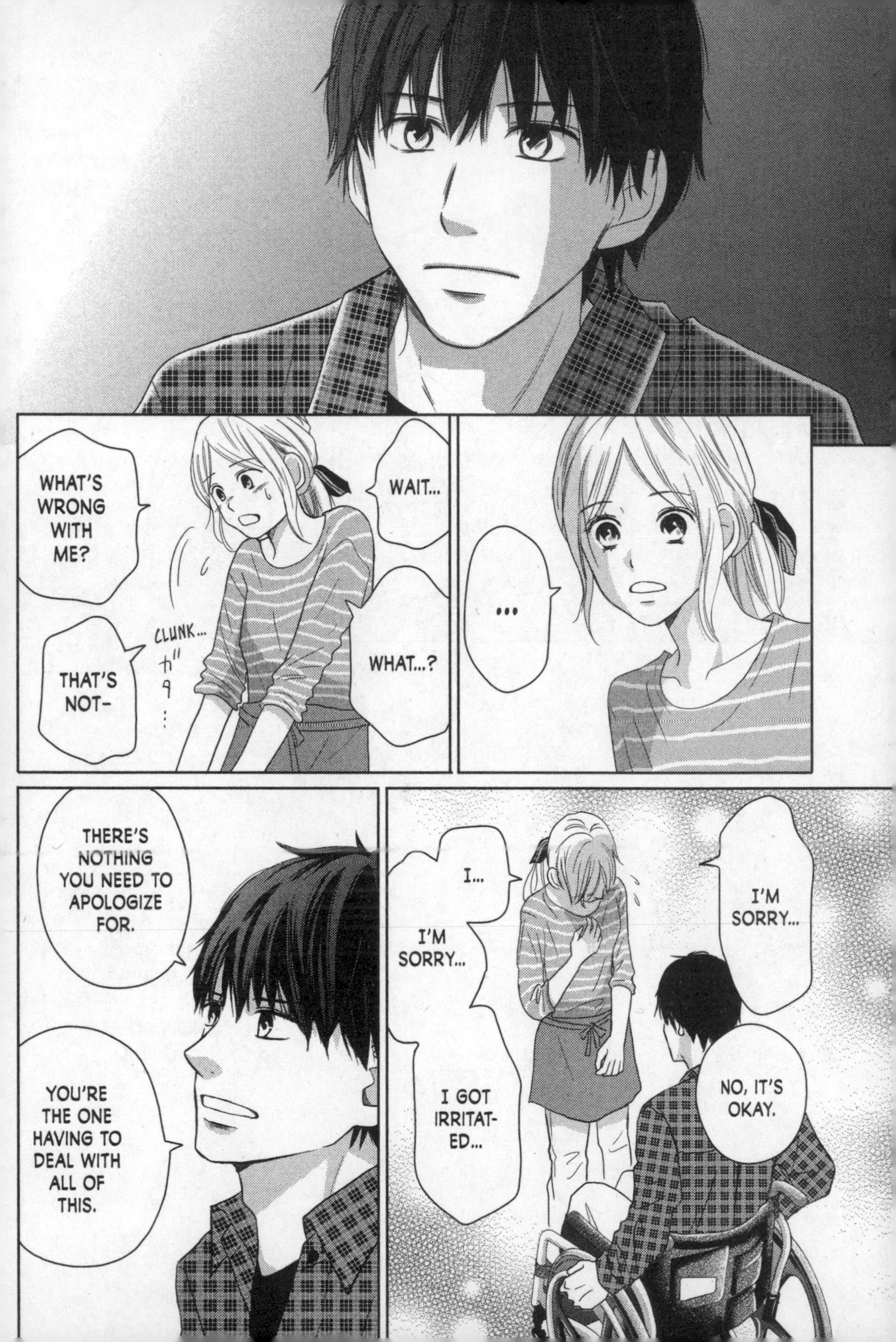
...
WAIT...
WHAT...?
WHAT'S WRONG WITH ME?
CLUNK...
ガタ...
THAT'S NOT-
I'M SORRY...
I...
I'M SORRY...
NO, IT'S OKAY.
I GOT IRRITAT-ED...
THERE'S NOTHING YOU NEED TO APOLOGIZE FOR.
YOU'RE THE ONE HAVING TO DEAL WITH ALL OF THIS.

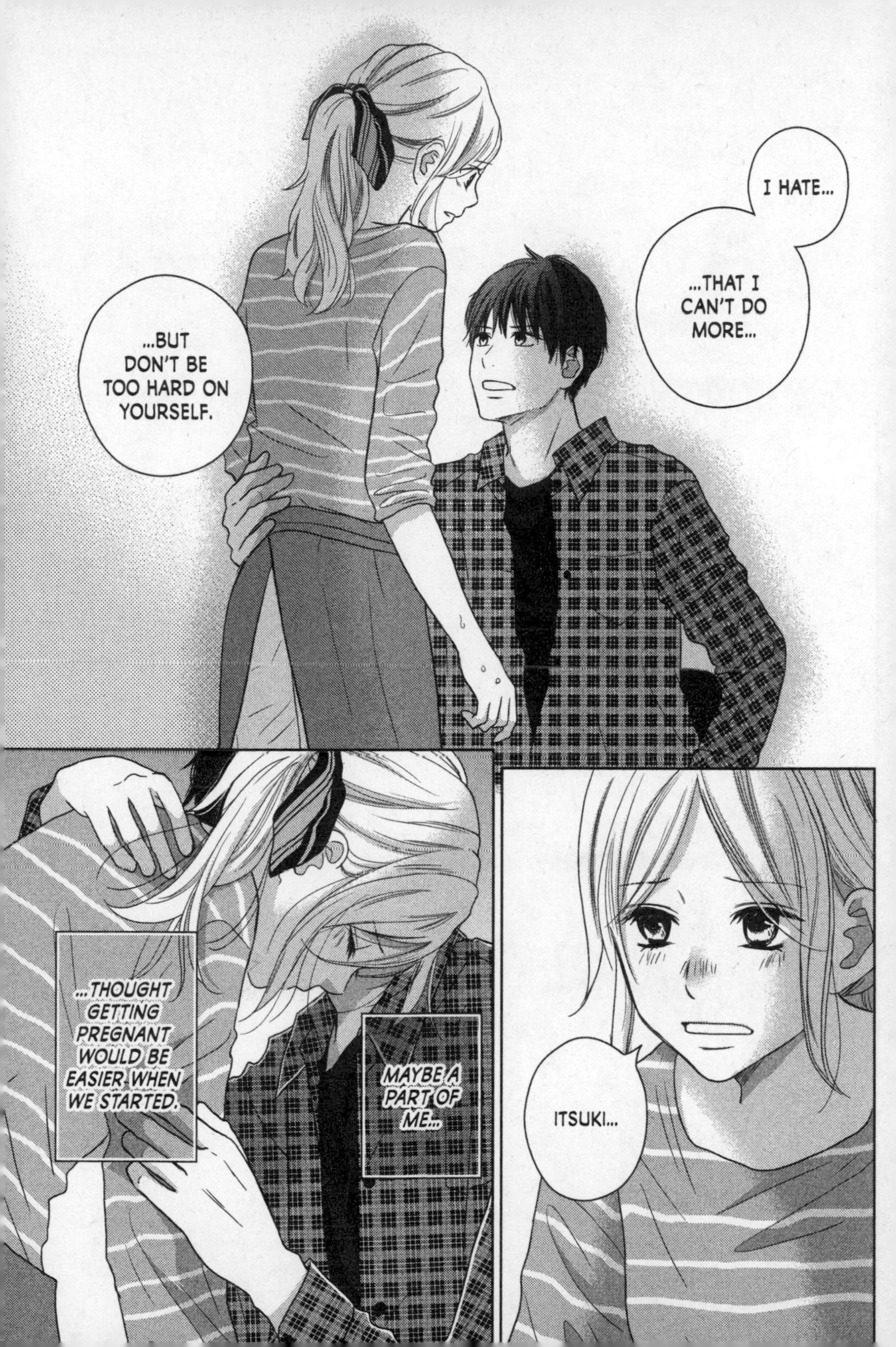
I HATE...
...THAT I CAN'T DO MORE...
...BUT DON'T BE TOO HARD ON YOURSELF.
ITSUKI...
MAYBE A PART OF ME...
...THOUGHT GETTING PREGNANT WOULD BE EASIER WHEN WE STARTED.

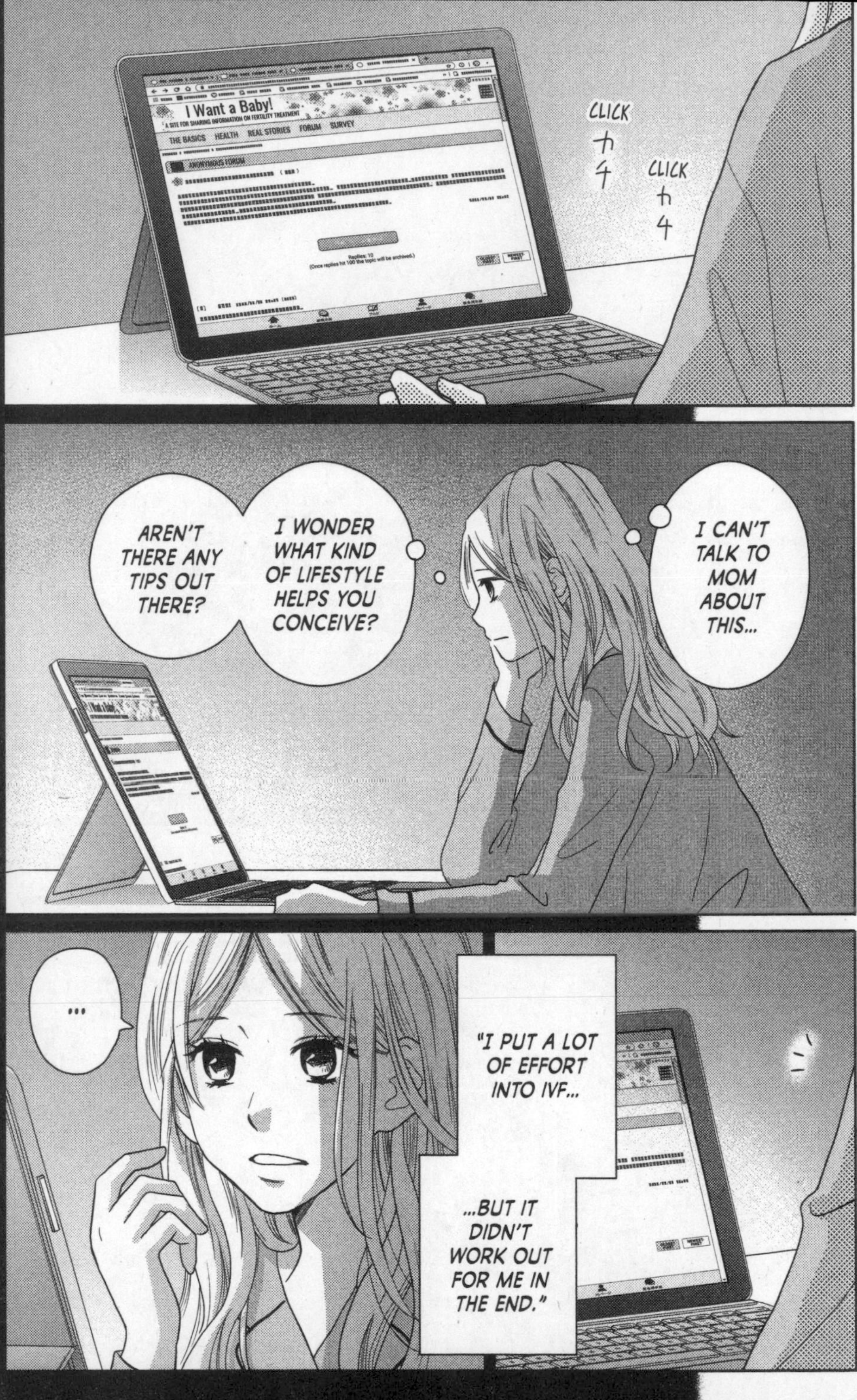
I Want a Baby!
A SITE FOR SHARING INFORMATION ON FERTILITY TREATMENT
THE BASICS HEALTH REAL STORIES FORUM SURVEY
ANONYMOUS FORUM
CLICK
カチ
CLICK
カチ
I CAN'T TALK TO MOM ABOUT THIS...
I WONDER WHAT KIND OF LIFESTYLE HELPS YOU CONCEIVE?
AREN'T THERE ANY TIPS OUT THERE?
"I PUT A LOT OF EFFORT INTO IVF...
...BUT IT DIDN'T WORK OUT FOR ME IN THE END."
...

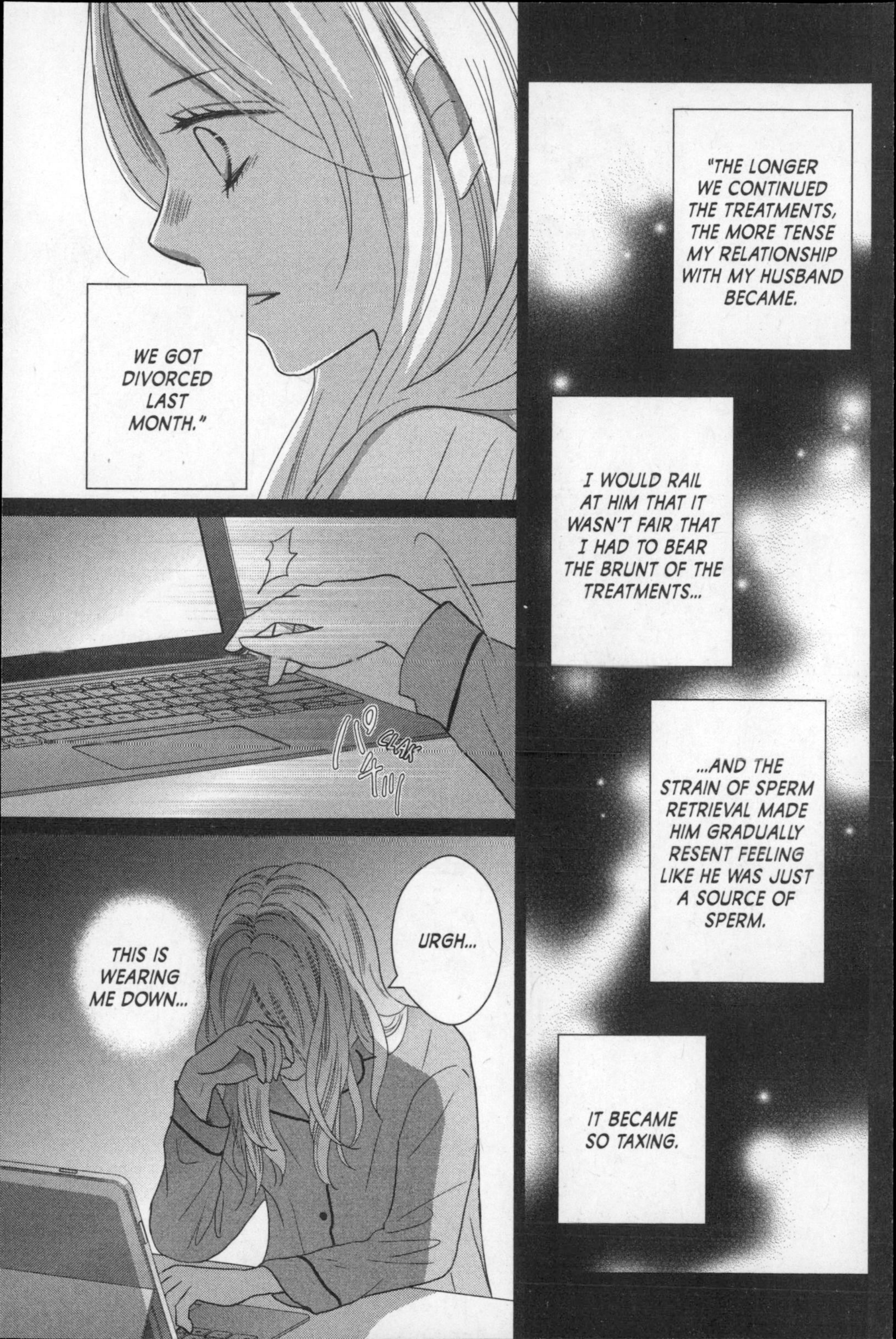
"THE LONGER WE CONTINUED THE TREATMENTS, THE MORE TENSE MY RELATIONSHIP WITH MY HUSBAND BECAME.
I WOULD RAIL AT HIM THAT IT WASN'T FAIR THAT I HAD TO BEAR THE BRUNT OF THE TREATMENTS...
...AND THE STRAIN OF SPERM RETRIEVAL MADE HIM GRADUALLY RESENT FEELING LIKE HE WAS JUST A SOURCE OF SPERM.
IT BECAME SO TAXING.
WE GOT DIVORCED LAST MONTH."
CLAK
URGH...
THIS IS WEARING ME DOWN...

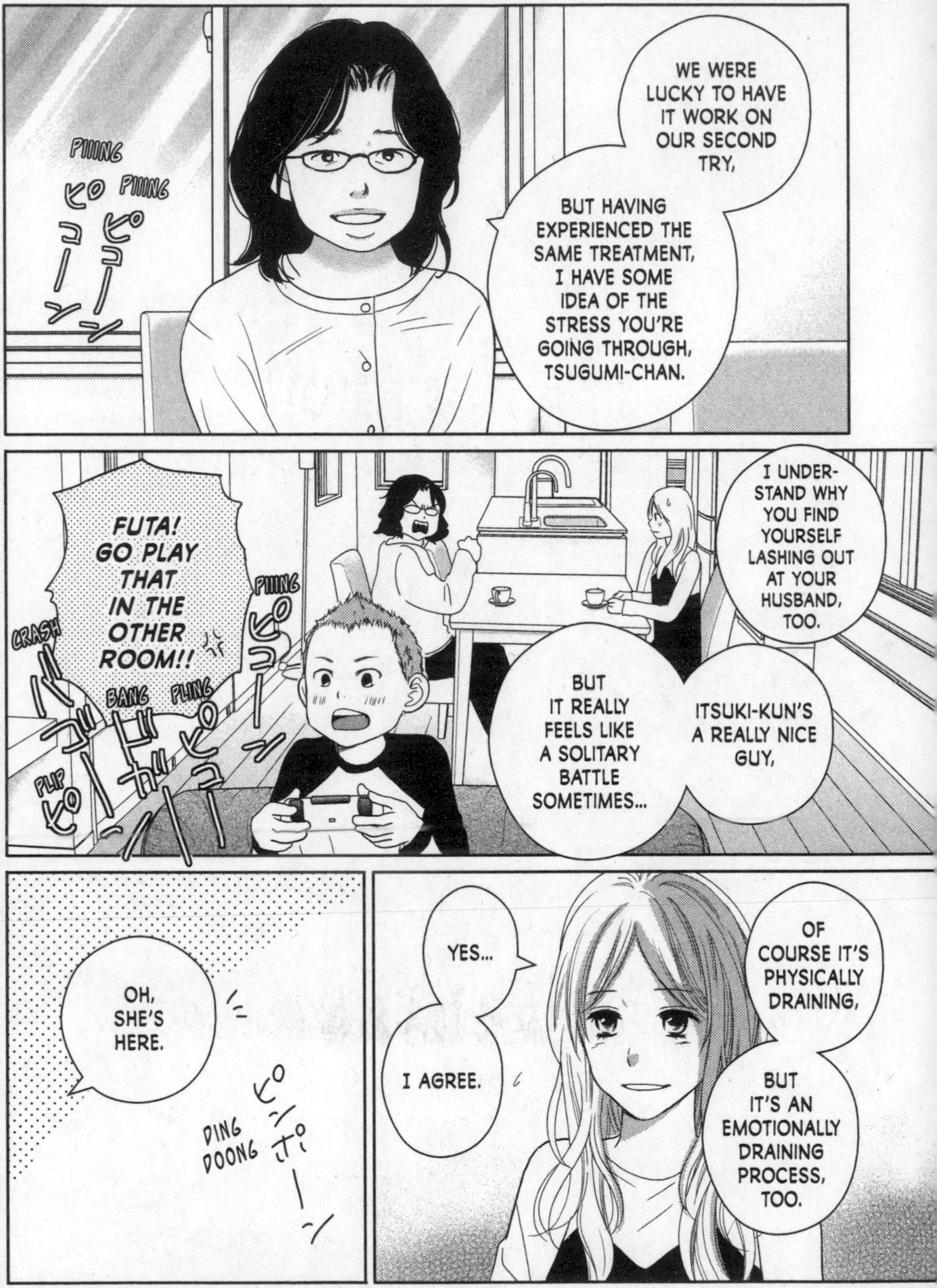
WE WERE LUCKY TO HAVE IT WORK ON OUR SECOND TRY,
BUT HAVING EXPERIENCED THE SAME TREATMENT, I HAVE SOME IDEA OF THE STRESS YOU'RE GOING THROUGH, TSUGUMI-CHAN.
PIIING
PIIING
I UNDER-STAND WHY YOU FIND YOURSELF LASHING OUT AT YOUR HUSBAND, TOO.
ITSUKI-KUN'S A REALLY NICE GUY,
BUT IT REALLY FEELS LIKE A SOLITARY BATTLE SOMETIMES...
FUTA! GO PLAY THAT IN THE OTHER ROOM!!
PIIING
CRASH
BANG
PLING
PLIP
OF COURSE IT'S PHYSICALLY DRAINING,
BUT IT'S AN EMOTIONALLY DRAINING PROCESS, TOO.
YES...
I AGREE.
OH, SHE'S HERE.
DING DOONG

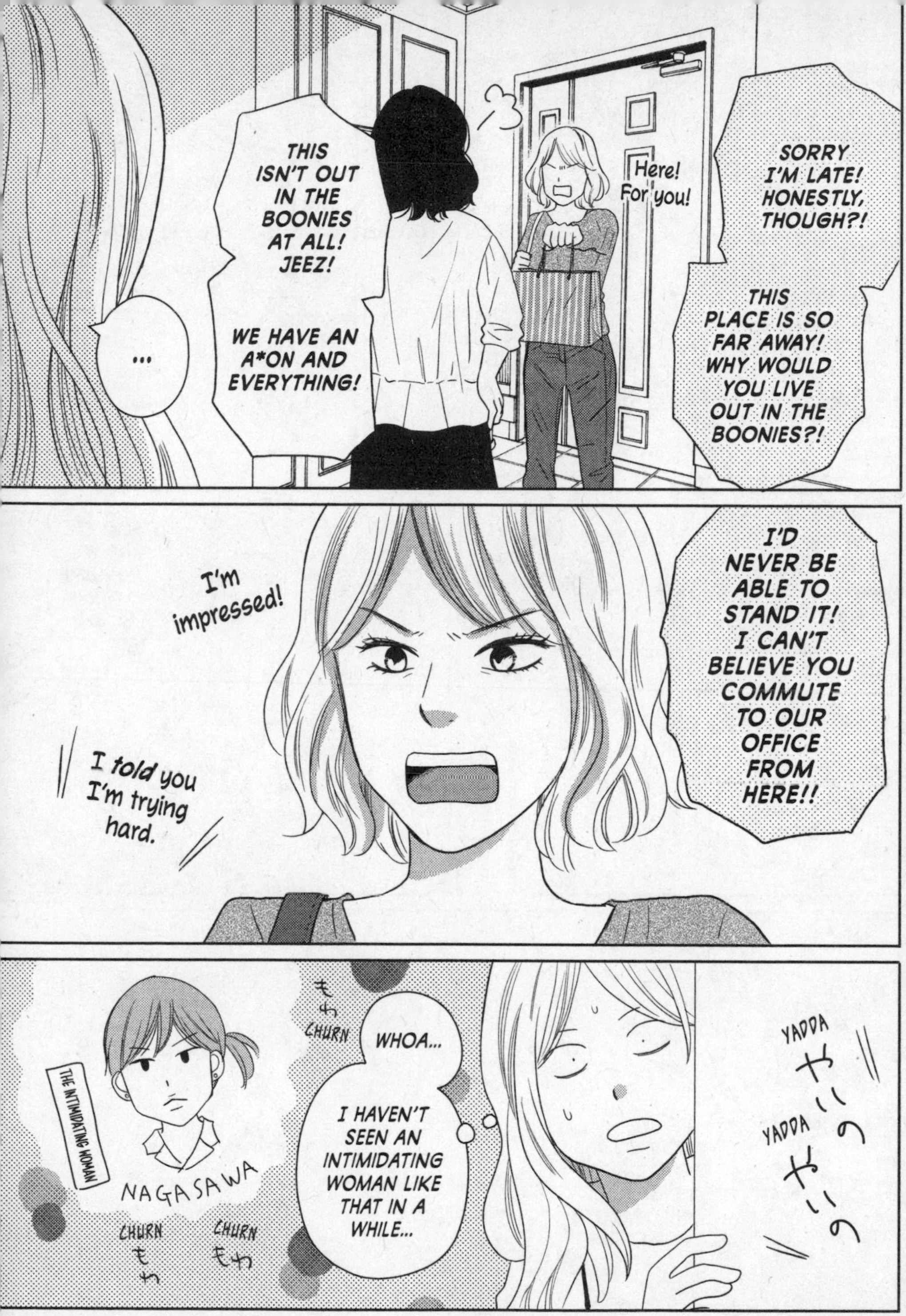
SORRY I'M LATE! HONESTLY, THOUGH?!
THIS PLACE IS SO FAR AWAY! WHY WOULD YOU LIVE OUT IN THE BOONIES?!
Here! For you!
THIS ISN'T OUT IN THE BOONIES AT ALL! JEEZ!
WE HAVE AN A*ON AND EVERYTHING!
...
I'D NEVER BE ABLE TO STAND IT! I CAN'T BELIEVE YOU COMMUTE TO OUR OFFICE FROM HERE!!
I'm impressed!
I *told* you I'm trying hard.
YADDA やいの
YADDA やいの
WHOA...
I HAVEN'T SEEN AN INTIMIDATING WOMAN LIKE THAT IN A WHILE...
CHURN もわ
THE INTIMIDATING WOMAN
NAGASAWA
CHURN もわ
CHURN もわ

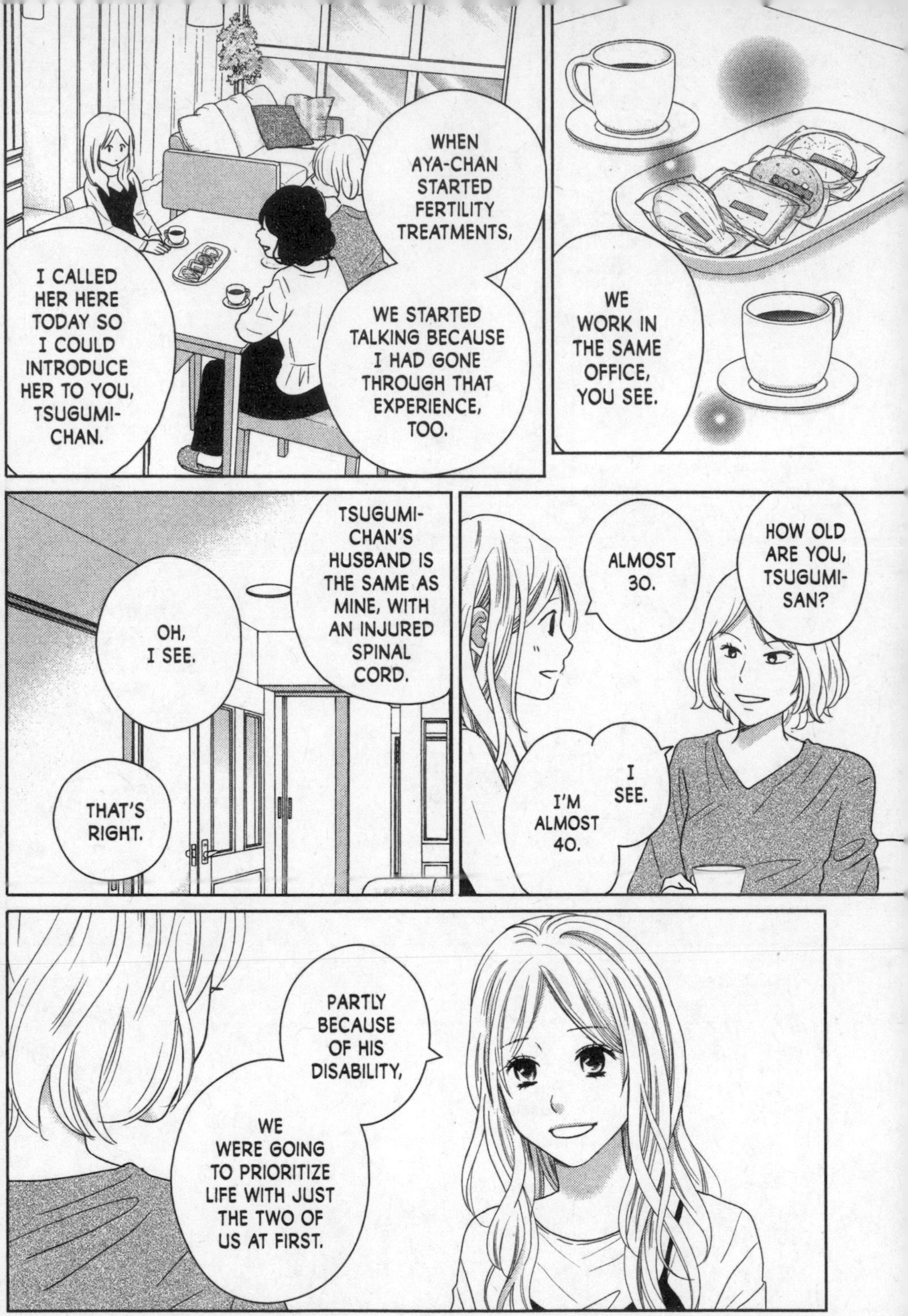
WE WORK IN THE SAME OFFICE, YOU SEE.
WHEN AYA-CHAN STARTED FERTILITY TREATMENTS,
WE STARTED TALKING BECAUSE I HAD GONE THROUGH THAT EXPERIENCE, TOO.
I CALLED HER HERE TODAY SO I COULD INTRODUCE HER TO YOU, TSUGUMI-CHAN.
HOW OLD ARE YOU, TSUGUMI-SAN?
ALMOST 30.
I SEE.
I'M ALMOST 40.
TSUGUMI-CHAN'S HUSBAND IS THE SAME AS MINE, WITH AN INJURED SPINAL CORD.
OH, I SEE.
THAT'S RIGHT.
PARTLY BECAUSE OF HIS DISABILITY,
WE WERE GOING TO PRIORITIZE LIFE WITH JUST THE TWO OF US AT FIRST.

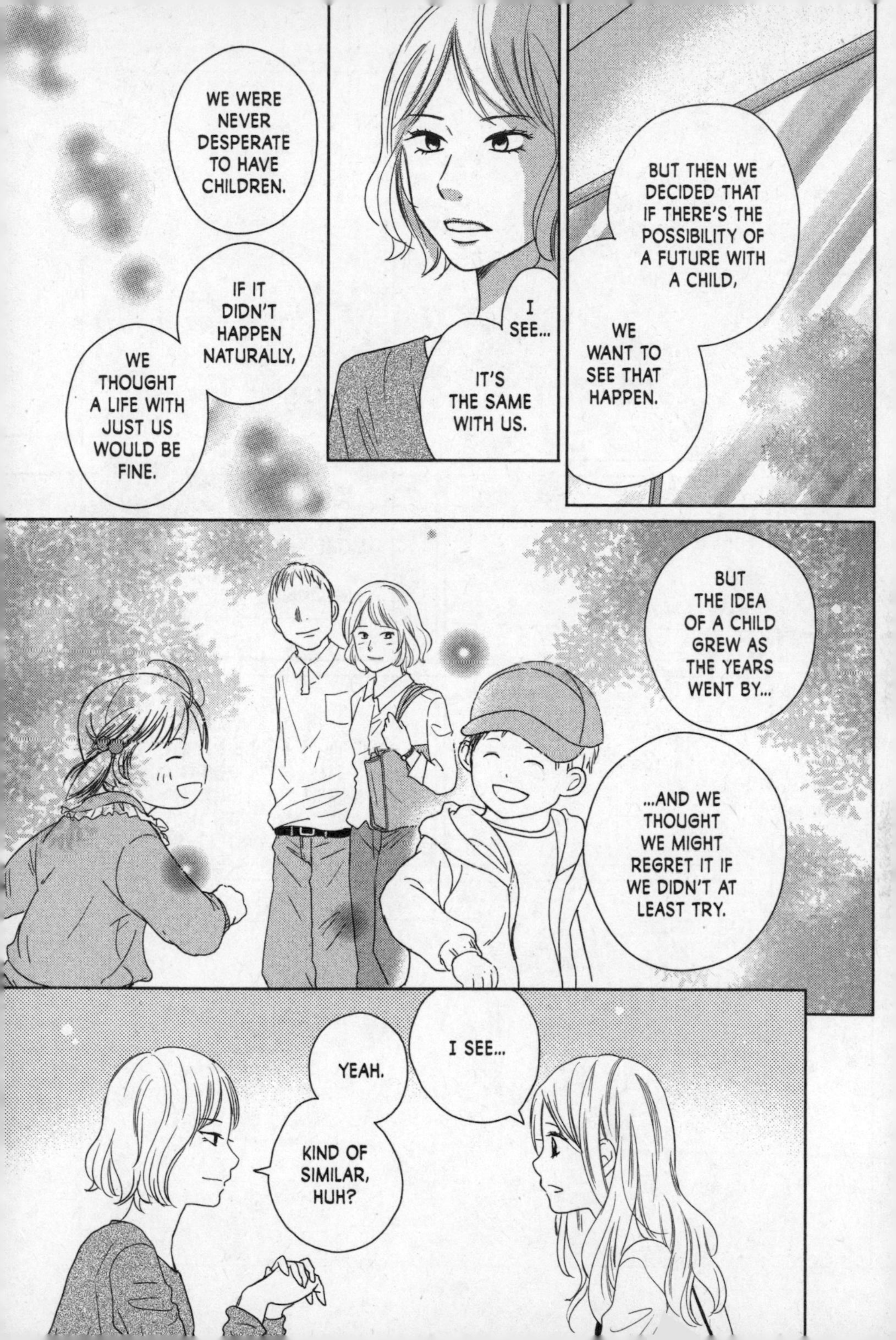
BUT THEN WE DECIDED THAT IF THERE'S THE POSSIBILITY OF A FUTURE WITH A CHILD,
WE WANT TO SEE THAT HAPPEN.
I SEE...
IT'S THE SAME WITH US.
WE WERE NEVER DESPERATE TO HAVE CHILDREN.
IF IT DIDN'T HAPPEN NATURALLY,
WE THOUGHT A LIFE WITH JUST US WOULD BE FINE.
BUT THE IDEA OF A CHILD GREW AS THE YEARS WENT BY...
...AND WE THOUGHT WE MIGHT REGRET IT IF WE DIDN'T AT LEAST TRY.
I SEE...
YEAH.
KIND OF SIMILAR, HUH?

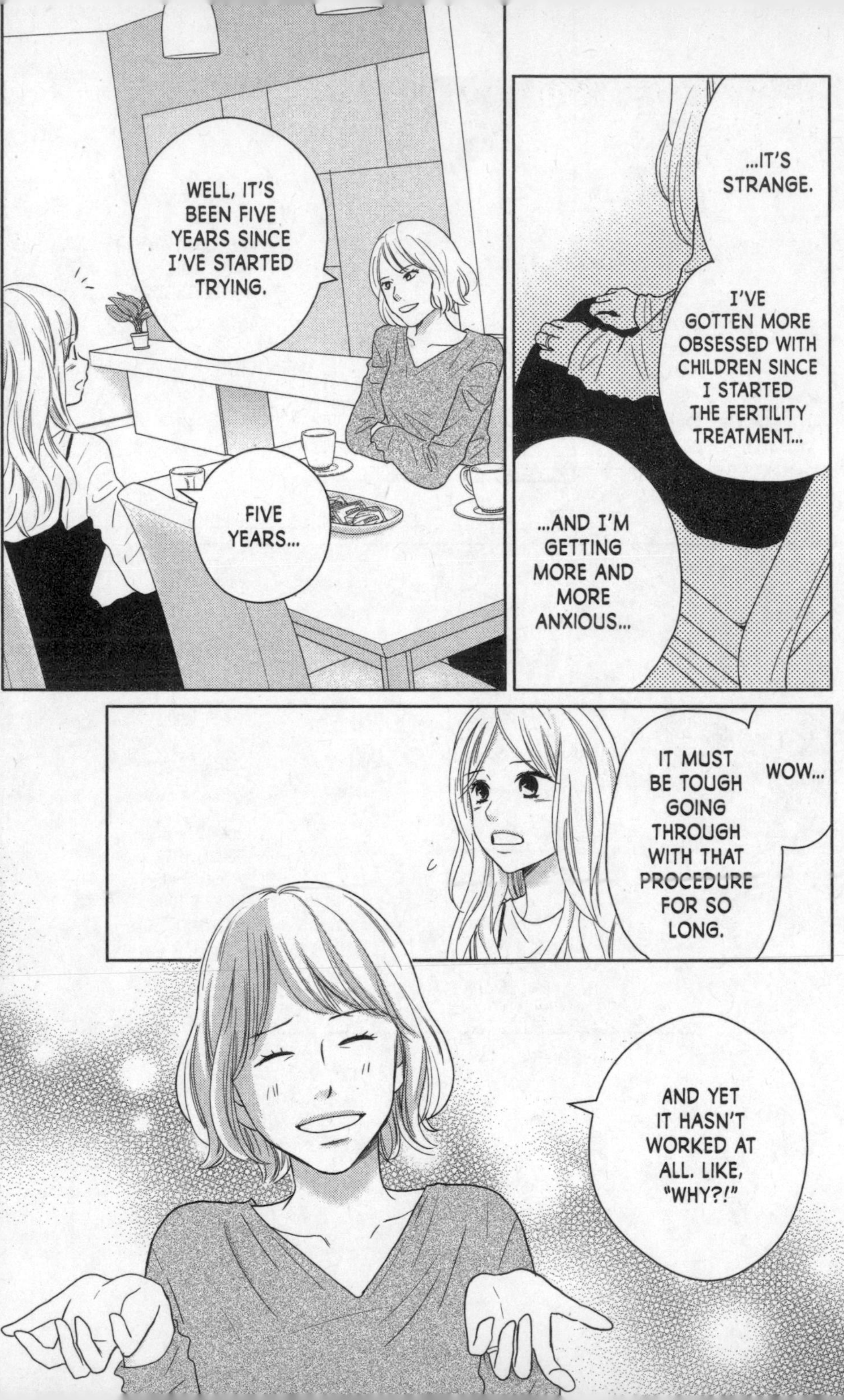
...IT'S STRANGE.
I'VE GOTTEN MORE OBSESSED WITH CHILDREN SINCE I STARTED THE FERTILITY TREATMENT...
...AND I'M GETTING MORE AND MORE ANXIOUS...
WELL, IT'S BEEN FIVE YEARS SINCE I'VE STARTED TRYING.
FIVE YEARS...
WOW...
IT MUST BE TOUGH GOING THROUGH WITH THAT PROCEDURE FOR SO LONG.
AND YET IT HASN'T WORKED AT ALL. LIKE, "WHY?!"

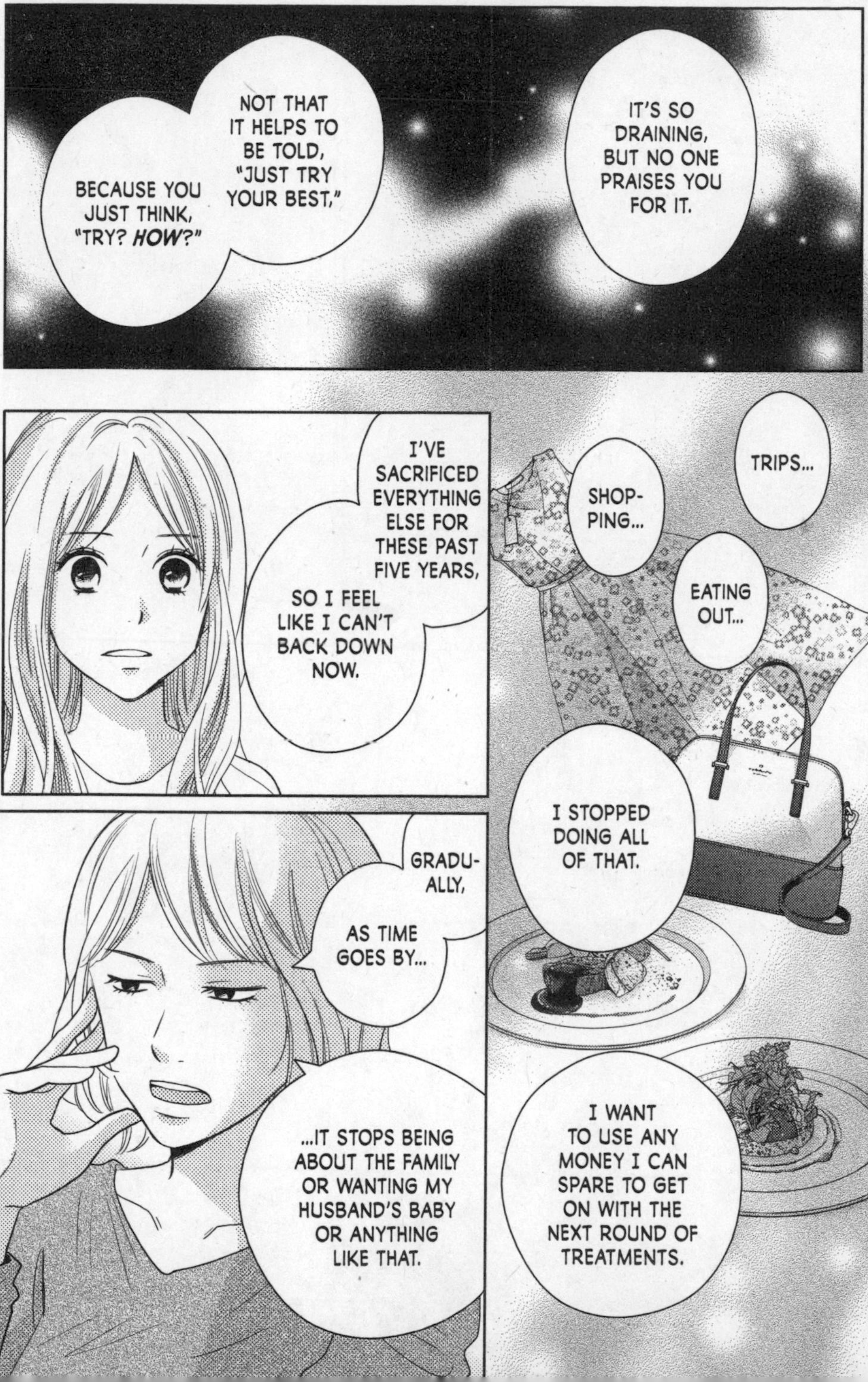
IT'S SO DRAINING, BUT NO ONE PRAISES YOU FOR IT.
NOT THAT IT HELPS TO BE TOLD, "JUST TRY YOUR BEST,"
BECAUSE YOU JUST THINK, "TRY? *HOW*?"
TRIPS...
SHOP-PING...
EATING OUT...
I STOPPED DOING ALL OF THAT.
I WANT TO USE ANY MONEY I CAN SPARE TO GET ON WITH THE NEXT ROUND OF TREATMENTS.
I'VE SACRIFICED EVERYTHING ELSE FOR THESE PAST FIVE YEARS,
SO I FEEL LIKE I CAN'T BACK DOWN NOW.
GRADU-ALLY,
AS TIME GOES BY...
...IT STOPS BEING ABOUT THE FAMILY OR WANTING MY HUSBAND'S BABY OR ANYTHING LIKE THAT.

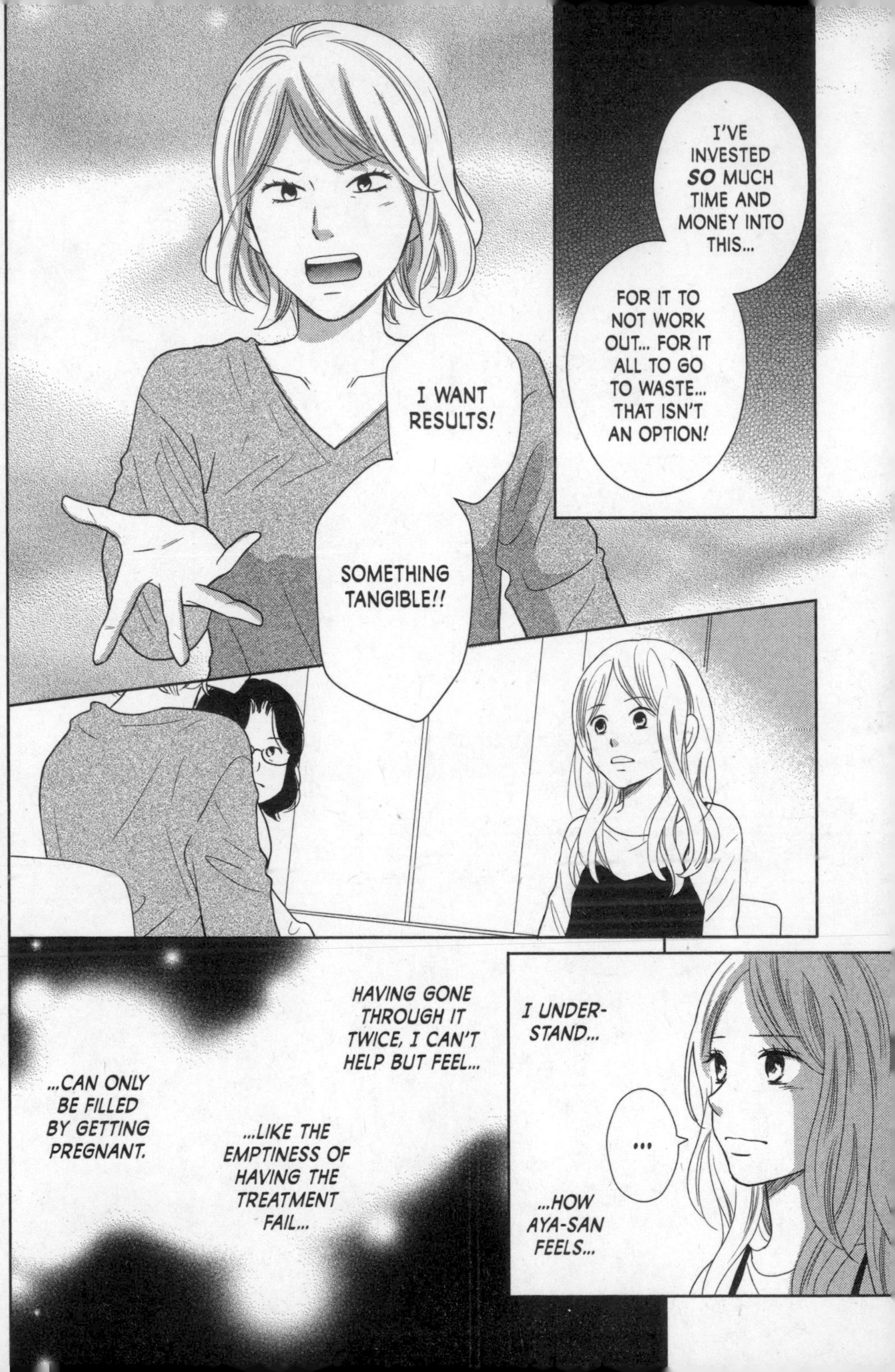
I'VE INVESTED *SO* MUCH TIME AND MONEY INTO THIS...
FOR IT TO NOT WORK OUT... FOR IT ALL TO GO TO WASTE... THAT ISN'T AN OPTION!
I WANT RESULTS!
SOMETHING TANGIBLE!!
I UNDER-STAND...
...
...HOW AYA-SAN FEELS...
HAVING GONE THROUGH IT TWICE, I CAN'T HELP BUT FEEL...
...LIKE THE EMPTINESS OF HAVING THE TREATMENT FAIL...
...CAN ONLY BE FILLED BY GETTING PREGNANT.

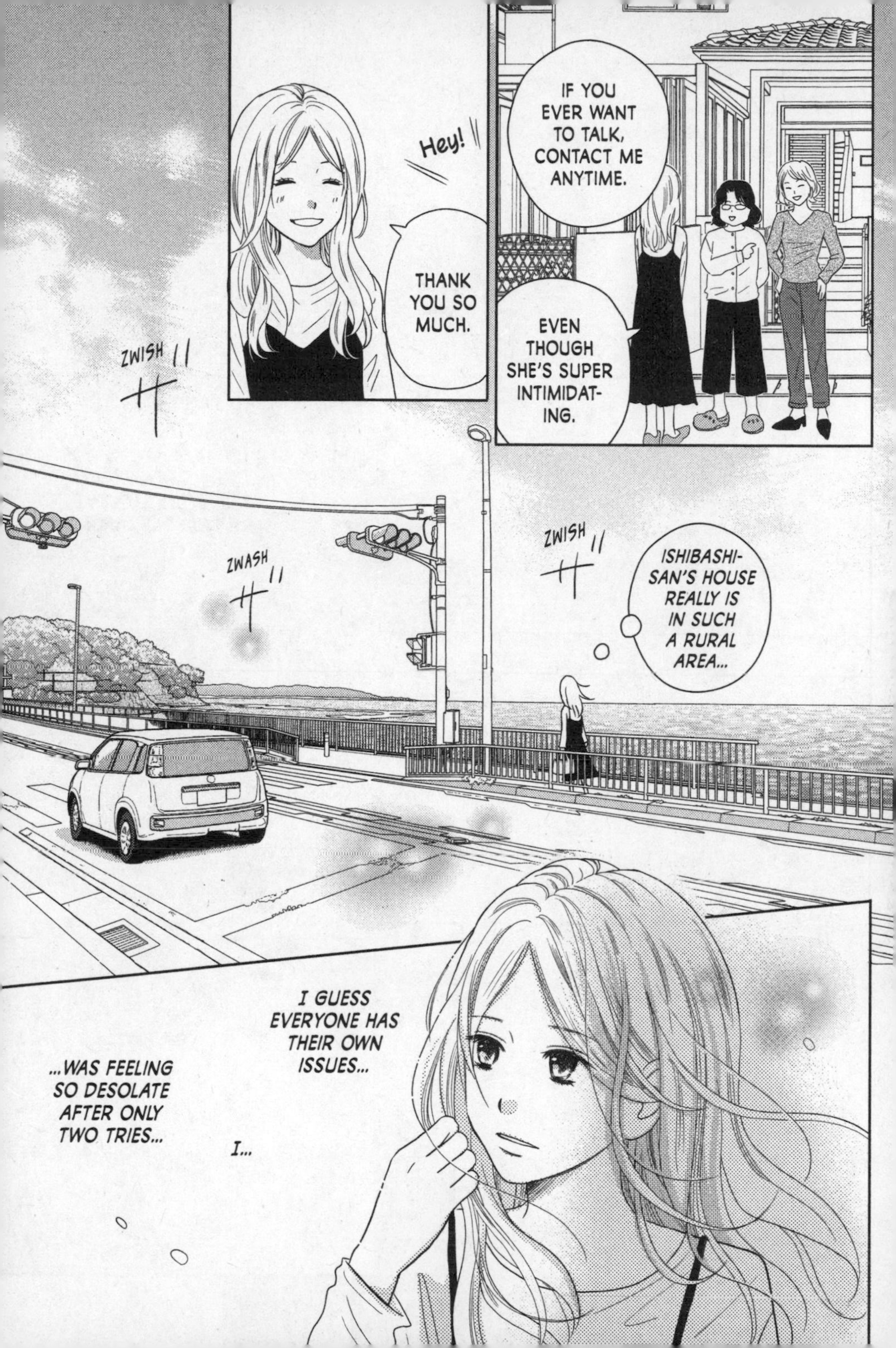
IF YOU EVER WANT TO TALK, CONTACT ME ANYTIME.
EVEN THOUGH SHE'S SUPER INTIMIDAT-ING.
Hey!
THANK YOU SO MUCH.
ZWISH
ISHIBASHI-SAN'S HOUSE REALLY IS IN SUCH A RURAL AREA...
ZWASH
ZWISH
I GUESS EVERYONE HAS THEIR OWN ISSUES...
I...
...WAS FEELING SO DESOLATE AFTER ONLY TWO TRIES...

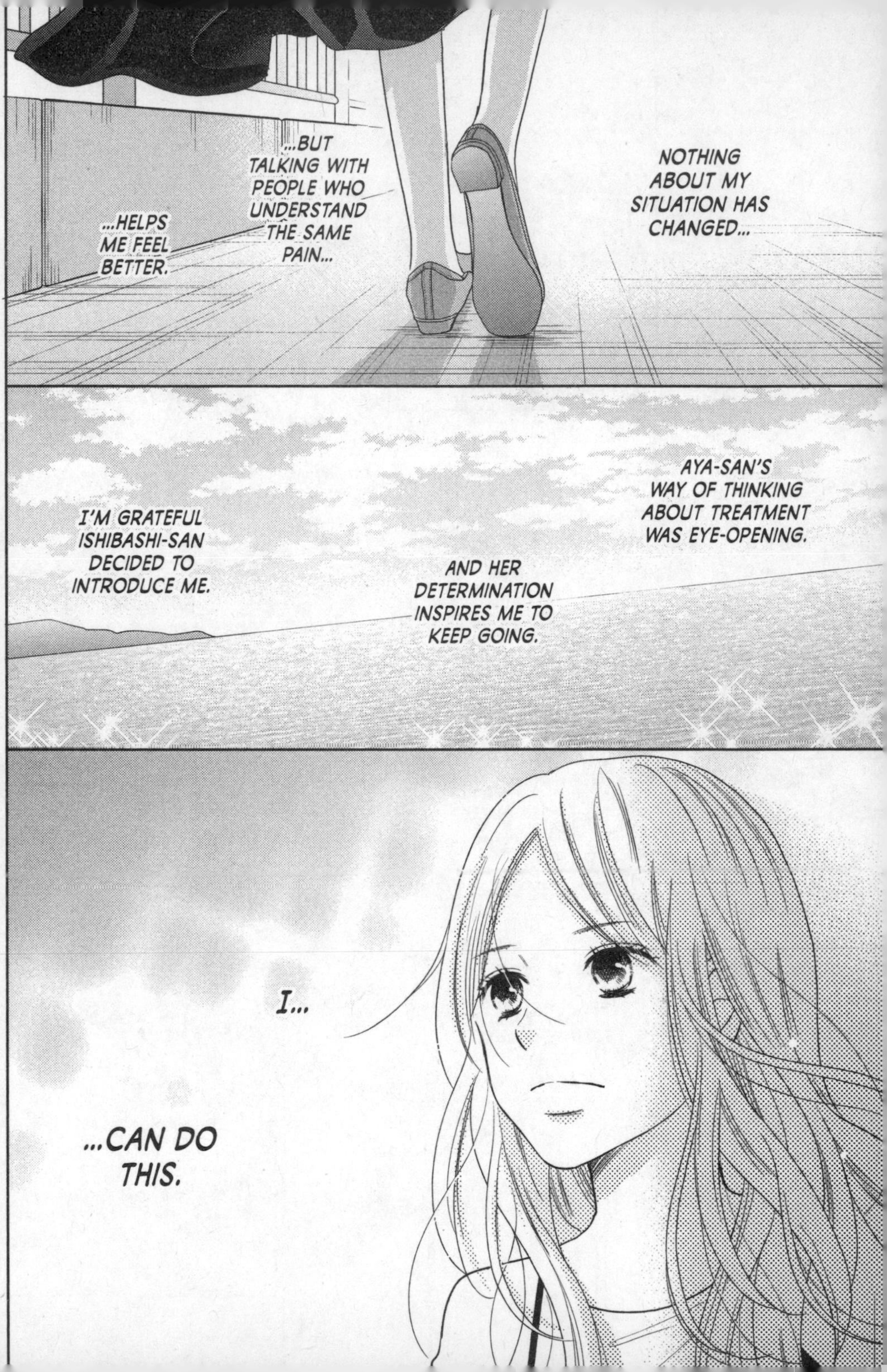
NOTHING ABOUT MY SITUATION HAS CHANGED...
...BUT TALKING WITH PEOPLE WHO UNDERSTAND THE SAME PAIN...
...HELPS ME FEEL BETTER.
AYA-SAN'S WAY OF THINKING ABOUT TREATMENT WAS EYE-OPENING.
AND HER DETERMINATION INSPIRES ME TO KEEP GOING.
I'M GRATEFUL ISHIBASHI-SAN DECIDED TO INTRODUCE ME.
I...
...CAN DO THIS.

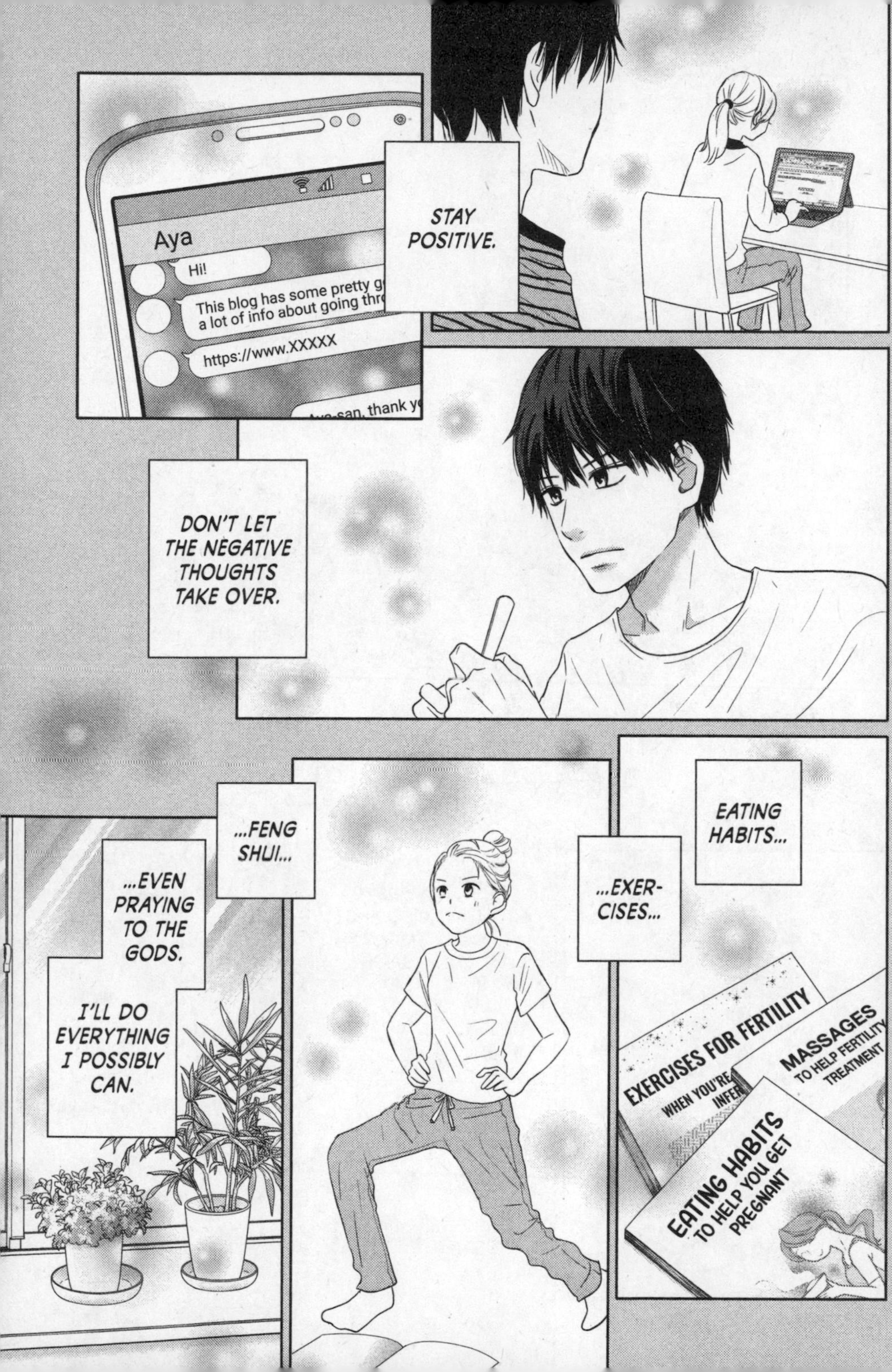
STAY POSITIVE.
Aya
Hi!
This blog has some pretty g
a lot of info about going thr
https://www.XXXXX
DON'T LET THE NEGATIVE THOUGHTS TAKE OVER.
EATING HABITS...
...EXER-CISES...
EXERCISES FOR FERTILITY
MASSAGES TO HELP FERTILITY TREATMENT
EATING HABITS TO HELP YOU GET PREGNANT
...FENG SHUI...
...EVEN PRAYING TO THE GODS.
I'LL DO EVERYTHING I POSSIBLY CAN.

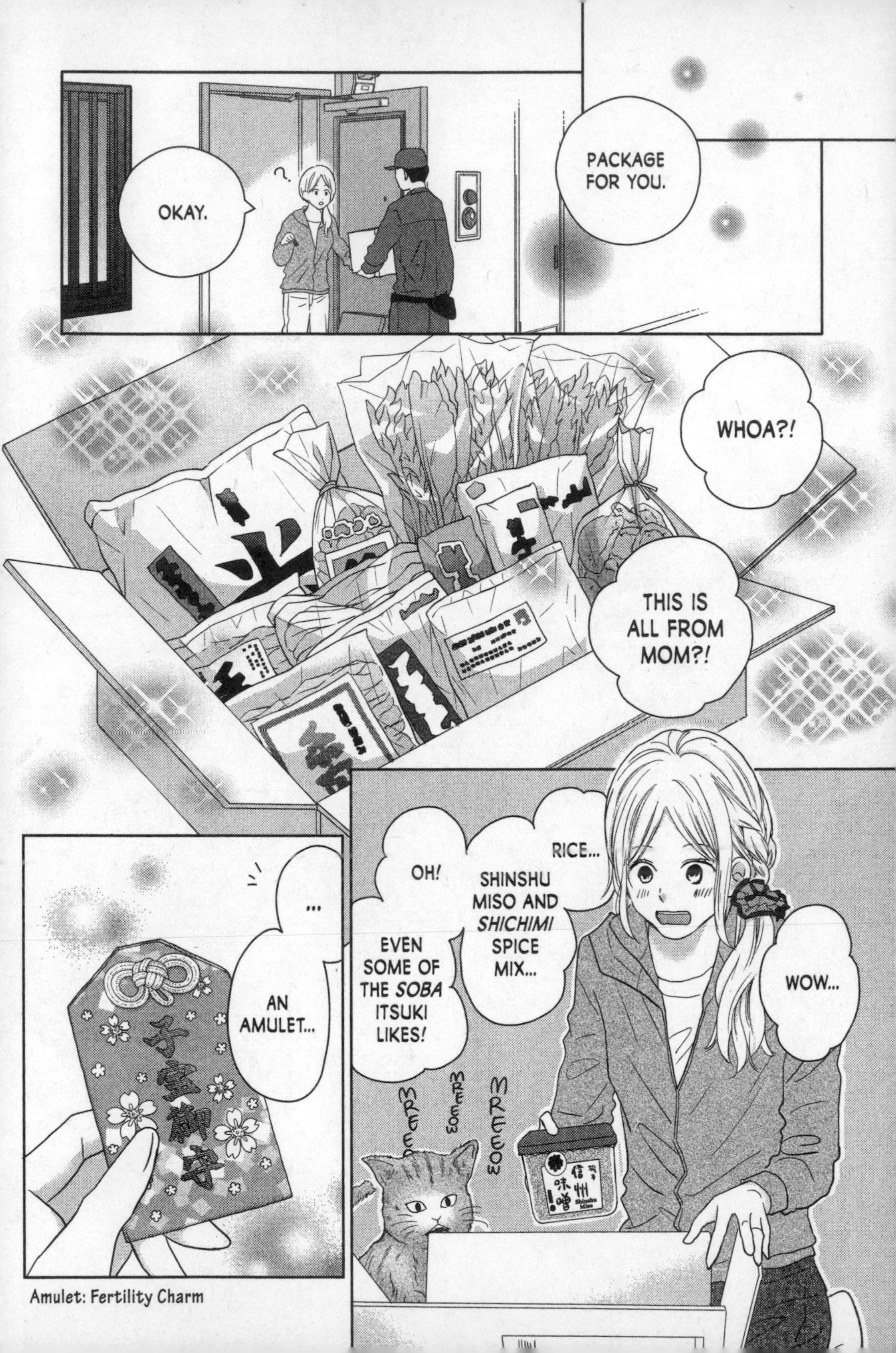
PACKAGE FOR YOU.
OKAY.
WHOA?!
THIS IS ALL FROM MOM?!
WOW...
RICE...
SHINSHU MISO AND *SHICHIMI* SPICE MIX...
OH!
EVEN SOME OF THE *SOBA* ITSUKI LIKES!
MREEOW
MREEOW
MREEOW
...
AN AMULET...

Amulet: Fertility Charm

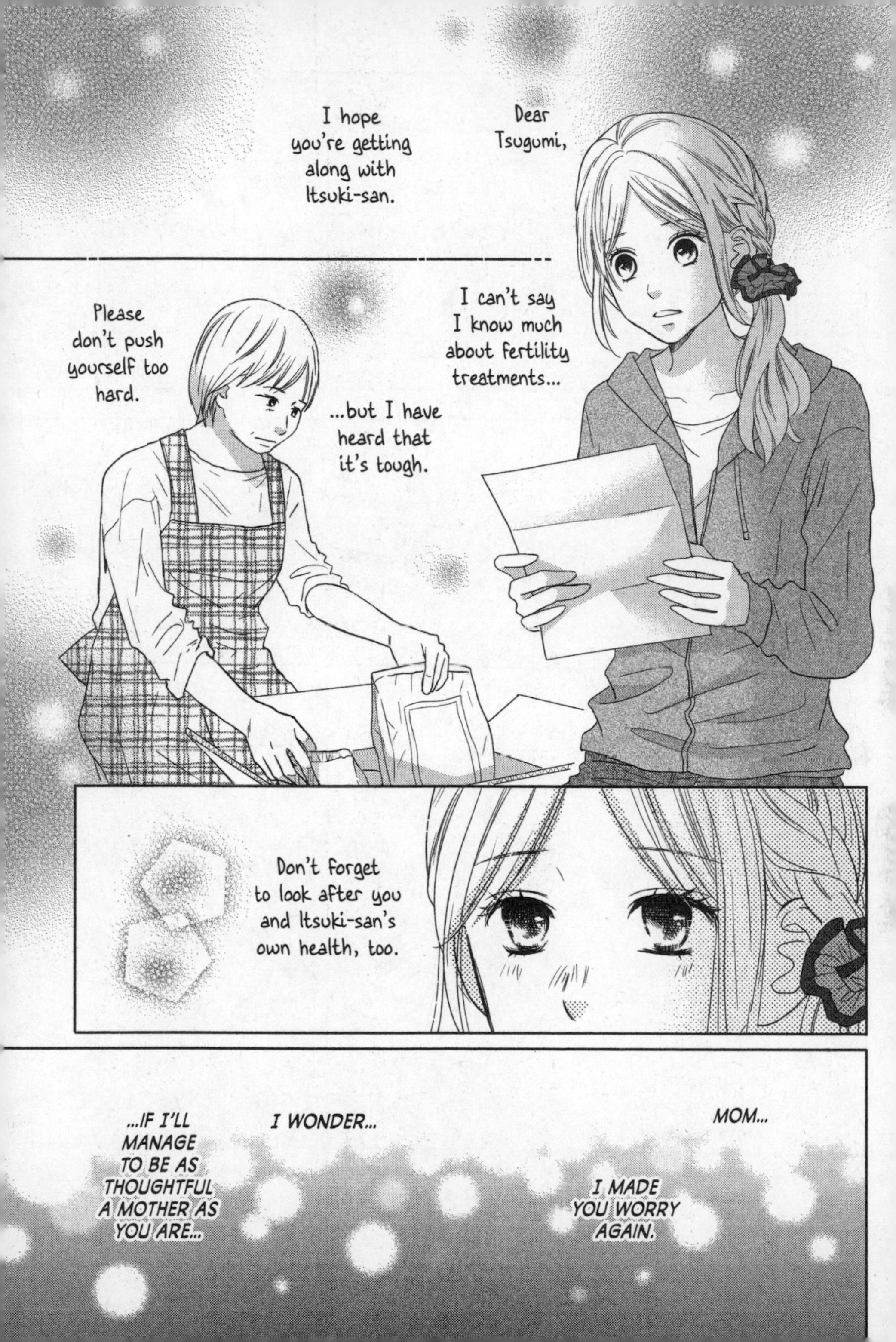
Dear Tsugumi,
I hope you're getting along with Itsuki-san.
I can't say I know much about fertility treatments...
...but I have heard that it's tough.
Please don't push yourself too hard.
Don't forget to look after you and Itsuki-san's own health, too.
MOM...
I MADE YOU WORRY AGAIN.
I WONDER...
...IF I'LL MANAGE TO BE AS THOUGHTFUL A MOTHER AS YOU ARE...

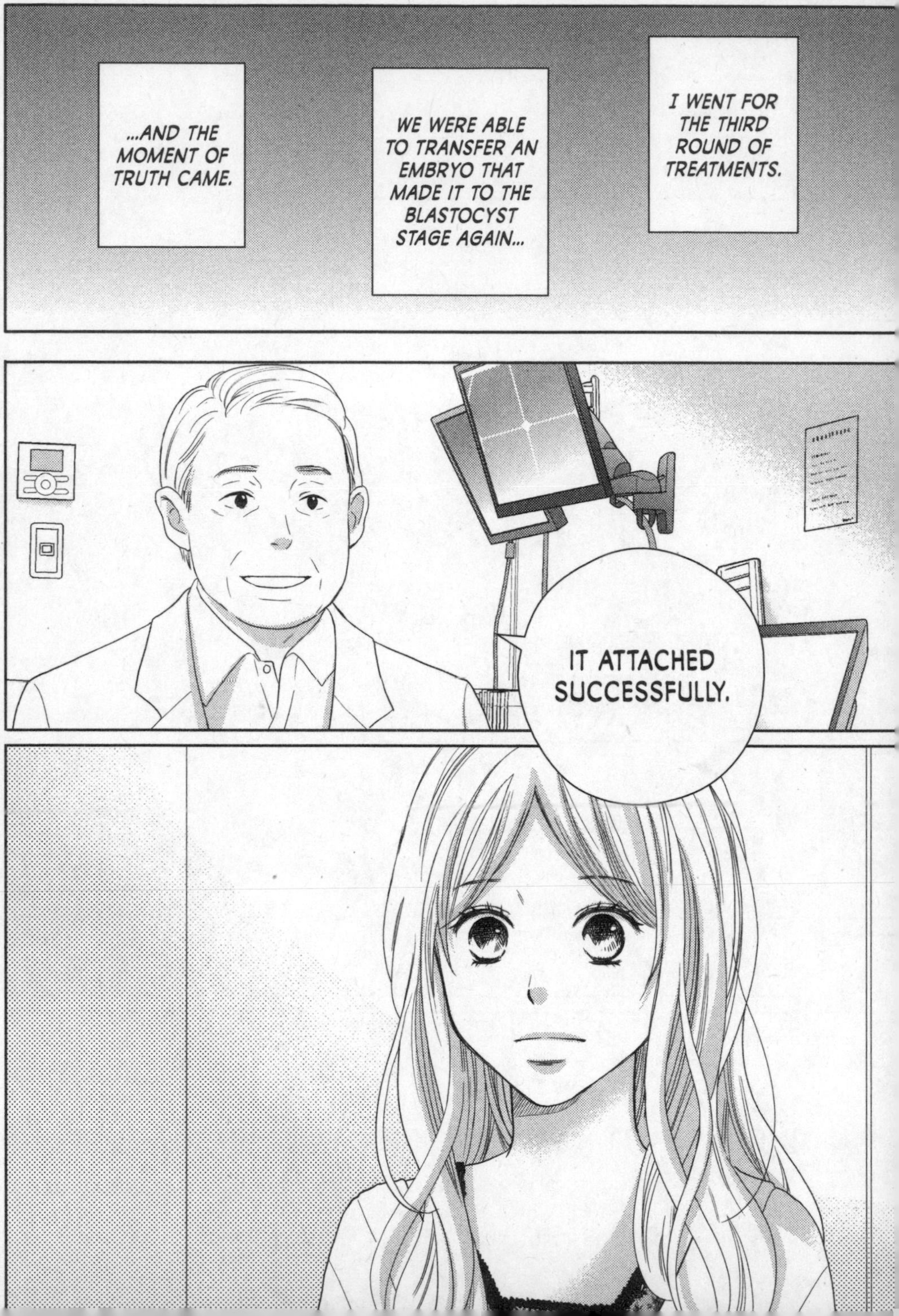
I WENT FOR THE THIRD ROUND OF TREATMENTS.
WE WERE ABLE TO TRANSFER AN EMBRYO THAT MADE IT TO THE BLASTOCYST STAGE AGAIN...
...AND THE MOMENT OF TRUTH CAME.
IT ATTACHED SUCCESSFULLY.

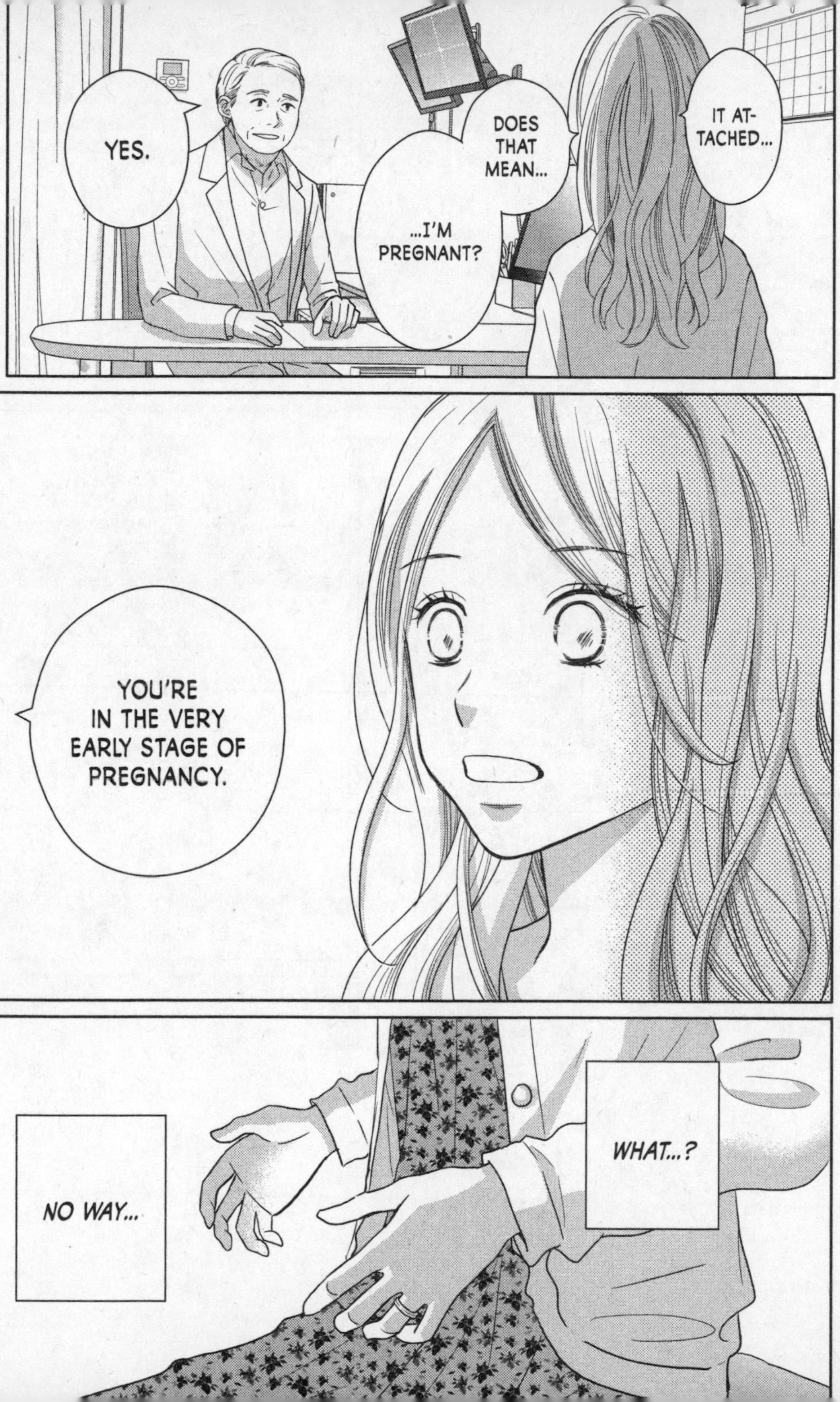
IT ATTACHED...
DOES THAT MEAN...
...I'M PREGNANT?
YES.
YOU'RE IN THE VERY EARLY STAGE OF PREGNANCY.
WHAT...?
NO WAY...

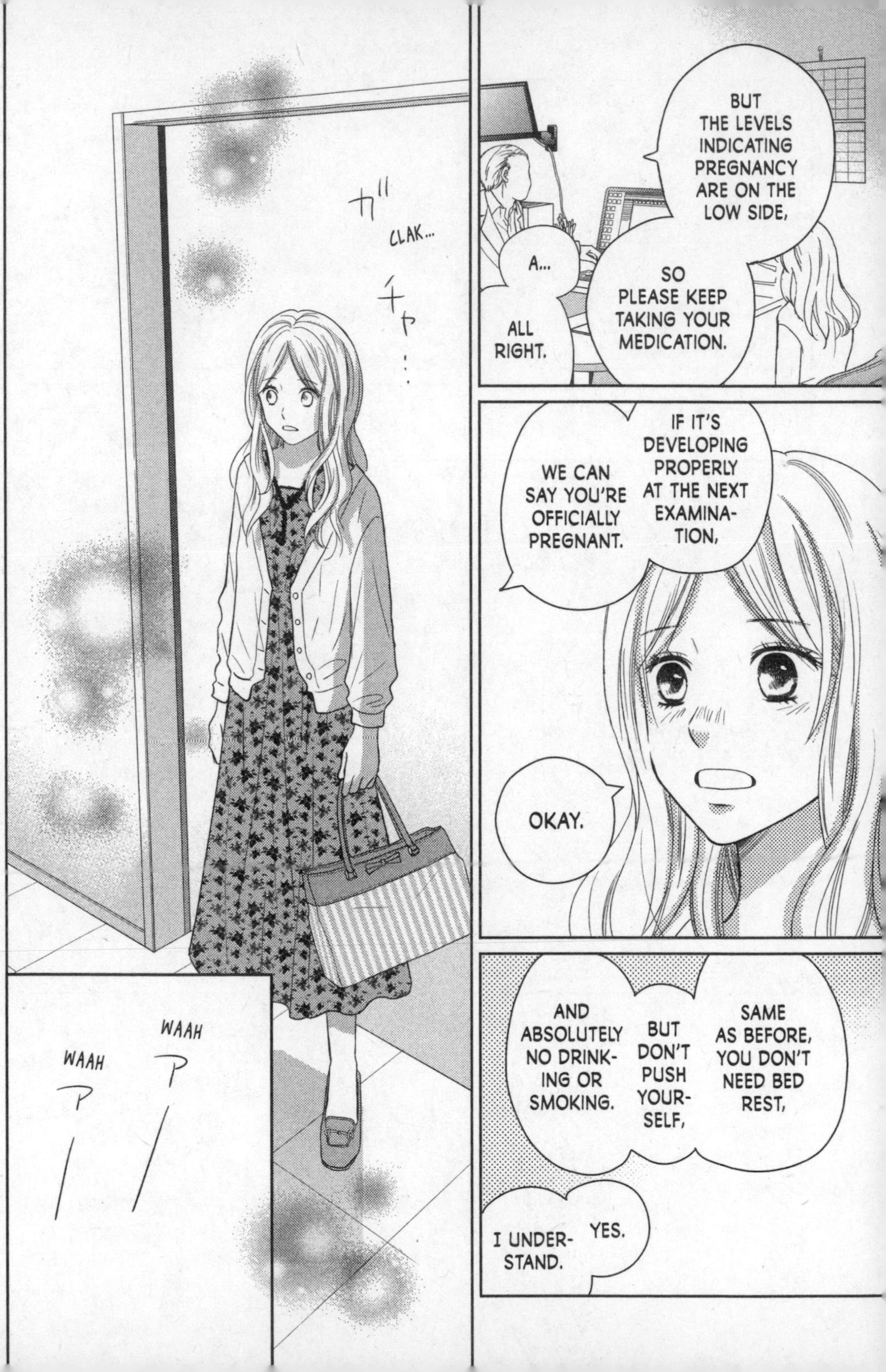
BUT THE LEVELS INDICATING PREGNANCY ARE ON THE LOW SIDE,
SO PLEASE KEEP TAKING YOUR MEDICATION.
A... ALL RIGHT.
IF IT'S DEVELOPING PROPERLY AT THE NEXT EXAMINATION,
WE CAN SAY YOU'RE OFFICIALLY PREGNANT.
OKAY.
SAME AS BEFORE, YOU DON'T NEED BED REST,
BUT DON'T PUSH YOURSELF,
AND ABSOLUTELY NO DRINKING OR SMOKING.
YES.
I UNDERSTAND.
CLAK...
WAAH
WAAH

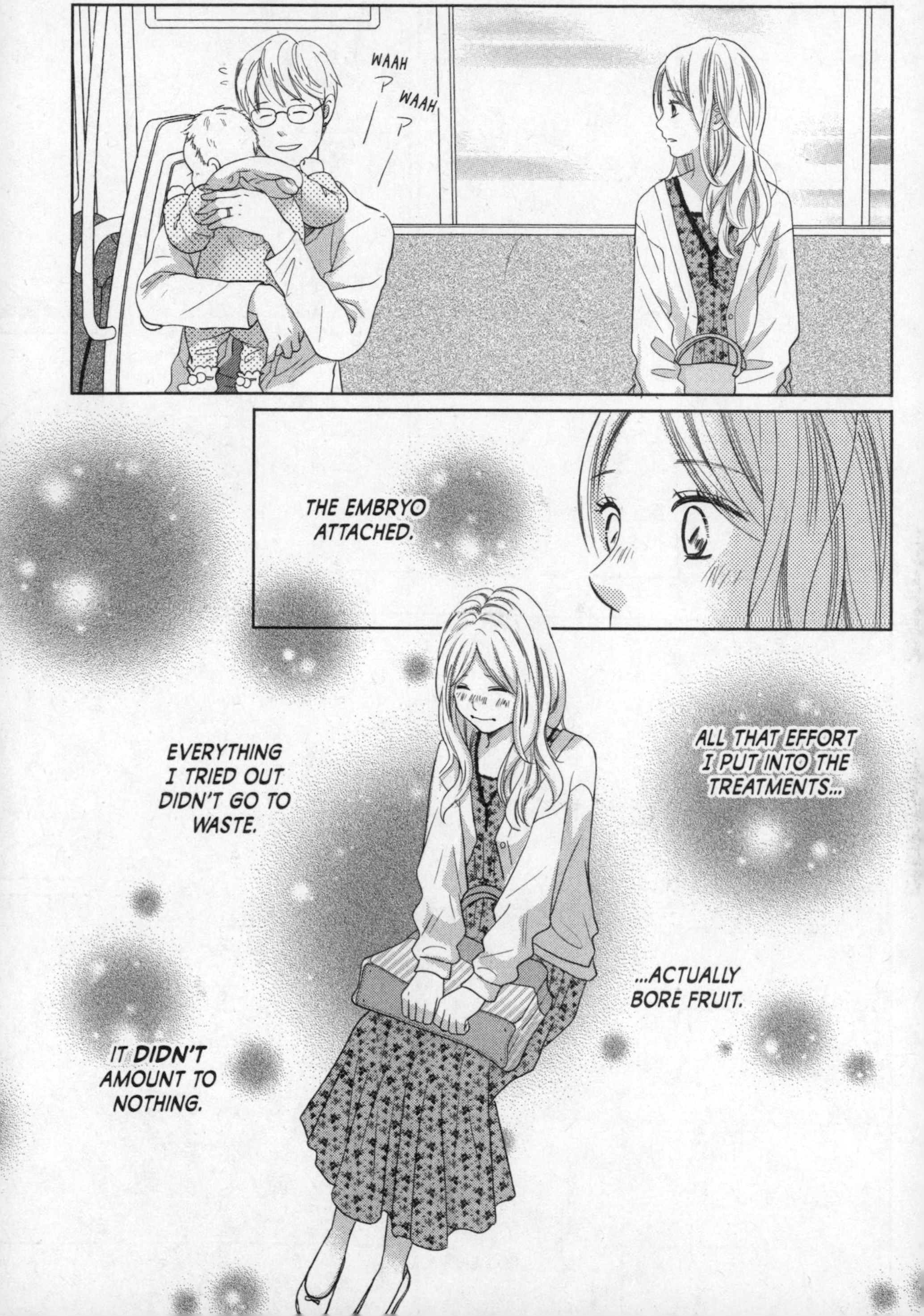
WAAH
WAAH
THE EMBRYO ATTACHED.
ALL THAT EFFORT I PUT INTO THE TREATMENTS...
...ACTUALLY BORE FRUIT.
EVERYTHING I TRIED OUT DIDN'T GO TO WASTE.
IT **DIDN'T** AMOUNT TO NOTHING.

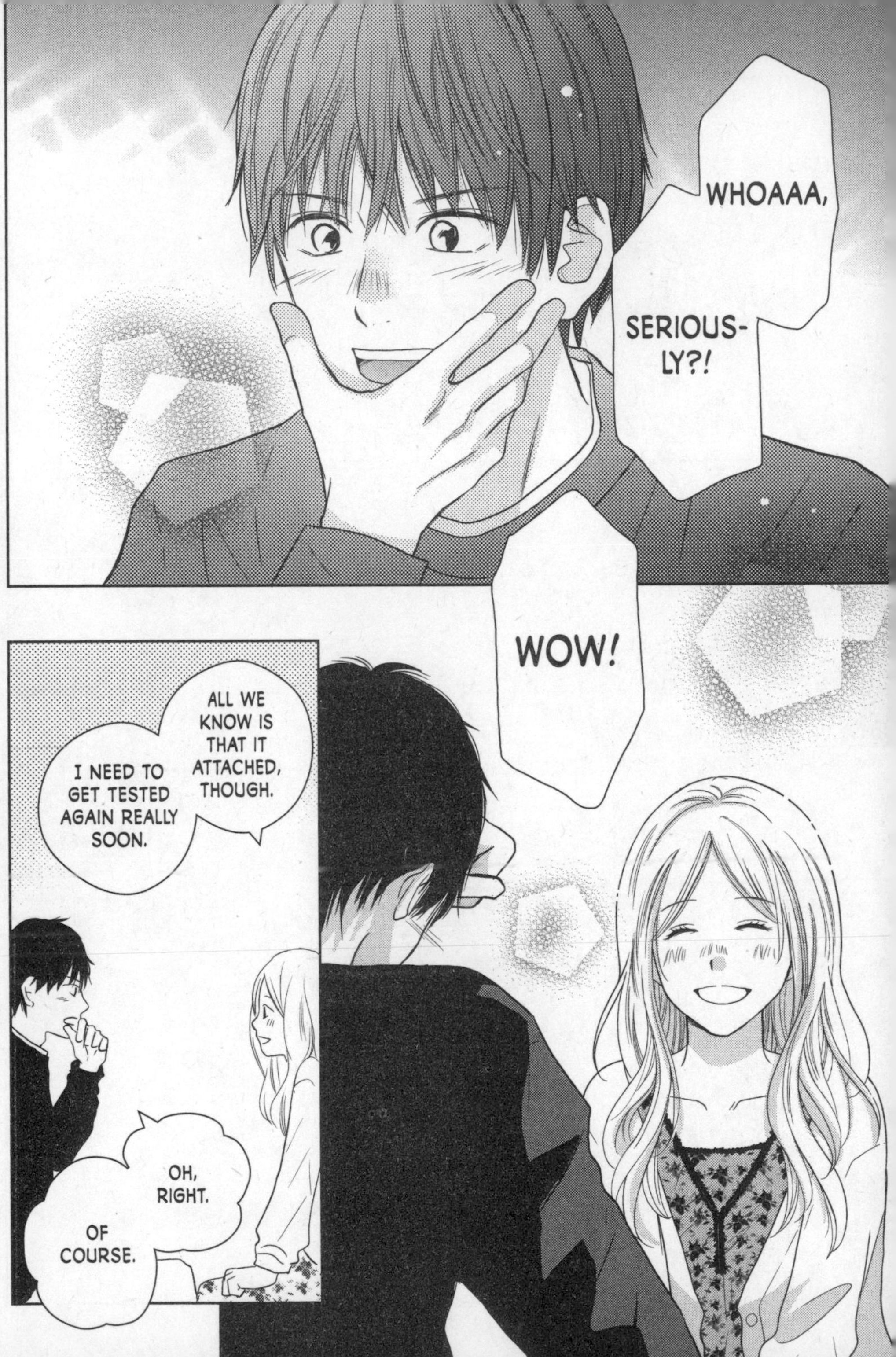
WHOAAA,
SERIOUS-LY?!
WOW!
ALL WE KNOW IS THAT IT ATTACHED, THOUGH.
I NEED TO GET TESTED AGAIN REALLY SOON.
OH, RIGHT.
OF COURSE.

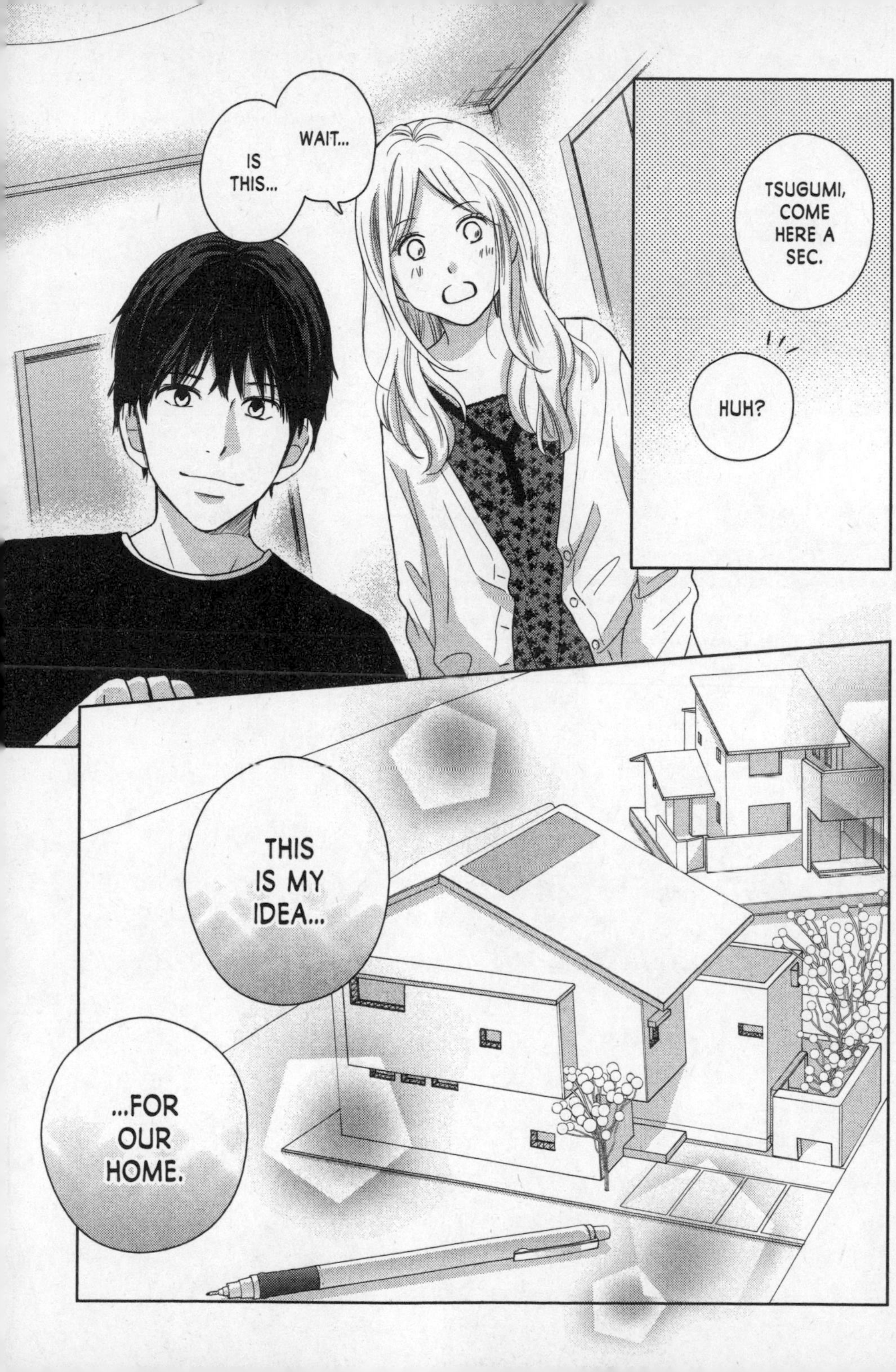
TSUGUMI, COME HERE A SEC.
HUH?
WAIT... IS THIS...
THIS IS MY IDEA...
...FOR OUR HOME.

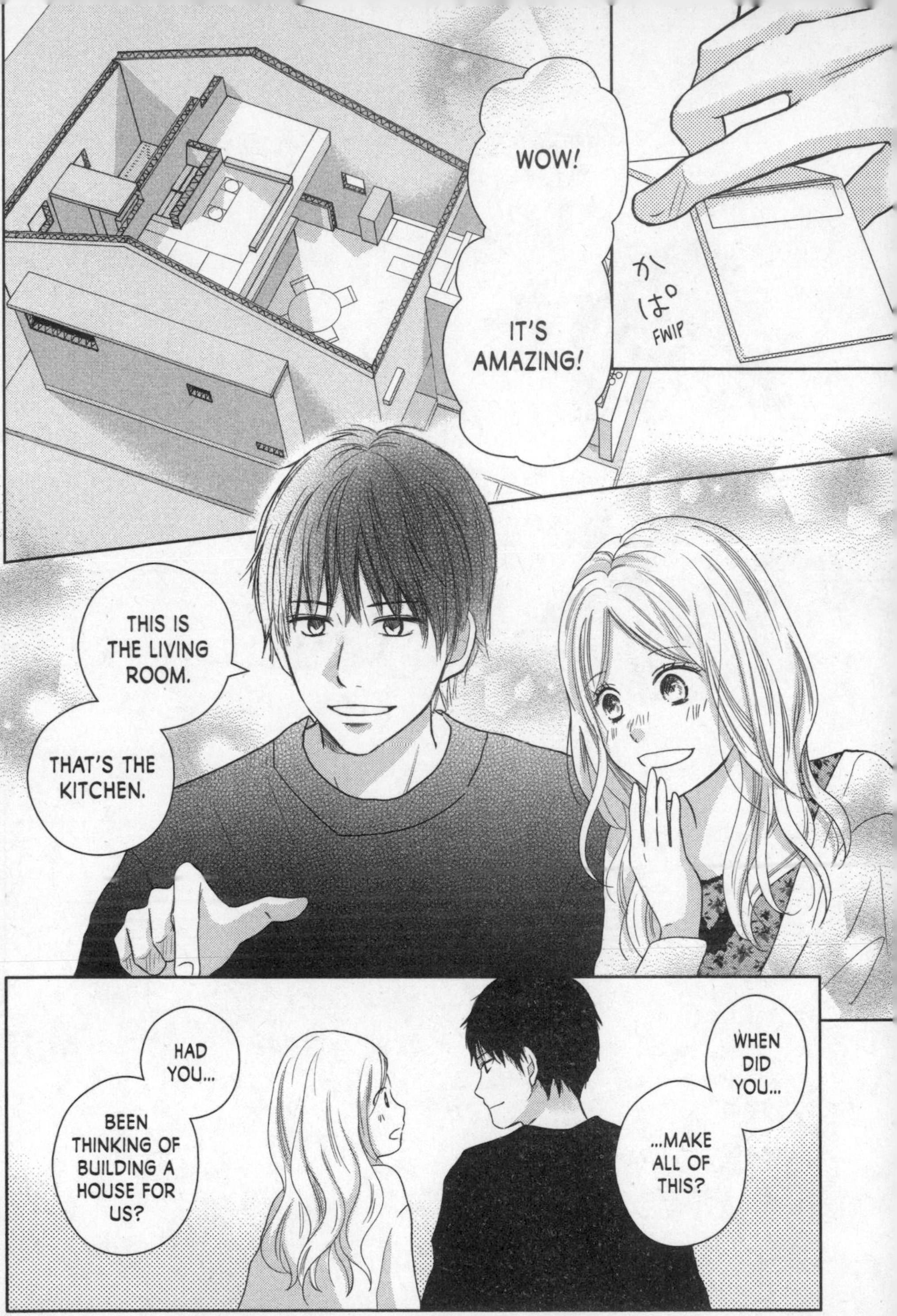
かぱ
FWIP
WOW!
IT'S AMAZING!
THIS IS THE LIVING ROOM.
THAT'S THE KITCHEN.
WHEN DID YOU...
...MAKE ALL OF THIS?
HAD YOU...
BEEN THINKING OF BUILDING A HOUSE FOR US?

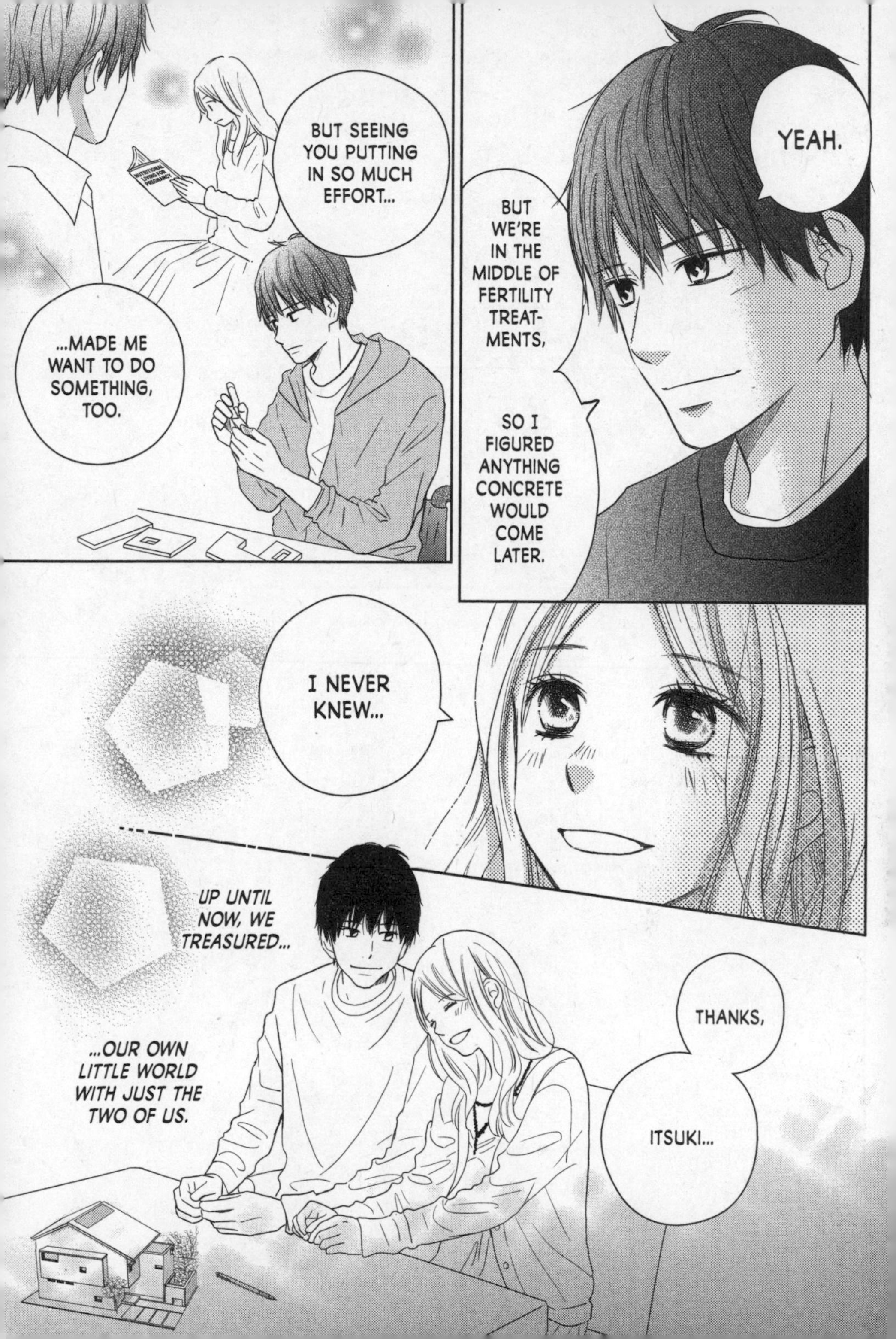
YEAH.
BUT WE'RE IN THE MIDDLE OF FERTILITY TREATMENTS,
SO I FIGURED ANYTHING CONCRETE WOULD COME LATER.
BUT SEEING YOU PUTTING IN SO MUCH EFFORT...
...MADE ME WANT TO DO SOMETHING, TOO.
I NEVER KNEW...
THANKS,
ITSUKI...
UP UNTIL NOW, WE TREASURED...
...OUR OWN LITTLE WORLD WITH JUST THE TWO OF US.

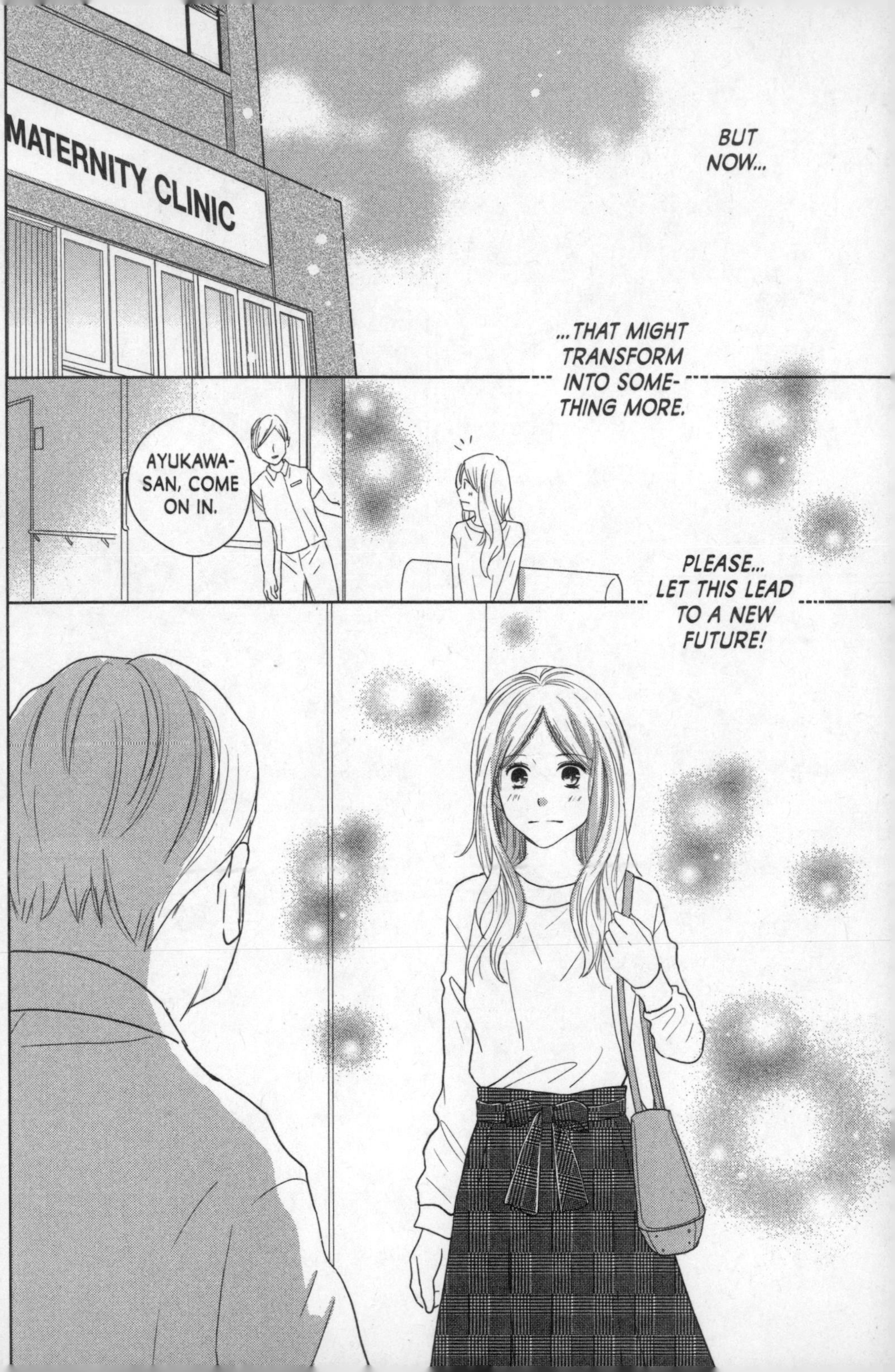
BUT NOW...
MATERNITY CLINIC
...THAT MIGHT TRANSFORM INTO SOME-THING MORE.
AYUKAWA-SAN, COME ON IN.
PLEASE... LET THIS LEAD TO A NEW FUTURE!

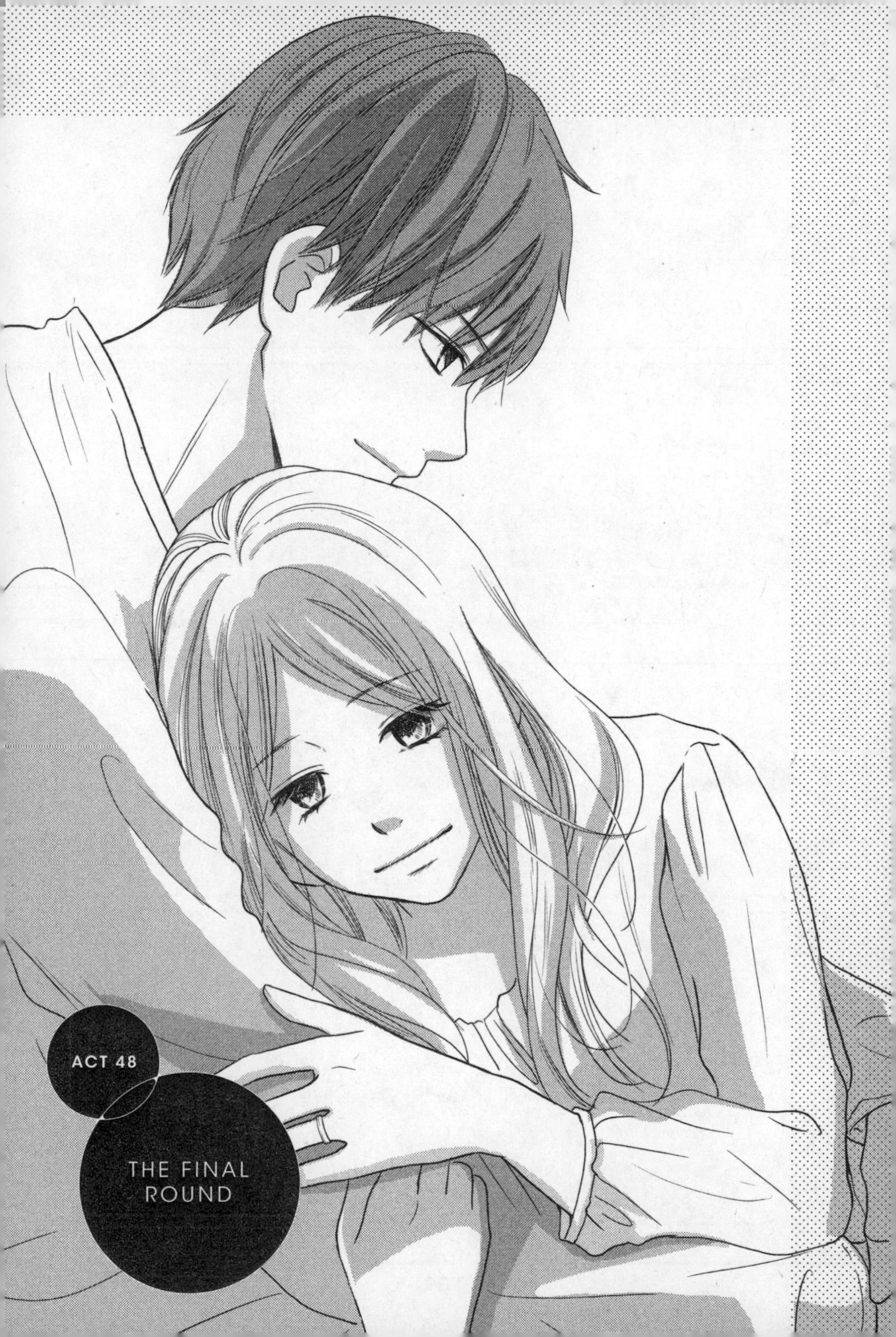
ACT 48
THE FINAL ROUND

THE EMBRYO FINALLY ATTACHED ON MY THIRD ROUND OF FERTILITY TREATMENTS...

...AND I ENTERED THE VERY EARLY STAGE OF PREGNANCY.

TODAY...

...I FIND OUT HOW IT'S GOING.

PLEASE...

...LET THIS LEAD TO A NEW FUTURE!

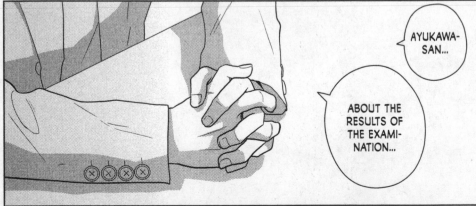

AYUKAWA-SAN...

ABOUT THE RESULTS OF THE EXAMI-NATION...

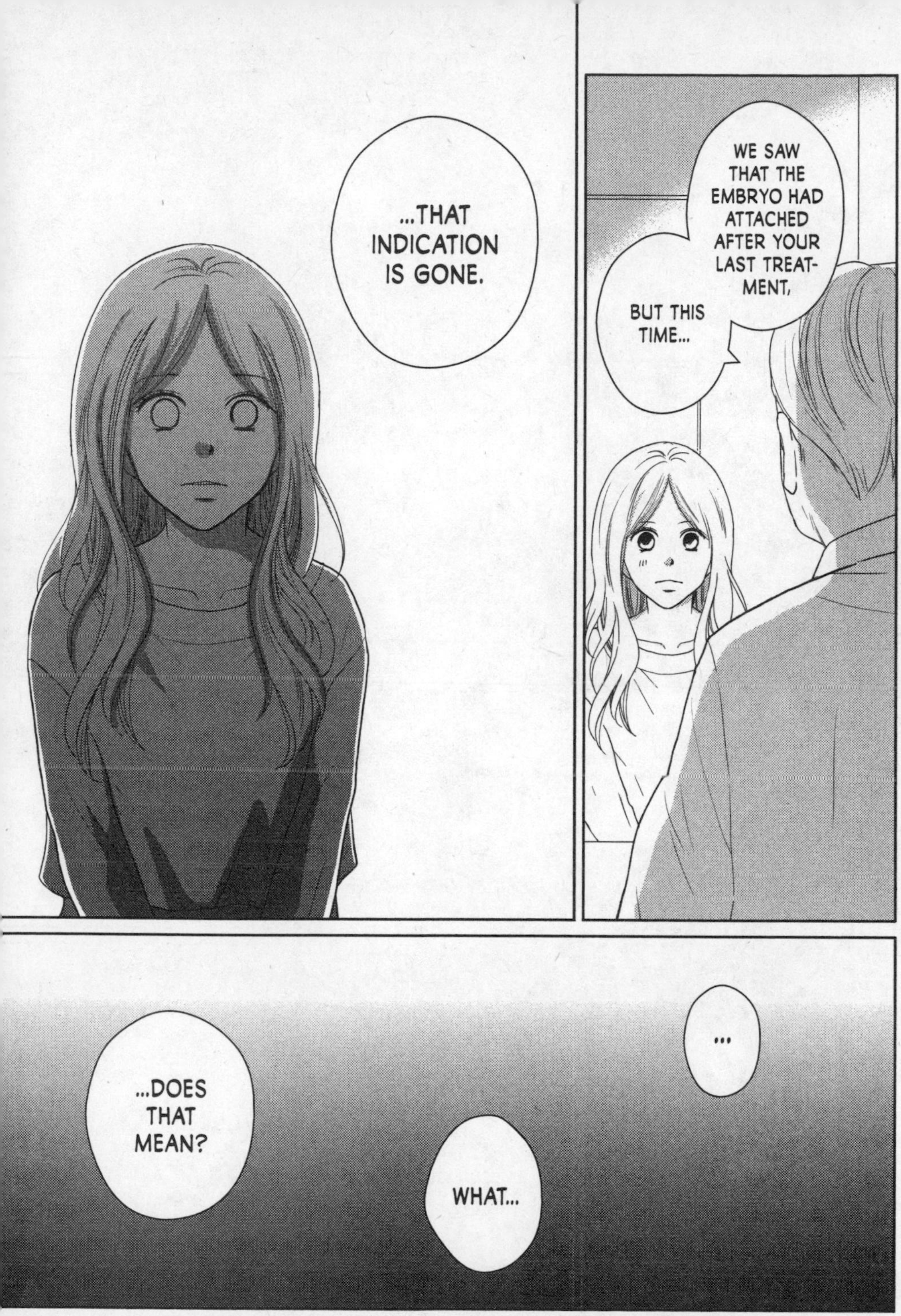
WE SAW THAT THE EMBRYO HAD ATTACHED AFTER YOUR LAST TREAT-MENT,
BUT THIS TIME...
...THAT INDICATION IS GONE.
...
WHAT...
...DOES THAT MEAN?

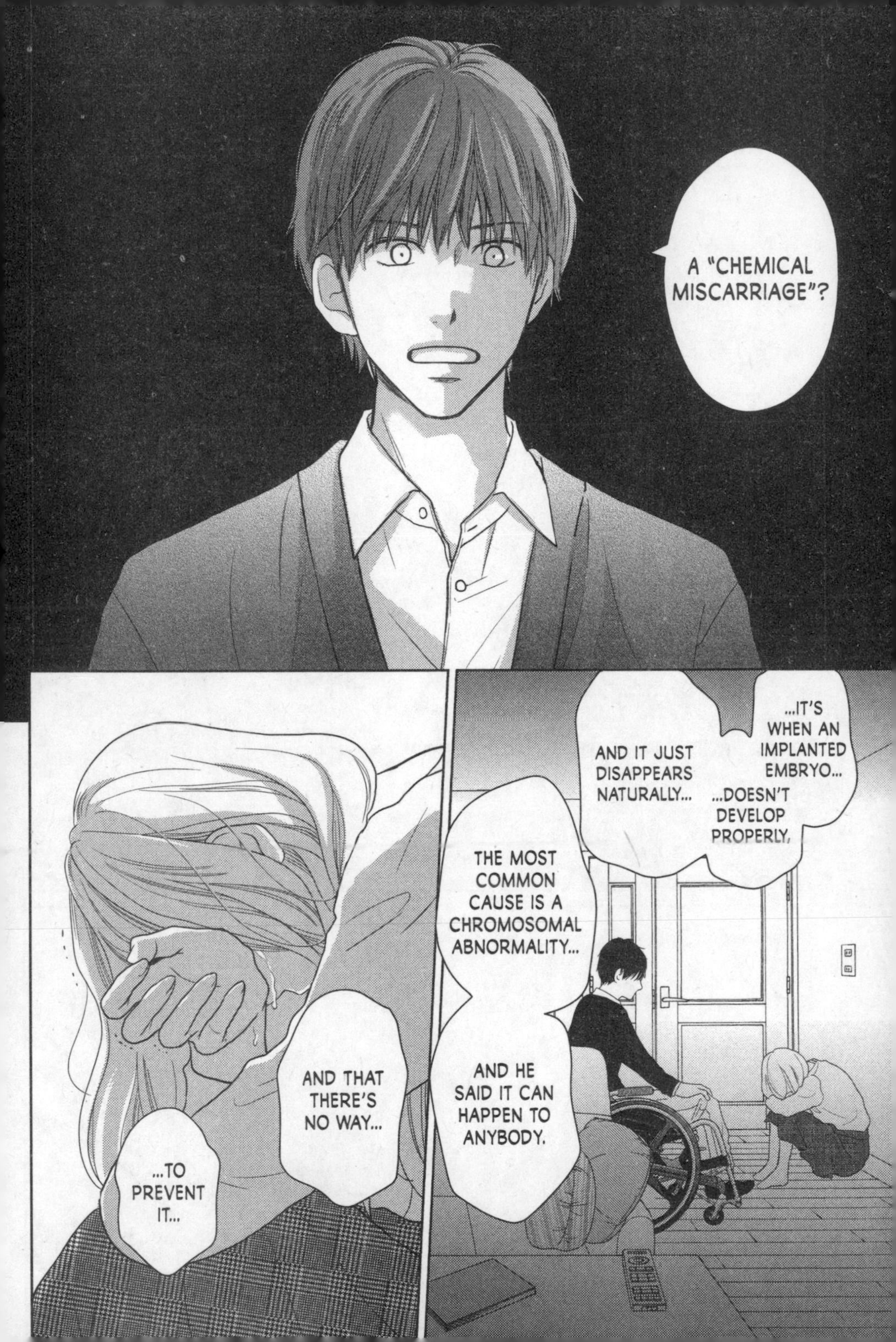
A "CHEMICAL MISCARRIAGE"?
...IT'S WHEN AN IMPLANTED EMBRYO...
...DOESN'T DEVELOP PROPERLY,
AND IT JUST DISAPPEARS NATURALLY...
THE MOST COMMON CAUSE IS A CHROMOSOMAL ABNORMALITY...
AND HE SAID IT CAN HAPPEN TO ANYBODY.
AND THAT THERE'S NO WAY...
...TO PREVENT IT...

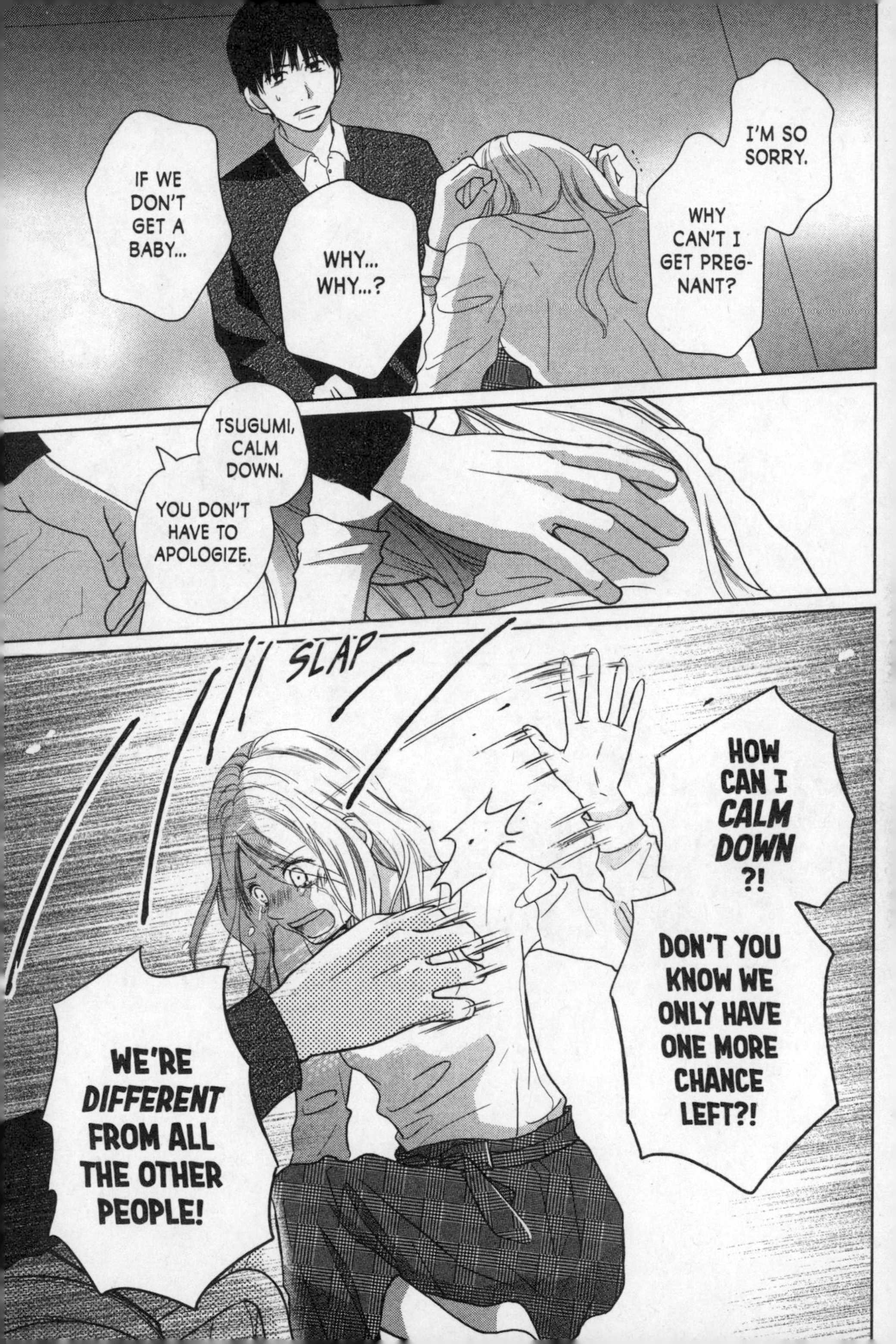
I'M SO SORRY.
WHY CAN'T I GET PREG-NANT?
WHY... WHY...?
IF WE DON'T GET A BABY...
TSUGUMI, CALM DOWN.
YOU DON'T HAVE TO APOLOGIZE.
SLAP
HOW CAN I CALM DOWN?!
DON'T YOU KNOW WE ONLY HAVE ONE MORE CHANCE LEFT?!
WE'RE DIFFERENT FROM ALL THE OTHER PEOPLE!

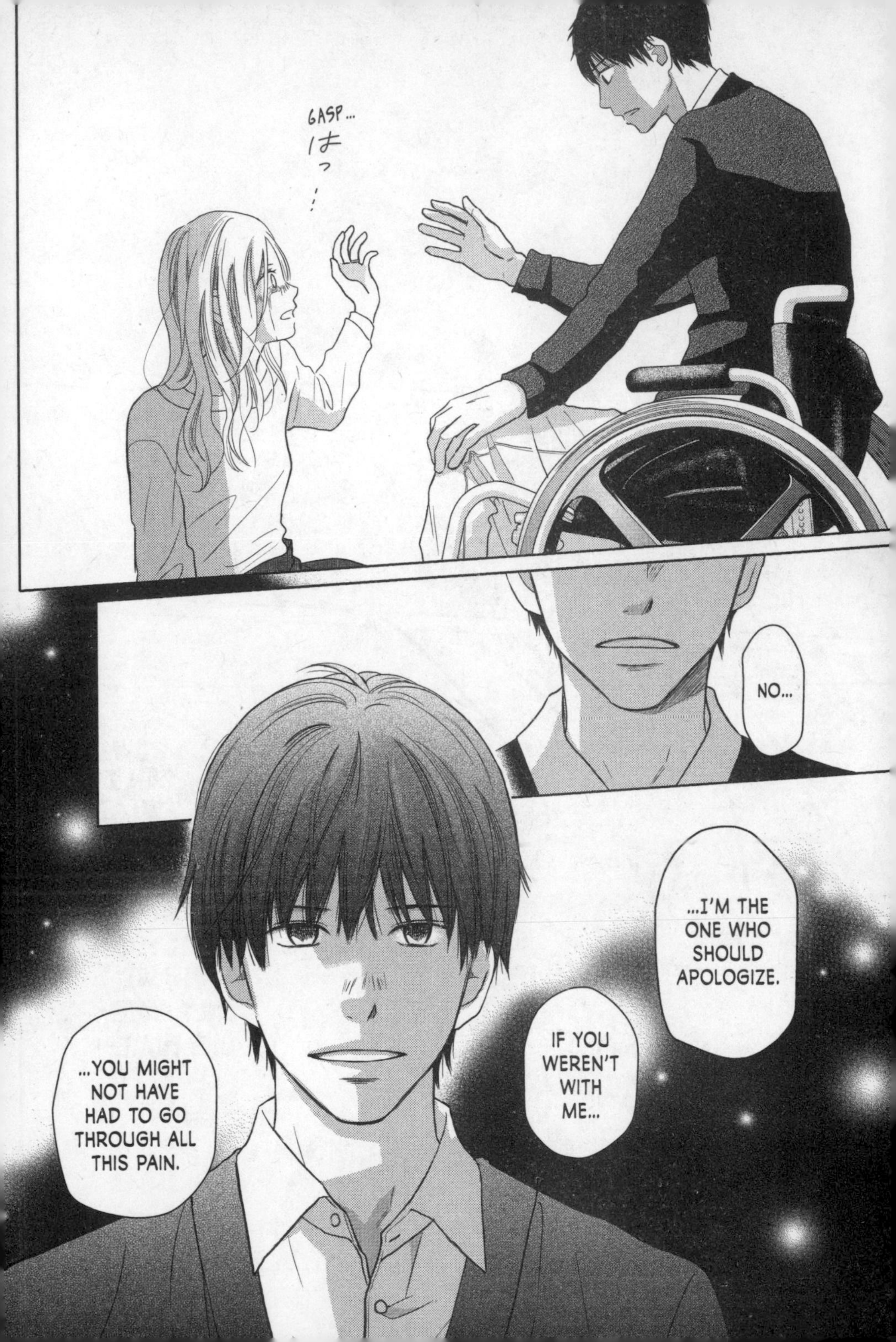
GASP...
はっ!
NO...
...I'M THE ONE WHO SHOULD APOLOGIZE.
IF YOU WEREN'T WITH ME...
...YOU MIGHT NOT HAVE HAD TO GO THROUGH ALL THIS PAIN.

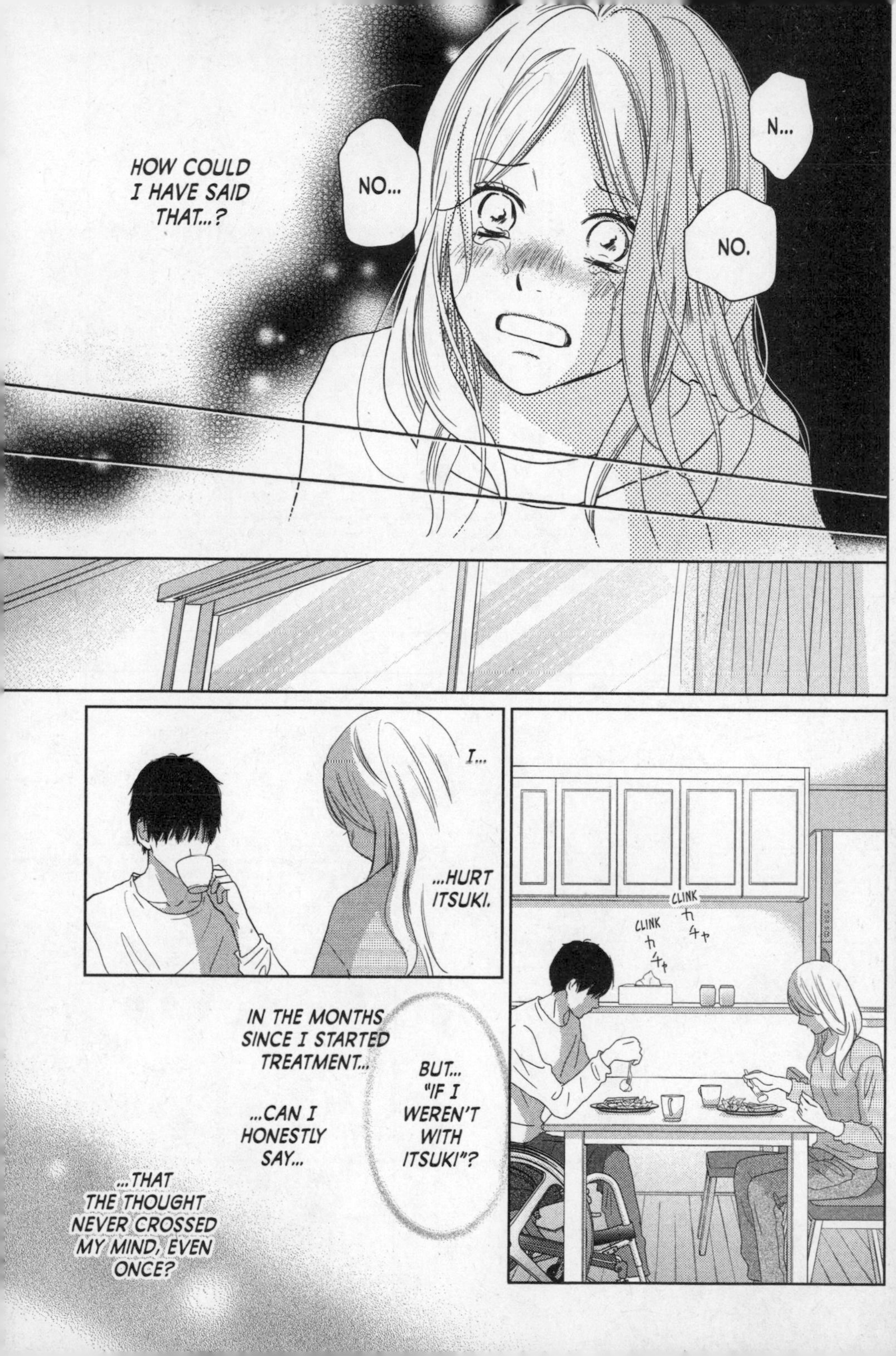
N...
NO.
NO...
HOW COULD I HAVE SAID THAT...?
CLINK
CLINK
I...
...HURT ITSUKI.
BUT... "IF I WEREN'T WITH ITSUKI"?
IN THE MONTHS SINCE I STARTED TREATMENT...
...CAN I HONESTLY SAY...
...THAT THE THOUGHT NEVER CROSSED MY MIND, EVEN ONCE?

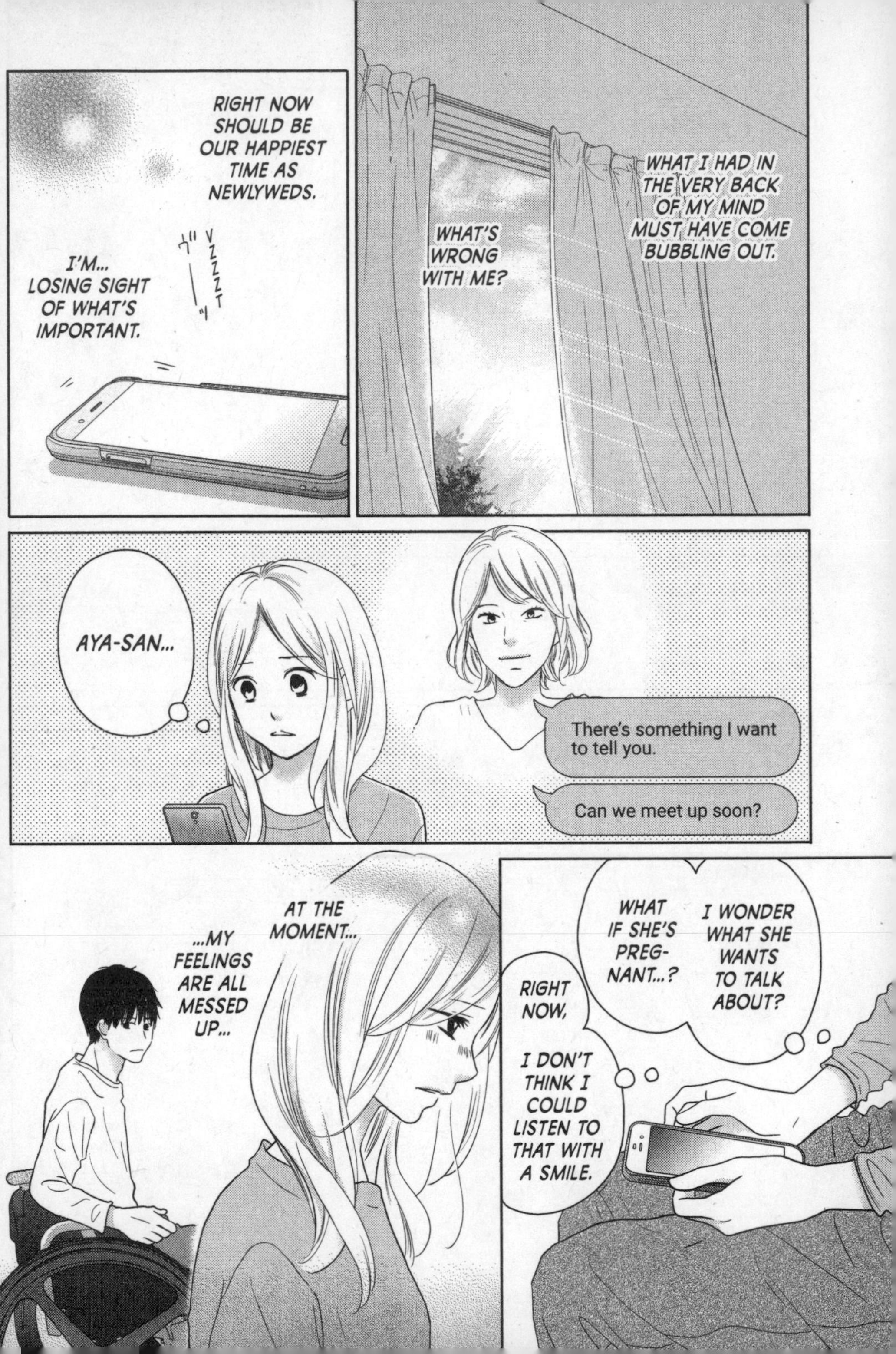
WHAT I HAD IN THE VERY BACK OF MY MIND MUST HAVE COME BUBBLING OUT.
WHAT'S WRONG WITH ME?
RIGHT NOW SHOULD BE OUR HAPPIEST TIME AS NEWLYWEDS.
I'M... LOSING SIGHT OF WHAT'S IMPORTANT.
VZZZT
There's something I want to tell you.
Can we meet up soon?
AYA-SAN...
I WONDER WHAT SHE WANTS TO TALK ABOUT?
WHAT IF SHE'S PREG-NANT...?
RIGHT NOW, I DON'T THINK I COULD LISTEN TO THAT WITH A SMILE.
AT THE MOMENT...
...MY FEELINGS ARE ALL MESSED UP...

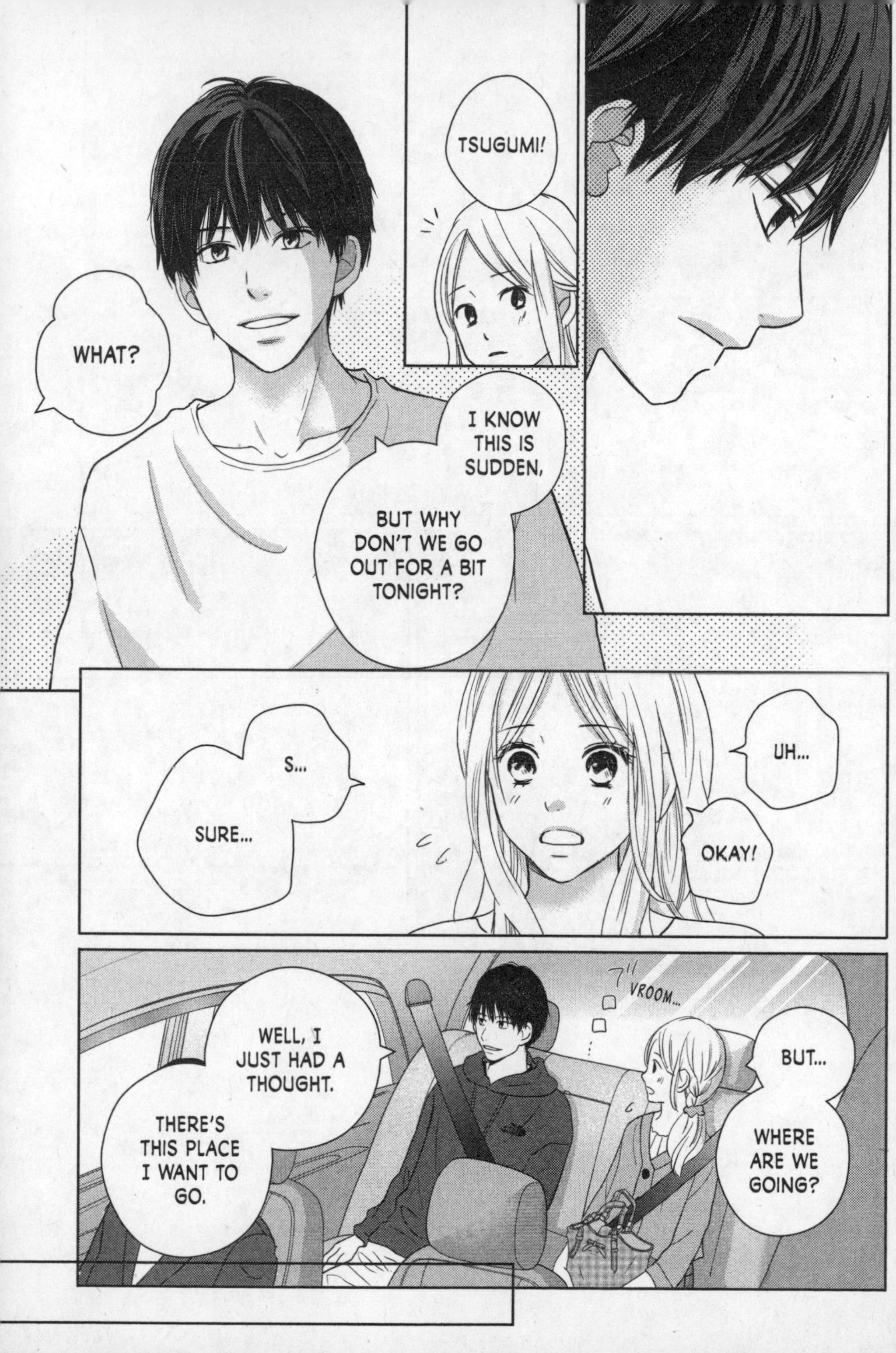
TSUGUMI!
WHAT?
I KNOW THIS IS SUDDEN,
BUT WHY DON'T WE GO OUT FOR A BIT TONIGHT?
UH...
OKAY!
S...
SURE...
VROOM...
BUT...
WHERE ARE WE GOING?
WELL, I JUST HAD A THOUGHT.
THERE'S THIS PLACE I WANT TO GO.

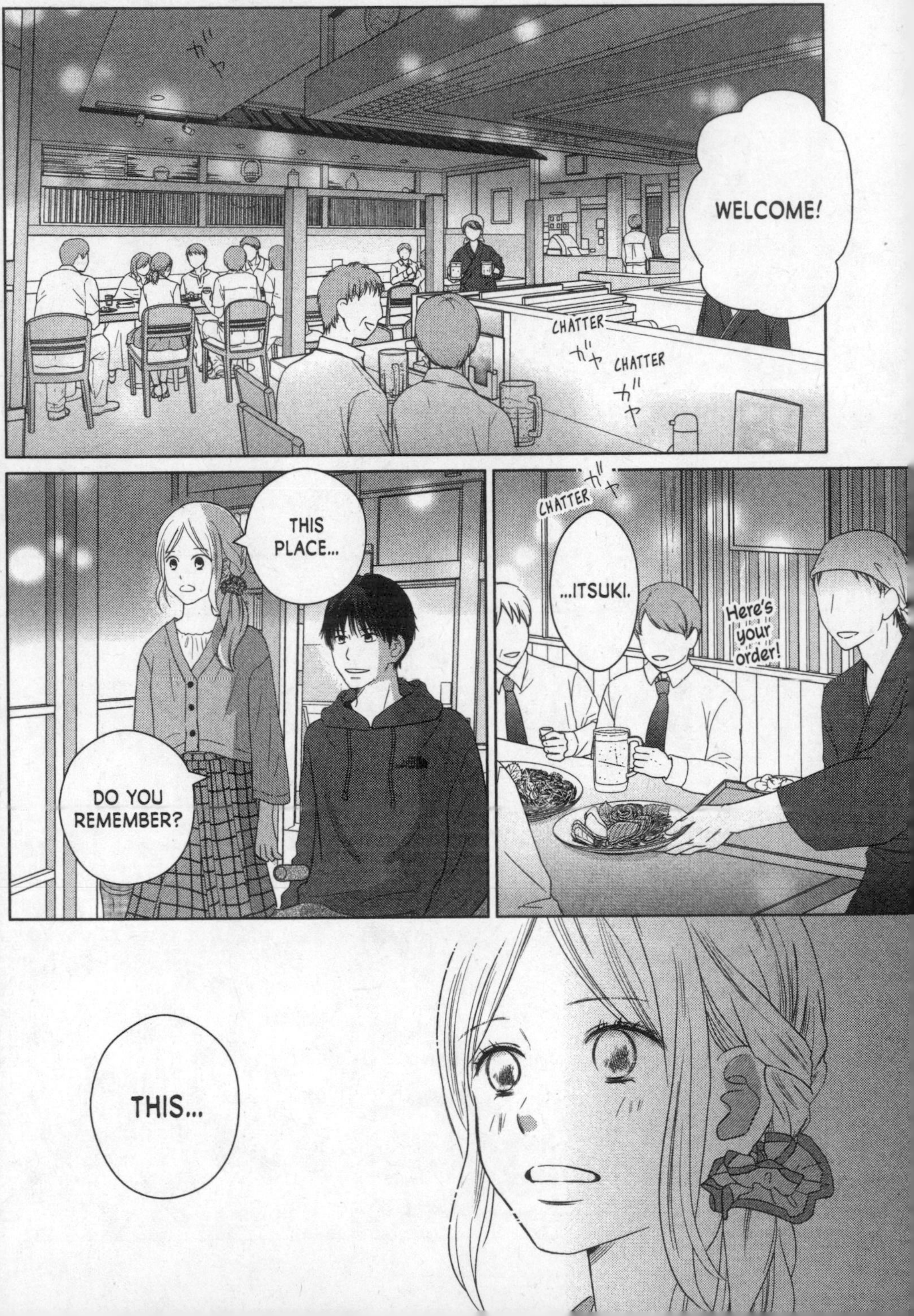
ガヤ
WELCOME!
CHATTER ガヤ
CHATTER ガヤ
CHATTER ガヤ
...ITSUKI.
Here's your order!
THIS PLACE...
DO YOU REMEMBER?
THIS...

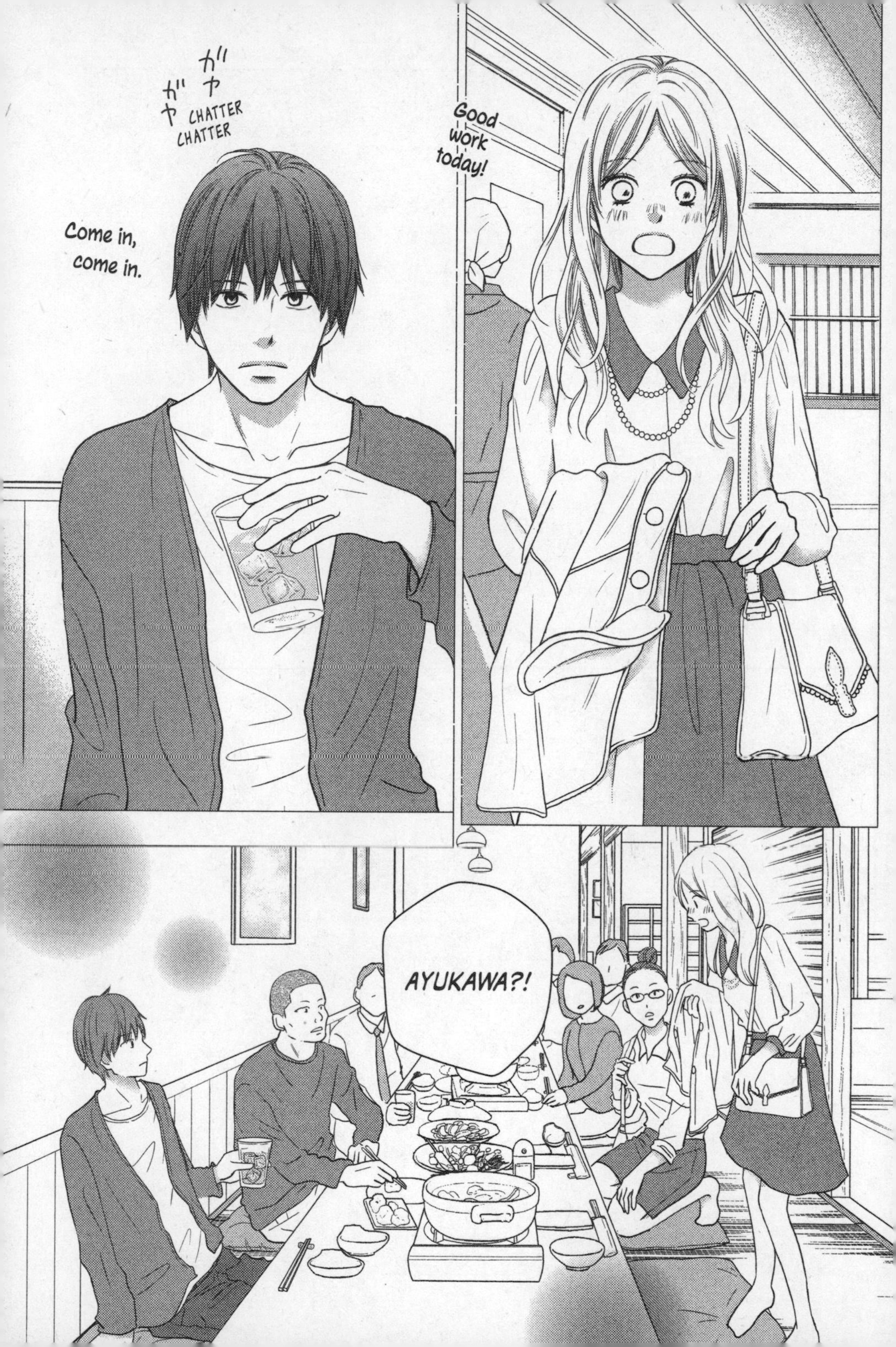
Good work today!
ガヤガヤ
CHATTER CHATTER
Come in, come in.
AYUKAWA?!

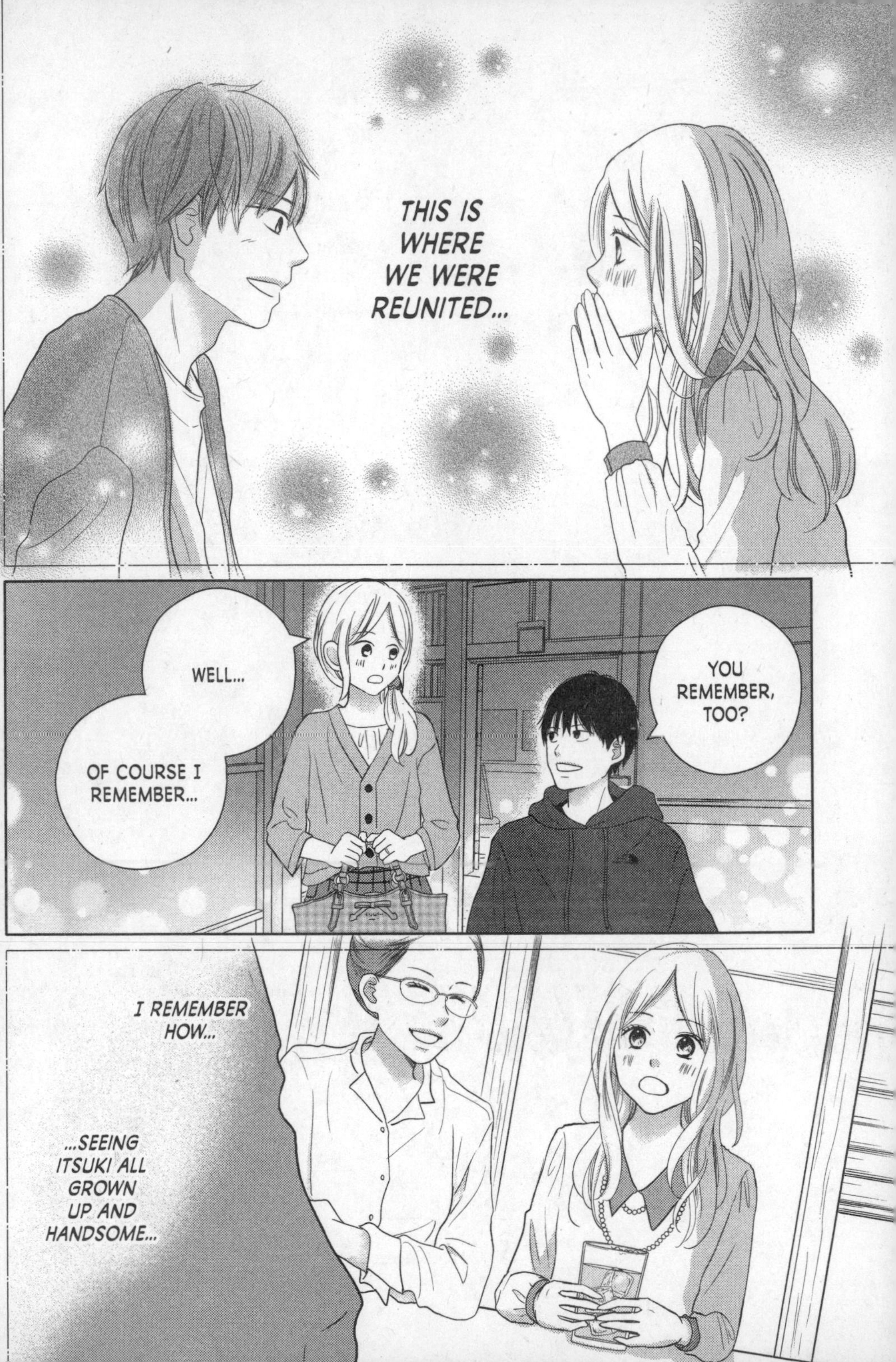
THIS IS WHERE WE WERE REUNITED...
YOU REMEMBER, TOO?
WELL...
OF COURSE I REMEMBER...
I REMEMBER HOW...
...SEEING ITSUKI ALL GROWN UP AND HANDSOME...

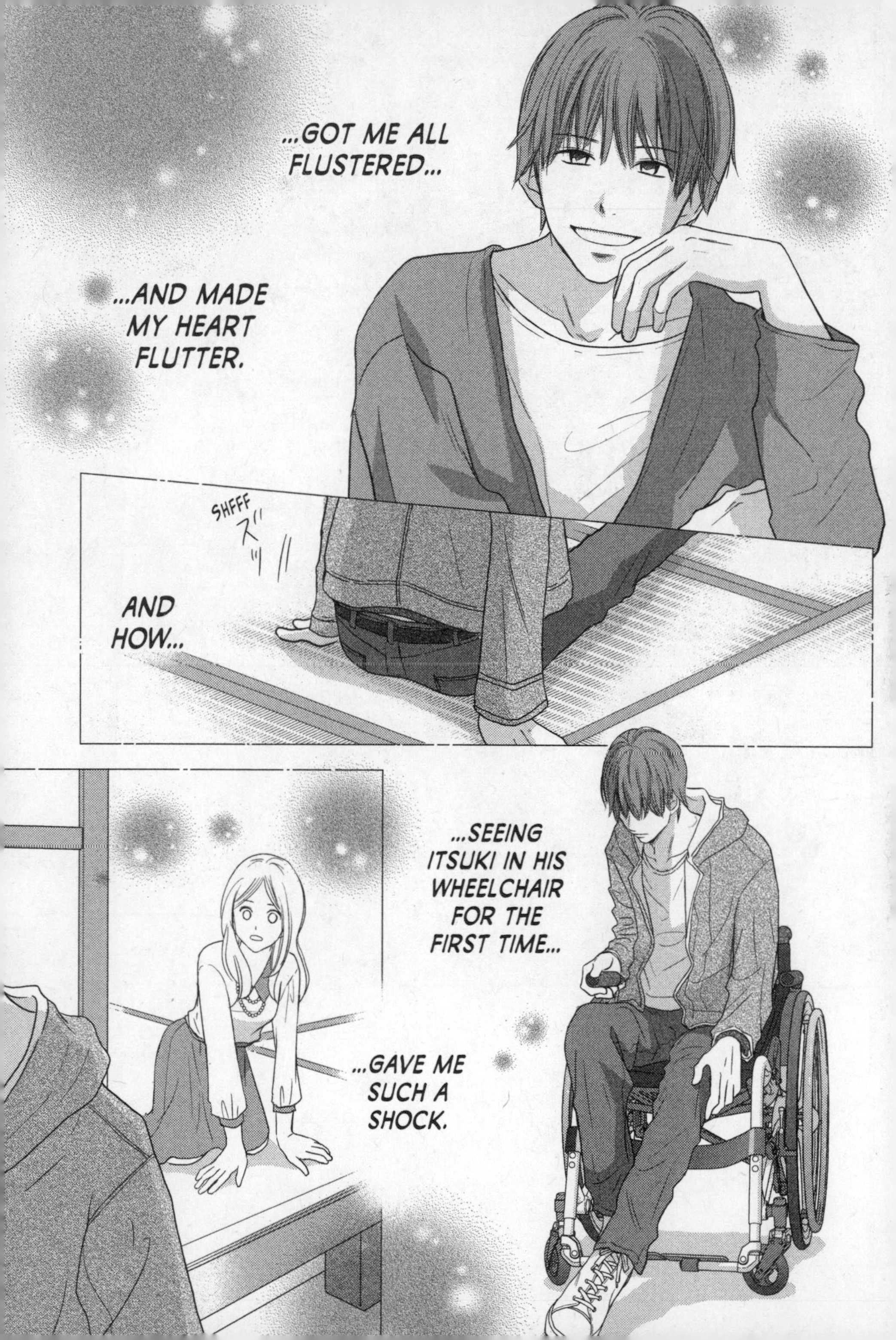
...GOT ME ALL FLUSTERED...
...AND MADE MY HEART FLUTTER.
SHFFF
ズッ
AND HOW...
...SEEING ITSUKI IN HIS WHEELCHAIR FOR THE FIRST TIME...
...GAVE ME SUCH A SHOCK.

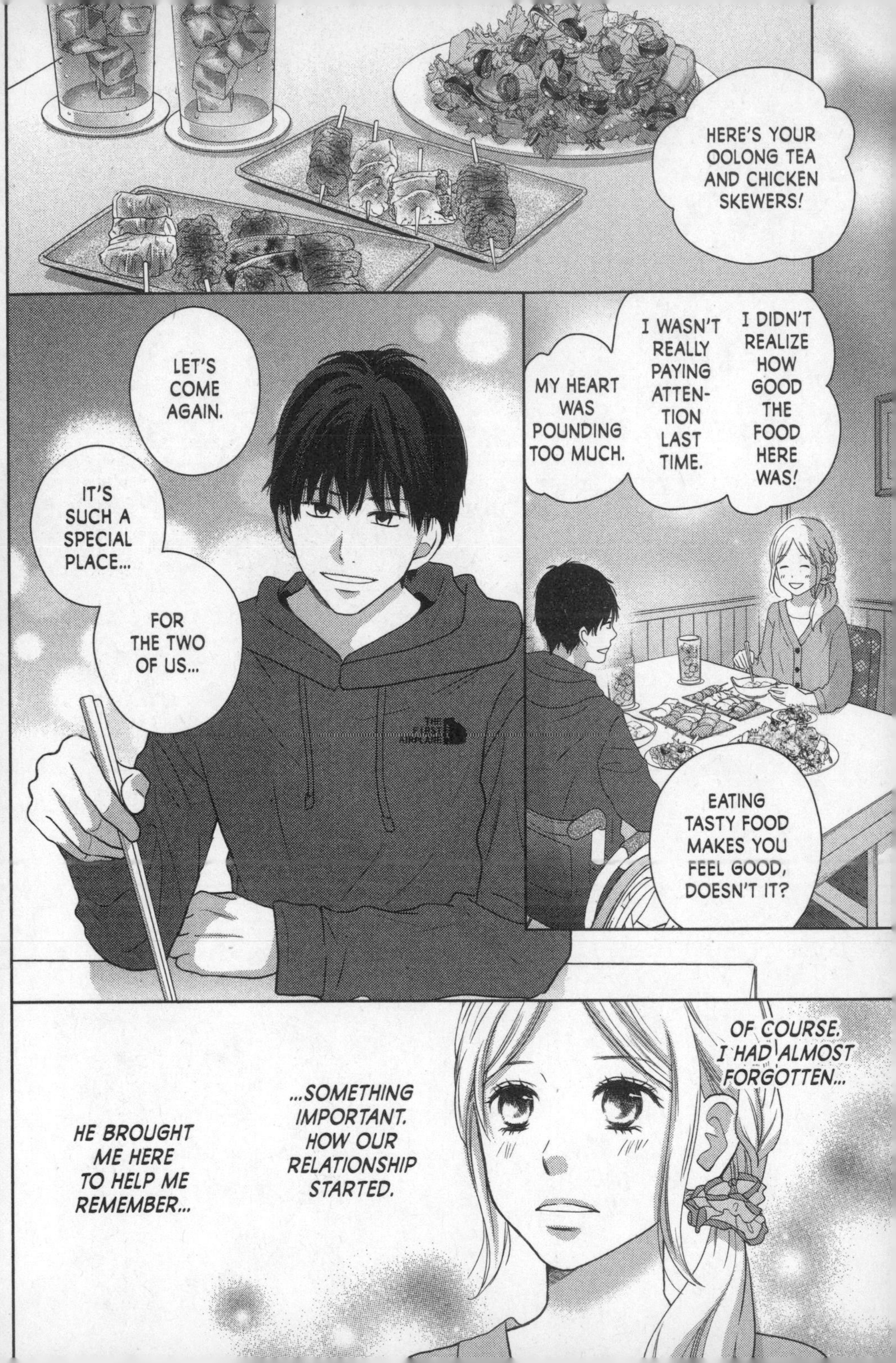
HERE'S YOUR OOLONG TEA AND CHICKEN SKEWERS!
I DIDN'T REALIZE HOW GOOD THE FOOD HERE WAS!
I WASN'T REALLY PAYING ATTEN-TION LAST TIME.
MY HEART WAS POUNDING TOO MUCH.
EATING TASTY FOOD MAKES YOU FEEL GOOD, DOESN'T IT?
LET'S COME AGAIN.
IT'S SUCH A SPECIAL PLACE...
FOR THE TWO OF US...
OF COURSE. I HAD ALMOST FORGOTTEN...
...SOMETHING IMPORTANT. HOW OUR RELATIONSHIP STARTED.
HE BROUGHT ME HERE TO HELP ME REMEMBER...

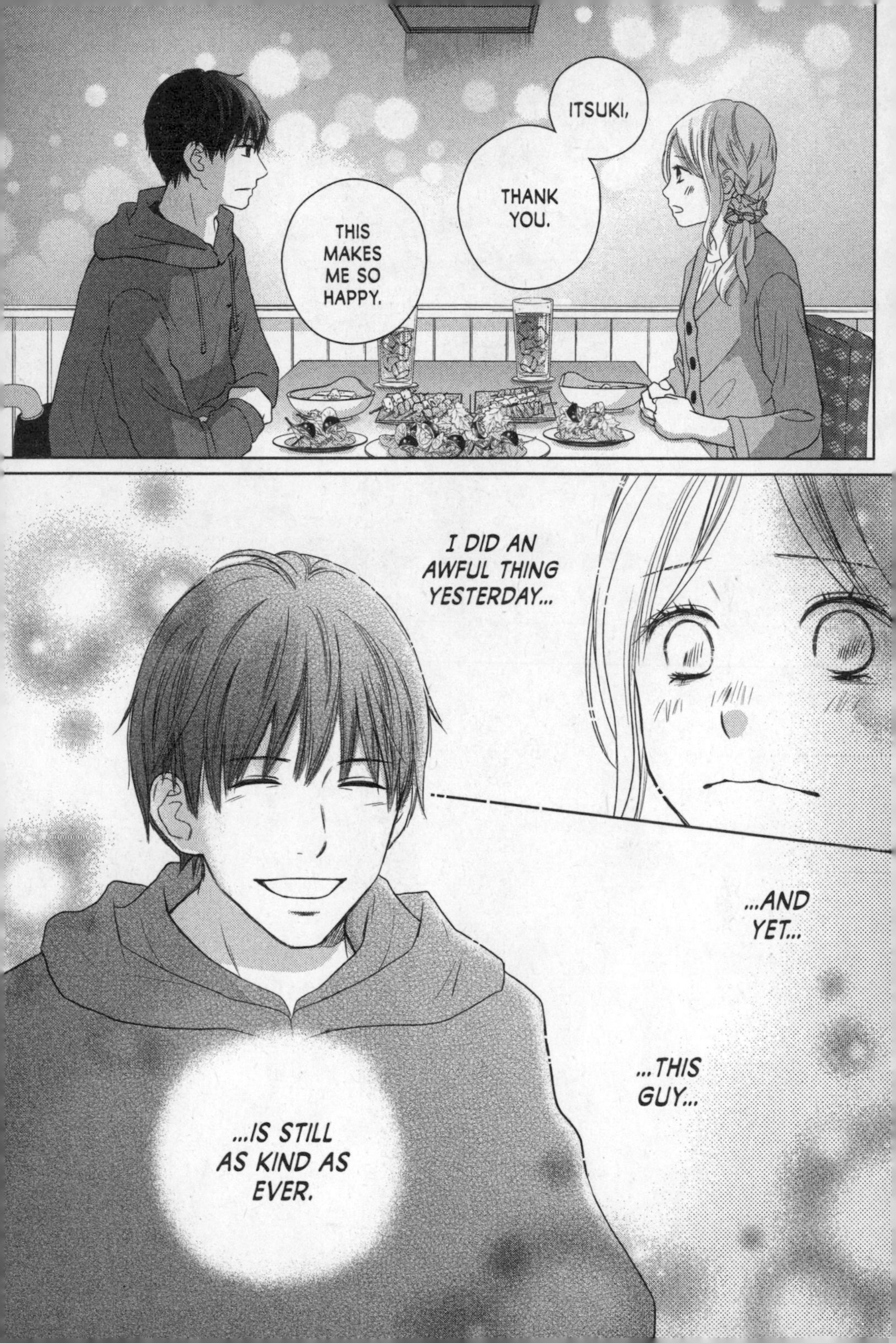
ITSUKI,
THANK YOU.
THIS MAKES ME SO HAPPY.
I DID AN AWFUL THING YESTERDAY...
...AND YET...
...THIS GUY...
...IS STILL AS KIND AS EVER.

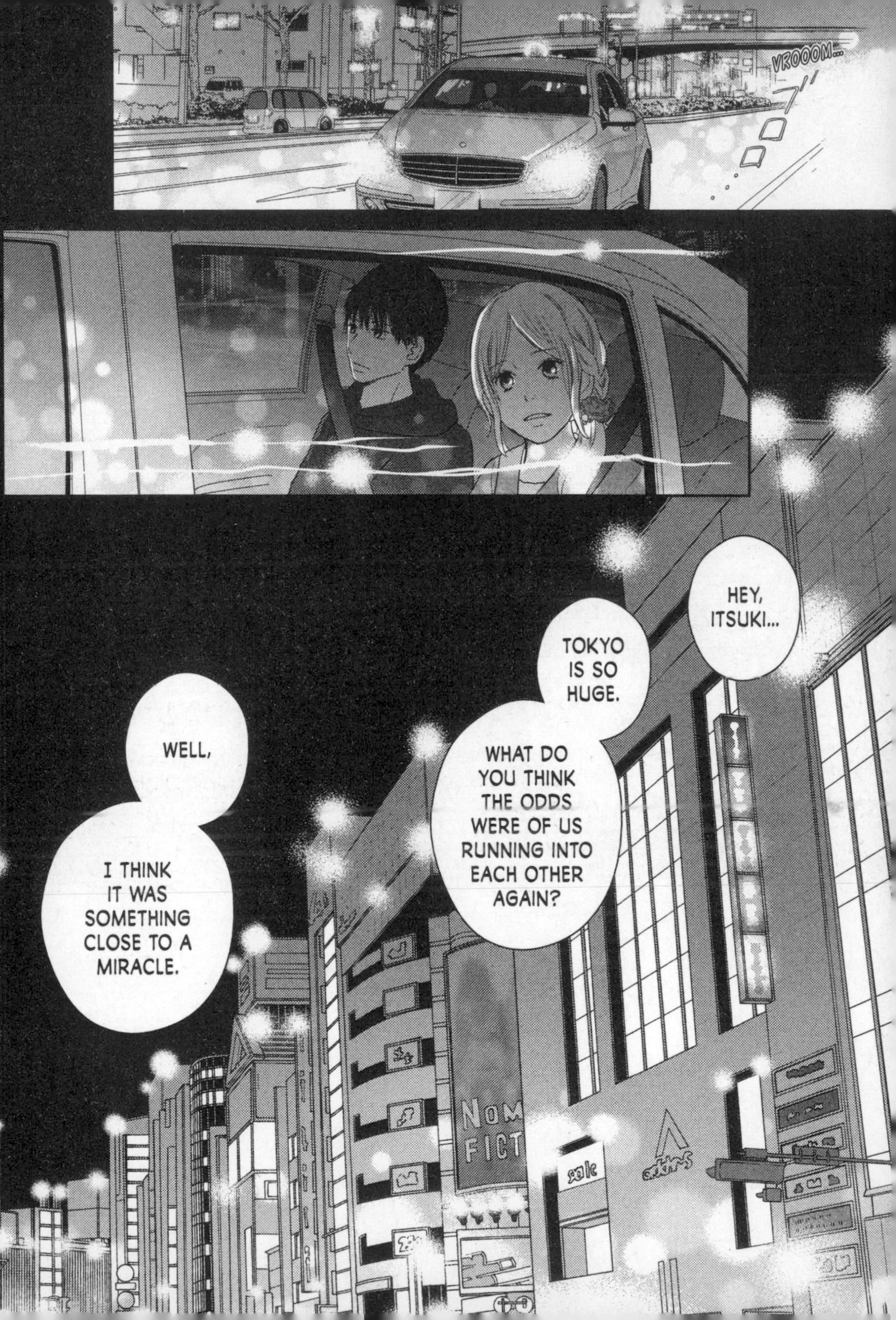
VROOOM...
HEY, ITSUKI...
TOKYO IS SO HUGE.
WHAT DO YOU THINK THE ODDS WERE OF US RUNNING INTO EACH OTHER AGAIN?
WELL,
I THINK IT WAS SOMETHING CLOSE TO A MIRACLE.

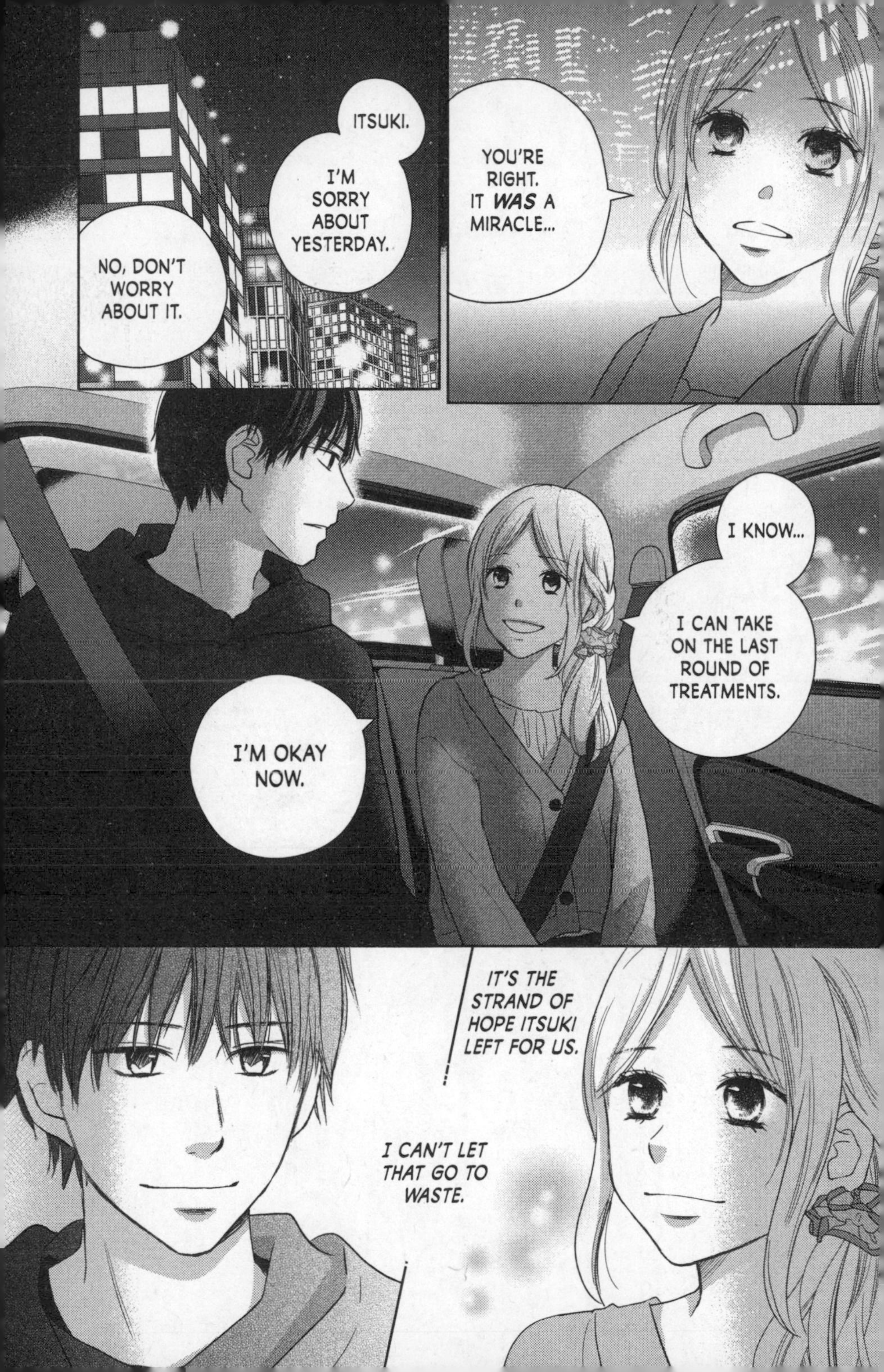
YOU'RE RIGHT. IT ***WAS*** A MIRACLE...
ITSUKI.
I'M SORRY ABOUT YESTERDAY.
NO, DON'T WORRY ABOUT IT.
I KNOW...
I CAN TAKE ON THE LAST ROUND OF TREATMENTS.
I'M OKAY NOW.
IT'S THE STRAND OF HOPE ITSUKI LEFT FOR US.
I CAN'T LET THAT GO TO WASTE.

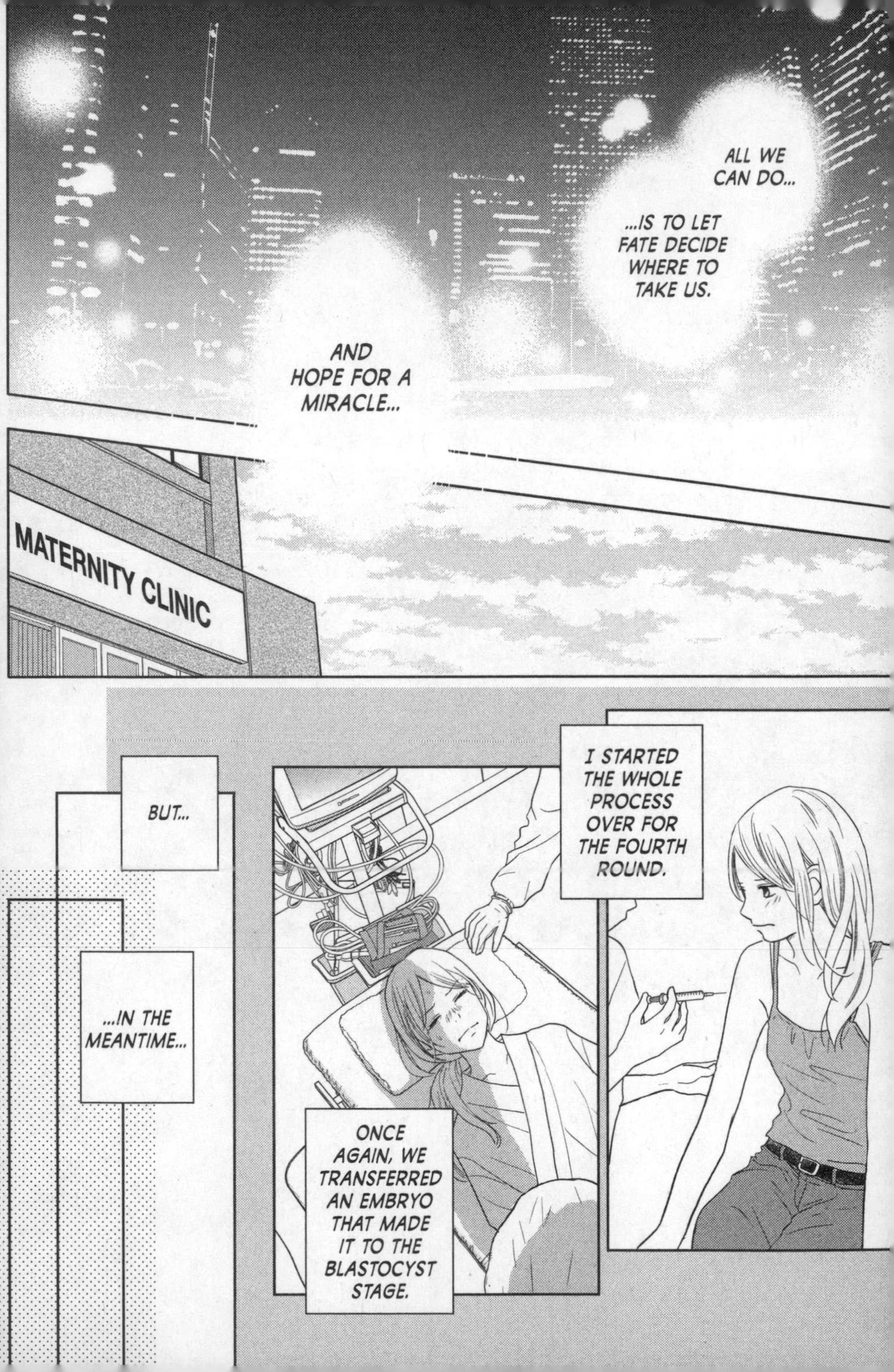
ALL WE CAN DO...
...IS TO LET FATE DECIDE WHERE TO TAKE US.
AND HOPE FOR A MIRACLE...
MATERNITY CLINIC
I STARTED THE WHOLE PROCESS OVER FOR THE FOURTH ROUND.
ONCE AGAIN, WE TRANSFERRED AN EMBRYO THAT MADE IT TO THE BLASTOCYST STAGE.
BUT...
...IN THE MEANTIME...

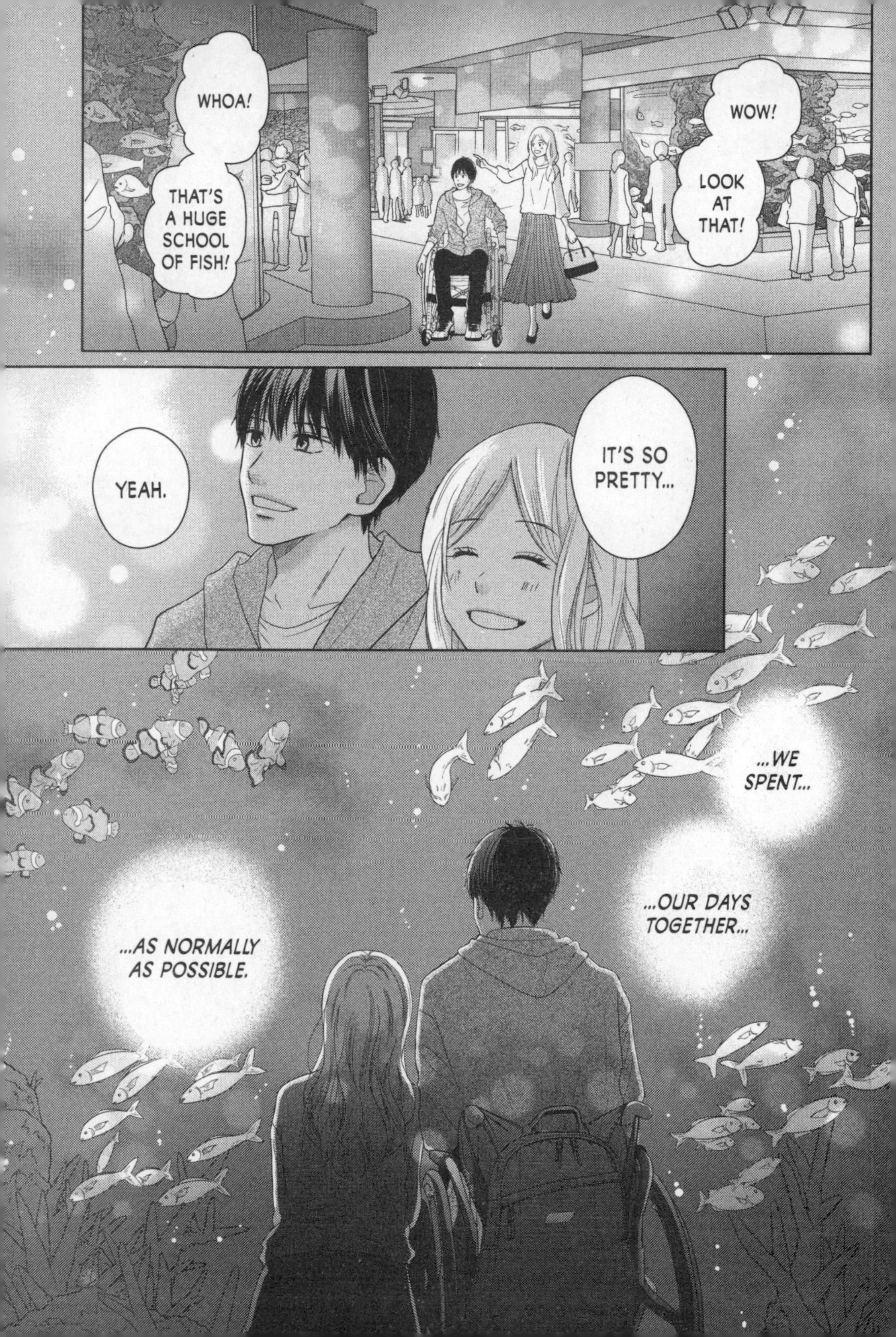
WOW!
LOOK AT THAT!
WHOA!
THAT'S A HUGE SCHOOL OF FISH!
IT'S SO PRETTY...
YEAH.
...WE SPENT...
...OUR DAYS TOGETHER...
...AS NORMALLY AS POSSIBLE.

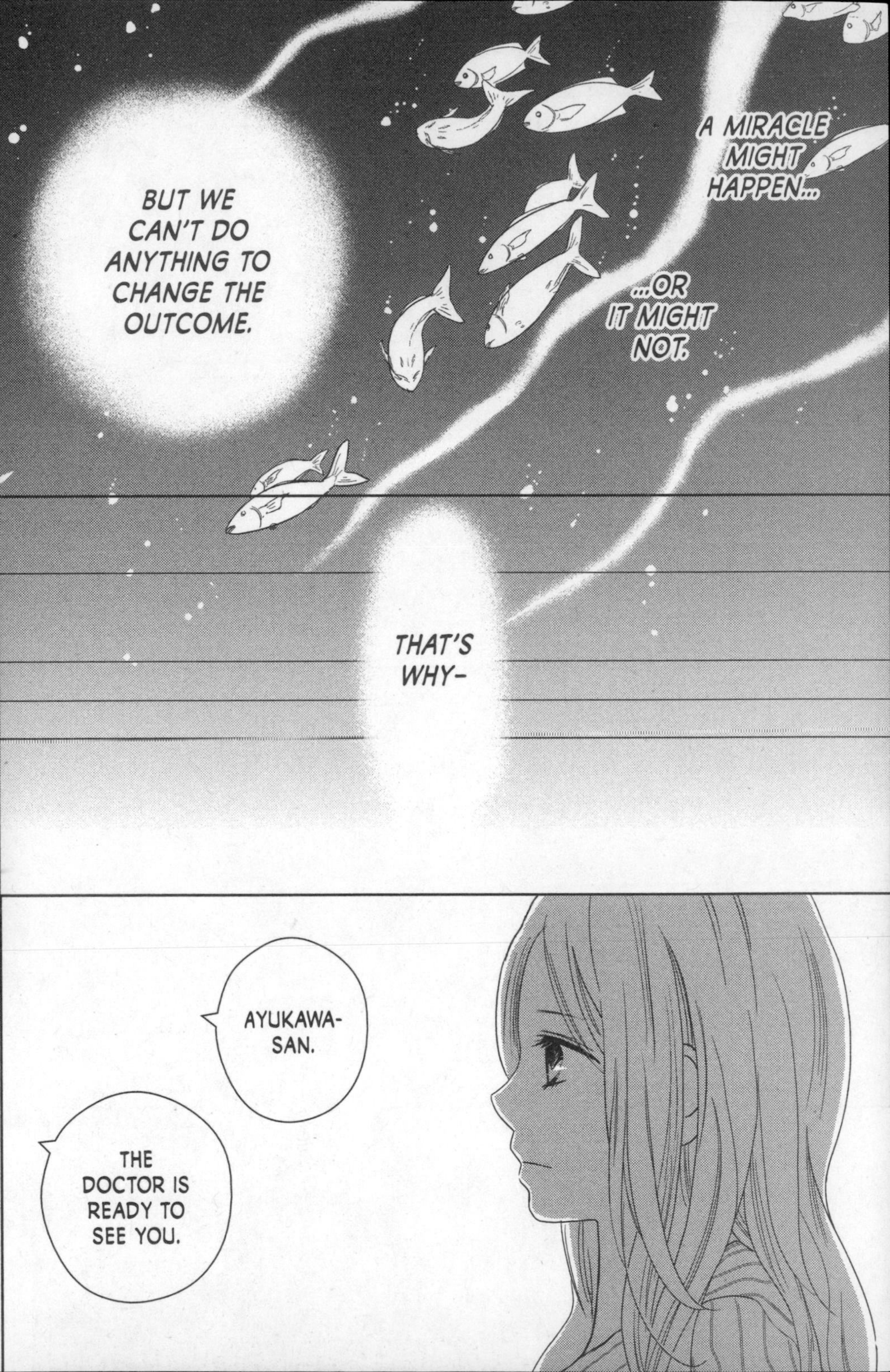
A MIRACLE MIGHT HAPPEN...
...OR IT MIGHT NOT.
BUT WE CAN'T DO ANYTHING TO CHANGE THE OUTCOME.
THAT'S WHY-
AYUKAWA-SAN.
THE DOCTOR IS READY TO SEE YOU.

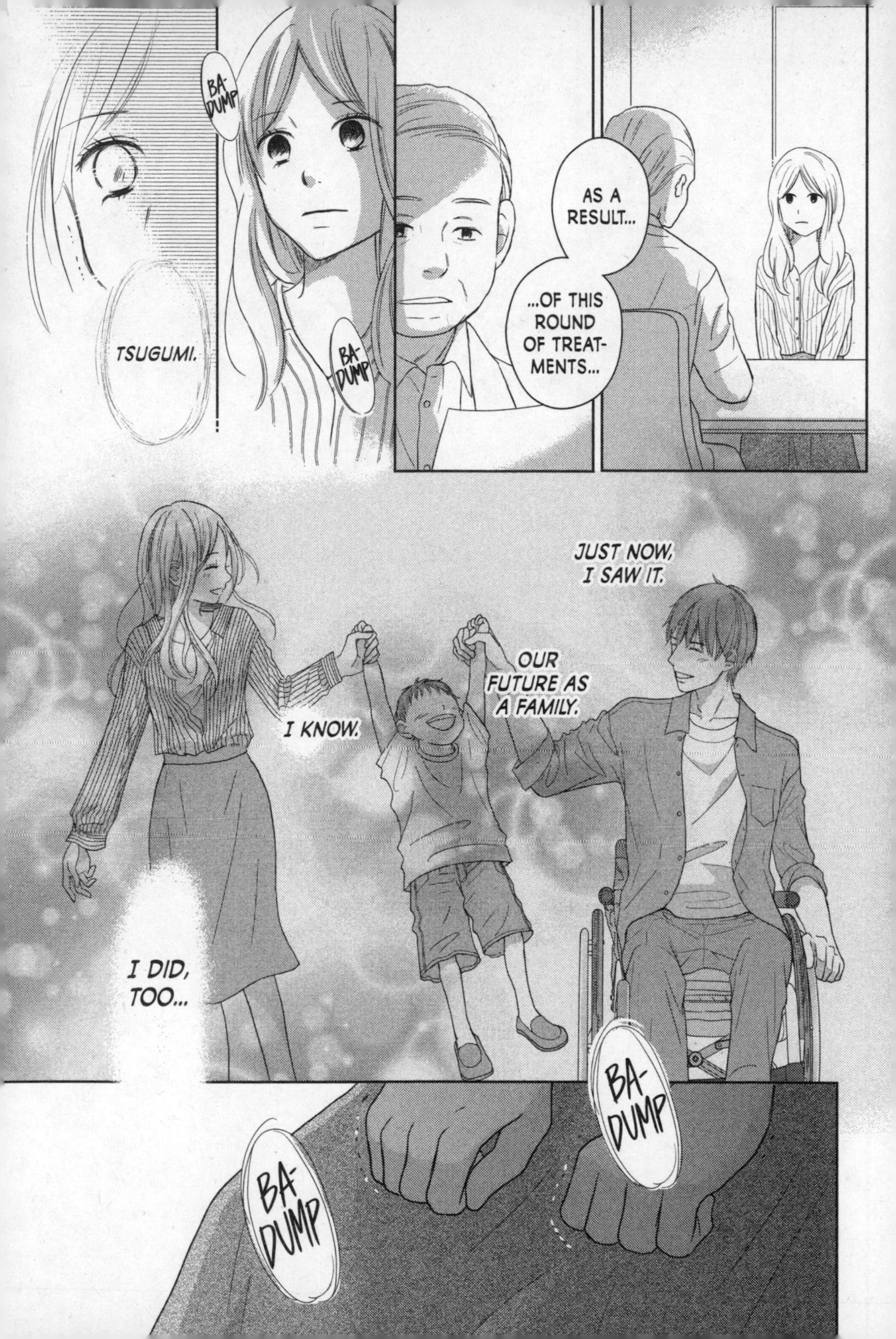
AS A RESULT...
...OF THIS ROUND OF TREATMENTS...
BA-DUMP
BA-DUMP
TSUGUMI.
JUST NOW, I SAW IT.
OUR FUTURE AS A FAMILY.
I KNOW.
I DID, TOO...
BA-DUMP
BA-DUMP

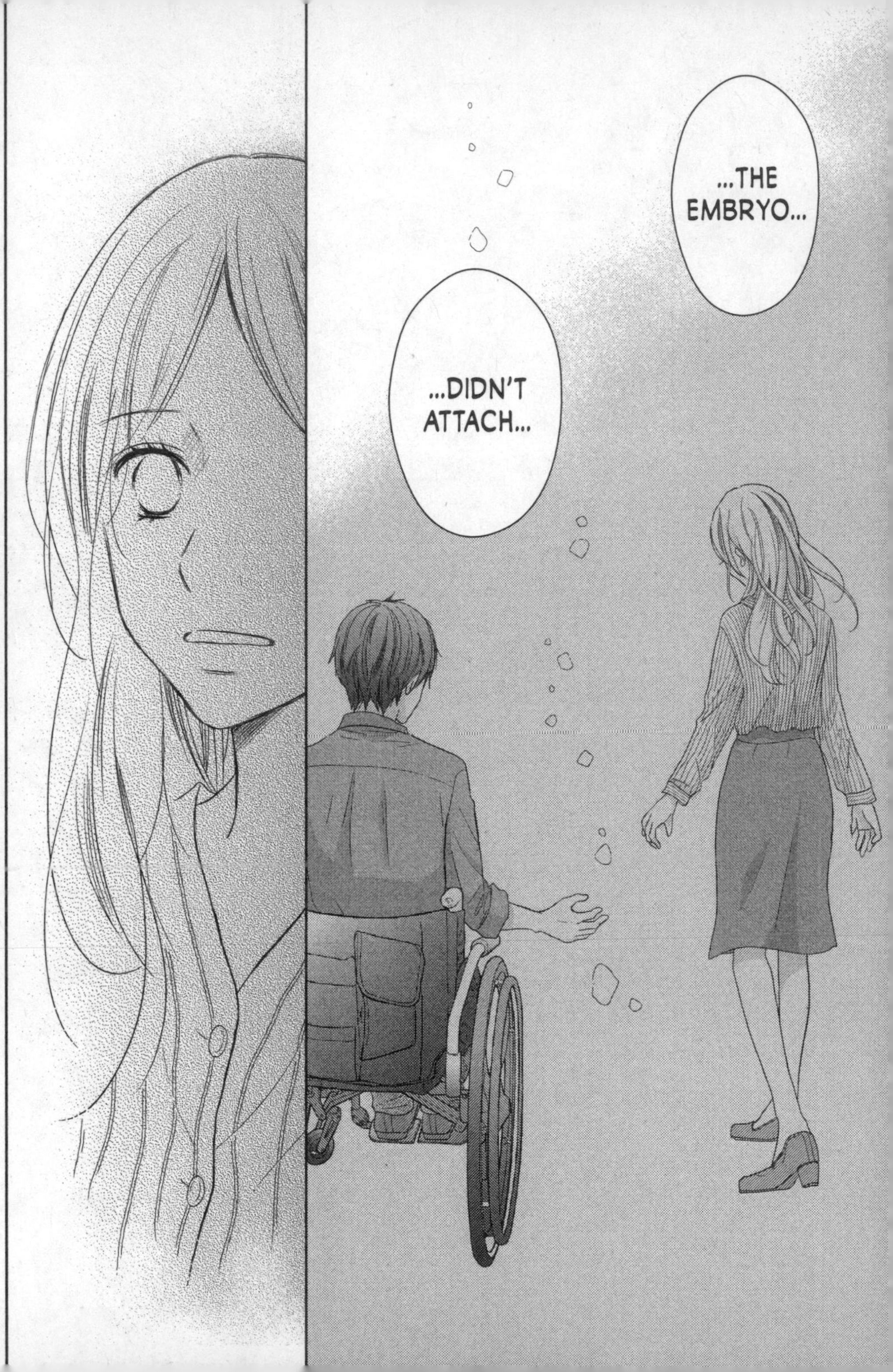
...THE EMBRYO...
...DIDN'T ATTACH...

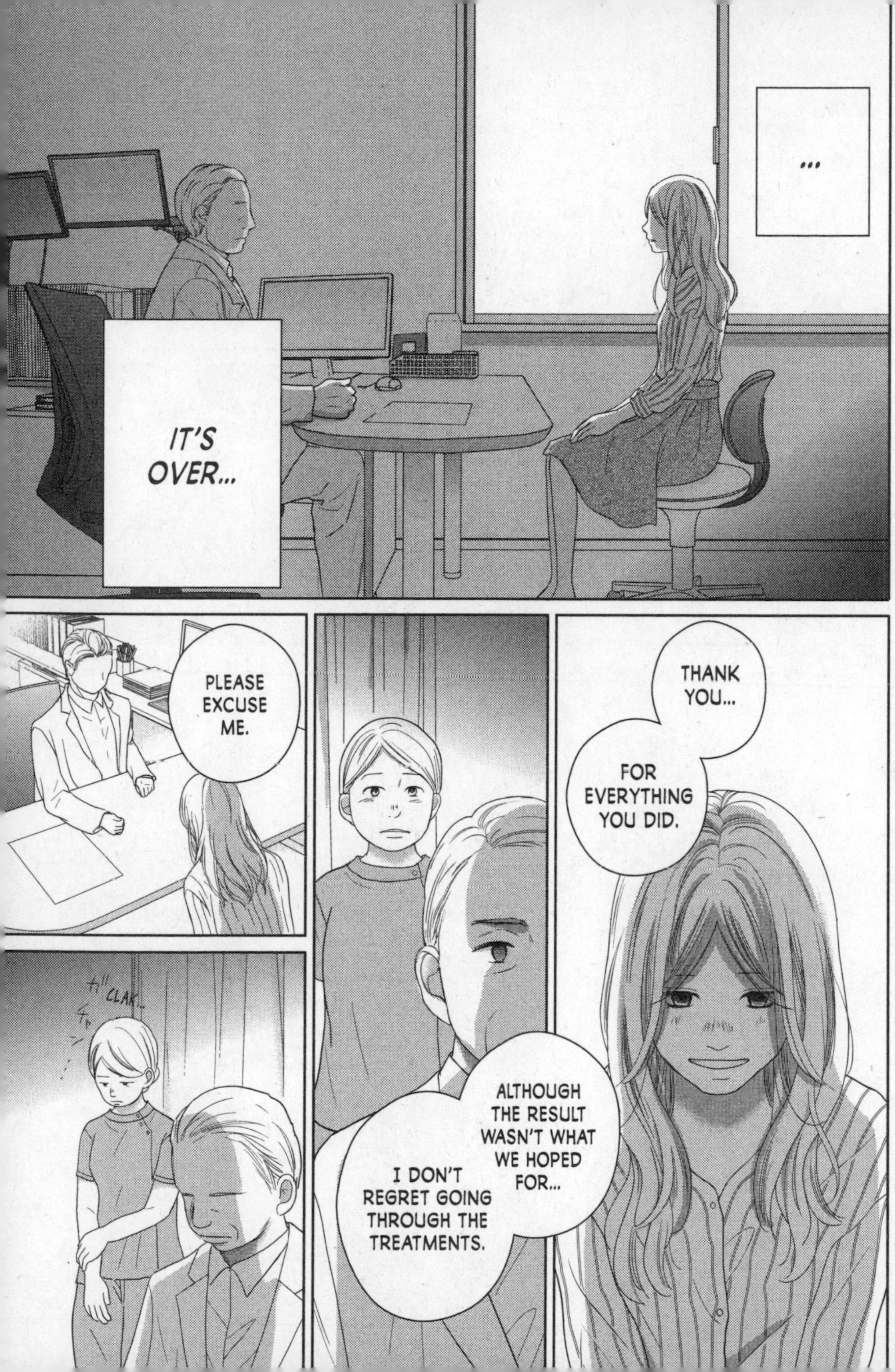
...
IT'S OVER...
THANK YOU...
FOR EVERYTHING YOU DID.
ALTHOUGH THE RESULT WASN'T WHAT WE HOPED FOR...
I DON'T REGRET GOING THROUGH THE TREATMENTS.
PLEASE EXCUSE ME.
CLAK...

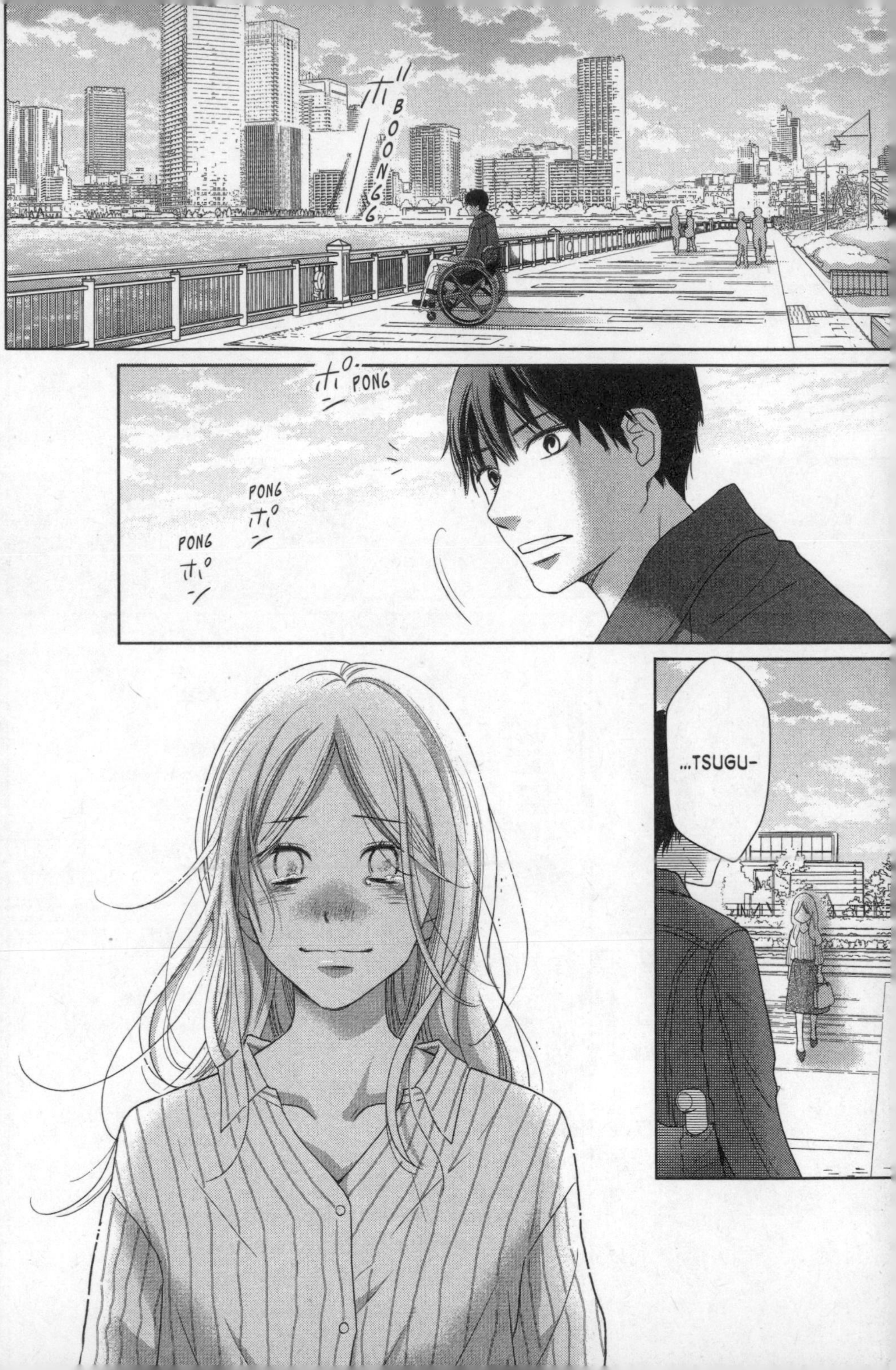
BOONGG
PONG
PONG
PONG
...TSUGU-

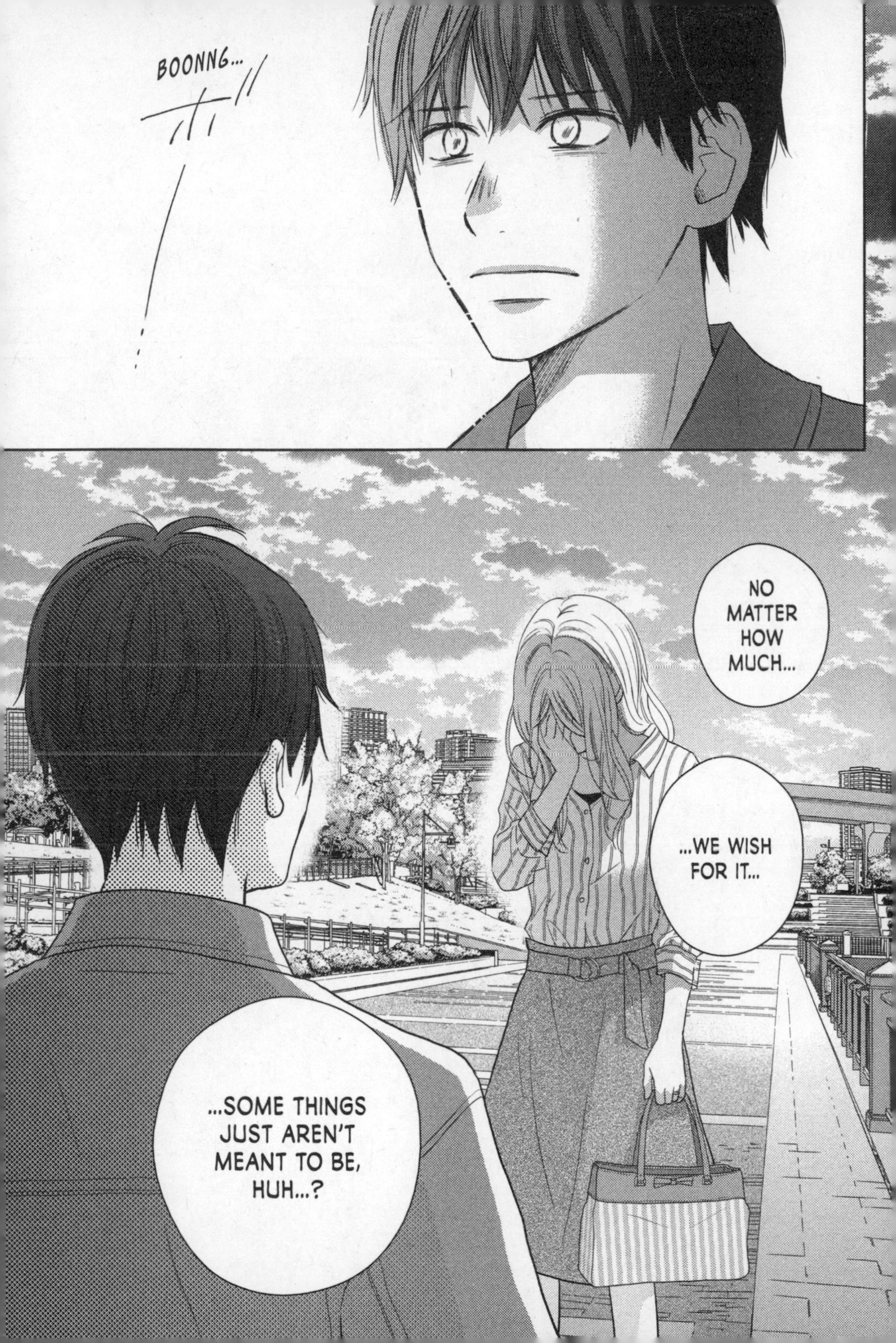
BOONNG...
NO MATTER HOW MUCH...
...WE WISH FOR IT...
...SOME THINGS JUST AREN'T MEANT TO BE, HUH...?

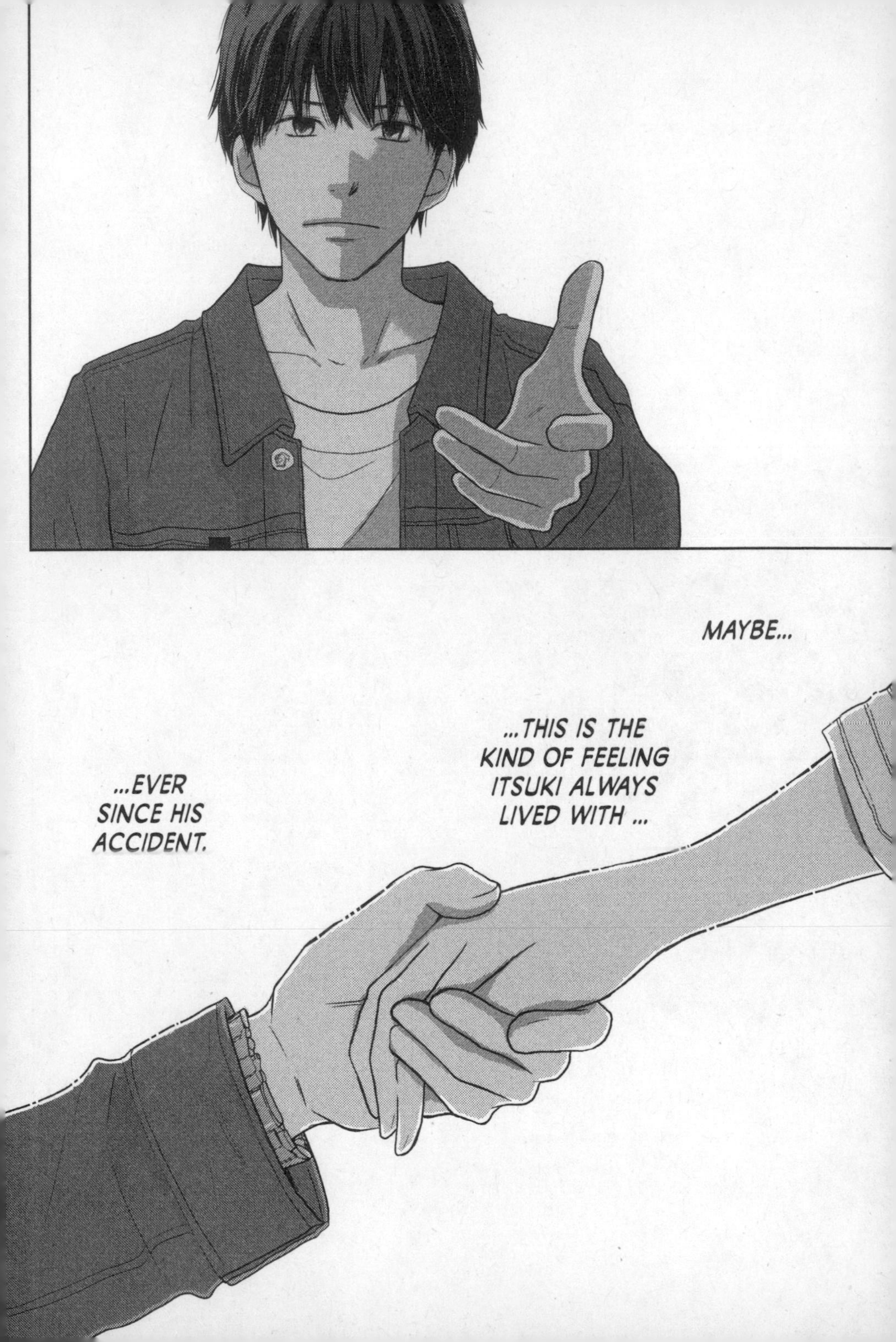
MAYBE...
...THIS IS THE KIND OF FEELING ITSUKI ALWAYS LIVED WITH ...
...EVER SINCE HIS ACCIDENT.

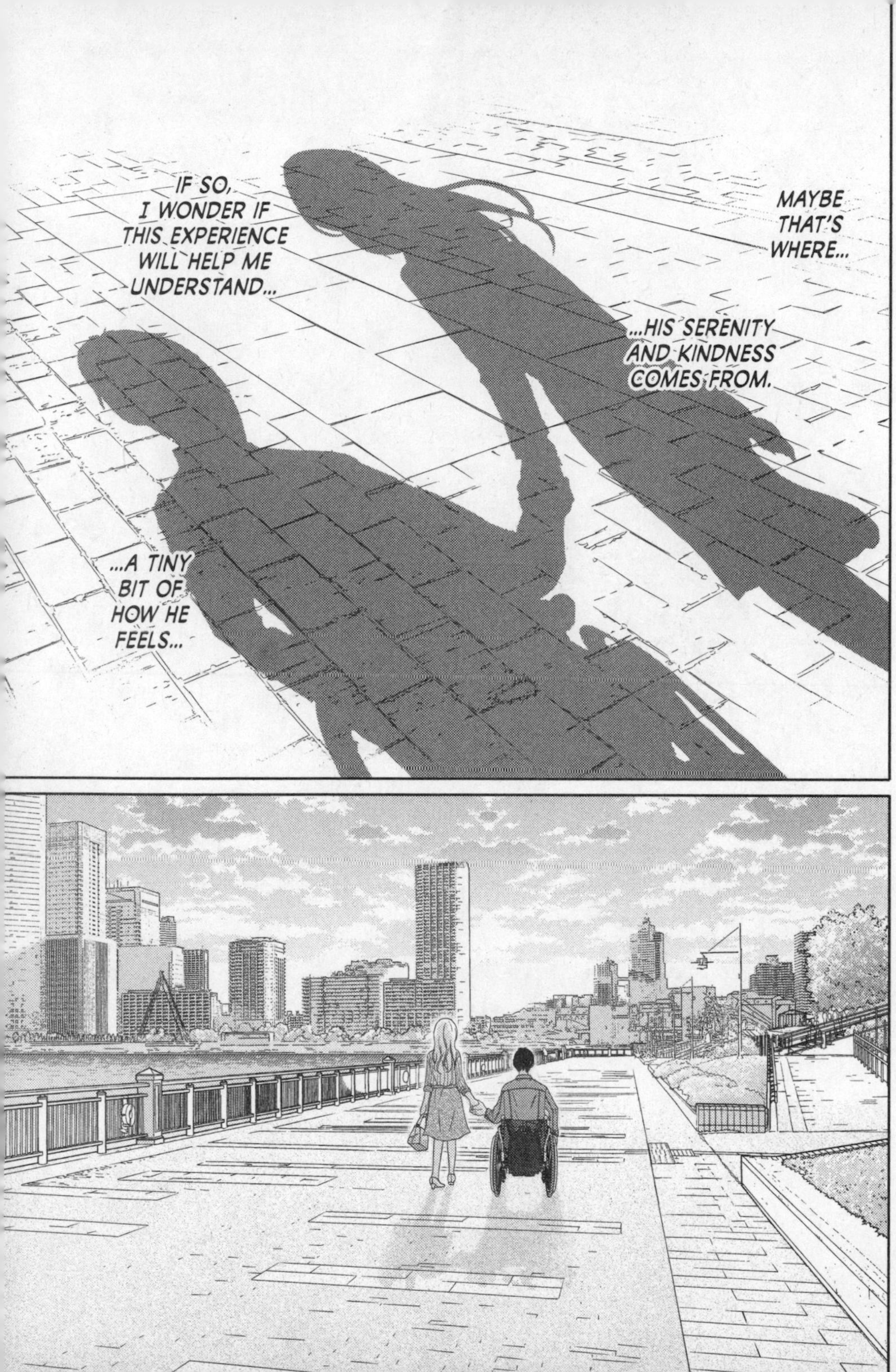
MAYBE THAT'S WHERE...
...HIS SERENITY AND KINDNESS COMES FROM.
IF SO, I WONDER IF THIS EXPERIENCE WILL HELP ME UNDERSTAND...
...A TINY BIT OF HOW HE FEELS...

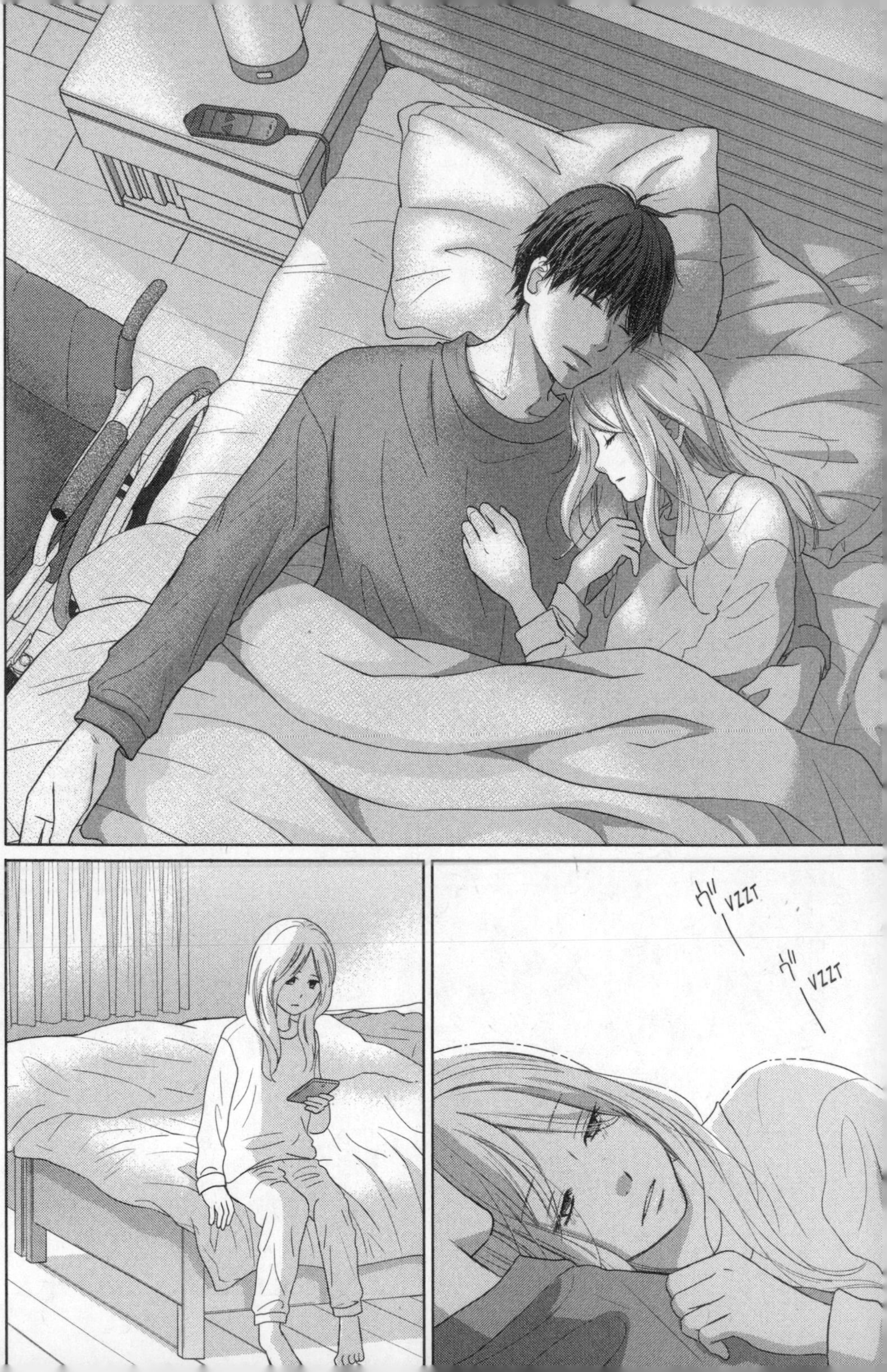
ヴ
VZZT
ヴ
VZZT

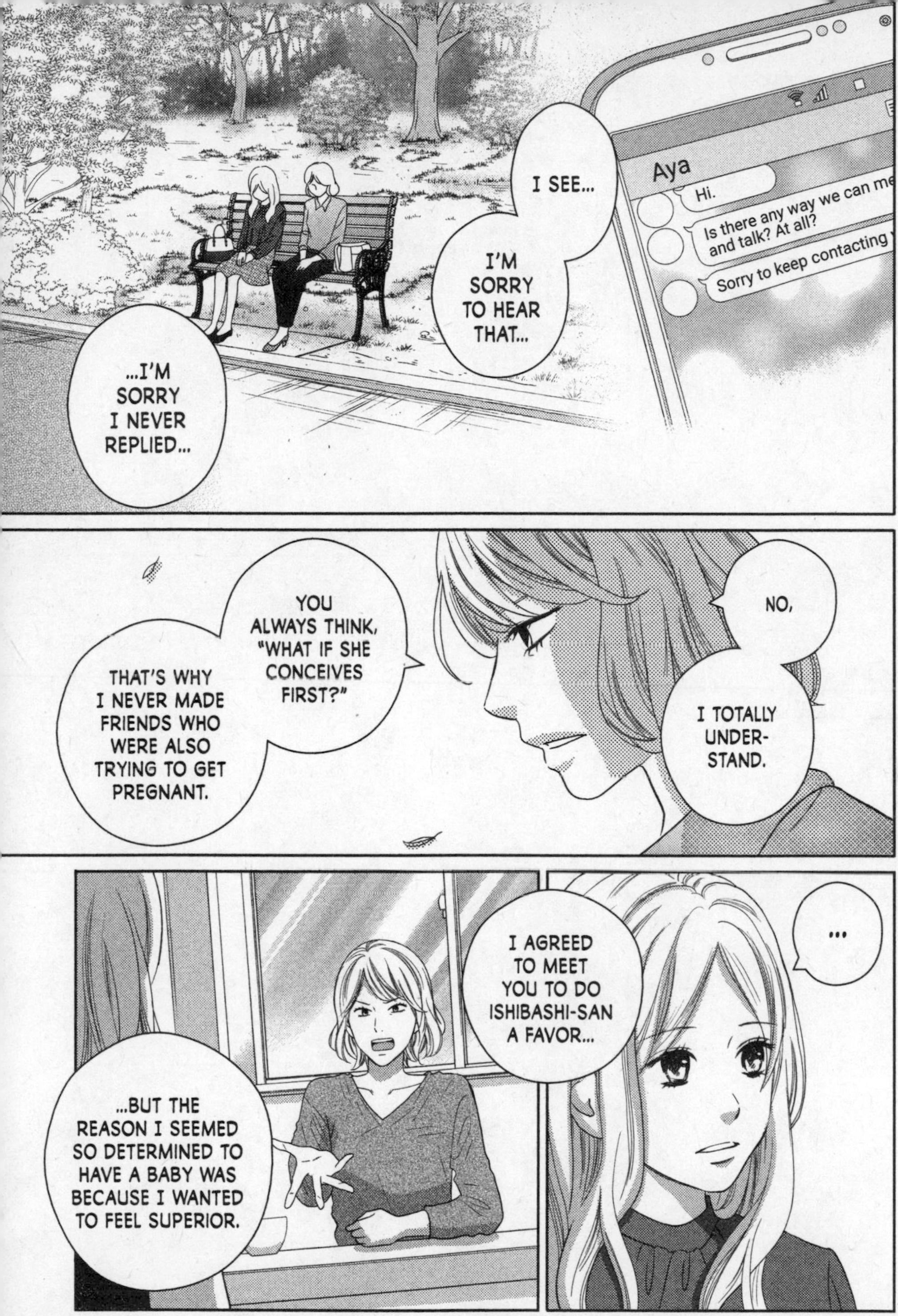
Aya
Hi.
Is there any way we can me
and talk? At all?
Sorry to keep contacting
I SEE...
I'M SORRY TO HEAR THAT...
...I'M SORRY I NEVER REPLIED...
NO,
I TOTALLY UNDER-STAND.
YOU ALWAYS THINK, "WHAT IF SHE CONCEIVES FIRST?"
THAT'S WHY I NEVER MADE FRIENDS WHO WERE ALSO TRYING TO GET PREGNANT.
...
I AGREED TO MEET YOU TO DO ISHIBASHI-SAN A FAVOR...
...BUT THE REASON I SEEMED SO DETERMINED TO HAVE A BABY WAS BECAUSE I WANTED TO FEEL SUPERIOR.

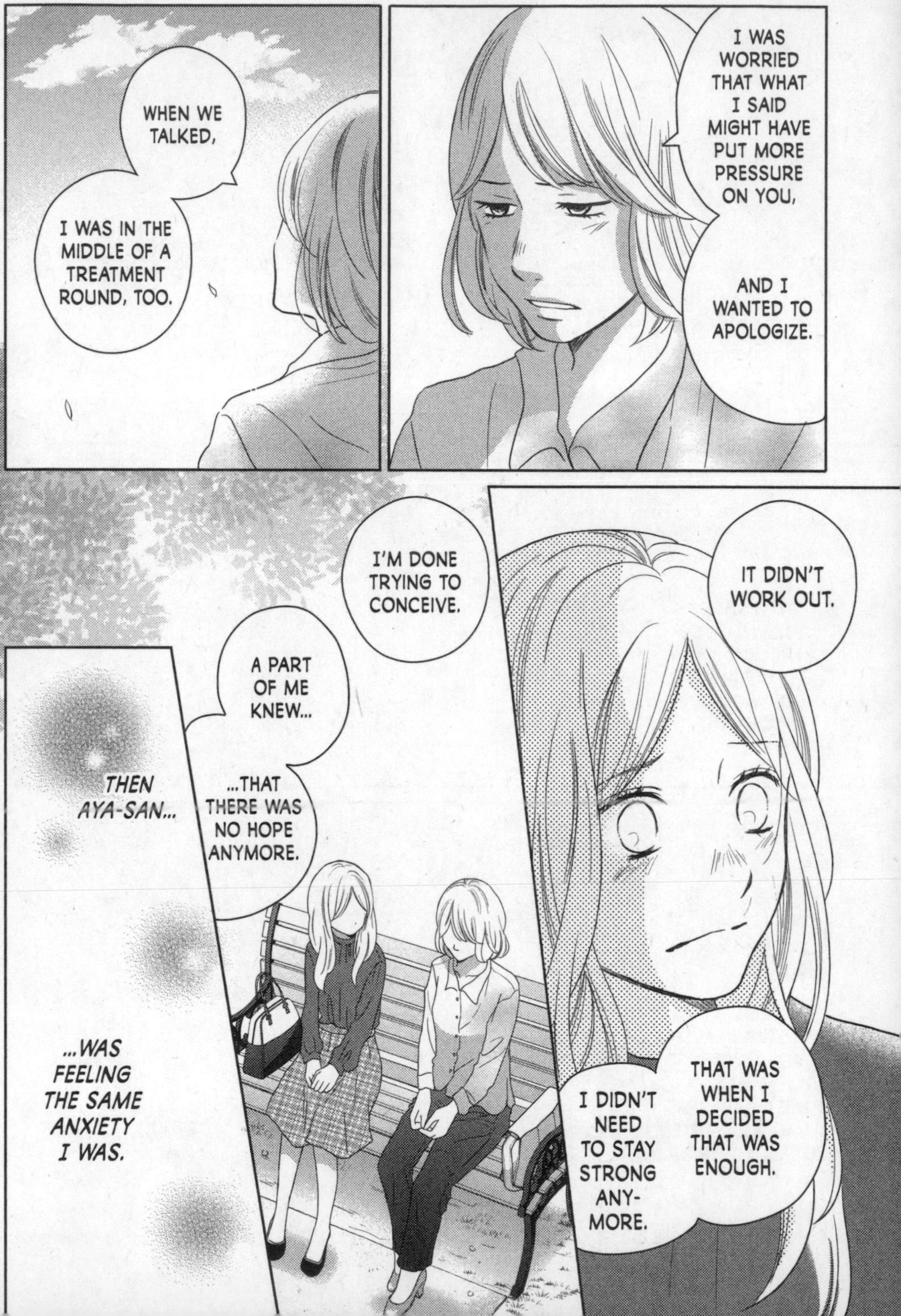
I WAS WORRIED THAT WHAT I SAID MIGHT HAVE PUT MORE PRESSURE ON YOU,
AND I WANTED TO APOLOGIZE.
WHEN WE TALKED,
I WAS IN THE MIDDLE OF A TREATMENT ROUND, TOO.
IT DIDN'T WORK OUT.
I'M DONE TRYING TO CONCEIVE.
A PART OF ME KNEW...
...THAT THERE WAS NO HOPE ANYMORE.
THAT WAS WHEN I DECIDED THAT WAS ENOUGH.
I DIDN'T NEED TO STAY STRONG ANY-MORE.
THEN AYA-SAN...
...WAS FEELING THE SAME ANXIETY I WAS.

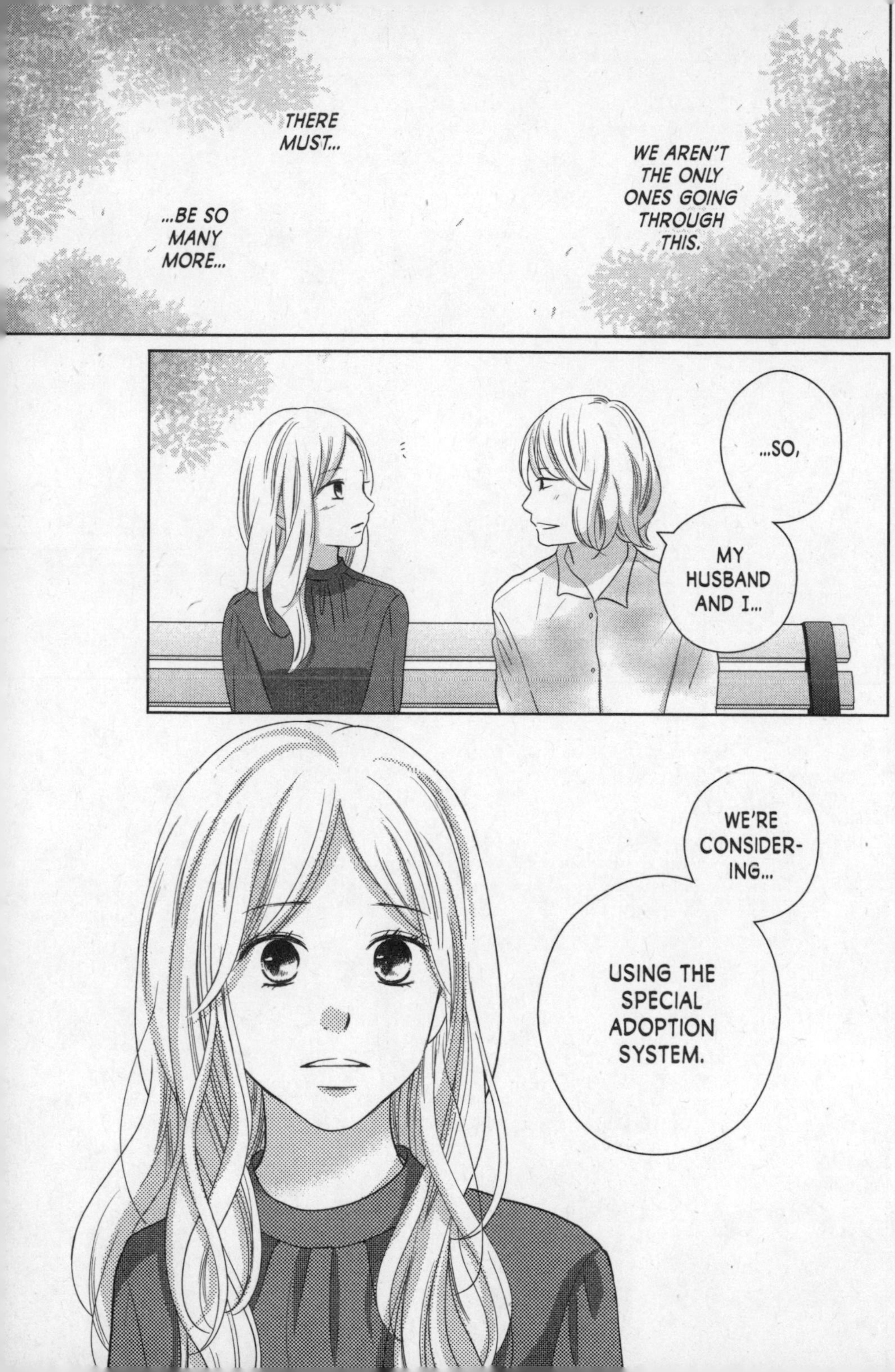
WE AREN'T THE ONLY ONES GOING THROUGH THIS.
THERE MUST...
...BE SO MANY MORE...
...SO,
MY HUSBAND AND I...
WE'RE CONSIDER-ING...
USING THE SPECIAL ADOPTION SYSTEM.

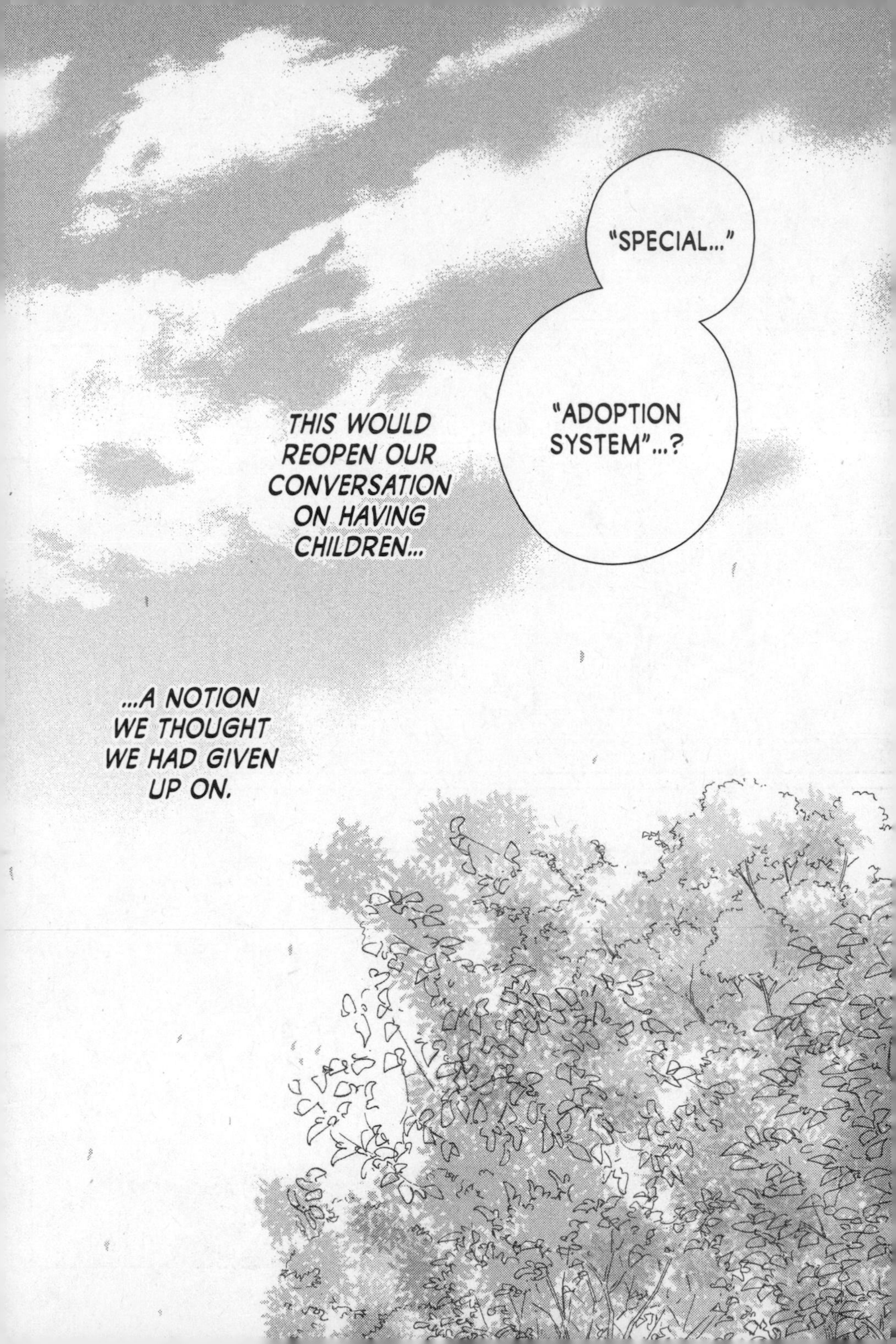
"SPECIAL..."
"ADOPTION SYSTEM"...?
THIS WOULD REOPEN OUR CONVERSATION ON HAVING CHILDREN...
...A NOTION WE THOUGHT WE HAD GIVEN UP ON.

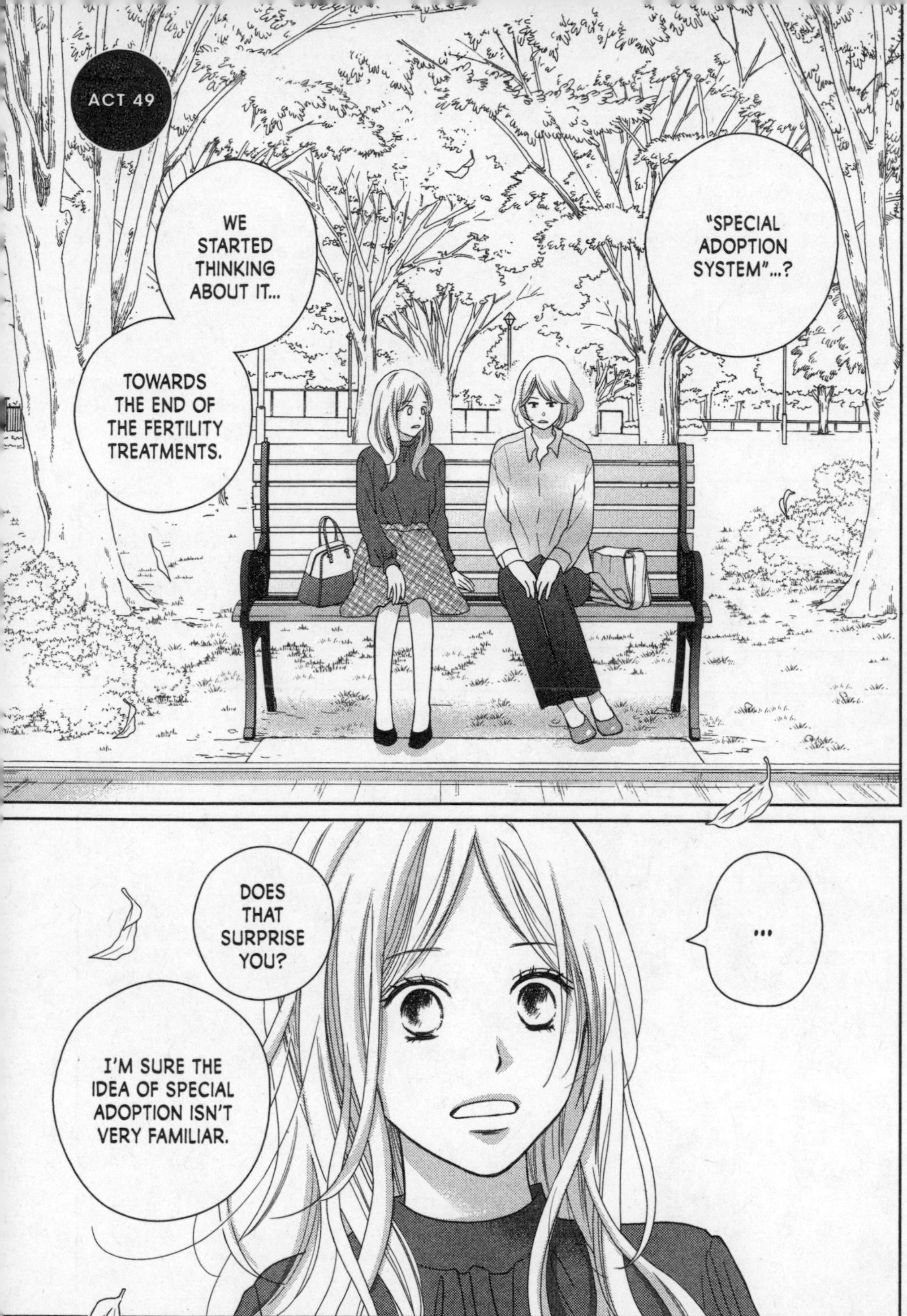
ACT 49
"SPECIAL ADOPTION SYSTEM"...?
WE STARTED THINKING ABOUT IT...
TOWARDS THE END OF THE FERTILITY TREATMENTS.
...
DOES THAT SURPRISE YOU?
I'M SURE THE IDEA OF SPECIAL ADOPTION ISN'T VERY FAMILIAR.

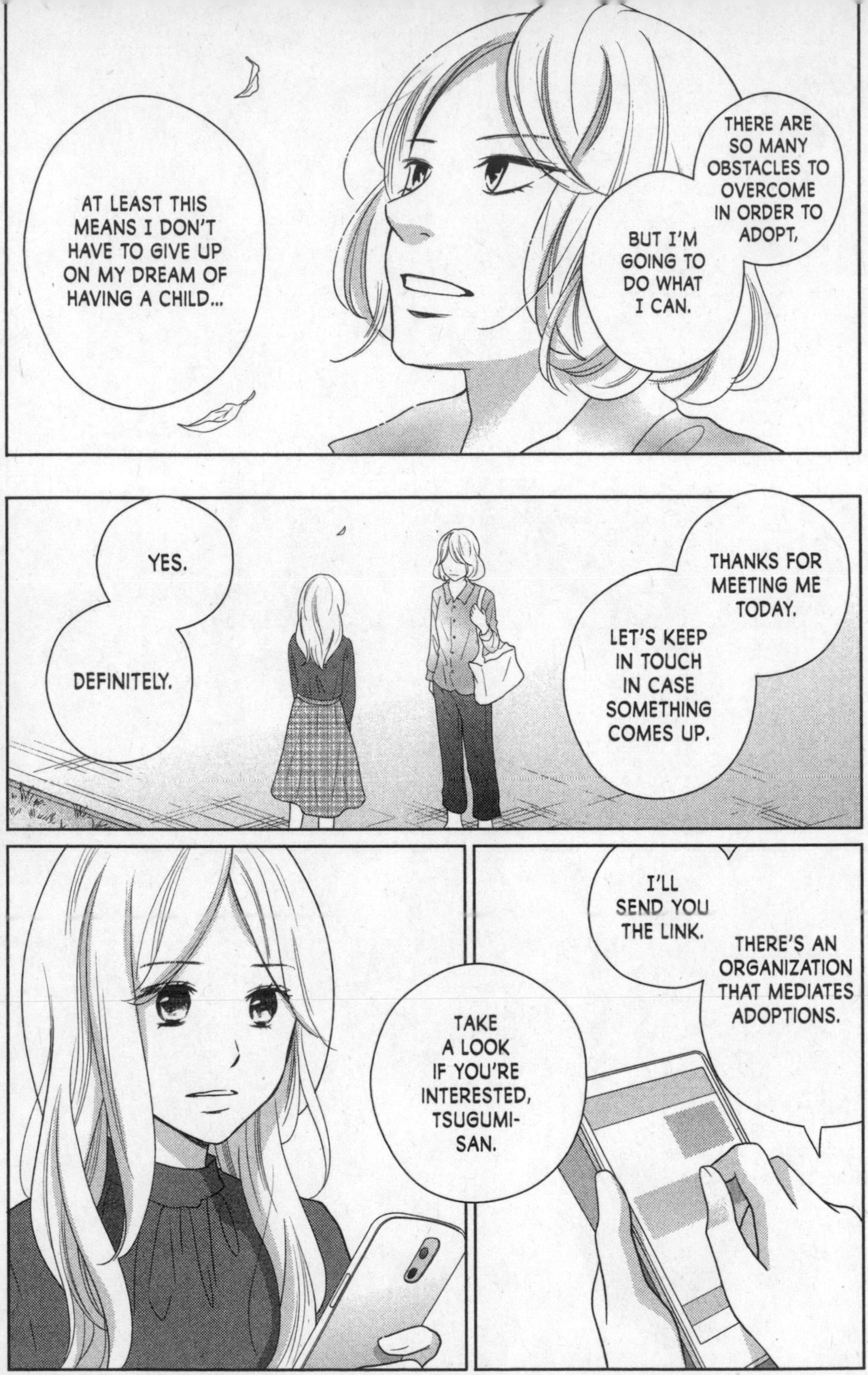
THERE ARE SO MANY OBSTACLES TO OVERCOME IN ORDER TO ADOPT,
BUT I'M GOING TO DO WHAT I CAN.
AT LEAST THIS MEANS I DON'T HAVE TO GIVE UP ON MY DREAM OF HAVING A CHILD...
THANKS FOR MEETING ME TODAY.
LET'S KEEP IN TOUCH IN CASE SOMETHING COMES UP.
YES.
DEFINITELY.
THERE'S AN ORGANIZATION THAT MEDIATES ADOPTIONS.
I'LL SEND YOU THE LINK.
TAKE A LOOK IF YOU'RE INTERESTED, TSUGUMI-SAN.

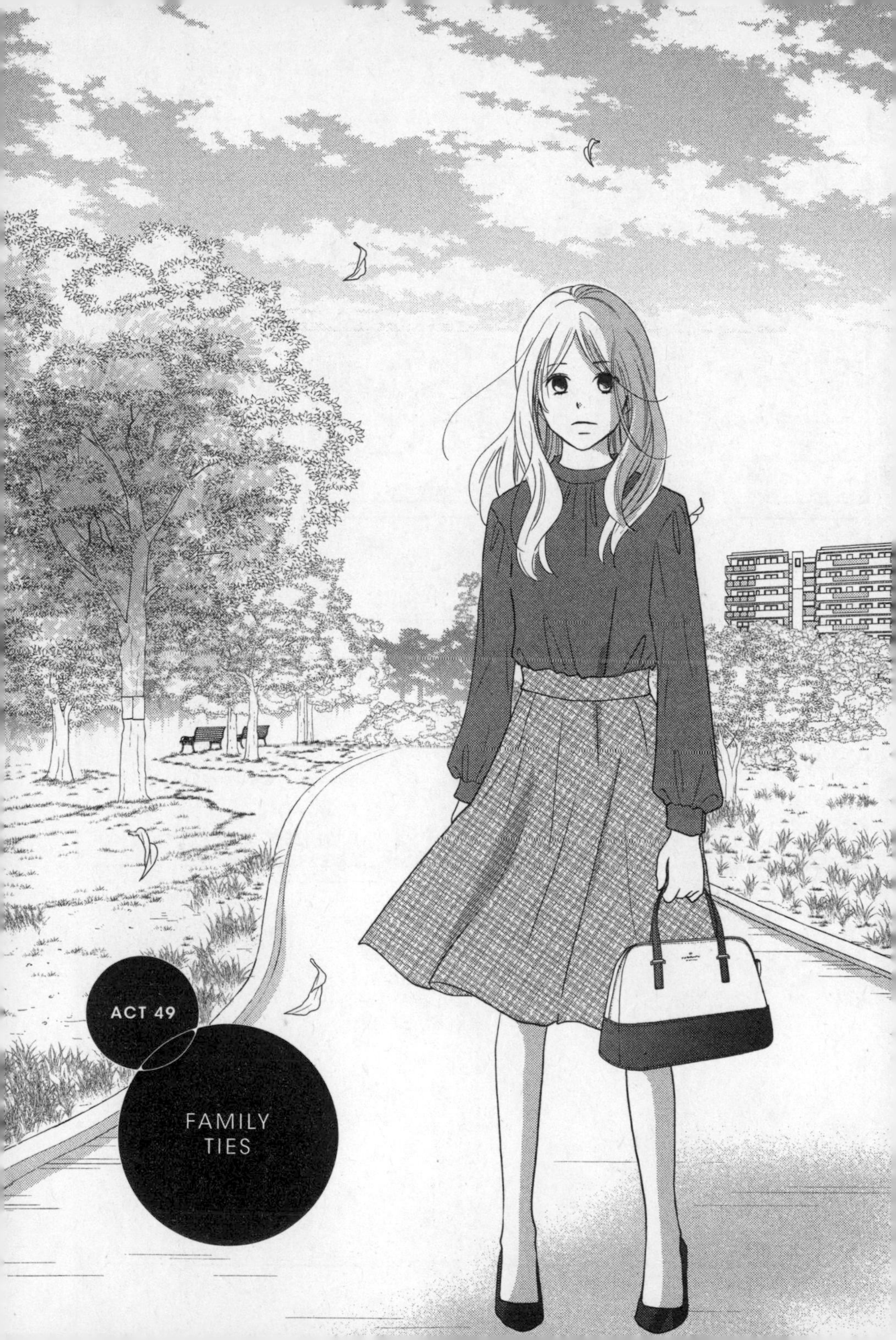
ACT 49
FAMILY TIES

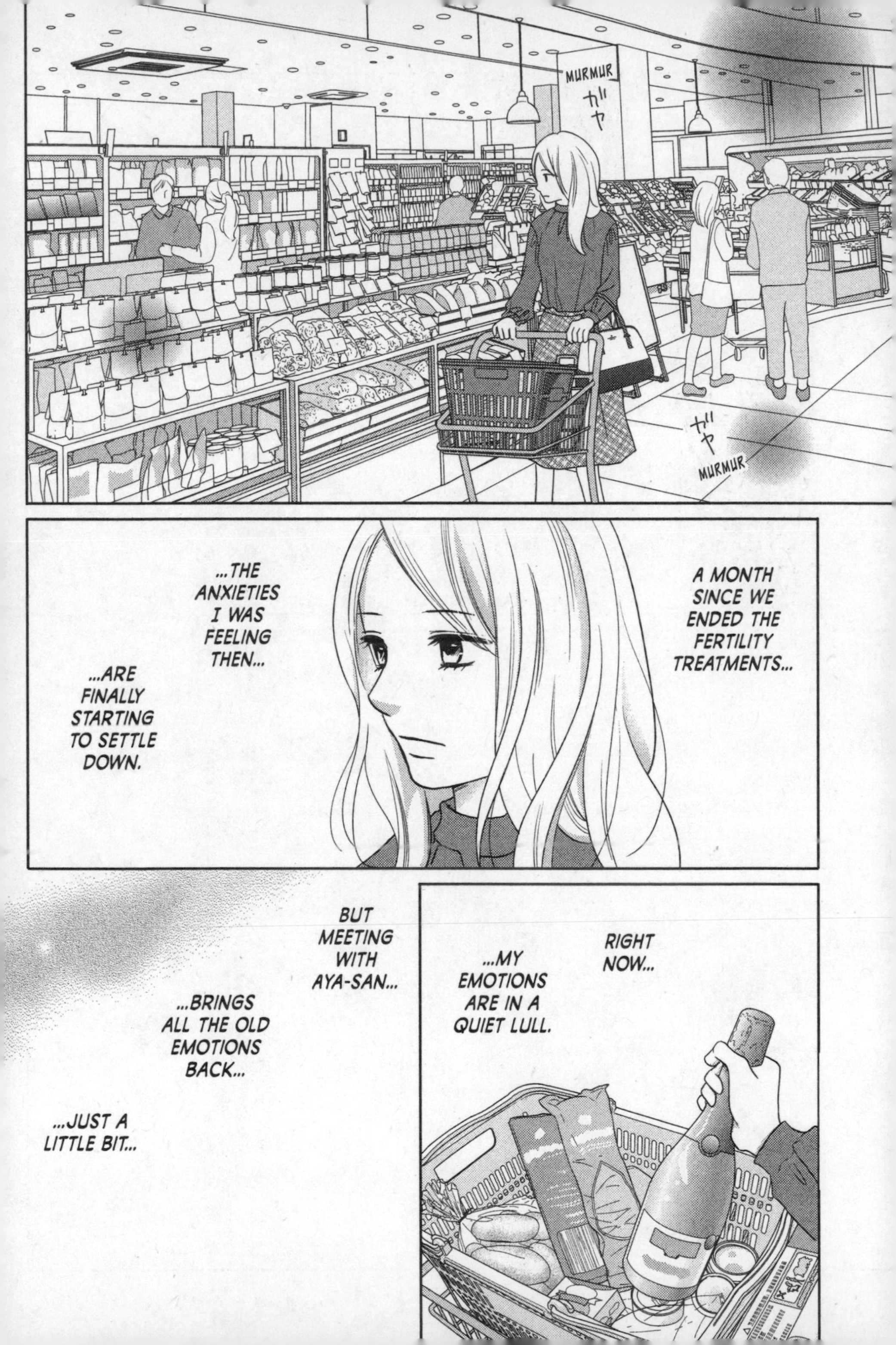

MURMUR
ガヤ
ガヤ
MURMUR
A MONTH SINCE WE ENDED THE FERTILITY TREATMENTS...
...THE ANXIETIES I WAS FEELING THEN...
...ARE FINALLY STARTING TO SETTLE DOWN.
RIGHT NOW...
...MY EMOTIONS ARE IN A QUIET LULL.
BUT MEETING WITH AYA-SAN...
...BRINGS ALL THE OLD EMOTIONS BACK...
...JUST A LITTLE BIT...

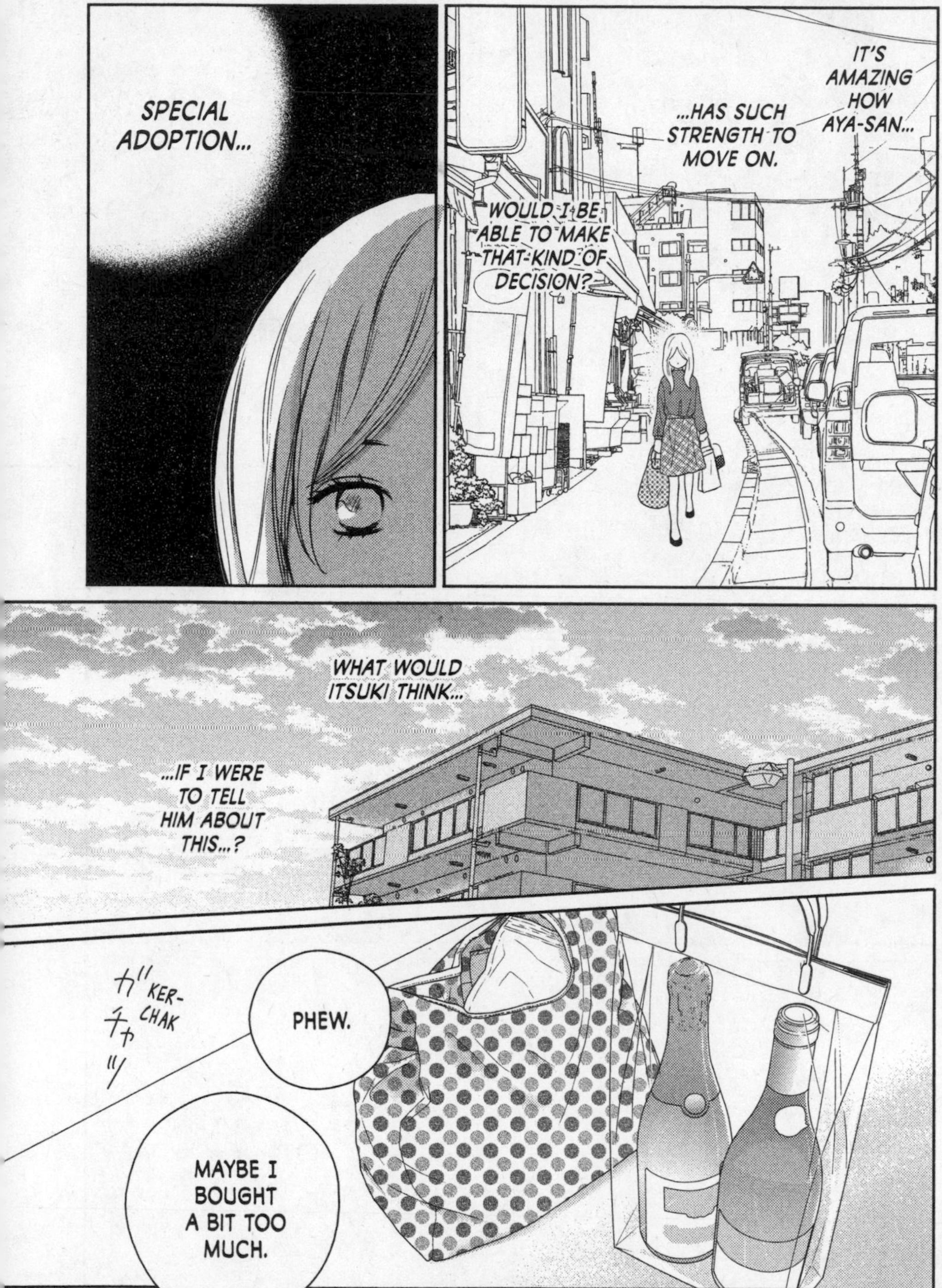
IT'S AMAZING HOW AYA-SAN...
...HAS SUCH STRENGTH TO MOVE ON.
WOULD I BE ABLE TO MAKE THAT KIND OF DECISION?
SPECIAL ADOPTION...
WHAT WOULD ITSUKI THINK...
...IF I WERE TO TELL HIM ABOUT THIS...?
ガチャッ KER-CHAK
PHEW.
MAYBE I BOUGHT A BIT TOO MUCH.

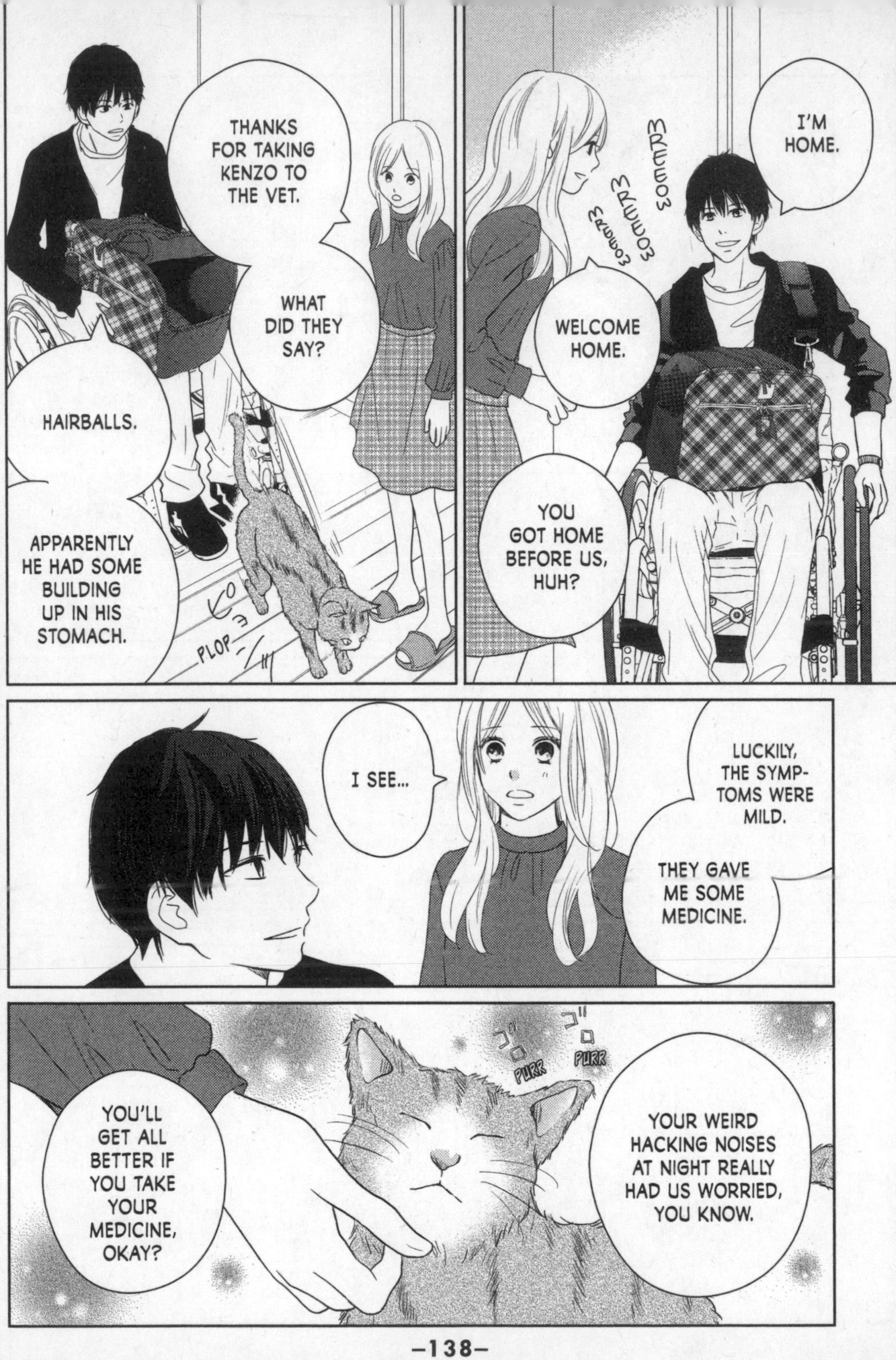
I'M HOME.
MREOW
MREOW
MREOW
WELCOME HOME.
YOU GOT HOME BEFORE US, HUH?
THANKS FOR TAKING KENZO TO THE VET.
WHAT DID THEY SAY?
HAIRBALLS.
APPARENTLY HE HAD SOME BUILDING UP IN HIS STOMACH.
PLOP
LUCKILY, THE SYMP-TOMS WERE MILD.
THEY GAVE ME SOME MEDICINE.
I SEE...
YOUR WEIRD HACKING NOISES AT NIGHT REALLY HAD US WORRIED, YOU KNOW.
ゴロ PURR
ゴロ PURR
YOU'LL GET ALL BETTER IF YOU TAKE YOUR MEDICINE, OKAY?

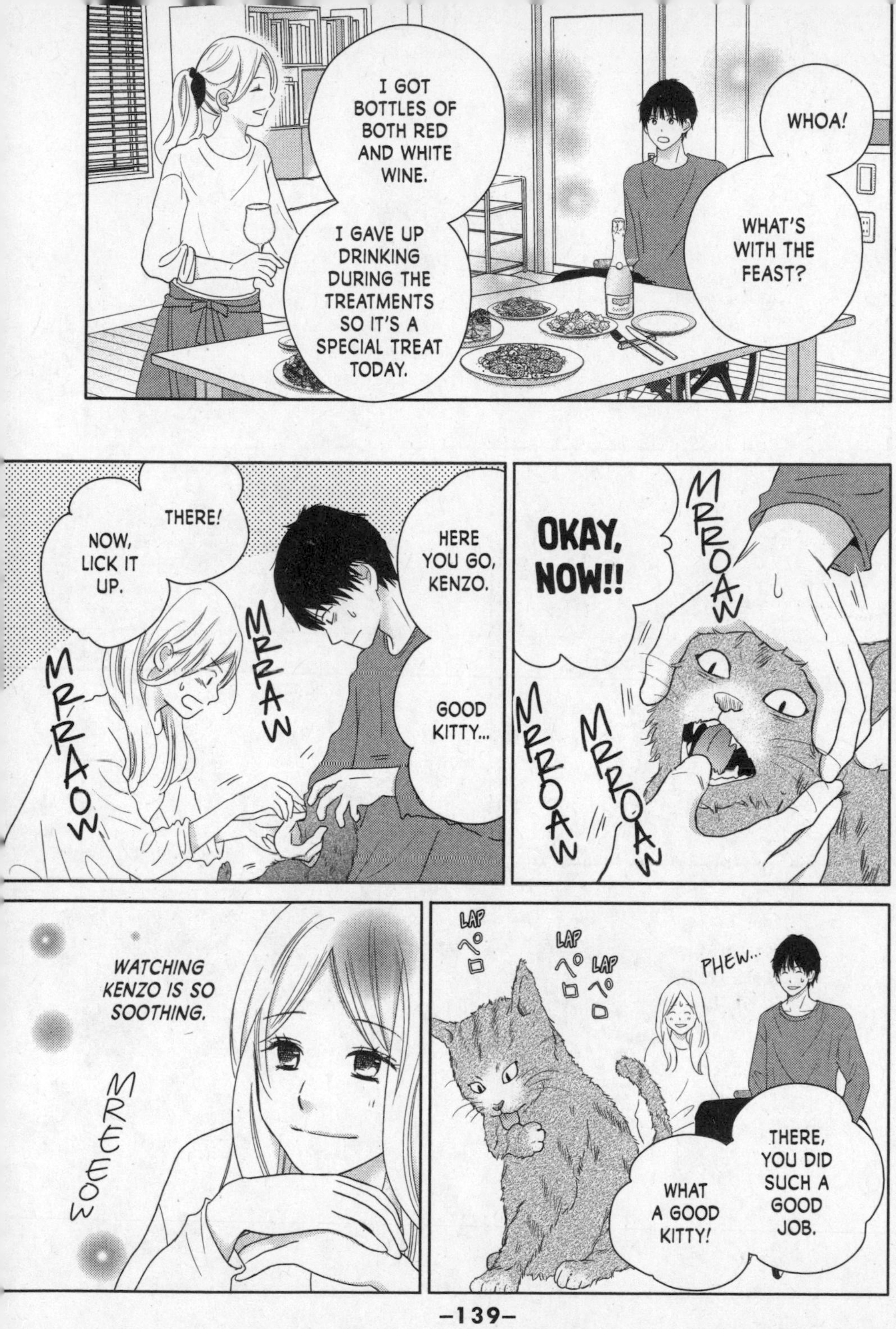
WHOA!
WHAT'S WITH THE FEAST?
I GOT BOTTLES OF BOTH RED AND WHITE WINE.
I GAVE UP DRINKING DURING THE TREATMENTS SO IT'S A SPECIAL TREAT TODAY.
MRROAW
OKAY, NOW!!
MRROAW
MRROAW
HERE YOU GO, KENZO.
GOOD KITTY...
MRRAW
THERE!
NOW, LICK IT UP.
MRRAOW
PHEW...
THERE, YOU DID SUCH A GOOD JOB.
WHAT A GOOD KITTY!
LAP
ペロ
LAP
ペロ
LAP
ペロ
WATCHING KENZO IS SO SOOTHING.
MREEOW

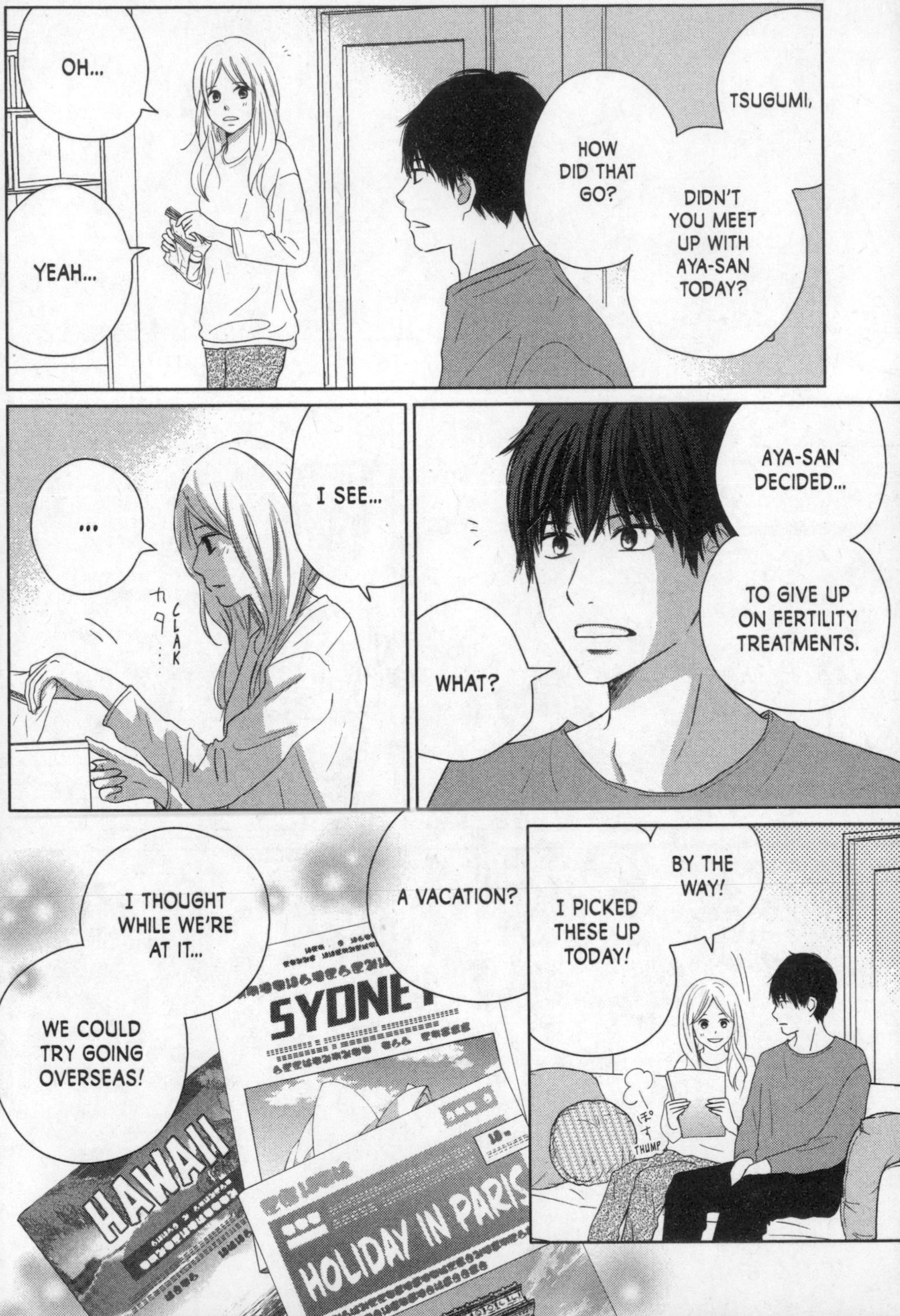
TSUGUMI,
DIDN'T YOU MEET UP WITH AYA-SAN TODAY?
HOW DID THAT GO?
OH...
YEAH...
AYA-SAN DECIDED...
TO GIVE UP ON FERTILITY TREATMENTS.
WHAT?
I SEE...
...
カタ CLAK
BY THE WAY!
I PICKED THESE UP TODAY!
ぽす THUMP
A VACATION?
I THOUGHT WHILE WE'RE AT IT...
WE COULD TRY GOING OVERSEAS!
HAWAII
HOLIDAY IN PARIS

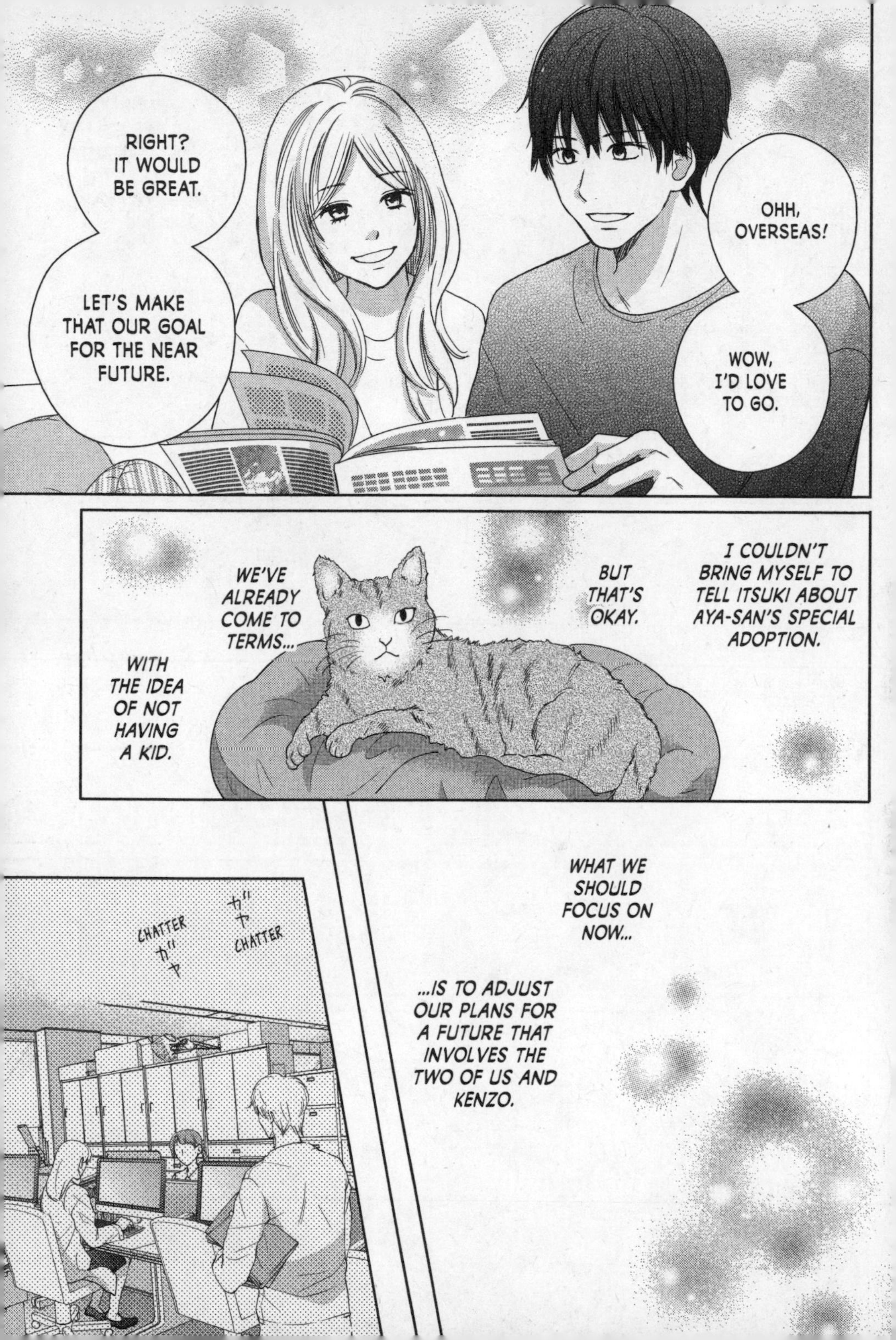
OHH, OVERSEAS!
WOW, I'D LOVE TO GO.
RIGHT? IT WOULD BE GREAT.
LET'S MAKE THAT OUR GOAL FOR THE NEAR FUTURE.
I COULDN'T BRING MYSELF TO TELL ITSUKI ABOUT AYA-SAN'S SPECIAL ADOPTION.
BUT THAT'S OKAY.
WE'VE ALREADY COME TO TERMS...
WITH THE IDEA OF NOT HAVING A KID.
WHAT WE SHOULD FOCUS ON NOW...
...IS TO ADJUST OUR PLANS FOR A FUTURE THAT INVOLVES THE TWO OF US AND KENZO.
ガヤ
CHATTER
ガヤ
CHATTER

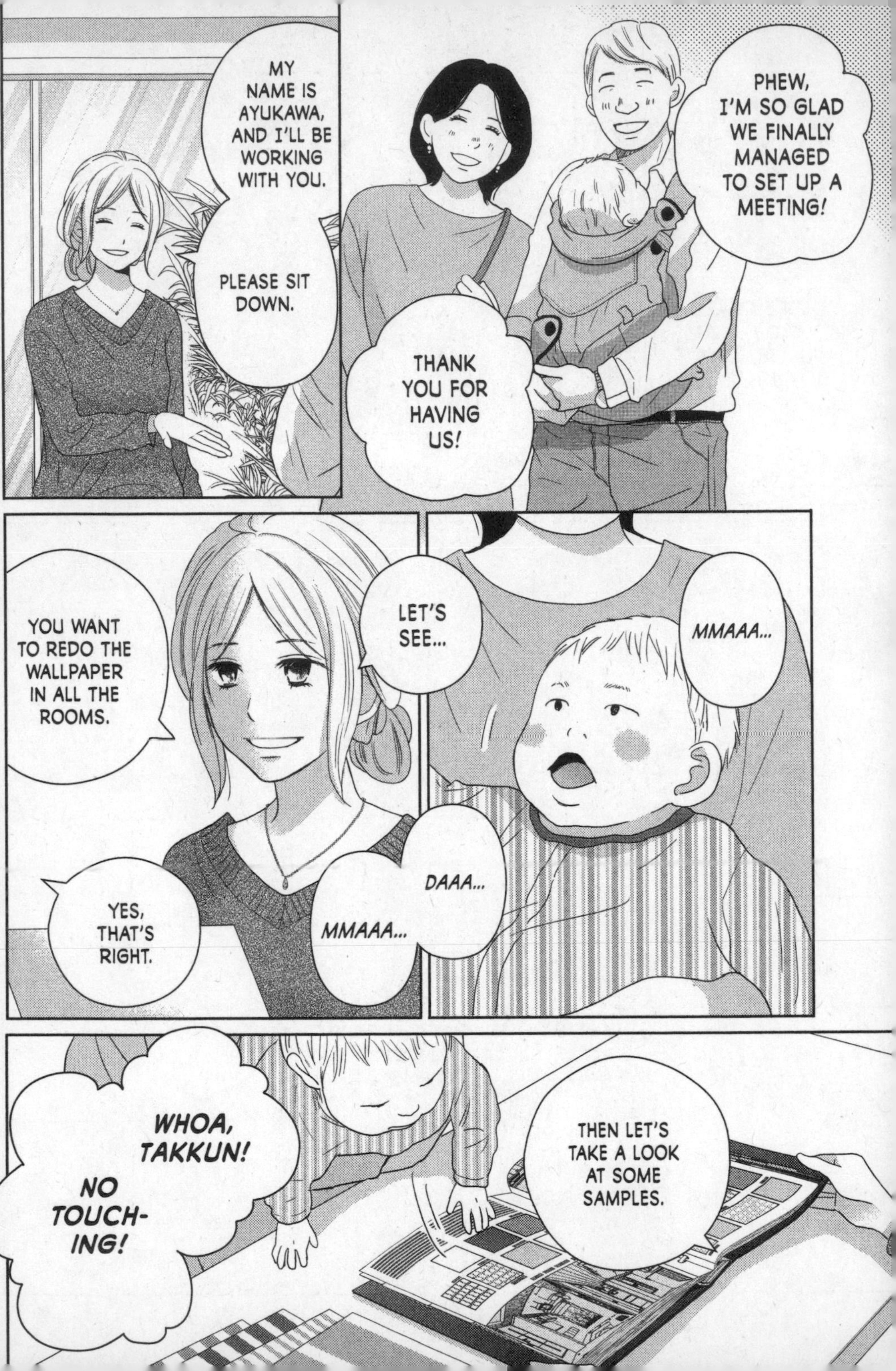
PHEW, I'M SO GLAD WE FINALLY MANAGED TO SET UP A MEETING!
THANK YOU FOR HAVING US!
MY NAME IS AYUKAWA, AND I'LL BE WORKING WITH YOU.
PLEASE SIT DOWN.
MMAAA...
DAAA...
MMAAA...
LET'S SEE...
YOU WANT TO REDO THE WALLPAPER IN ALL THE ROOMS.
YES, THAT'S RIGHT.
THEN LET'S TAKE A LOOK AT SOME SAMPLES.
WHOA, TAKKUN!
NO TOUCH-ING!

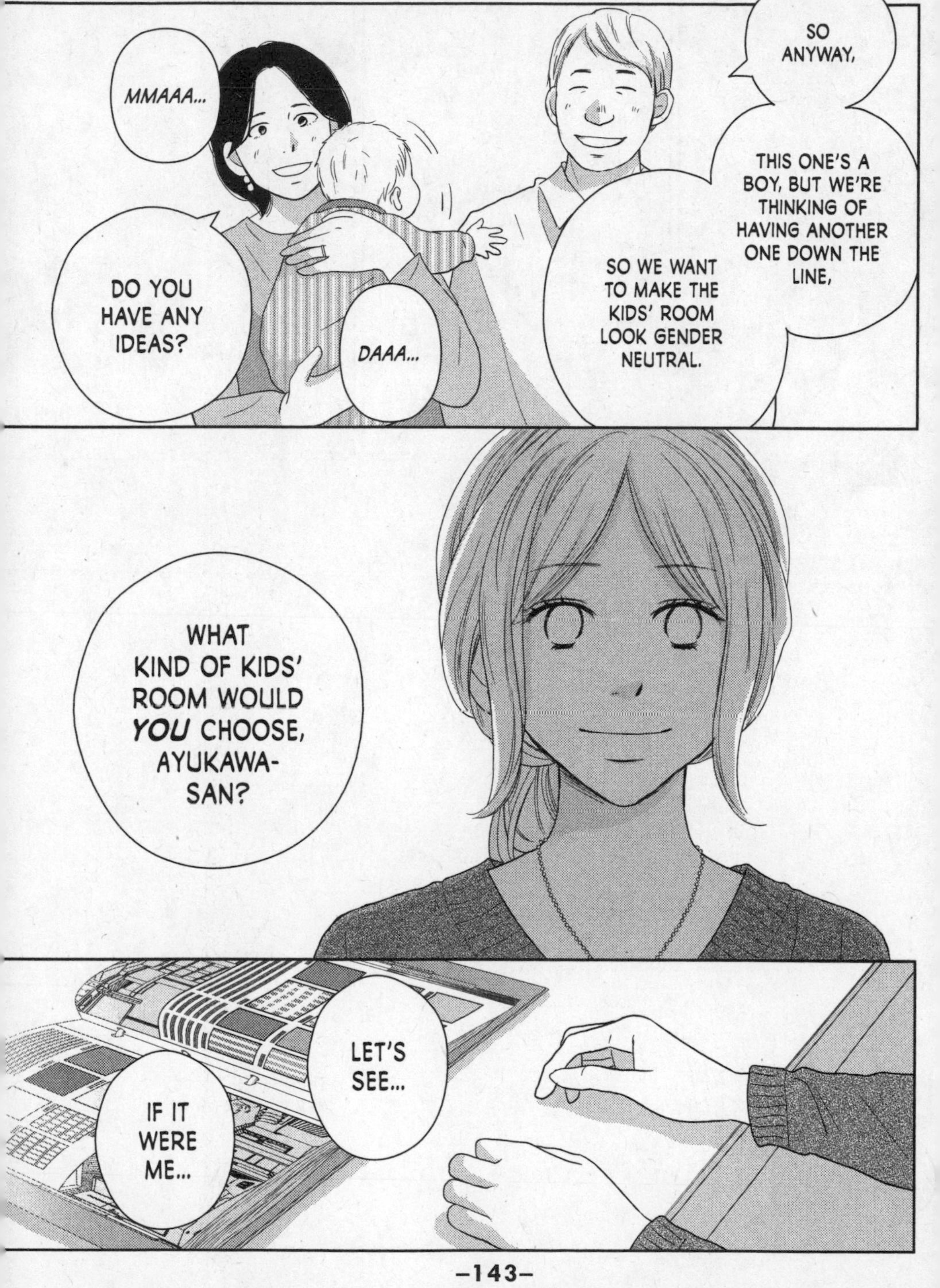
SO ANYWAY,
THIS ONE'S A BOY, BUT WE'RE THINKING OF HAVING ANOTHER ONE DOWN THE LINE,
SO WE WANT TO MAKE THE KIDS' ROOM LOOK GENDER NEUTRAL.
MMAAA...
DAAA...
DO YOU HAVE ANY IDEAS?
WHAT KIND OF KIDS' ROOM WOULD *YOU* CHOOSE, AYUKAWA-SAN?
LET'S SEE...
IF IT WERE ME...

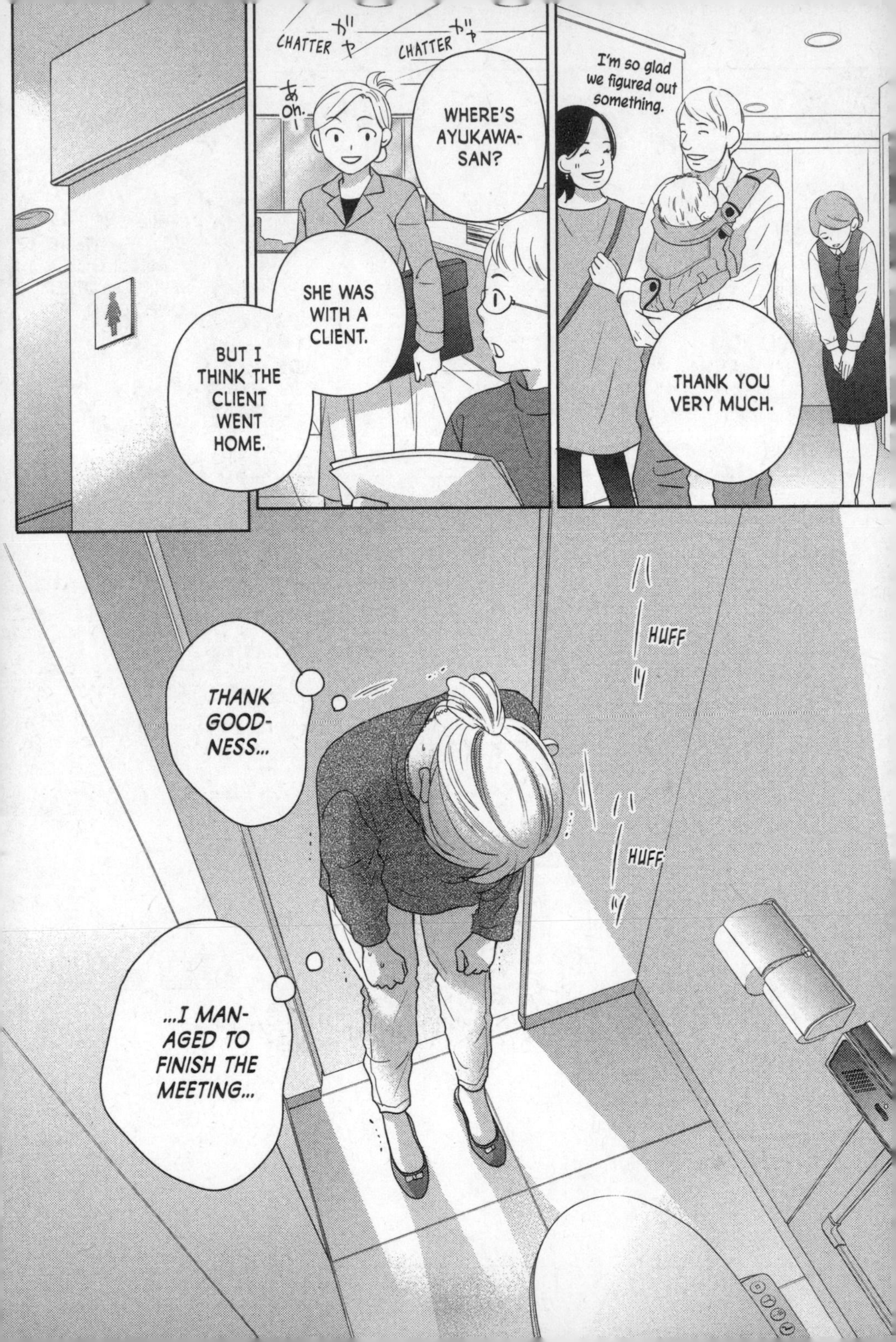
I'm so glad we figured out something.
THANK YOU VERY MUCH.
CHATTER ガヤ
CHATTER ガヤ
WHERE'S AYUKAWA-SAN?
あ Oh.
SHE WAS WITH A CLIENT.
BUT I THINK THE CLIENT WENT HOME.
ハーッ HUFF
ハーッ HUFF
THANK GOODNESS...
...I MANAGED TO FINISH THE MEETING...

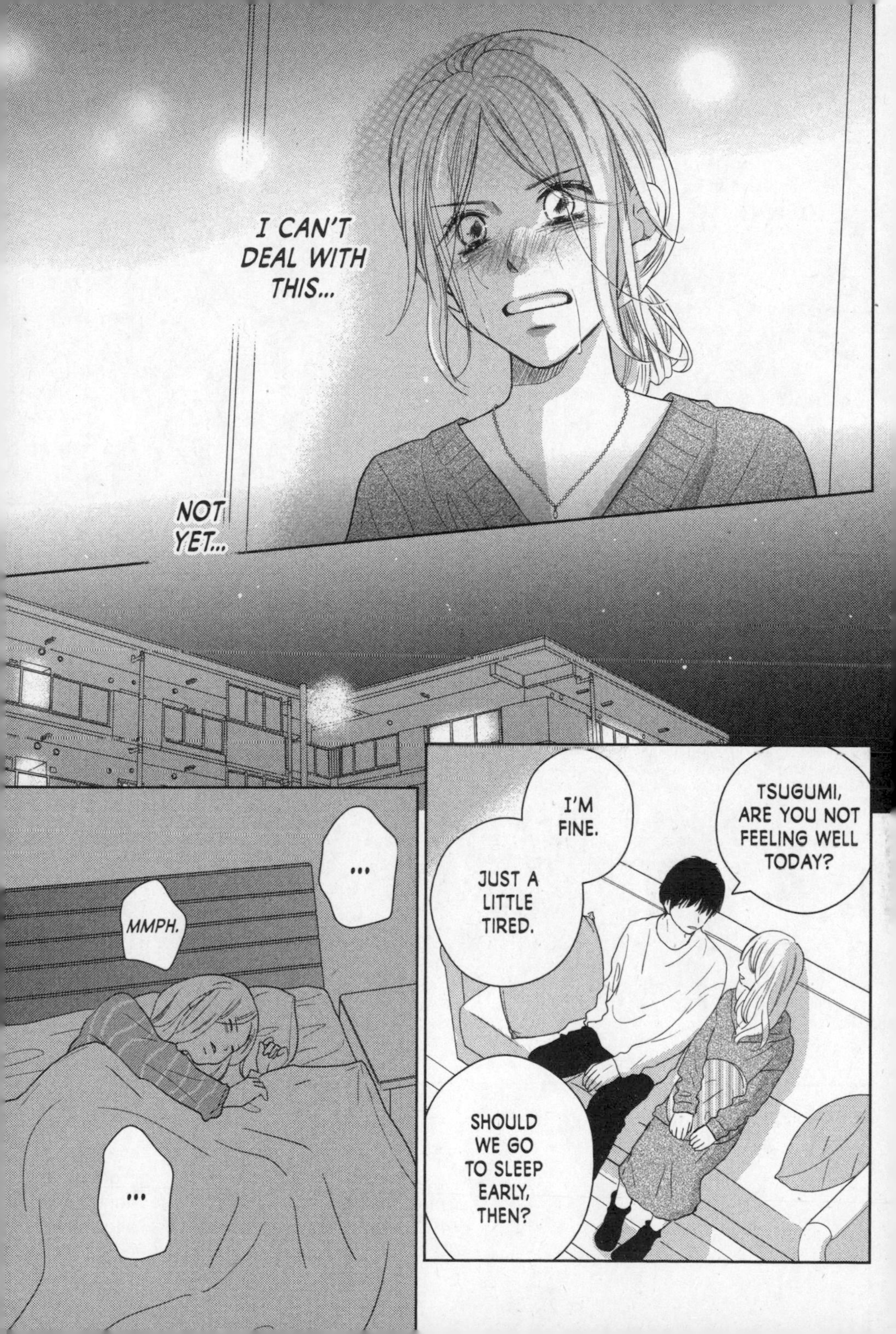
I CAN'T DEAL WITH THIS...
NOT YET...
TSUGUMI, ARE YOU NOT FEELING WELL TODAY?
I'M FINE.
JUST A LITTLE TIRED.
SHOULD WE GO TO SLEEP EARLY, THEN?
...
MMPH.
...

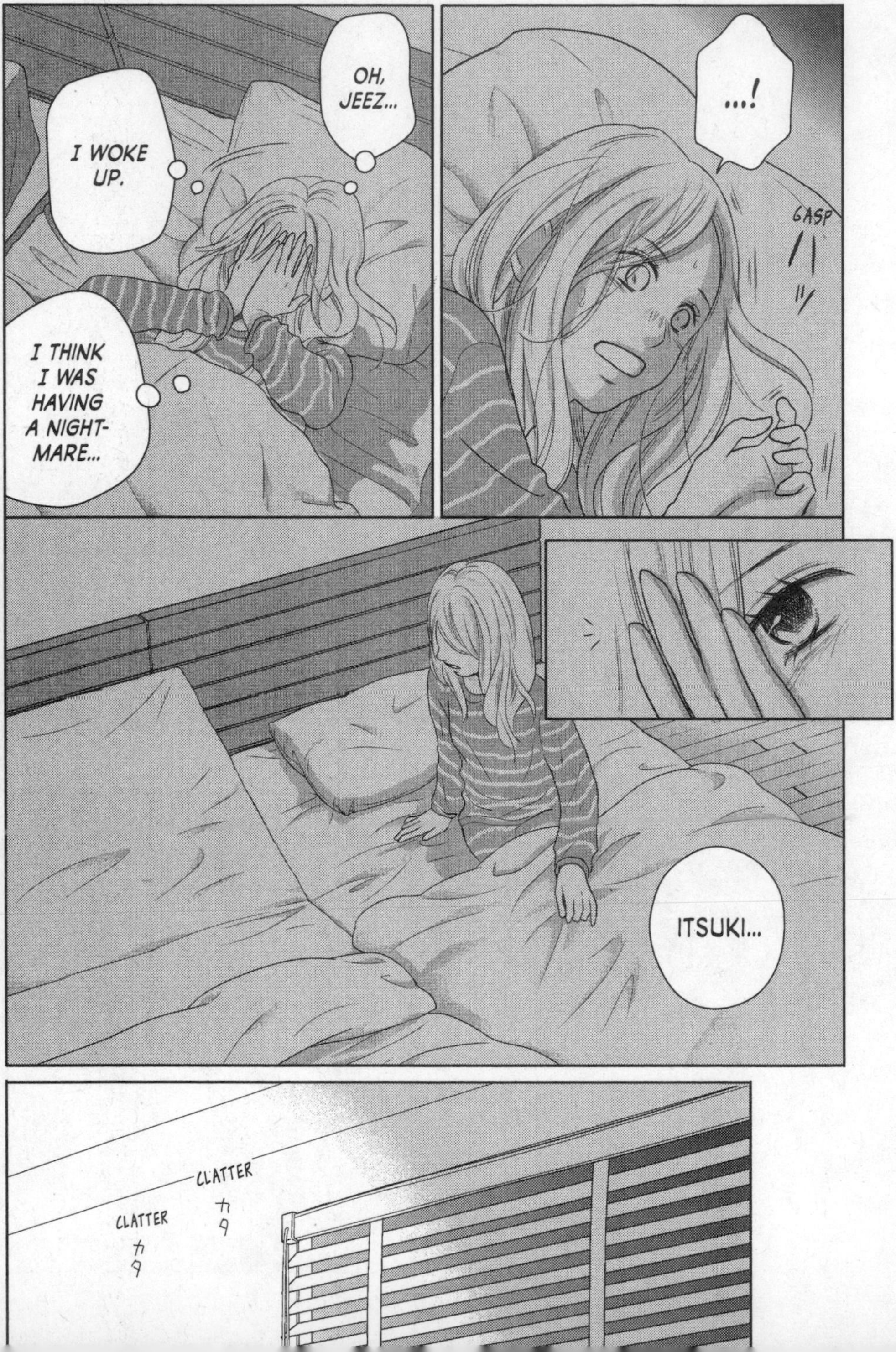
...!
GASP
OH, JEEZ...
I WOKE UP.
I THINK I WAS HAVING A NIGHT-MARE...
ITSUKI...
CLATTER
カタ
CLATTER
カタ

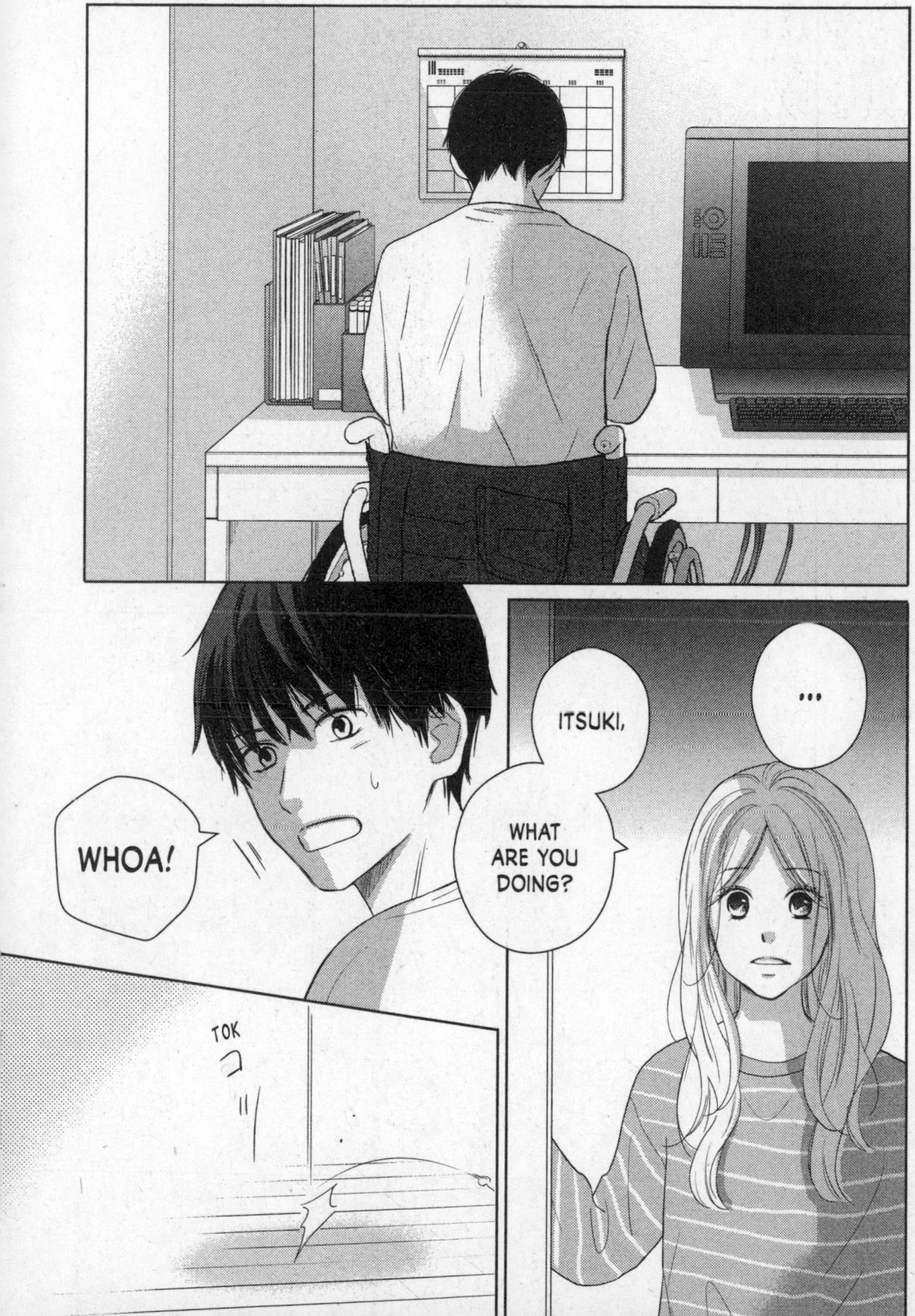
...
ITSUKI,
WHAT ARE YOU DOING?
WHOA!
TOK

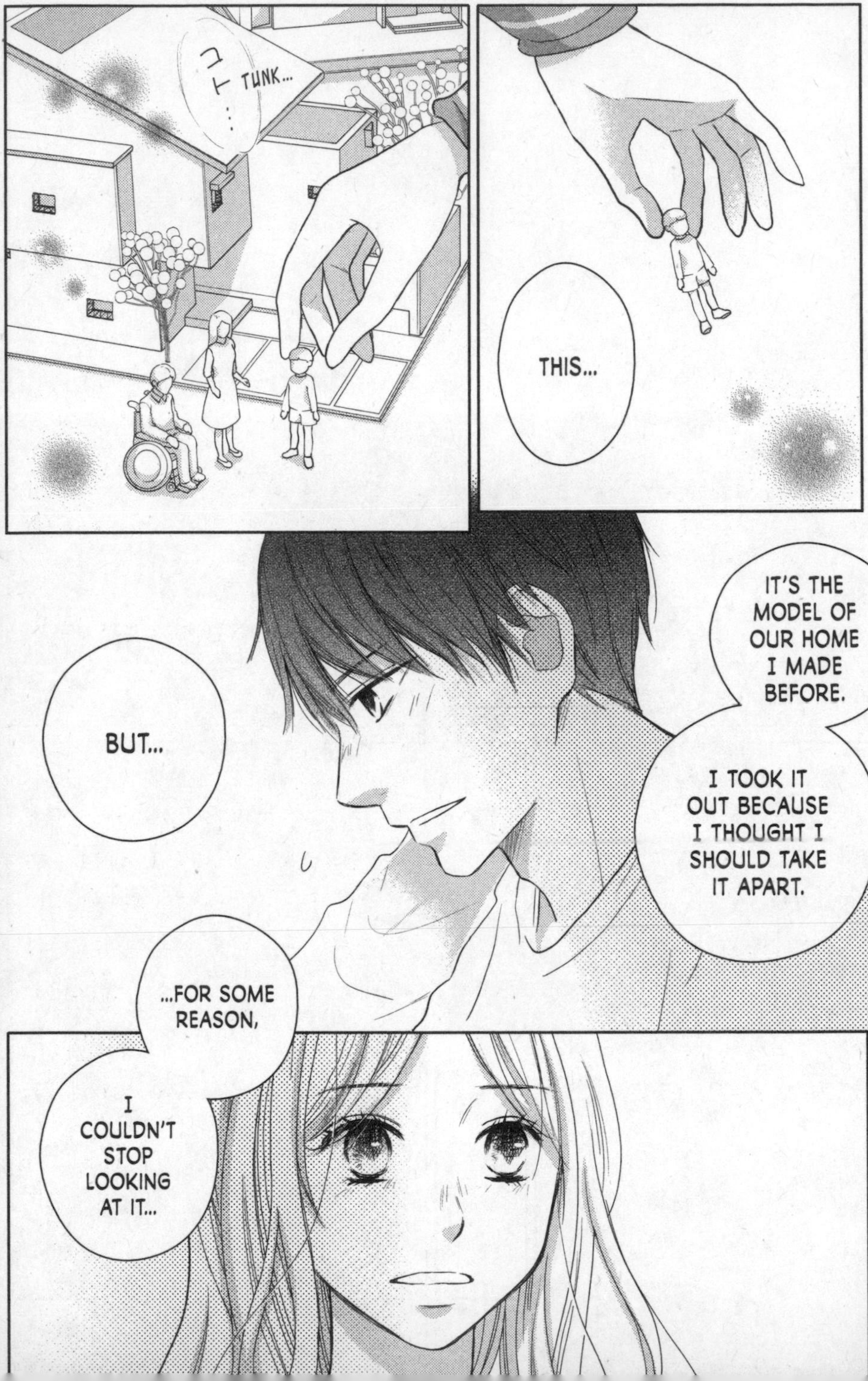
THIS...
コト
TUNK...
IT'S THE MODEL OF OUR HOME I MADE BEFORE.
I TOOK IT OUT BECAUSE I THOUGHT I SHOULD TAKE IT APART.
BUT...
...FOR SOME REASON,
I COULDN'T STOP LOOKING AT IT...

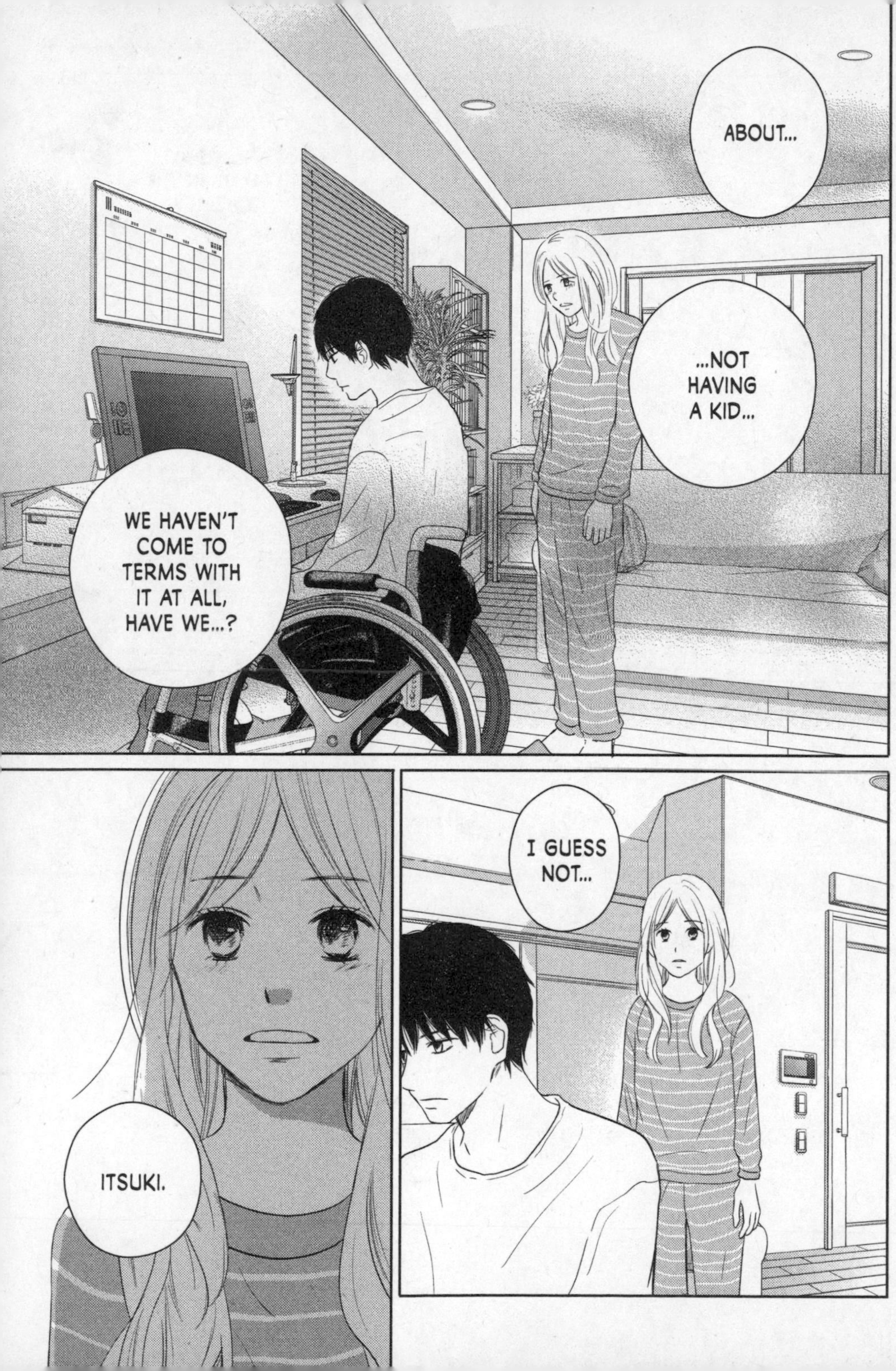
ABOUT...
...NOT HAVING A KID...
WE HAVEN'T COME TO TERMS WITH IT AT ALL, HAVE WE...?
I GUESS NOT...
ITSUKI.

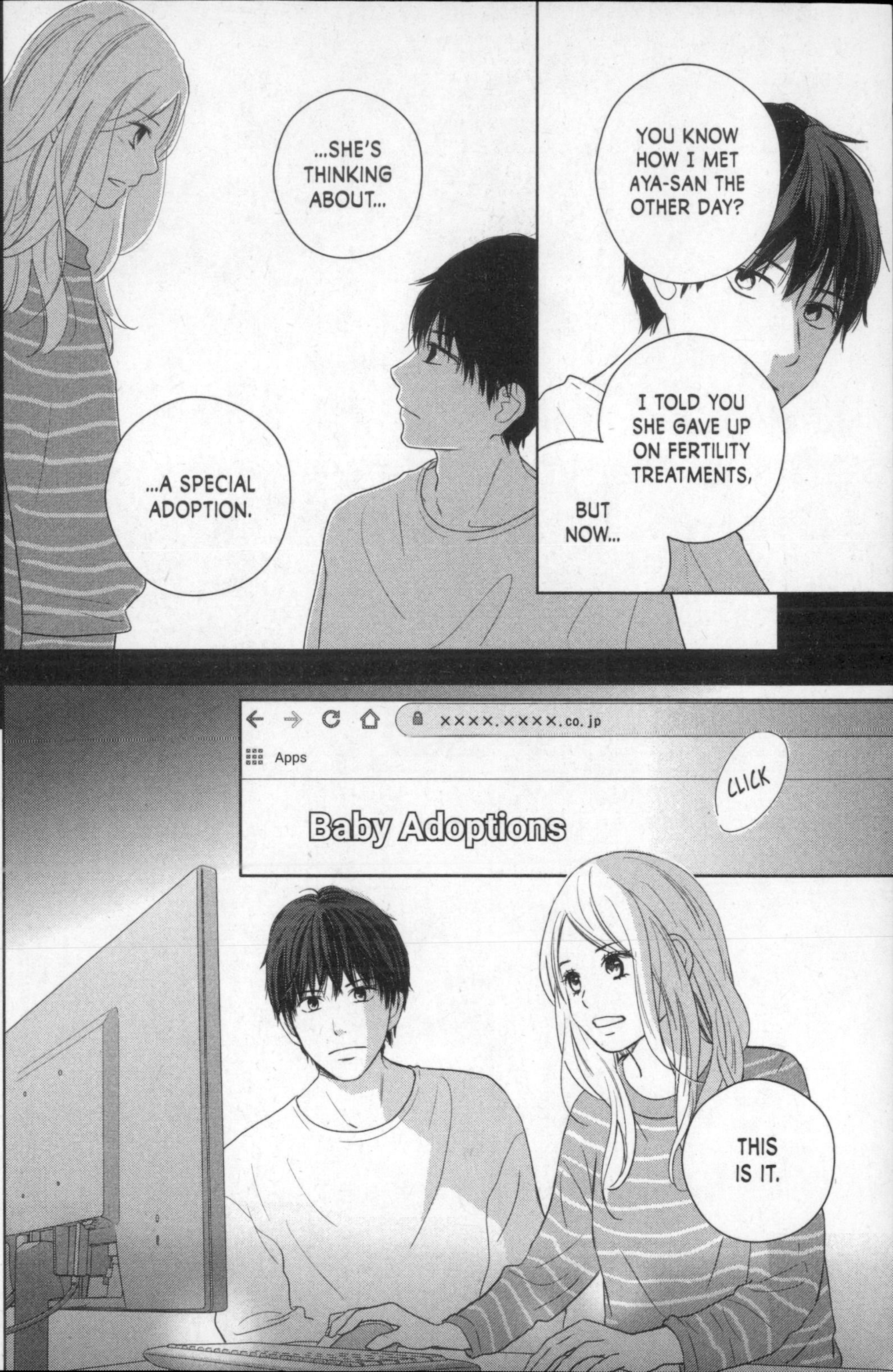
YOU KNOW HOW I MET AYA-SAN THE OTHER DAY?
I TOLD YOU SHE GAVE UP ON FERTILITY TREATMENTS,
BUT NOW...
...SHE'S THINKING ABOUT...
...A SPECIAL ADOPTION.
xxxx.xxxx.co.jp
Apps
Baby Adoptions
CLICK
THIS IS IT.

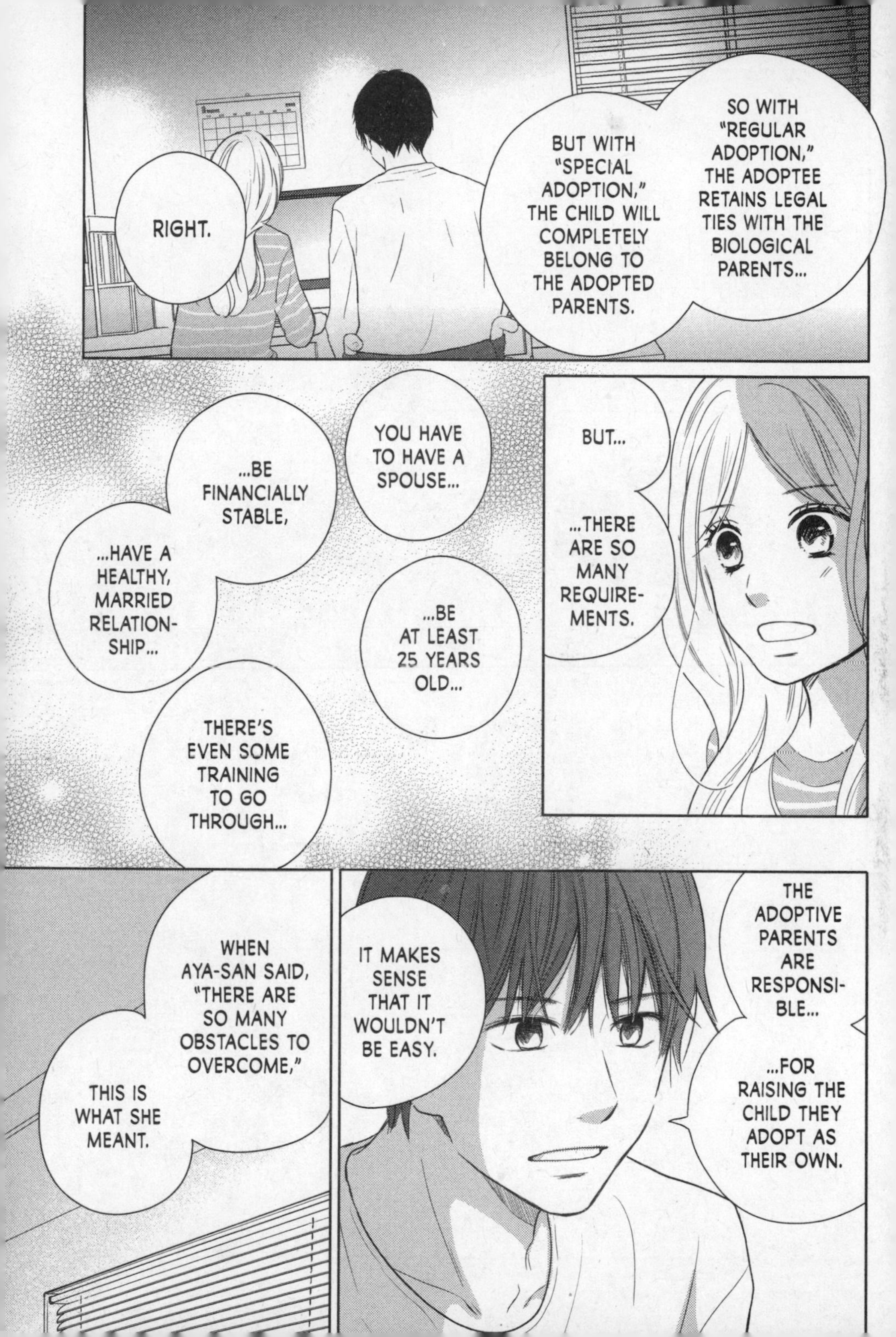
SO WITH "REGULAR ADOPTION," THE ADOPTEE RETAINS LEGAL TIES WITH THE BIOLOGICAL PARENTS...
BUT WITH "SPECIAL ADOPTION," THE CHILD WILL COMPLETELY BELONG TO THE ADOPTED PARENTS.
RIGHT.
BUT...
...THERE ARE SO MANY REQUIREMENTS.
YOU HAVE TO HAVE A SPOUSE...
...BE FINANCIALLY STABLE,
...HAVE A HEALTHY, MARRIED RELATIONSHIP...
...BE AT LEAST 25 YEARS OLD...
THERE'S EVEN SOME TRAINING TO GO THROUGH...
THE ADOPTIVE PARENTS ARE RESPONSIBLE...
...FOR RAISING THE CHILD THEY ADOPT AS THEIR OWN.
IT MAKES SENSE THAT IT WOULDN'T BE EASY.
WHEN AYA-SAN SAID, "THERE ARE SO MANY OBSTACLES TO OVERCOME,"
THIS IS WHAT SHE MEANT.

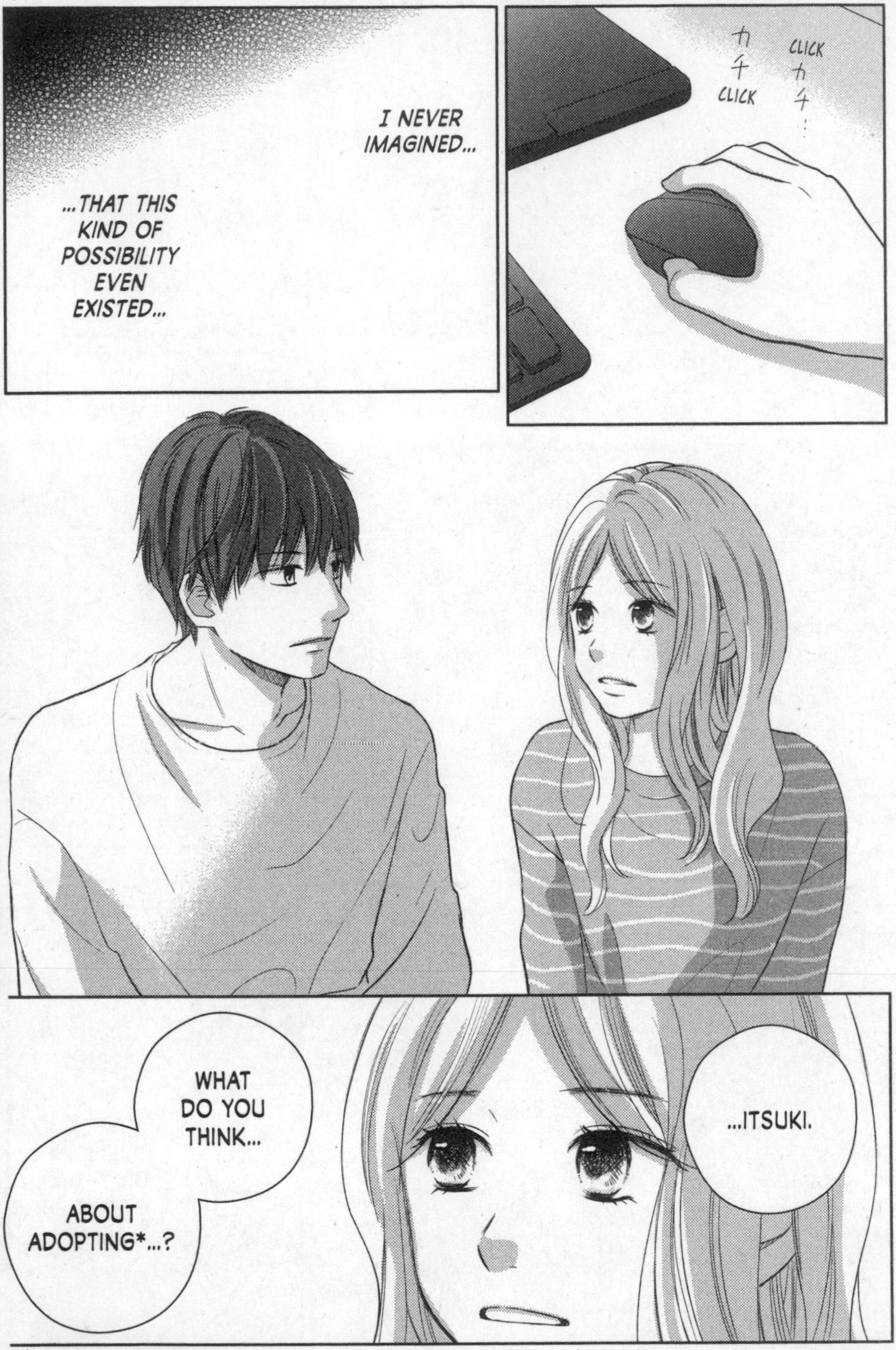

カチ
CLICK
カチ…
CLICK
I NEVER IMAGINED...
...THAT THIS KIND OF POSSIBILITY EVEN EXISTED...
...ITSUKI.
WHAT DO YOU THINK...
ABOUT ADOPTING*...?

*The requirements for special adoption described here are those given by the NPO the author consulted for this series.

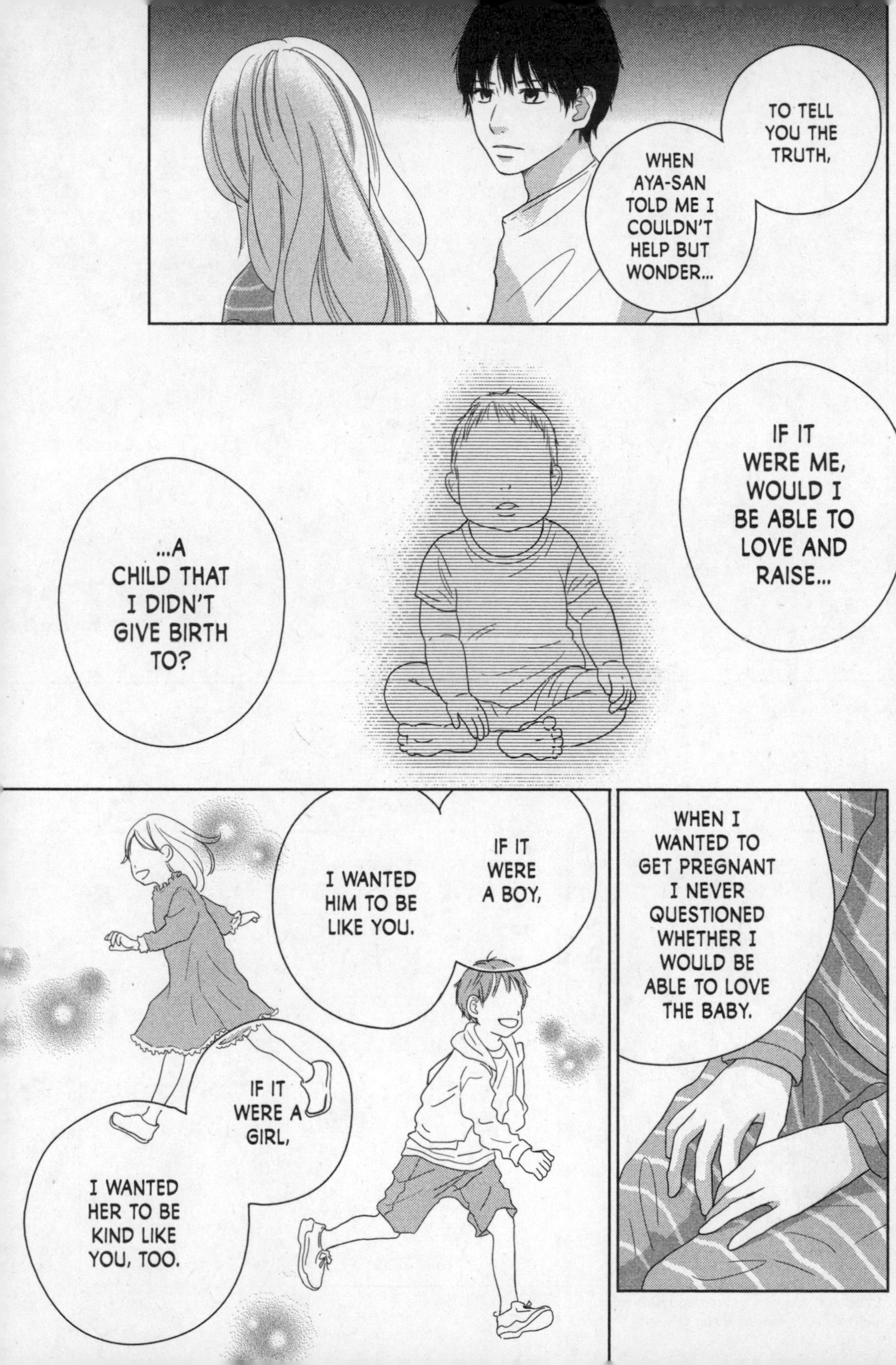
TO TELL YOU THE TRUTH,
WHEN AYA-SAN TOLD ME I COULDN'T HELP BUT WONDER...
IF IT WERE ME, WOULD I BE ABLE TO LOVE AND RAISE...
...A CHILD THAT I DIDN'T GIVE BIRTH TO?
WHEN I WANTED TO GET PREGNANT I NEVER QUESTIONED WHETHER I WOULD BE ABLE TO LOVE THE BABY.
IF IT WERE A BOY,
I WANTED HIM TO BE LIKE YOU.
IF IT WERE A GIRL,
I WANTED HER TO BE KIND LIKE YOU, TOO.

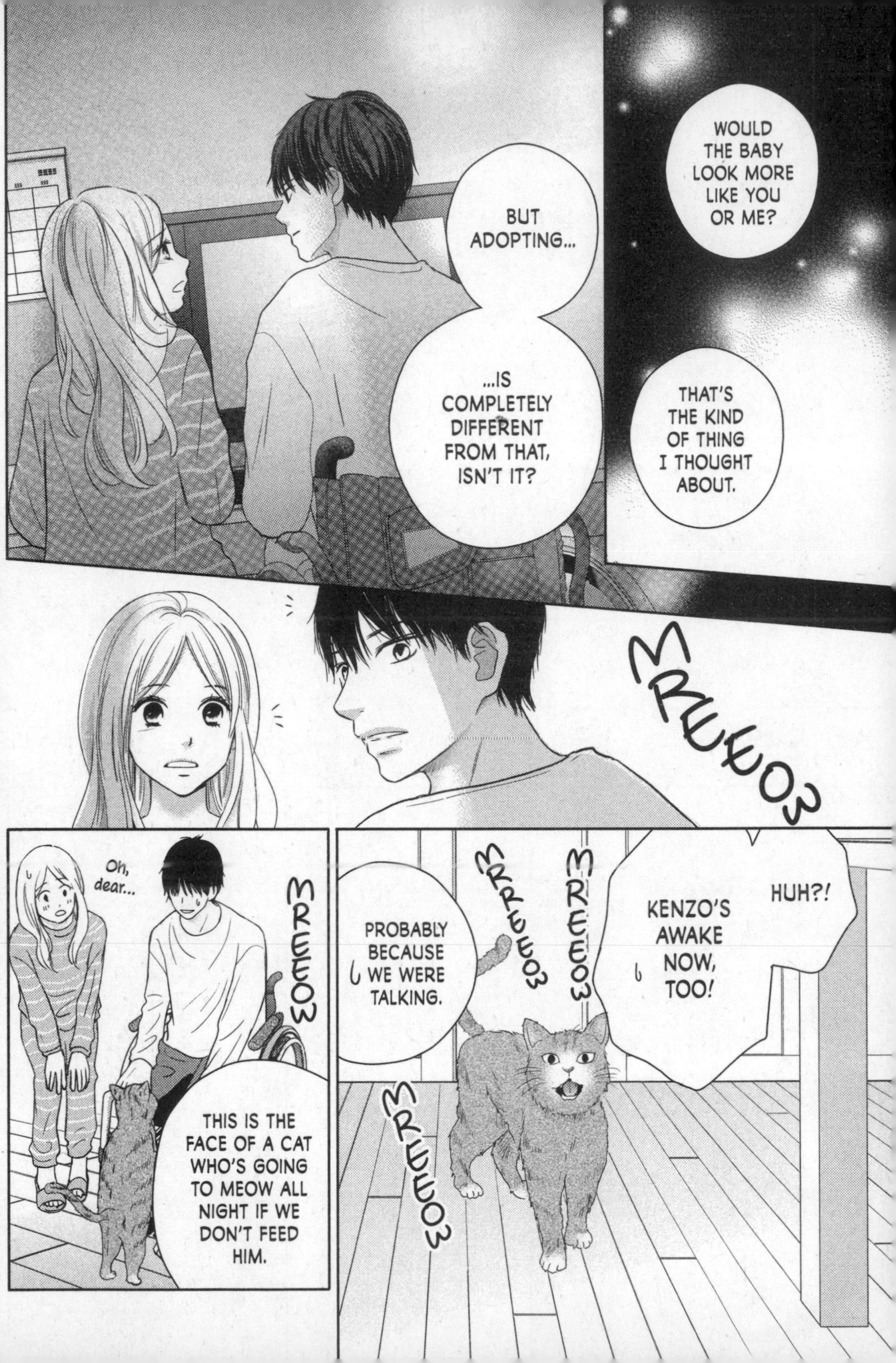
WOULD THE BABY LOOK MORE LIKE YOU OR ME?
THAT'S THE KIND OF THING I THOUGHT ABOUT.
BUT ADOPTING...
...IS COMPLETELY DIFFERENT FROM THAT, ISN'T IT?
MREEEOW
HUH?!
KENZO'S AWAKE NOW, TOO!
MREEOW
MREEOW
PROBABLY BECAUSE WE WERE TALKING.
MREEOW
Oh, dear...
MREEOW
THIS IS THE FACE OF A CAT WHO'S GOING TO MEOW ALL NIGHT IF WE DON'T FEED HIM.

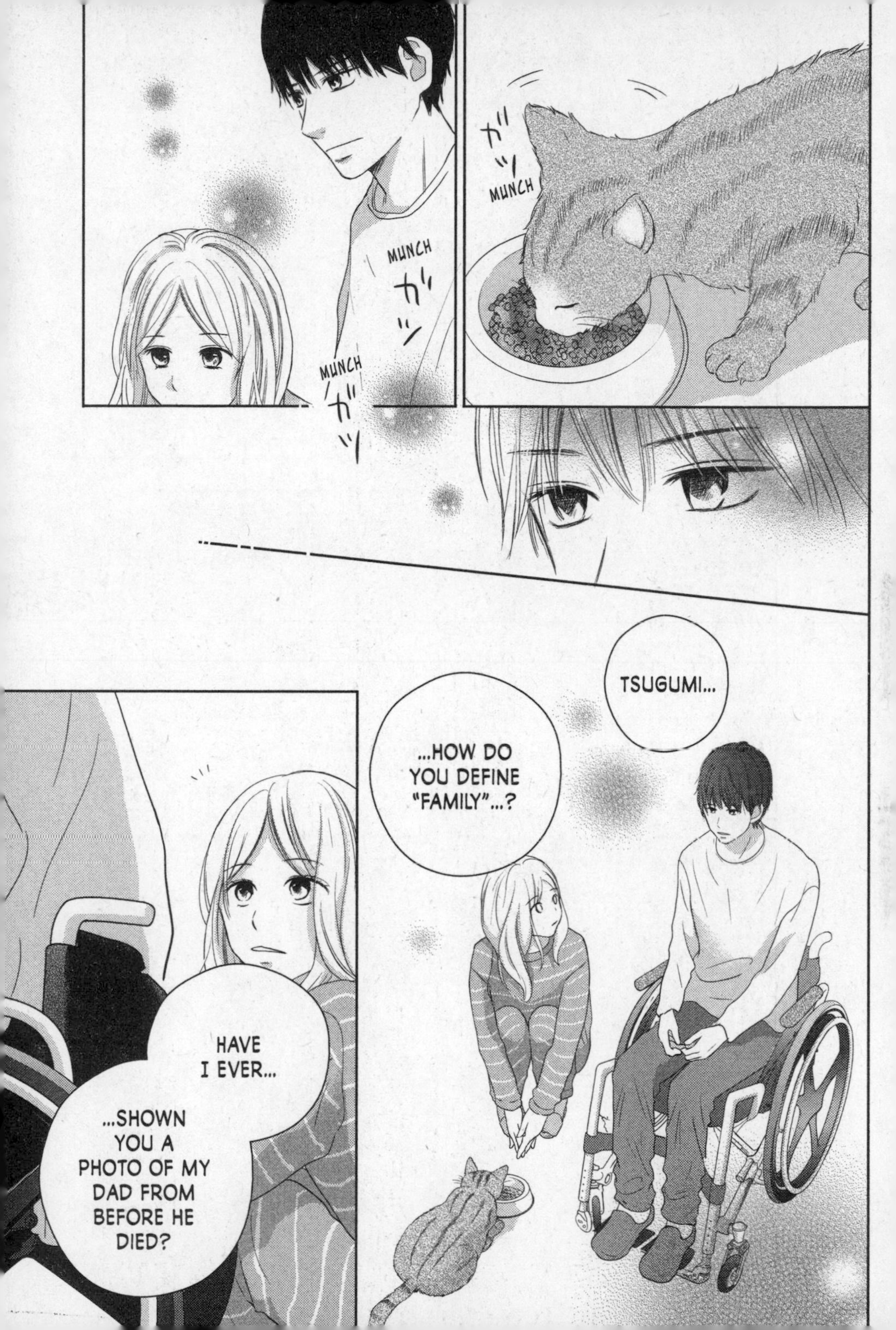
ガツ
MUNCH
MUNCH
ガツ
MUNCH
ガツ
TSUGUMI...
...HOW DO YOU DEFINE "FAMILY"...?
HAVE I EVER...
...SHOWN YOU A PHOTO OF MY DAD FROM BEFORE HE DIED?

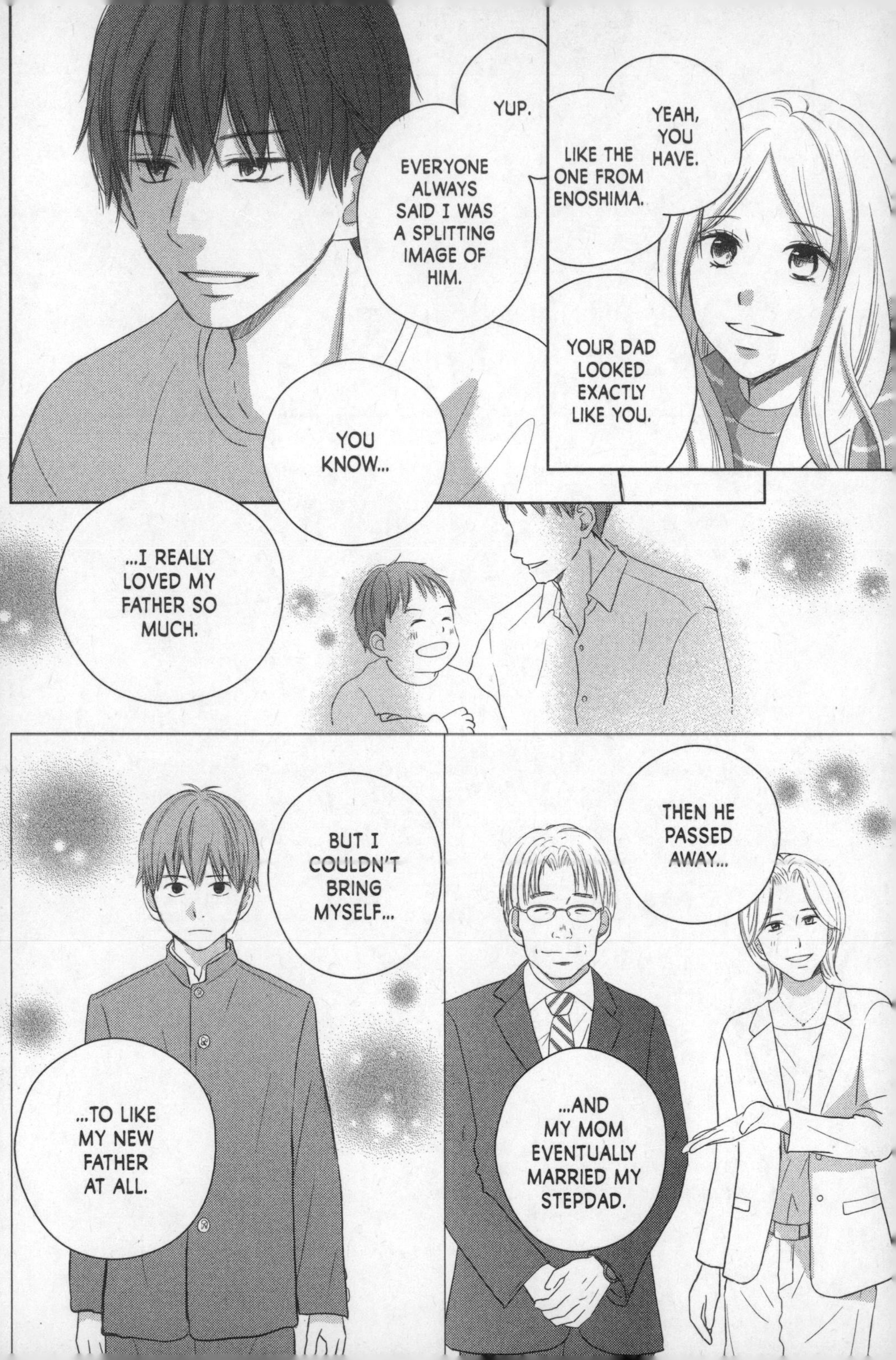
YEAH, YOU HAVE.
LIKE THE ONE FROM ENOSHIMA.
YOUR DAD LOOKED EXACTLY LIKE YOU.
YUP.
EVERYONE ALWAYS SAID I WAS A SPLITTING IMAGE OF HIM.
YOU KNOW...
...I REALLY LOVED MY FATHER SO MUCH.
THEN HE PASSED AWAY...
...AND MY MOM EVENTUALLY MARRIED MY STEPDAD.
BUT I COULDN'T BRING MYSELF...
...TO LIKE MY NEW FATHER AT ALL.

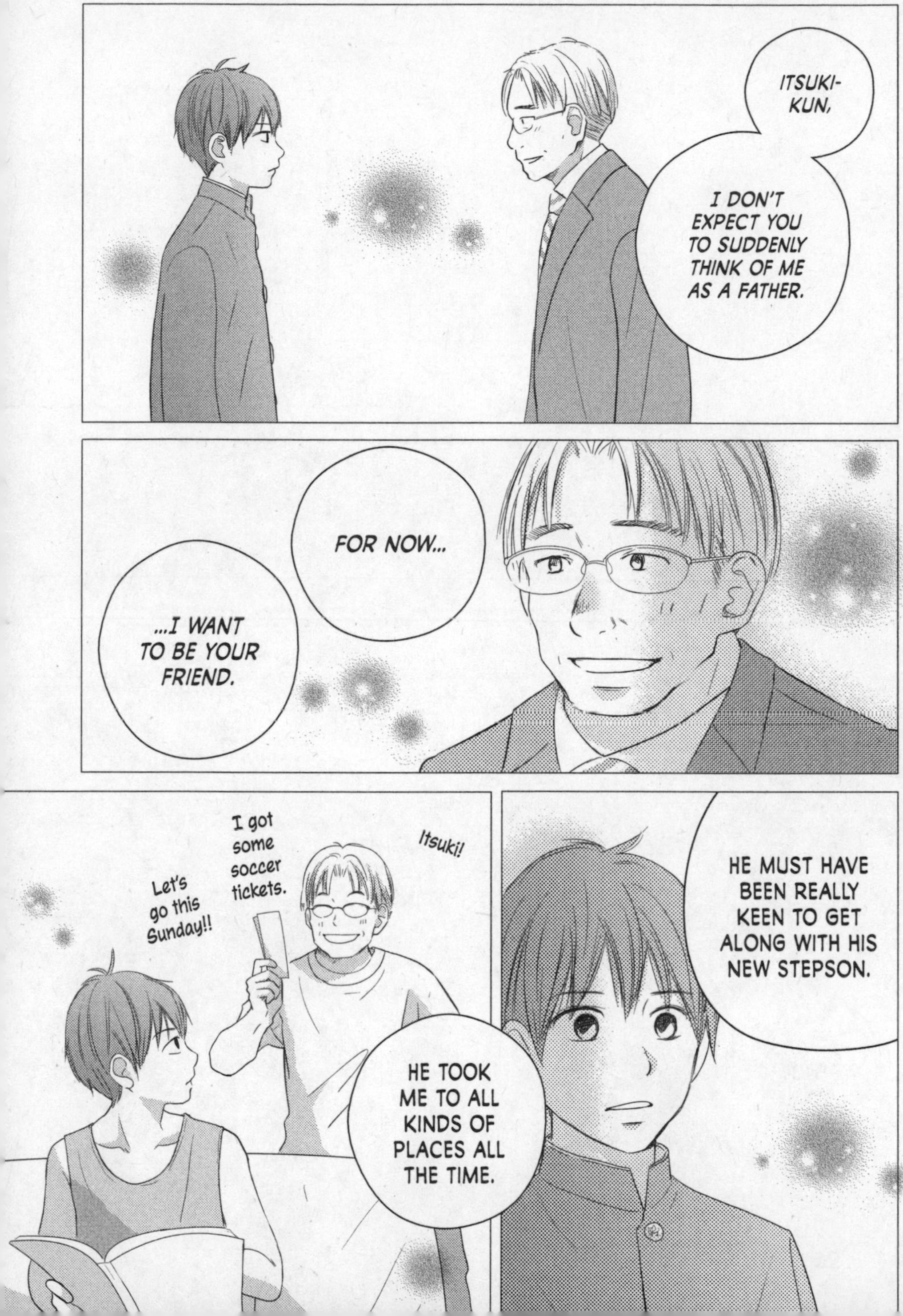
ITSUKI-KUN,
I DON'T EXPECT YOU TO SUDDENLY THINK OF ME AS A FATHER.
FOR NOW...
...I WANT TO BE YOUR FRIEND.
HE MUST HAVE BEEN REALLY KEEN TO GET ALONG WITH HIS NEW STEPSON.
HE TOOK ME TO ALL KINDS OF PLACES ALL THE TIME.
Itsuki!
I got some soccer tickets.
Let's go this Sunday!!

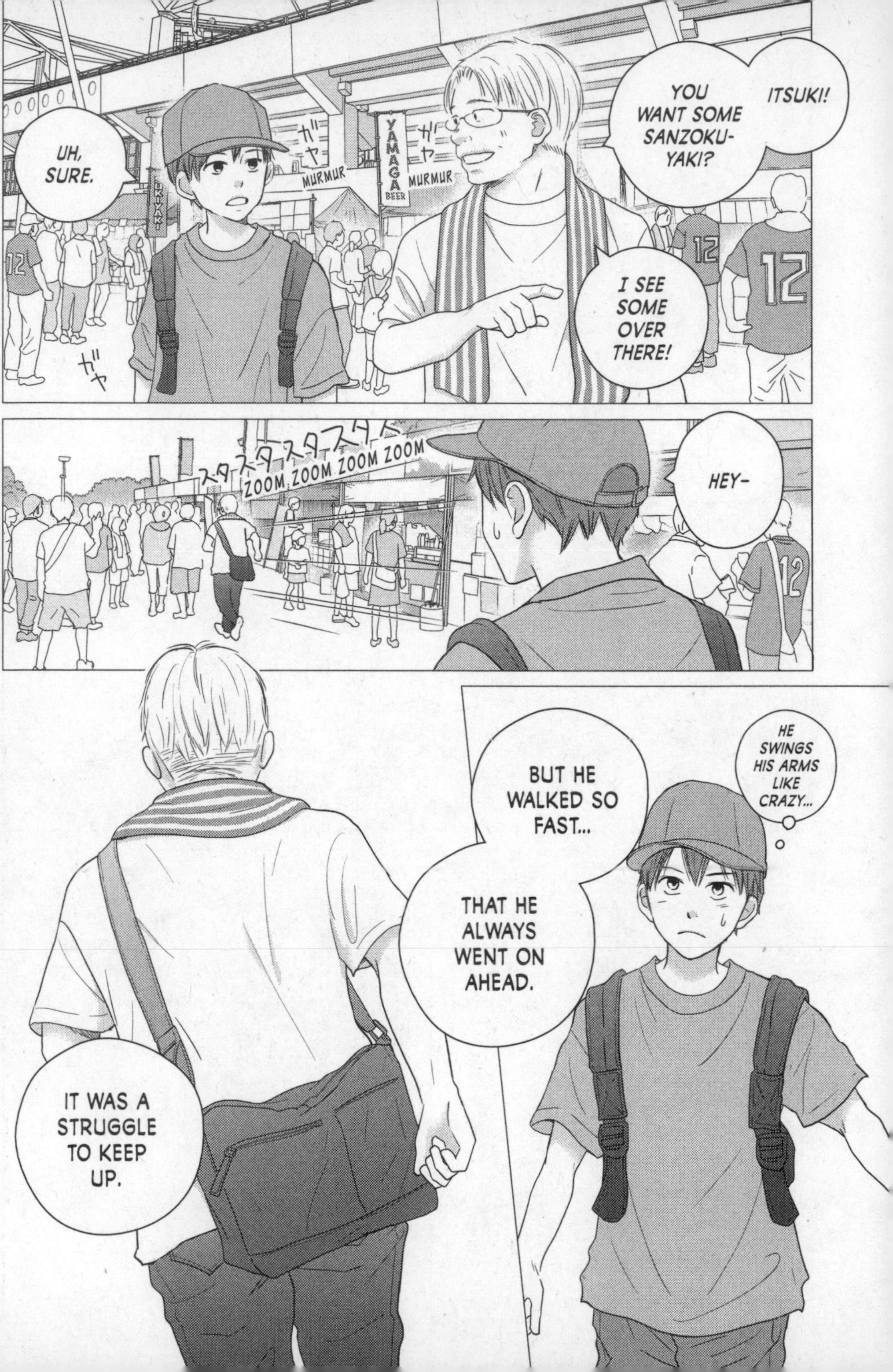
ITSUKI!
YOU WANT SOME SANZOKU-YAKI?
YAMAGA BEER
MURMUR
MURMUR
UH, SURE.
I SEE SOME OVER THERE!
HEY-
ZOOM ZOOM ZOOM ZOOM
HE SWINGS HIS ARMS LIKE CRAZY...
BUT HE WALKED SO FAST...
THAT HE ALWAYS WENT ON AHEAD.
IT WAS A STRUGGLE TO KEEP UP.

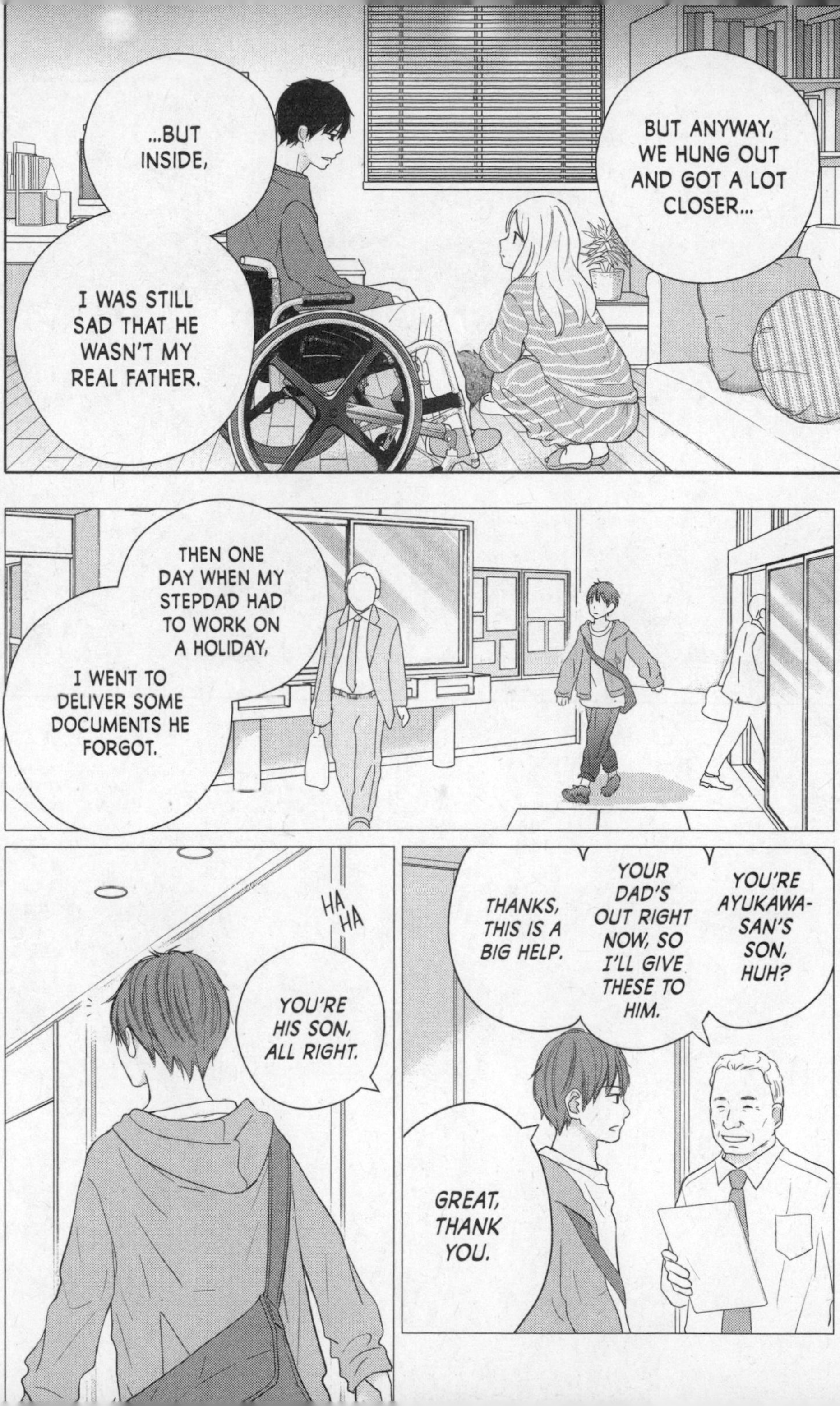
BUT ANYWAY, WE HUNG OUT AND GOT A LOT CLOSER...
...BUT INSIDE,
I WAS STILL SAD THAT HE WASN'T MY REAL FATHER.
THEN ONE DAY WHEN MY STEPDAD HAD TO WORK ON A HOLIDAY,
I WENT TO DELIVER SOME DOCUMENTS HE FORGOT.
YOU'RE AYUKAWA-SAN'S SON, HUH?
YOUR DAD'S OUT RIGHT NOW, SO I'LL GIVE THESE TO HIM.
THANKS, THIS IS A BIG HELP.
GREAT, THANK YOU.
HA HA
YOU'RE HIS SON, ALL RIGHT.

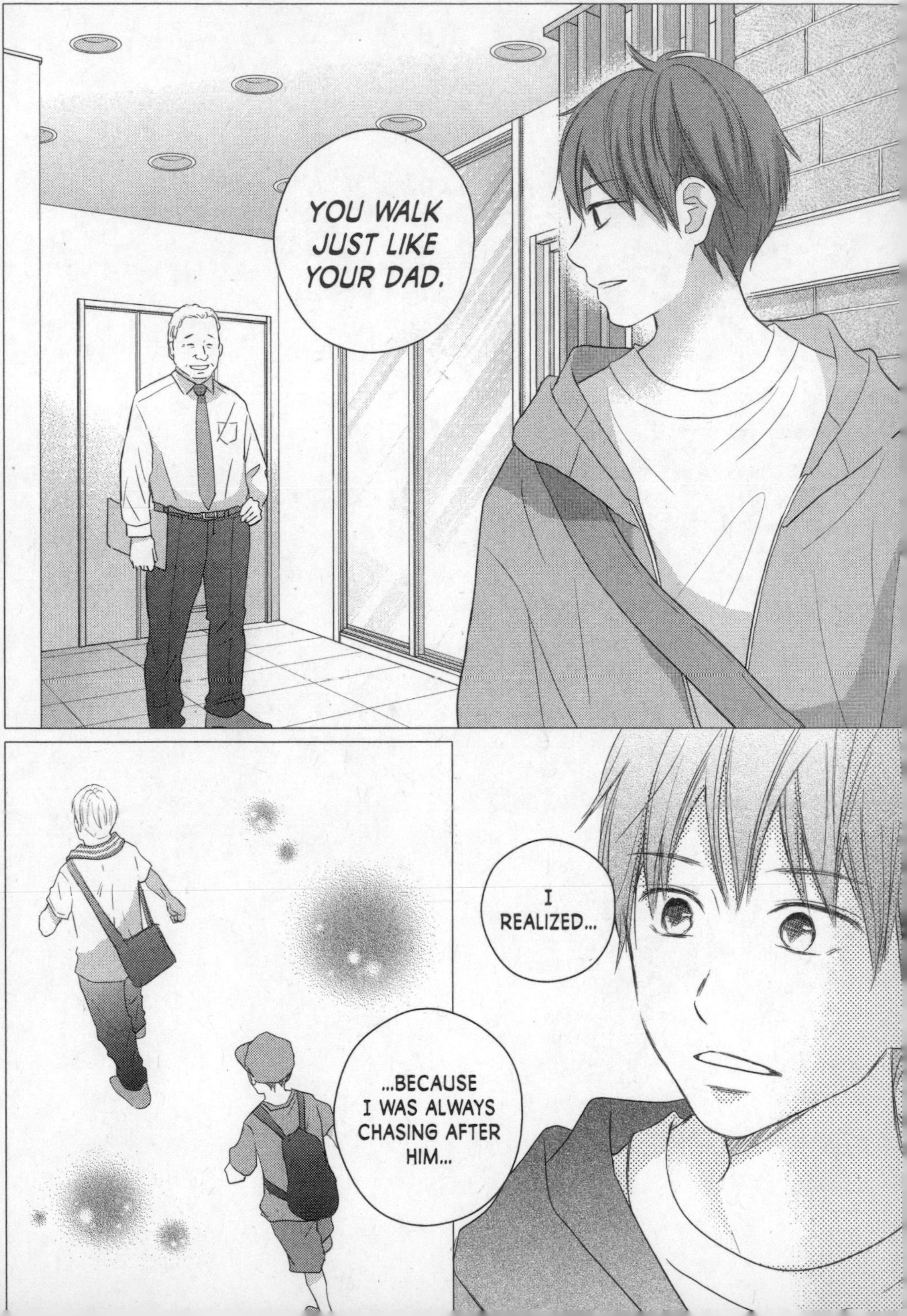
YOU WALK JUST LIKE YOUR DAD.
I REALIZED...
...BECAUSE I WAS ALWAYS CHASING AFTER HIM...

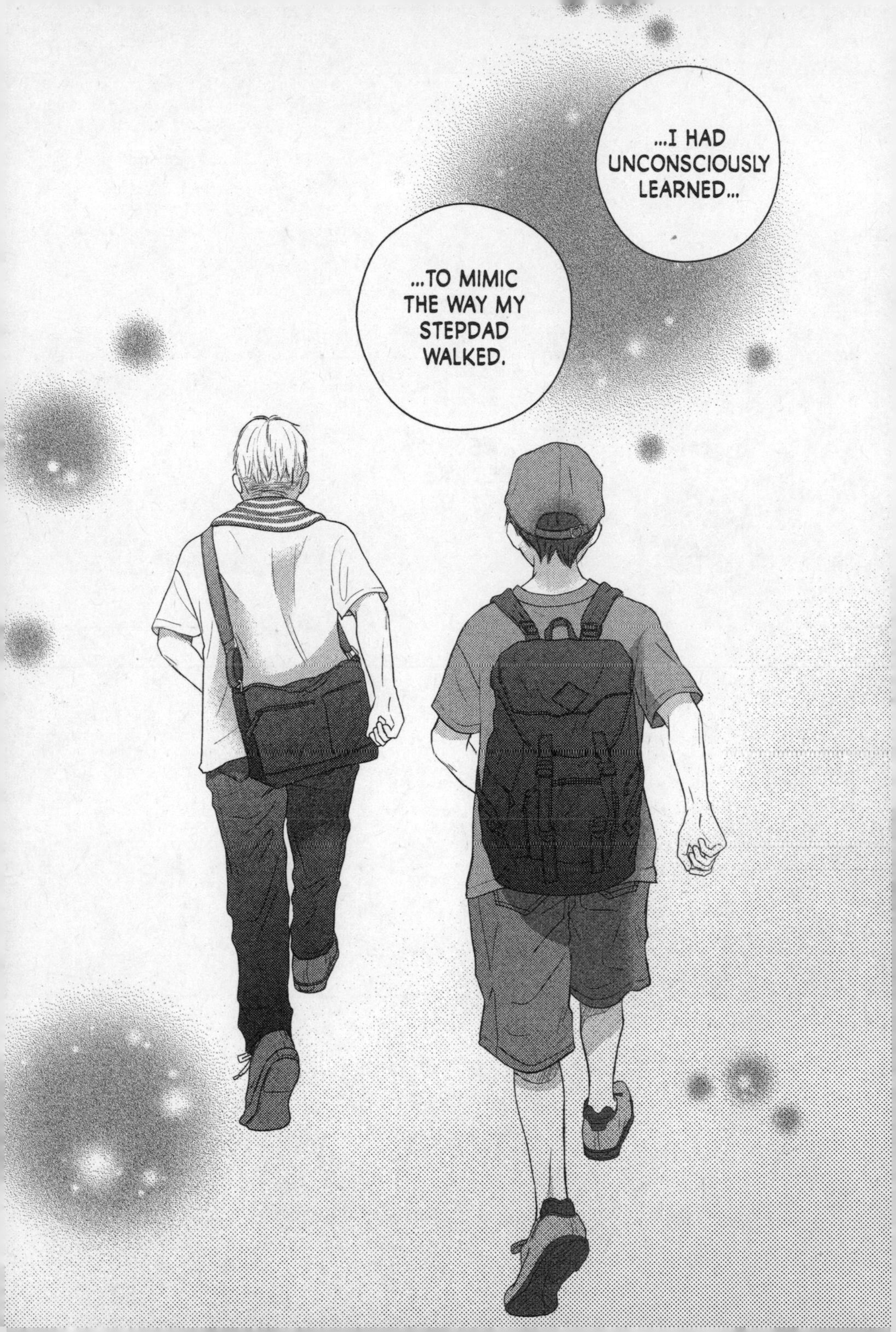
...I HAD UNCONSCIOUSLY LEARNED...
...TO MIMIC THE WAY MY STEPDAD WALKED.

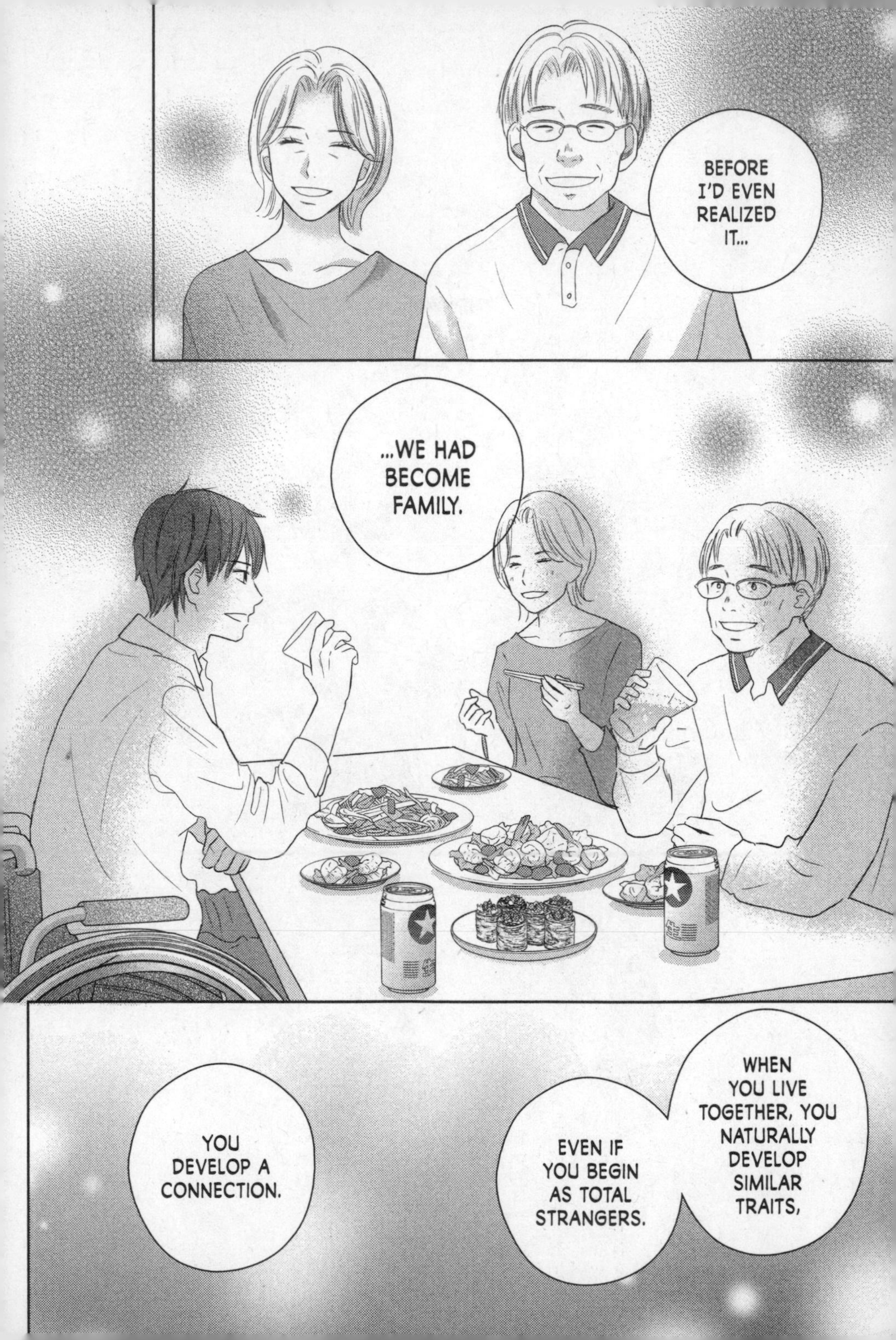
BEFORE I'D EVEN REALIZED IT...
...WE HAD BECOME FAMILY.
WHEN YOU LIVE TOGETHER, YOU NATURALLY DEVELOP SIMILAR TRAITS,
EVEN IF YOU BEGIN AS TOTAL STRANGERS.
YOU DEVELOP A CONNECTION.

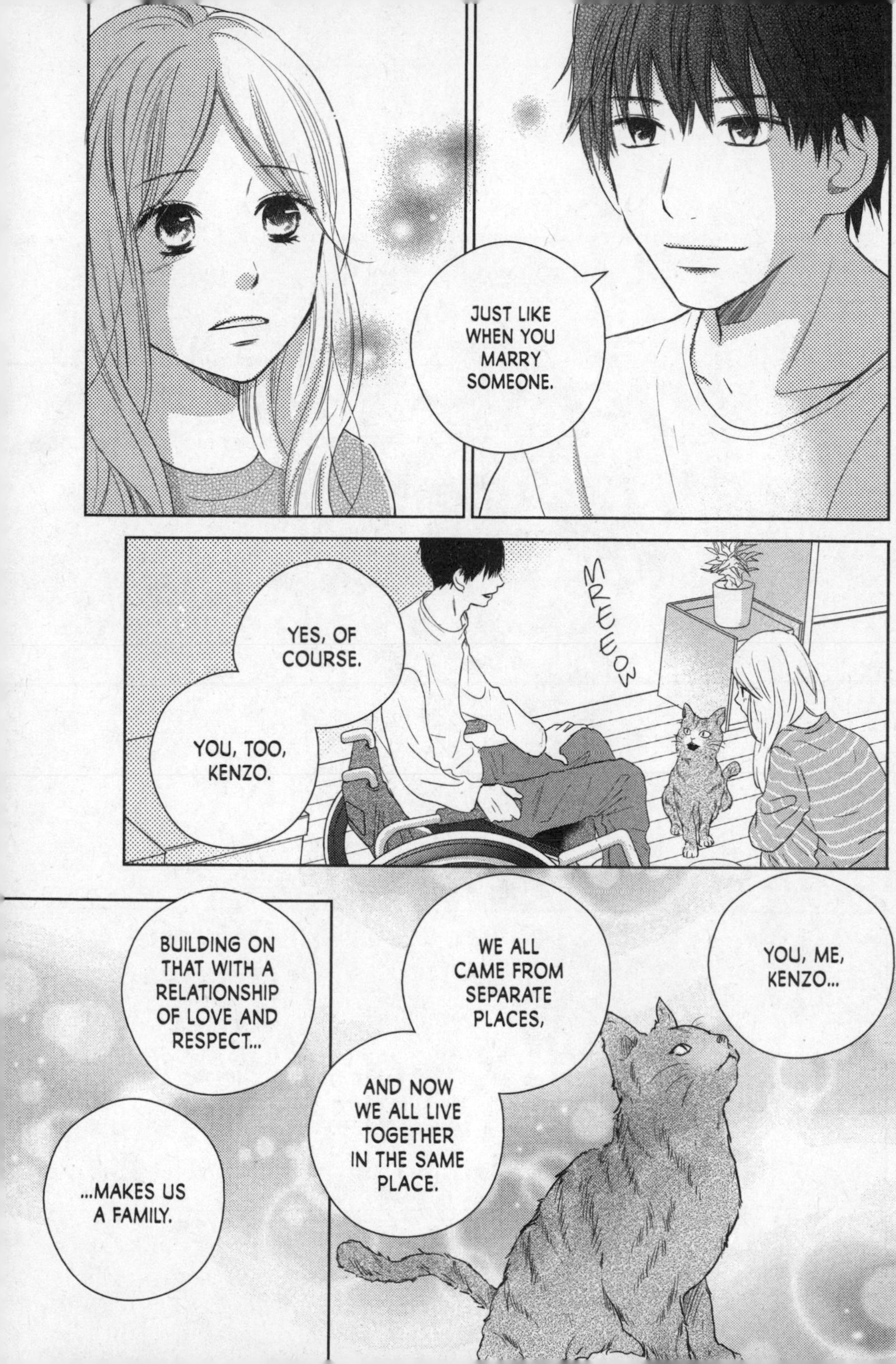
JUST LIKE WHEN YOU MARRY SOMEONE.
MREEOW
YES, OF COURSE.
YOU, TOO, KENZO.
YOU, ME, KENZO...
WE ALL CAME FROM SEPARATE PLACES,
AND NOW WE ALL LIVE TOGETHER IN THE SAME PLACE.
BUILDING ON THAT WITH A RELATIONSHIP OF LOVE AND RESPECT...
...MAKES US A FAMILY.

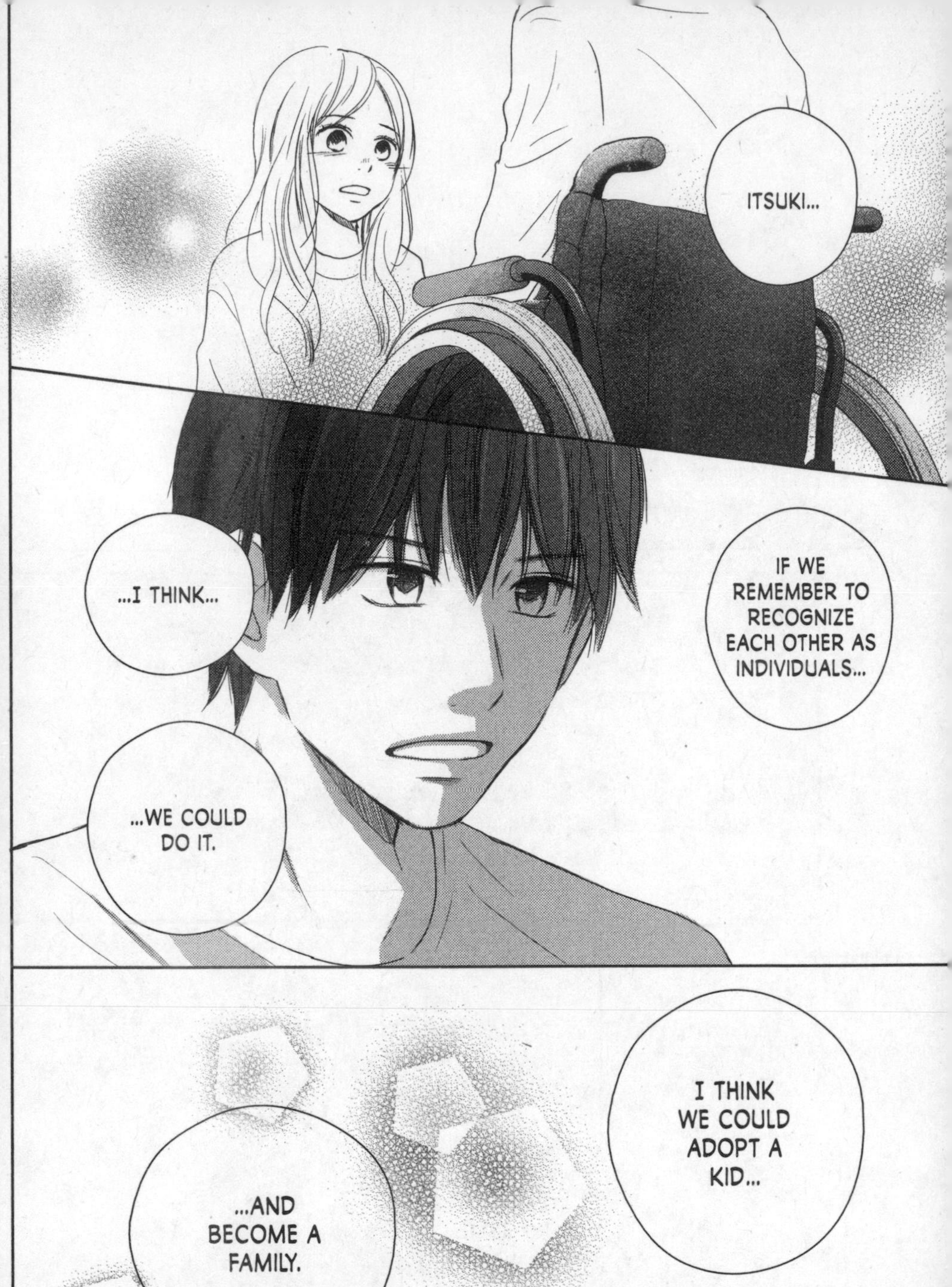
ITSUKI...
IF WE REMEMBER TO RECOGNIZE EACH OTHER AS INDIVIDUALS...
...I THINK...
...WE COULD DO IT.
I THINK WE COULD ADOPT A KID...
...AND BECOME A FAMILY.

PERFECT WORLD 10 / THE END

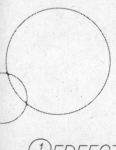

PERFECT WORLD

Thank you so much for reading volume ten of *Perfect World!*

Tsugumi and Itsuki's married life starts from this volume. I hope you'll continue following their story!

This summer, *Perfect World* received the 43rd Kodansha Manga Award for Best Shojo Manga.
I hadn't expected to receive an award in the slightest, so when I received the call at a train station I was so surprised that I started wandering around, not really sure what to do with myself.

For the awards ceremony, I got to invite the architect, Abe-san, and individuals and their families I've consulted, the hospital and rehab staff who helped me out, and the producers who made the film and TV drama adaptations.
(I'm sorry I couldn't invite those who lived too far away).

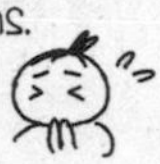

I had the honor to have amazing manga artists like Tetsuya Chiba-sensei telling me, "You did a terrific job. Congratulations!" and Waki Yamato-sensei commenting, "It really is a great series. It's wonderful!" I almost cried. The award seems far too grand for my abilities, but I was happy that it brought joy to so many people. Thank you so much.

With the support from my readers and everyone who has given me encouragement, I hope to draw this series to the end.

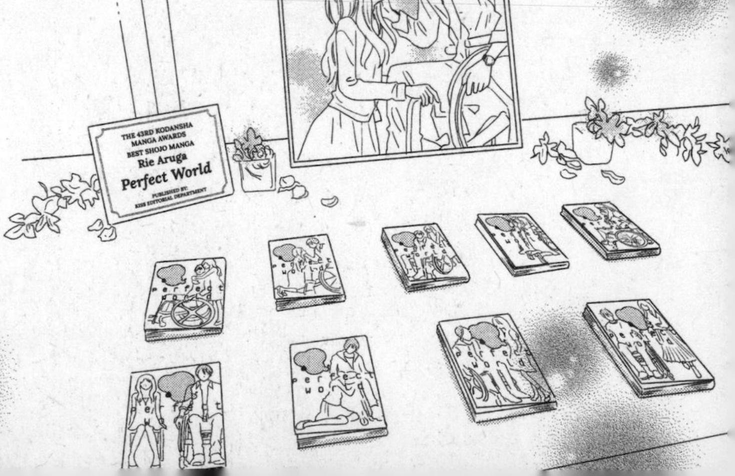
PERFECT WORLD
rie aruga
THE 43RD KODANSHA MANGA AWARDS
BEST SHOJO MANGA
Rie Aruga
Perfect World
PUBLISHED BY:
KISS EDITORIAL DEPARTMENT

— From the bottom of my heart, thank you to all of those who helped me. —

- Kazuo Abe-sama from Abe Kensetsu Inc.
- Ouchi-sama · Kimura-sama · Nakamura-sama
- Kamakura Rehabilitation St. Therese Hospital
- Certified NPO Florence · OX Kanto Vivit Minami Funabashi
- My editor, Ito-sama · Everyone from editorial at Kiss
- The designer, Kusume-sama
- My assistants, T-sama, K-sama, and TN-sama
- My family and friends
- Everyone involved in getting this sold
- My readers

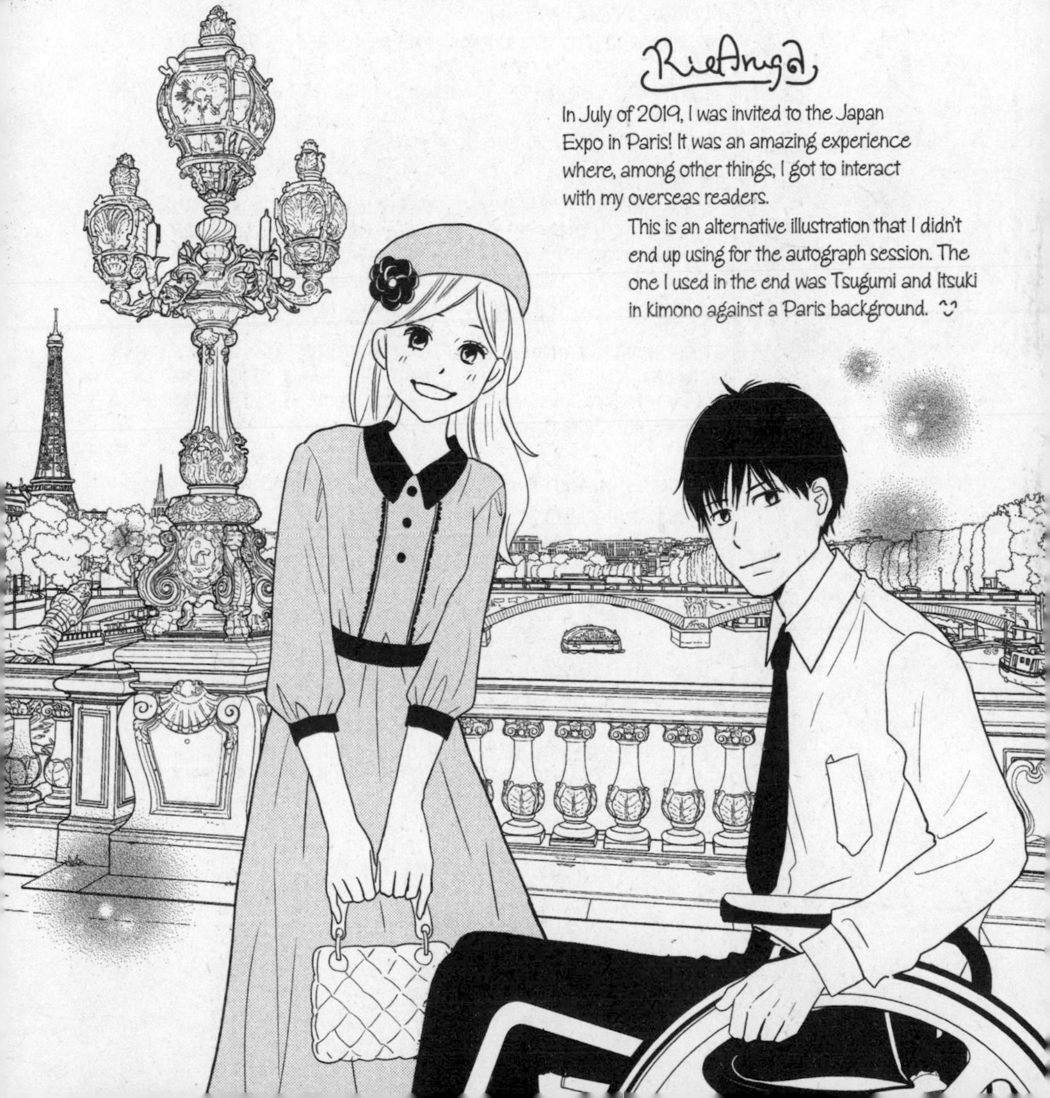

Rie Aruga

In July of 2019, I was invited to the Japan Expo in Paris! It was an amazing experience where, among other things, I got to interact with my overseas readers.

This is an alternative illustration that I didn't end up using for the autograph session. The one I used in the end was Tsugumi and Itsuki in kimono against a Paris background. ◡̈

TRANSLATION NOTES

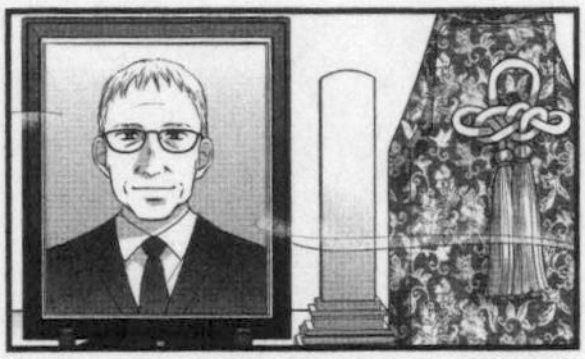

49 DAYS, PAGE 5

IN JAPAN, MANY FAMILIES FOLLOW THE BUDDHIST TRADITION OF MOURNING WHERE THE SPIRIT OF THE DECEASED IS ASSUMED TO LINGER IN AN INTERMEDIATE STATE FOR 49 DAYS. DURING THIS TIME, THE CREMATED REMAINS ARE KEPT ON AN ALTAR AT HOME. A CEREMONY IS HELD ON THE 49TH DAY, AFTER WHICH THE SPIRIT OF THE DECEASED WILL MOVE ON AND THE REMAINS ARE INTERRED AT A GRAVE.

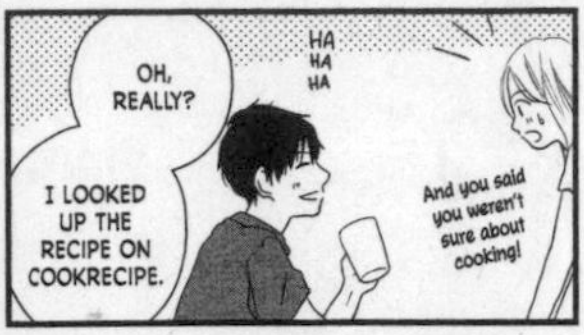
And you said you weren't sure about cooking!
HA HA HA
OH, REALLY?
I LOOKED UP THE RECIPE ON COOKRECIPE.

COOKRECIPE, PAGE 48

A REFERENCE TO "COOKPAD," AN ONLINE RECIPE SHARING SITE WHERE USERS POST THEIR OWN RECIPES AND PHOTOS. IT IS CURRENTLY THE MOST POPULAR, GO-TO SITE FOR FINDING RECIPES IN JAPAN.

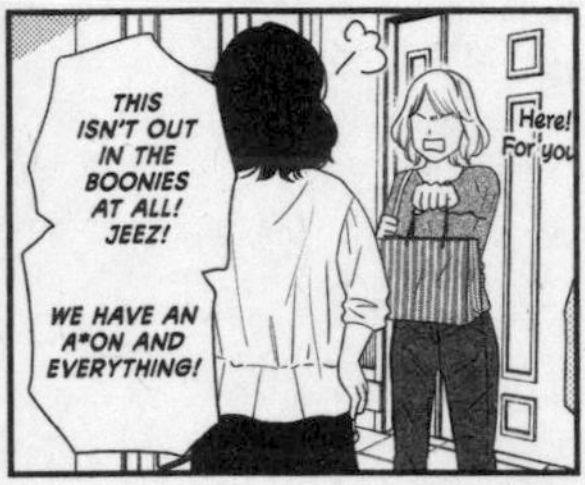
Here! For you
THIS ISN'T OUT IN THE BOONIES AT ALL! JEEZ!
WE HAVE AN A*ON AND EVERYTHING!

A*ON, PAGE 81

ISHIBASHI-SAN IS REFERRING TO A SHOPPING COMPLEX RUN BY THE AEON CORPORATION, WHICH USUALLY HAS GROCERIES, SUNDRY GOODS, A SELECTION OF SPECIALTY STORES, AND RELATIVELY AFFORDABLE, FAMILY-FRIENDLY PLACES TO EAT. ALTHOUGH AEON HAS SOME VERY LARGE MALLS WITH HUNDREDS OF SPECIALTY STORES, SMALL ONES IN LESS URBAN AREAS WILL ONLY HAVE A HANDFUL OF SPECIALTY STORES AND RESTAURANTS, SIMILAR TO WHAT YOU MIGHT FIND IN A SMALL STRIP MALL. ISHIBASHI-SAN'S CLAIM THAT THEIR AREA IS NOT RURAL BECAUSE IT HAS AN AEON IS NOT VERY CONVINCING.

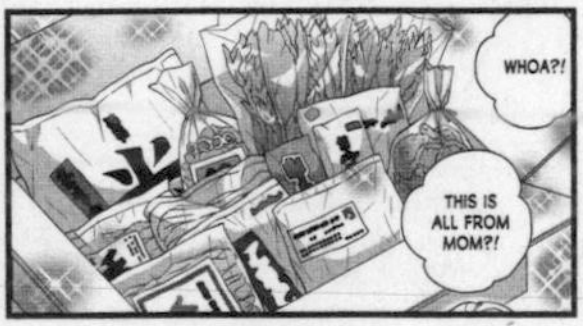
WHOA?!
THIS IS ALL FROM MOM?!

SHINSHU MISO, SHICHIMI SPICE MIX, AND SOBA, PAGE 90

THESE ARE ALL FOOD ITEMS THAT TSUGUMI AND ITSUKI'S HOMETOWN IS FAMOUS FOR. THE TWO COME FROM MATSUMOTO CITY IN NAGANO PREFECTURE, WHICH IS A REGION THAT WAS ONCE CALLED SHINSHU. *SHICHIMI* IS A SPICE MIX FEATURING CHILI PEPPERS, AND *SOBA* ARE NOODLES MADE OF BUCKWHEAT.

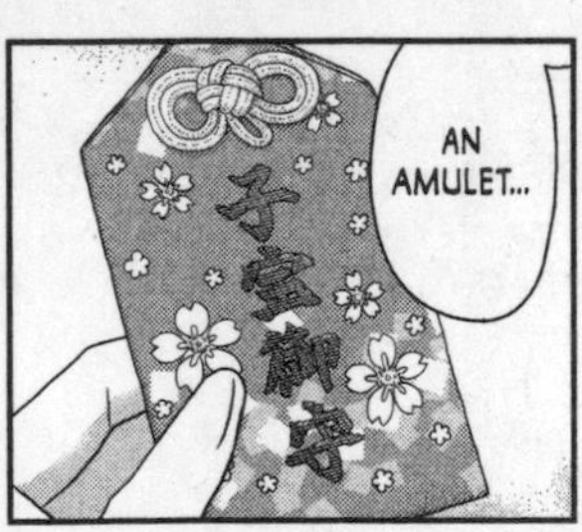
AN AMULET...
子宝御守

FERTILITY CHARM, PAGE 90

THESE TYPES OF AMULETS ARE SOLD AT TEMPLES AND SHRINES AND ARE KEPT TO BRING A PARTICULAR TYPE OF FORTUNE TO ITS OWNER. THERE ARE MANY TYPES OF WISHES THEY CAN GRANT, INCLUDING TRAFFIC SAFETY, SUCCESS IN AN ENTRANCE EXAM, FERTILITY, OR GOOD HEALTH.

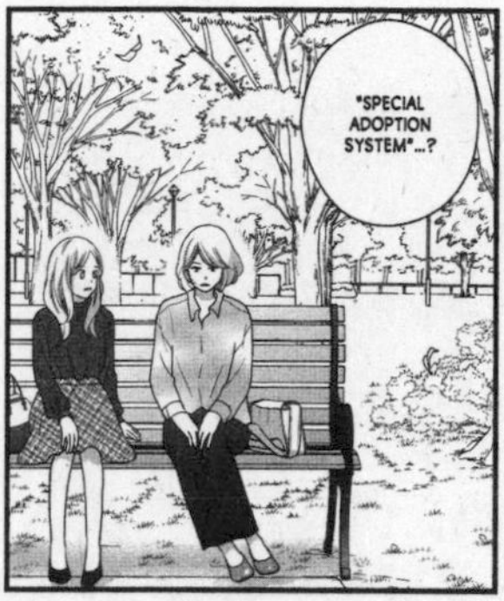
"SPECIAL ADOPTION SYSTEM"...?

SPECIAL ADOPTION SYSTEM, **PAGE 133**

IN JAPAN, THERE ARE TWO CATEGORIES OF ADOPTION: "REGULAR" AND "SPECIAL." HISTORICALLY IN JAPAN, ADOPTION PRIMARILY WAS AND STILL REMAINS A SYSTEM FOR ADOPTING AN INDIVIDUAL, OFTEN AN ADULT, INTO THE FAMILY AS A WAY TO SECURE AN HEIR OR FOR OTHER (OFTEN FINANCIAL) REASONS. FOR EXAMPLE, A BUSINESS THAT NEEDS A MALE HEIR MIGHT ADOPT A SON-IN-LAW THAT MARRIES INTO THE FAMILY TO ENSURE THE FAMILY NAME AND INHERITANCE GETS PASSED DOWN. THIS IS "REGULAR" ADOPTION, AND THE ADOPTED PERSON RETAINS LEGAL TIES TO HIS OR HER BIOLOGICAL FAMILY. THE SPECIAL ADOPTION SYSTEM WAS INTRODUCED IN 1988 IN LINE WITH MORE INTERNATIONAL CONCEPTS OF ADOPTION. SPECIAL ADOPTION SEVERS LEGAL TIES WITH THE ADOPTEE'S BIOLOGICAL PARENTS SO THAT THE ADOPTIVE PARENTS TRULY BECOME THE SOLE PARENTS OF THE CHILD, WHO HAS TO BE UNDER SIX YEARS OLD. SPECIAL ADOPTION IS STILL FAIRLY UNCOMMON, WHICH IS WHY AYA ASSUMES THAT TSUGUMI MAY NOT BE FAMILIAR WITH THE CONCEPT.

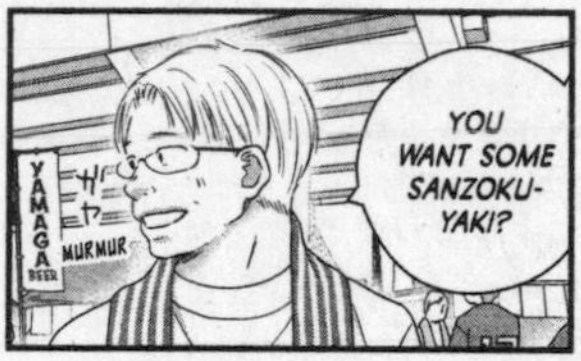
YOU WANT SOME SANZOKU-YAKI?
YAMAGA
BEER
MURMUR

SANZOKU-YAKI, YAMAGA BEER, **PAGE 158**

ITSUKI AND HIS STEPDAD ARE AT THE HOME STADIUM OF THE MATSUMOTO YAMAGA F.C., A DIVISION 1 TEAM IN THE J-LEAGUE, WHICH IS JAPAN'S PROFESSIONAL NATIONAL SOCCER LEAGUE. THE STADIUM SELLS ICONIC REGIONAL FOOD AND SPECIAL THEMED REFRESHMENTS, SUCH AS THE GREEN YAMAGA BEER MADE TO MATCH THE TEAM COLOR AND SANZOKU-YAKI, A TYPE OF GARLIC FRIED CHICKEN SPECIFIC TO THE REGION.

TETSUYA CHIBA, **PAGE 166**

ARTIST OF THE LEGENDARY BOXING MANGA *ASHITA NO JOE* (TOMORROW'S JOE).

WAKI YAMATO, **PAGE 166**

ONE OF THE MOST PROMINENT SHOJO MANGA ARTISTS FROM THE 1970S TO 1990S, BEST KNOWN FOR THE TAISHO ERA LOVE STORY OF A MODERN-SPIRITED GIRL, *HAIKARA-SAN: HERE COMES MISS MODERN*, WHICH WON THE 1ST KODANSHA MANGA AWARD FOR BEST SHOJO MANGA AND *ASAKI YUME MISHI*, AN ADAPTATION OF MURASAKI SHIKIBU'S *THE TALE OF GENJI*.

Young characters and steampunk setting, like *Howl's Moving Castle* and *Battle Angel Alita*

Beyond the Clouds © 2018 Nicke / Ki-oon

A boy with a talent for machines and a mysterious girl whose wings he's fixed will take you beyond the clouds! In the tradition of the high-flying, resonant adventure stories of Studio Ghibli comes a gorgeous tale about the longing of young hearts for adventure and friendship!

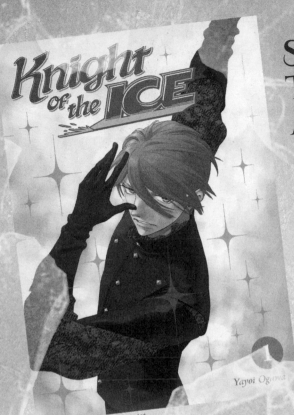

Knight of the Ice ©Yayoi Ogawa/Kodansha Ltd.

SKATING THRILLS AND ICY CHILLS WITH THIS NEW TINGLY ROMANCE SERIES!

A rom-com on ice, perfect for fans of *Princess Jellyfish* and *Wotakoi*. Kokoro is the talk of the figure-skating world, winning trophies and hearts. But little do they know... he's actually a huge nerd! From the beloved creator of *You're My Pet* (*Tramps Like Us*).

Chitose is a serious young woman, working for the health magazine *SASSO*. Or at least, she would be, if she wasn't constantly getting distracted by her childhood friend, international figure skating star Kokoro Kijinami! In the public eye and on the ice, Kokoro is a gallant, flawless knight, but behind his glittery costumes and breathtaking spins lies a secret: He's actually a hopelessly romantic otaku, who can only land his quad jumps when Chitose is on hand to recite a spell from his favorite magical girl anime!

A SMART, NEW ROMANTIC COMEDY FOR FANS OF *SHORTCAKE CAKE* AND *TERRACE HOUSE*!

Living-Room Matsunaga-san © Keiko Iwashita / Kodansha Ltd.

KC KODANSHA COMICS

A romance manga starring high school girl Meeko, who learns to live on her own in a boarding house whose living room is home to the odd (but handsome) Matsunaga-san. She begins to adjust to her new life away from her parents, but Meeko soon learns that no matter how far away from home she is, she's still a young girl at heart — especially when she finds herself falling for Matsunaga-san.

Something's Wrong With Us

NATSUMI ANDO

The dark, psychological, sexy shojo series readers have been waiting for!

A spine-chilling and steamy romance between a Japanese sweets maker and the man who framed her mother for murder!

Following in her mother's footsteps, Nao became a traditional Japanese sweets maker, and with unparalleled artistry and a bright attitude, she gets an offer to work at a world-class confectionary company. But when she meets the young, handsome owner, she recognizes his cold stare...

KC
KODANSHA
COMICS

Something's Wrong With Us © Natsumi Ando / Kodansha Ltd.

THE SWEET SCENT OF LOVE IS IN THE AIR! FOR FANS OF OFFBEAT ROMANCES LIKE *WOTAKOI*

Sweat and Soap © Kintetsu Yamada / Kodansha Ltd.

In an office romance, there's a fine line between sexy and awkward... and that line is where Asako — a woman who sweats copiously — meets Koutarou — a perfume developer who can't get enough of Asako's, er, scent. Don't miss a romcom manga like no other!

KC
KODANSHA
COMICS

The adorable new odd-couple cat comedy manga from the creator of the beloved *Chi's Sweet Home*, in full color!

Praise for *Chi's Sweet Home*

"Nearly impossible to turn away... a true all-ages title that anyone, young or old, cat lover or not, will enjoy. The stories will bring a smile to your face and warm your heart."

—School Library Journal

Sue & Tai-chan

Konami Kanata

Sue is an aging housecat who's looking forward to living out her life in peace... but her plans change when the mischievous black tomcat Tai-chan enters the picture! Hey! Sue never signed up to be a catsitter! *Sue & Tai-chan* is the latest from the reigning meow-narch of cute kitty comics, Konami Kanata.

Sue & Tai-chan © Konami Kanata/Kodansha Ltd.

KC
KODANSHA
COMICS